THE BANGLADESH ECONOMY IN TRANSITION

THE BANGLADESH ECONOMY IN TRANSITION

Edited by

M. G. QUIBRIA

Published for the Asian Development Bank

DELHI
OXFORD UNIVERSITY PRESS
CALCUTTA CHENNAI MUMBAI
1997

Oxford University Press, Walton Street, Oxford OX2 6DP

Oxford New York
Athens Auckland Bangkok Calcutta
Cape Town Chennai Dar es Salaam Delhi
Florence Hong Kong Istanbul Karachi
Kuala Lumpur Madrid Melbourne Mexico City
Mumbai Nairobi Paris Singapore
Taipei Tokyo Toronto

and associates in

Berlin Ibadan

ISBN 0 19 564011 X

Printed at Pauls Press, New Delhi 110020
and published by Manzar Khan, Oxford University Press
YMCA Library Building, Jai Singh Road, New Delhi 110001

TABLE OF CONTENTS

TABLES

FIGURES

FOREWORD

Bangladesh has undertaken a wide range of economic reform measures in recent years. To discuss these reforms as well as to review the state of the economy, the Asian Development Bank, in collaboration with the Academy for Planning and Development, Ministry of Planning, Government of Bangladesh, organized a conference in Bangladesh in the autumn of 1993. This volume is the collection of papers presented in the conference. We hope that the papers would generate further discussions and debates within and outside the country regarding policy reforms in Bangladesh, so that it could improve its policy framework. Such debates and discussions are helpful in clarifying policy choices not only in Bangladesh but also in other Asian developing countries facing similar choices.

The views and opinions expressed in this volume are those of the authors and do not necessarily reflect the views and policies of the Asian Development Bank.

Vishvanath V. Desai
Director and Chief Economist
Economics and Development Resource Center
Asian Development Bank

PREFACE

The Asian Development Bank, in collaboration with the Academy for Planning and Development of the Ministry of Planning, Government of Bangladesh, organized a conference on the economy of Bangladesh in Dhaka on 15-16 September 1993. The conference, which was inaugurated by the Minister of Finance of the Government of Bangladesh, M. Saifur Rahman, was attended by academic economists, policymakers, officials from international development organizations, and representatives from various private sector organizations. The present volume is essentially the outcome of the papers presented at the conference.

The success of the conference was largely due to the cooperation, support and encouragement of many individuals. S.C. Jha, at that time Chief Economist, and J.M. Dowling, Assistant Chief Economist of the Economic Analysis and Research Division, provided the necessary support and encouragement for organizing the conference. The smooth conduct of the conference would have been impossible without the unstinting support of the Bank's Bangladesh Resident Mission, particularly its chief, G.H.P.B. Van der Linden, as well as of its staff. The contributions of Nurul Huda, Syed Alaur Rahman, M. Enamul Aziz, and Rezaul K. Khan are especially noteworthy. At the Bank's Headquarters in Manila, the staff of Programs Department (West) and the staff of the Economics and Development Resource Center, in particular, Lutgarda T. Labios, Elizabeth E. Leuterio, and Ma. Lourdes Antonio, worked conscientiously to make the conference a success. However, without the important contributions of the staff of the Academy for Planning and Development, the conference would not have materialized.

The papers presented in this volume have benefitted from the comments of session chairs, who include: Talukder Moniruzzaman, Dhaka University; K.F. Rahman, Former Adviser to the President; Haroonur Rashid, Secretary, Ministry of Planning; S.A.L. Reza, Director General, Bangladesh Institute of Development Studies; the designated discussants, who include Kabir U. Ahmed, Kamaluddin Ahmed, Momtaz Uddin Ahmed, Quazi Mesbahuddin Ahmed, Mohammad Mustafa Alam, Ayubur Rahman Bhuyan, Faruq A. Chowdhury, Taufiq-e-Elahi Chowdhury, A.T.M. Zahurul

Huq, Chowdhury Aminul Huq, Barkat-e-Khuda, Nasreen Khundker, A. Hye Mondal, A.M.A. Muhit, and Mamunur Rashid; and the referees, who include Ahmed Ahsan, Quazi Mesbahuddin Ahmed, Syed M. Ahsan, A.T.M. Nurul Amin, Mahmudul Anam, Steven Haggblade, Wahidul Haque, Shaikh Iftekhar Hossain, Mirza Azizul Islam, Rizwanul Islam, Faizul Kabir Khan, Habibullah Khan, Syed Akhtar Mahmud, M. Muqtada, Munir Quddus, Salim Rashid, and M.A. Taslim.

The following individuals deserve special appreciation for their contribution in converting the conference papers into a publishable manuscript. Fakrul Alam, the editorial consultant, handled the principal editorial responsibility diligently and efficiently. Further editorial assistance was provided by Judith Banning and Cherry Lynn T. Zafaralla, who also coordinated the production of the volume. Finally, the manuscript was processed by a team of efficient word processors, consisting of Anita P. Angeles, Zenaida M. Acacio, Helen K. Buencamino, Evelyn Gelano, and Ma. Luisa Sinco, who worked on several versions of the manuscript.

M.G. Quibria

March 1996
Manila

CONTRIBUTORS

ABU ABDULLAH, Research Director,
Bangladesh Institute of Development Studies

A. K. MONAW-WAR UDDIN AHMAD, Professor of Economics,
Department of Economics, University of Dhaka

SALEHUDDIN AHMED, Director General,
NGO Affairs Bureau, Government of Bangladesh

ZAID BAKHT, Senior Research Fellow,
Bangladesh Institute of Development Studies

AKHTAR HOSSAIN, Senior Lecturer,
Department of Economics, University of New Castle
Australia

ZAHID HOSSAIN, National Board of Revenue,
Government of Bangladesh

MOHAMMAD MOHABBAT KHAN, Department of Public Administration
University of Dhaka

MUSTAFA K. MUJERI, Programme Officer (Research),
Centre on Integrated Rural Development for Asia and the Pacific

M. G. QUIBRIA, Senior Economist
Asian Development Bank

MASIHUR RAHMAN, Secretary
Ministry of Communications, Government of Bangladesh

PRADUMNA B. RANA, Senior Project Officer/Economist
Bangladesh Resident Mission, Asian Development Bank

M. ALI RASHID, Professor,
Department of Economics, University of Dhaka

SALIM RASHID, Professor,
Department of Economics, University of Illinois at Urbana-Champaign

SADREL REZA, Director General,
Bangladesh Institute of Development Studies

ZAIDI SATTAR, Macroeconomist and Domestic Resource Mobilization Specialist, Planning Commission, Government of Bangladesh

QUAZI SHAHABUDDIN, Research Director,
Bangladesh Institute of Development Studies

TERMS AND ABBREVIATIONS

ADB	Asian Development Bank
ASEAN	Association of Southeast Asian Nations
BBS	Bangladesh Bureau of Statistics
BNP	Bangladesh Nationalist Party
BSCIC	Bangladesh Small Cottage Industries Corporation
CMI	Census of Manufacturing Industries
CIRDAP	Centre on Integrated Rural Development for Asia and the Pacific
EPZ	Export Processing Zones
IMF	International Monetary Fund
SKOP	United Front of Workers and Employees
UNDP	United Nations Development Programme
UNCTC	United Nations Centre for Transnational Corporations
USAID	United States Agency for International Development

1 INTRODUCTION

M.G. QUIBRIA

Bangladesh has been dubbed many things, from the " basket case" to the "test case" for economic development.[1] Despite these gloomy and pessimistic characterizations, it has made significant economic strides in a number of areas, even though the country remains one of the poorest in the developing world (its per capita income is estimated at less than $250 at the market exchange rate, and about $1,230 at the purchasing-power-parity exchange rate).[2] In recent years the country has made notable progress in the following areas:

- Food production has improved considerably over the years, increasing at 3 percent per annum since the 1980s. The country is on the verge of self-sufficiency in food, thereby opening up the possibility of food export, if further improvements are made in food production.

- In the last decade or so, with the widespread adoption of family planning practices, fertility has declined sharply, leading to a reduction in the population growth rate, which is now estimated at around 2 percent. The case of Bangladesh has demonstrated that demographic transition is attainable at a considerably lower level of income than previously considered feasible.

- The country has achieved significant reduction in poverty, with poverty incidence declining from over 70 percent of the population in the early 1980s to less than 50 percent in the early 1990s. Partially, this reflects the relatively egalitarian distribution of assets, including land, but more importantly, it is mainly the result of the broad-based growth that took place in the economy during this period. The seed-fertilizer technology that spearheaded the agricultural breakthrough led to a significant growth in employment in the rural sector (though some of the positive effect was offset by the still high population growth). Similarly, the industrial expansion that took place, including in the so-called nontraditional sectors (e.g., garments, light electronics, etc.) was essentially labor-intensive. Finally, there was a rapid growth of the informal service sector that now absorbs a significant portion of the urban labor force.

- The country has achieved notable success in maintaining macroeconomic stability. In 1980, the country had a national savings rate of about 6 percent of GDP, of which 2 percent was accounted for by workers' remittances from abroad. During the same period, the country maintained an investment rate of about 13 percent of GDP, relying predominantly on foreign resources for financing investment. However, the national savings rate has increased significantly in the meantime, and is estimated to be about 13 percent of GDP in 1994, reflecting enhanced public savings (made possible by the success of the newly introduced value-added tax and improved tax collection), and private savings (partly reflecting greater remittances from abroad). The budget deficit has remained under 6 percent of GDP. Similarly, the country has reduced its reliance on foreign resources and the current account deficit was reduced to less than 2 percent of GDP in 1994. This has been made possible partly by improved performance of merchandise exports, particularly garments, and partly by a steady increase of foreign remittances. The country has successfully maintained a competitive, effective real exchange rate. Finally, the country has been successful in maintaining a very low rate of inflation: with an inflation rate of about 5 percent per annum in the 1990s, it has one of the lowest inflation rates in developing Asia.

Despite the above successes, the country faces a number of critical constraints in further economic development. These constraints relate to:

- *The low level of human resource development*. The country has a high adult illiteracy rate of 65 percent, and the general level of education for its population remains commensurately low. The health and nutritional status of a large segment of the population remains unsatisfactory.

- *Relatively low savings and investment rates.* The country's savings and investment rates, though much improved in recent years, remain low. The economy is now trapped in a growth rate of about 4 to 5 percent. To improve the existing poverty situation, the country needs to accelerate its growth rate significantly, and that will require much higher rates of investment and savings than obtains currently.

- *Narrow export base.* Despite the considerable increase in the value of nontraditional exports, the export base has remained narrow and is limited to a few products. The country needs to significantly diversify its exportables as well as increase the supply elasticities of existing export products.

- *Efficiency of the public sector.* Despite considerable reform, the level of efficiency of public sector enterprises remains unsatisfactory. Public sector deficits still claim a considerable amount of budgetary outlays. Notwithstanding some recent improvements, there is significant scope for enhancing the efficiency of the public sector in the delivery of services.

The chapters that follow focus on selected development issues facing the Bangladesh economy. Chapter 2, by P.B. Rana, describes the various policy reforms undertaken by Bangladesh and how these compare with other South Asian economies. In doing so, Rana brings out some important issues related to design and sequencing of policies. In particular, he stresses the need for broadening the reform process at the microeconomic level, addressing institutional and enterprise reforms. Chapter 3, by Abu Abdullah and Quazi Shahabuddin, reviews the performance of the agricultural sector in conjunction with the various policy reforms implemented in the past. It also analyzes the policy agenda that should be adopted in the future, in particular, the need for crop diversification. Chapter 4, by Masihur Rahman and Zaid Bakht, highlights the constraints to industrial development and recommends policy and institutional reforms to improve the performance of the sector. The authors suggest a collaborative relationship between the government and the private sector along the line of East Asian economies. Chapter 5, by Mustafa K. Mujeri and Salehuddin Ahmed, provides an account of the poverty and human development situation in the country. The authors adopt a perspective where human development has both an instrumental value in eradicating poverty and is an end in itself. Chapter 6, by Zaidi Sattar, provides a critical assessment of the prospects for nontraditional exports and highlights some important issues affecting expansion of exports. Chapter 7, by Sadrel Reza and M. Ali Rashid, examines why the country has failed to attract foreign investment and suggests regulatory and policy measures to improve this unsatisfactory situation. Chapter 8, by Akhtar Hossain and Salim Rashid, reviews the financial sector reforms undertaken in the economy and indicates further reforms are needed to improve the functioning of this critical sector. Chapter 9, by M. Zahid Hossain, provides a summary of domestic resource mobilization in the public sector, identifies its problems, and suggests steps including administrative reforms to improve it. Finally, Chapter 10, by Mohammad Mohabbat Khan and A.K. Monaw-War Uddin Ahmad, reviews the state of governance in the country and emphasizes the need for further improvement since governance has a critical bearing on the development process.

As evident from the various chapters, economic reforms in Bangladesh have helped stabilize the economy and yielded moderate economic growth. However, as all the chapters have consistently emphasized, if the economy is to move from a low-growth to a high-growth trajectory, reforms need to be sustained.

For the reforms to be successful, they need to be *credible*. However, the political instability that has existed in the past 20 years or so has not been particularly helpful in inspiring confidence in the credibility of the reforms. Nevertheless, a consensus exists across the political spectrum in favor of these reforms which makes it almost certain that these reforms will continue.

Besides the issue of credibility of reforms, the other issues critical to the economic success of the country, which are largely political-economic in nature, relate to *labor market flexibility* and *governance*. The industrial labor force is highly politicized and the consequent strikes and lockouts have prevented industrial output from reaching its full potential. Similarly, the management of public sector enterprises remains inefficient. Regulation and enforcement of government policies remain mired in various levels of red tape and corruption. The capability of the government to maintain law and order and enforce contracts remains circumscribed and needs to be further strengthened. All these issues, which are related to the larger political environment, require broad-based societal support for their resolution in favor of the process of economic development.

In sum, the economy seems to be at a crossroads. If the economic reforms already initiated can be sustained and further reinforced; if the economic, political, and social institutions can be reformed to suit economic development; and if the broad consensus that exists in favor of reforms can be further nourished, the economy has a fairly bright future, despite many difficult economic and social constraints. However, if the present consensus in favor of reforms flounders, and the reform process becomes unsustainable; if the structure of governance remains weak; if the labor market remains inflexible; if political stability remains as fragile as it is today, then further economic progress will not only be difficult but may suffer an irreversible setback. In this particular sense, the present economic situation represents a transition which may lead either to a virtuous circle of growth and development or to a vicious cycle of poverty and backwardness.

Notes

1. The "basket case" label is attributed to Henry Kissinger, former secretary of state of President Richard Nixon, and subsequently, President Gerald Ford. The "test case" label for economic development is to be found in one of the first books on the economy of Bangladesh by Just Faaland and J.R. Parkinson (1976). The title implies that in view of extreme resource constraints, Bangladesh represents "the world's most difficult problem of economic development". The authors argue, "If the problem of Bangladesh can be solved, there can be reasonable confidence that less difficult problems of development can also be solved" (p. 5).

2. Data cited herein are derived from such Asian Development Bank publications as *Key Indicators of Developing Asian and Pacific Countries 1995* and *Asian Development Outlook 1995-1996.*

References

Asian Development Bank, 1995. *Asian Development Outlook 1995-1996*. Hong Kong: Oxford University Press.

Asian Development Bank, 1995. *Key Indicators of Developing Asian and Pacific Countries 1995*. Hong Kong: Oxford University Press.

Faaland, J., and J.R. Parkinson, 1976. *Bangladesh: The Test Case of Development*. London: C. Hurst and Company.

2 Reforms in Bangladesh: A Comparative Assessment in Relation to Other South Asian Countries

Pradumna B. Rana

Introduction

It is well established that the East and the Southeast Asian countries are, economically, among the most dynamic and resilient in the world. Economic forecasters expect this dynamism to continue into the foreseeable future. The People's Republic of China, presently the fastest growing country in the world, is expected to become an economic superpower in the next millennium. The factors behind this expectation are well discussed, among others, in Rana (1990) and various issues of the *Asian Development Outlook* of the Asian Development Bank.

The South Asian countries, whose inward-looking and highly protectionist policies of the post-independence era are almost legendary, were basically left out of this process of Asian economic dynamism. Chakravarty (1990) notes that most South Asian countries started moving away from import-substituting development regimes in the late 1970s and adopted market-oriented policy reforms. Initial policy reform measures were piecemeal and fragmented and had little impact on the economy.

It was only in the early 1990s when multiparty elections were held in Bangladesh and Nepal and reform-oriented governments took over in India and Pakistan, that the pace of reforms in South Asia picked up. With the adoption of a wide range of stabilization and structural reform measures, there was some optimism that these countries would, at some point, get on the bandwagon of Asian economic dynamism. Evidence presented in this paper suggests that although some signs of improved economic performance including booming stock markets are becoming visible in South Asian countries, and even though a certain amount of macroeconomic stability has been achieved, reforms have yet to be translated into improved economic performance on a sustained basis.

The political turmoils many South Asian countries experienced in recent years have raised new questions as to the depth and pace of reforms. In Bangladesh and Pakistan, despite their parliamentary democracies, a good deal of opposition against reforms was expressed through political strikes and boycotts. In Nepal, it appears that much of the political instability was related to the issue of market reforms instituted in recent years. In India, although the political landscape is somewhat more stable than its neighbors, there is an ongoing national debate about the depth and pace of reforms, which are widely perceived to have adversely affected the poorer sections of the population.

In this context, this discussion aims to outline the progress made by the South Asian countries (namely, Bangladesh, India, Nepal, Pakistan, and Sri Lanka) in the area of economic reforms; assess the impact of the reforms measures; and outline the prospects for South Asia.

Rather than limiting itself to a discussion of reforms in South Asia, this chapter addresses a set of analytical issues related to the design and sequencing of policies. One of its findings is that the impact of reforms on the real sector of South Asia is yet to be fully established. This raises an important question, Is the sluggish economic performance an inevitable outcome of the stabilization program which is the familiar J-curve argument,[1] or is it due to an inappropriate design and sequencing of reform policies? These questions are important because if the J-curve scenario holds, then over time, the growth process will resume and ultimately a higher trajectory will be reached. If it is a question of flaws in the design and sequencing of reforms then the growth process might not resume until and unless complementary reforms are undertaken in various other areas.

The question whether economic policies matter is a subject of considerable debate in the literature. At one extreme are Easterly et al. (1993) who argue that much of the country variation in economic growth is due to random and exogenous shocks including fortuitous events, and policies only have minimal impact. At the other end are the new growth theorists who attribute much of the variation to endogenous country characteristics including policies on research and development (De Long and Summers 1993); human capital (Lucas 1988, Barro 1991); investment in physical capital (Romer 1991); government spending (Barro 1990); tax policy (King and Rebelo 1990); financial policy (Levine 1991); trade policy (Young 1991); and macroeconomic policy (Fischer 1993).

If policies matter, as appears to be the majority opinion, then issues related to design and sequencing, and credibility and consistency of policies become critically important. McKinnon (1993) argues that it is neither theoretically defensible nor practically feasible to implement all aspects of policy reforms simultaneously. Inappropriate design and sequence can lead to the failure of the reform program. Economic history has recorded numerous such instances. An example is the Southern Cone Latin American case where efforts to reform the financial and trade sectors failed in the mid-1980s (Diaz-Alejandro 1985). The debate that exists in relation to reforming transitional economies (the formerly centrally planned economies) is also relevant (see Sachs and Woo 1993, Rana and Hamid 1994, and Rana 1995).

Another important dimension of a reform package which determines its success or failure is the question of credibility and consistency of policies. Unless a package is perceived to be credible and consistent, it cannot work. This issue is, however, not very different from that of design and sequencing reforms because an ill-designed and poorly sequenced package cannot be credible.

An important hypothesis of this paper is that macroeconomic and sector reforms, while necessary, are by themselves not enough for enhanced economic efficiency and growth. Creating an enabling environment for the private sector requires action in the microeconomic areas as well (institutional and enterprise reforms in various sectors such as agriculture and industries, public administration reform, and reforms of the legal system and labor laws). Rana (1995) and Rana and Hamid (1994) argues that supply responses were relatively quick in People's Republic of China and the Socialist Republic of Viet Nam because of the success in dismantling communes and introducing farm households at an early stage of the reform process in the early 1970s. Increased agricultural productivity and savings of the sector could finance the fiscal deficit of the government. At a later stage the dynamism of the township and village enterprises, which were market-driven and outside the web of price and output controls that dominated the heavy industries, supported the reform process (Rana and Hamid 1994). It is also well-known that the partnership between the government and the private business sector was an important factor contributing to the "East Asian Miracle" (see, for example, World Bank 1993).

This paper argues that the South Asian countries are lagging behind in micro reforms and that this is an important reason for their lackluster performance in the real sector. Micro reforms are more painful than macro and sector reforms because they involve curtailing the power of the bureaucracy along with layoffs and retrenchment of the labor force.

The rest of this chapter is organized as follows: the second section summarizes the major reforms undertaken by the South Asian countries; the third section analyzes the impact of the reform measures; the fourth section focuses on the experience of Bangladesh; and finally, the fifth section outlines the prospects for South Asia.

Survey of Policy Reforms in South Asia

Among the five major South Asian countries, the process of policy reforms began the earliest in Sri Lanka in the late 1970s supported by various facilities provided by the International Monetary Fund. The measures involved a stabilization package together with structural measures in the areas of trade and financial sector reforms, including deregulation of interest rates. There were delays in implementing the reform program in the mid-1980s due to political turmoil. Since late 1989, in spite of continuing difficulties, a new and rigorous liberalization program was introduced.

In Pakistan the reform process began in 1990 with a macroeconomic and structural adjustment program. The process accelerated in July 1993 when a caretaker government came to power. Subsequently, the democratically elected Bhutto government, despite backpedalling in certain politically sensitive areas such as taxation of income from agriculture, by and large has continued the reform agenda.

In contrast to these countries, the latest spurt in the reform program occurred in the other South Asian countries of India, Nepal, and Bangladesh only a year later in 1991 as newly elected governments took over[2]. In India, the Narasimha Rao government, which assumed power in mid-1991 reversed the previous inward-looking approach. A number of high-level committees were established to design reform programs in many sectors of the economy. The collapse of the former Soviet Union, with which the country had close trade and investment relations, also added some urgency to the reform process in India. Similarly, Nepal and Bangladesh are now pursuing an export-led development strategy.

In summarizing the status of reforms in South Asia, let us distinguish between three categories of policies: macroeconomic policies referring to indirect tools of monetary management, budget tightening and exchange rate adjustment; sector reforms referring to fiscal, financial and trade policy reforms; and microeconomic reforms, as defined earlier, which relate to the organization of a firm or unit or union.

The information in Table 2.1 suggests that the South Asian countries have achieved considerable progress in the areas of industrial deregulation and in macroeconomic and sector reforms (including trade, exchange rate, and financial and fiscal sector reforms). Whereas a few years ago a license was required to establish just about any type of business venture and to procure inputs (including imported inputs), presently such activities are significantly deregulated in all South Asian countries. Both tariffs and nontariff barriers have also been reduced significantly and the exchange rate, barring the existence of some regulations, is largely market-determined. Foreign investment is being eagerly sought after and current account convertibility has been announced. The financial sector (including interest rate) has been deregulated to some extent. In fact, since the late 1970s Sri Lanka has been one of the few developing countries with a totally deregulated interest rate regime. Private banks and other types of financial institutions are being established and capital markets developed. In the area of fiscal reforms, Bangladesh, Sri Lanka, and Nepal have introduced the value-added tax (VAT) while the other South Asian countries are in the process of introducing it. In an attempt to mobilize larger amounts of resources in the public sector, India and Pakistan have simplified their taxation system and expanded coverage. The public expenditure system has been streamlined in many countries.

In contrast, the implementation of microeconomic reforms, except in the areas of industrial deregulation, has been relatively slow. Aside from Bangladesh, attempts to reform the agriculture sector and remove subsidies to the sector have been slow.[3] Pakistan is facing political difficulties in implementing the farm development package. Similarly, although privatization policies have been announced in several South Asian countries and several enterprises have been privatized, implementation of industrial restructuring policies has been slow.

Table 2.1

Policy Reforms in Selected South Asian Countries

	Bangladesh	*India*	*Nepal*	*Pakistan*	*Sri Lanka*
I. Macroeconomic and Sector Reforms					
A. *Fiscal Reforms and Public Resource Management*	VAT introduced in July 1991. Personal income tax rate reduced in 1993-1994. A number of procedural changes in ADP implementation introduced including the 3-year rolling plan.	Personal income taxation: maximum marginal rate reduced to 40%; surcharge abolished; exemption limit raised. Excise duties being simplified to resemble a VAT system. Tax administration being modernized. Octroi being slowly abolished.	VAT being introduced in a phased manner. Octroi to be abolished. Introduced 3-year rolling plan system.	Coverage of general sales tax expanded. Provinces initiating measures to implement agriculture income tax.	VAT introduced in 1994. Defence levy of 3% introduced in 1992. Introduced 5-year rolling plan in the 1980s.
B. *Financial Sector*	Significant deregulation of interest rates. Role of directed credit declined and NCBs given greater freedom. Securities Exchange Commission established in 1993. Loan provisioning system introduced. Several new private and foreign banks allowed. NCBs have been partially recapitalized. One development finance institution (Bangladesh Shilpa Rin Sangstha) has initiated commercial transactions. Rupali Bank to be privatized soon.	Gradual deregulation of interest rates and reduction of allocated credit to priority sectors. Prudential accounting and capital adequancy norms introduced. Private sector banks being allowed to expand and new private banks are being established. Securities Exchange Board of India with regulatory and prosecuting powers established. A regulatory framework for insurance sector being finalized as a prelude to liberalization. National Stock Exchange established.	Open market operations have been introduced. Four new private banks established. Several new nonbank financial institutions (such as leasing and finance companies) established. Nepal Stock Exchange established.	Open market operations have been introduced. Of the five state-owned banks, two have been privatized and two others are earmarked for privatization.	Several financial institutions privatized. Since 1991 foreign banks allowed to establish branches outside Colombo. Securities Council strengthened. Credit Information Bureau established. Stock Exchange opened to foreign investors beginning 1990.

(Continued next page)

Table 2.1 *(continued)*

	Bangladesh	*India*	*Nepal*	*Pakistan*	*Sri Lanka*
C. *Trade*	System of export incentives deepened by introducing bonded warehouses, duty drawback schemes, and back-to-back letters of credit. Tax exemption on import of capital machinery for 100% export-oriented industries. Quantitative restrictions on imports liberalized considerably: 192 to 112 items in 1993 and about 30 items by the end of the present fiscal year. Level and structure of tariff rates improved: Presently only two products (cigarette paper and alcoholic beverages) still have tariffs over 100%. Maximum rate on others is 60%.	Except for a small list of negative items, import licensing virtually abolished. Quantitative restrictions replaced by tariffs. Tariffs reduced in stages: Maximum rate reduced from 400% in 1990-1991 to 65% in 1994 and 50% in 1995, and the average duty from about 50% to 27% during the same period.	75% of foreign exchange earnings can be sold at market-determined rates. System of export incentives being developed. Import licensing system abolished for most raw materials and imported inputs. Tariffs reduced in stages: present range is from 5-100% and 8 sub-rates.	System of export incentives strengthened through concessional tariff treatment of imported inputs and freight subsidy. Import licensing system liberalized by reducing negative list. Tariffs reduced in stages: from 225% in 1988 to 70% in 1994.	The import licensing system liberalized; only 11 reserved items require license. Export taxes eliminated. Foreign exchange surrender system lifted in March 1993. Import surcharge abolished in 1991. Since 1991 import tariffs regrouped into a new four-band structure and rates reduced progressively since 1997.
D. *Exchange Rate*	Dual exchange rate system abolished in 1992. The taka is freely convertible for current account transactions.	Exchange rate of the rupee is basically market-determined: peg with the Indian rupee still maintained. Rupee is freely convertible for current account transactions.	Exchange rate of the rupee is basically market-determined. Rupee is freely convertible for current account transactions.	Exchange rate of the rupee is basically market-determined. Rupee is freely convertible for current account transactions (since July 1994).	Exchange rate of the rupee is basically market-determined. Rupee is freely convertible for current account transactions.
II. Microeconomic Reforms					
E. *Agriculture Sector and Land Issues*	Significant deregulation of inputs have occurred. Subsidies have been eliminated. Some actions taken in land reform during the mid-1980s.	Slow: massive subsidies for water, electricity, and fertilizer.	Distribution of agricultural inputs liberalized.	Slow: Awami Tractor Scheme introduced. Farm development package introduced to encourage crop diversification.	Privatized management of tea plantations.

(Continued next page)

Table 2.1 *(continued)*

	Bangladesh	*India*	*Nepal*	*Pakistan*	*Sri Lanka*
F. *Industrial Policy and Public Enterprise*	Industrial licensing system abolished. Significantly liberalized foreign investment regulations. Incentive scheme upgraded. Institutional reforms including restructuring and privatization have been slow.	Industrial licenses abolished for all except 14 industries in the areas of defence, health, safety and environment. Liberal stance even in these 14 industries. Restrictions on expansion of large business houses abolished. Significantly liberalized foreign investment regulations: approvals for up to 51% foreign equity participation is automatic (January 1993). Five-year tax holiday for private investors in power generation, port, airlines, and telecom and infrastructure. A new policy announced in 1991, but institutional reforms including restructuring and privatization of public enterprises has been slow.	Industrial licenses abolished for all except those in defence, health, and environment. Significantly liberalized foreign investment regulations: 100% ownership permitted in medium and large-scale industries and "one window" established. Privatization Act is in place and several industries including airline industry have been privatized: restructuring policies have been slow.	Board of Investment established to reduce the multiplicity of institutions involved in investment decisions. Significantly liberalized foreign investment for power generation. New privatization policy approved in February 1994: restructuring policies have been slow.	New liberal guidelines for foreign investment announced in 1991. Third investment promotion zone established in 1991. Over 30 state-owned enterprises have been privatized.
G. *Public Administration*	Slow: various studies and reports prepared but little action.	Slow	Slow: Several thousand civil servants retrenched.	Slow	Serious efforts being made to reduce size of bureaucracy.
H. *Labor Market*	Slow	Slow: Industrial Disputes Act and Companies Act are being revised. National Renewal Fund for training and redeploying workers established.	Slow	Slow	Slow

Sources: Asian Development Bank, *Asian Development Outlook* (various years).

The impact of reforms cannot be felt at the level of the individual entrepreneur unless the institutions and the bureaucracy can deliver the announced services and benefits. The reform of the public administration system is, therefore, a necessity in all of the South Asian countries which have inherited the old British system from their colonial days. Similarly, in all of the South Asian countries there is an urgent need to establish a code of conduct for labor and employees and to promote greater partnership between the management, the labor force, and the government.

Impact of Policy Reforms

As noted earlier, all the countries of South Asia have, in the past few years, undertaken wide-ranging reform programs that have led to the dismantling of many rigid controls and the removal or relaxation of restrictive policies. Reforms, which covered all sectors of the economy, have had a major impact on trade, finance, public enterprises, foreign investment, and taxation. The liberalization measures have led to booming exports. They have attracted the attention of foreign investors and the size of the middle class has started to increase. For example, in India foreign investments have shot up from a low level of $120 million a year in the second half of the 1980s to over $1.2 billion in 1993 and are expected to keep rising. In addition, foreign portfolio investment in Indian stock exchanges totalled $2.4 billion in July 1994—up from almost nothing a year ago.

The precise impact of reforms on the economy is, nevertheless, more difficult to establish because of the difficulty in isolating the impact of individual policies in an environment where many other reforms are being implemented simultaneously. However, a review of data in Table 2.2, where various macroeconomic stability and growth indicators for the pre-reform and post-reform years are provided, leads to several interesting findings:

- Reforms have led to macroeconomic stability in all the countries with the sole exception of perhaps Pakistan. For example, the growth rate of money supply and the inflation rate (although starting to increase recently) has slowed considerably in India in the post-1991 period. The fiscal and current account deficits have also been reduced significantly although the former has still overshot the target. Foreign exchange reserves now stand at about $20 billion

Table 2.2[a]

Economic Indicators for Selected South Asian Countries

Country	*1988*	*1989*	*1990*	*1991*	*1992*	*1993*	*1994*[b]	*1995*[b]	*1996*[b]
Bangladesh									
GDP growth rate	2.9	2.5	6.6	**3.4**	4.2	4.5	4.5	5.5	...
Inflation rate	9.4	10.0	8.1	**7.2**	4.3	1.9	2.5	2.5	...
Broad money supply (percentage change)	9.1	16.3	16.9	**12.1**	14.1	10.6	12.0	14.0	...
Fiscal deficit (percent of GDP)	-7.1	-7.3	-7.7	**-6.8**	-5.0	-5.3	...	...	...
Current account deficit (percent of GDP)	-1.5	-5.4	-1.9	**0.3**	0.8	0.9	0.5	0.2	...
India									
GDP growth rate	9.9	6.6	5.2	**0.7**	4.6	3.8	5.4	5.8	6.3
Inflation rate	9.4	6.1	11.6	**13.5**	9.6	7.5	10.0	9.0	8.0
Broad money supply (percentage change)	21.9	15.3	15.1	**19.3**	15.7	18.2	18.5	16.5	15.0
Fiscal deficit (percent of GDP)	-7.8	-7.8	-8.4	**-5.9**	-5.7	-7.5	-6.7	-5.5	-5.0
Current account deficit (percent of GDP)	-2.9	-2.5	-3.3	**-0.9**	-1.5	-0.1	-1.0	-1.0	-1.0
Nepal									
GDP growth rate	7.0	5.4	4.9	**6.4**	4.6	2.9	7.8	3.5	5.0
Inflation rate	9.0	8.8	8.3	**15.6**	17.1	8.9	9.1	8.0	7.0
Broad money supply (percentage change)	22.4	24.2	18.6	**19.5**	21.1	27.7	21.2	18.0	16.0
Fiscal deficit (percent of GDP)	-8.8	-11.5	-10.0	**-10.7**	-8.6	-8.3	-6.7	-12.3	...
Current account deficit (percent of GDP)	-8.2	-7.4	-8.2	**-9.4**	-5.2	-6.0	-6.5	-7.1	-8.2

(Continued next page)

Table 2.2 (*continued*)

Country	*1988*	*1989*	*1990*	*1991*	*1992*	*1993*	*1994*[b]	*1995*[b]	*1996*[b]
Pakistan									
GDP growth rate	6.4	4.8	**4.6**	5.6	7.7	2.3	4.0	6.5	...
Inflation rate	8.8	7.9	**9.0**	11.8	9.5	4.2	8.8	8.0	...
Broad money supply (percentage change)	12.2	4.6	**12.6**	16.3	30.3	18.0	16.0	14.5	...
Fiscal deficit (percent of GDP)	-8.5	-7.4	**-6.5**	-8.7	-7.4	-7.9	-5.8	...	...
Current account deficit (percent of GDP)	-3.8	-3.6	**4.2**	-3.3	-3.9	-6.1	...	-4.7	...
Sri Lanka									
GDP growth rate	2.7	2.3	**6.2**	4.6	4.3	7.0	6.0	6.6	6.4
Inflation rate	14.0	11.5	**21.5**	12.2	11.4	11.7	7.7	11.3	9.1
Broad money supply (percentage change)	16.5	12.5	**19.1**	23.6	16.6	23.6	17.1	6.8	12.9
Fiscal deficit (percent of GDP)	-15.3	-11.0	**-9.8**	-11.5	-7.2	-7.9	-9.9	-9.5	-7.9
Current account deficit (percent of GDP)	-5.5	-5.8	**3.7**	-6.5	-4.6	-3.6	-2.6	-1.9	-1.9

... means data not available

[a]All data are on a calendar year basis except GDP growth rate and fiscal deficit which are on a fiscal year (FY) basis. The fiscal year for Bangladesh and Pakistan ends on 30 June, while it ends on 31 March and 15 July for India and Nepal, respectively. For Bangladesh, Nepal, and Pakistan, for example, 1994 refers to FY1993/1994 whereas for India it refers to FY1994/1995. The data for the year when the pace of reforms picked up considerably are in bold.

[b]ADB Staff projections.

Source: *Asian Development Outlook 1995 and 1996* (ADB 1995).

today as compared to $1.1 billion in June 1991. Stability has also been commendable in Bangladesh where the inflation rate stands at around 2.5 per cent per annum; the fiscal deficit at around 5 per cent of GDP; and foreign exchange reserves at 8 months imports.

- The data in Table 2.2, however, suggest that the reform programs have yet to lead to a sustained improvement in the real sector of the South Asian countries. In Bangladesh, India, and Nepal, the GDP growth rate is running at around 4 percent per annum on average. This rate is not very different from the rates prevailing during the years preceding the reforms. Some encouraging trends of higher growth levels are, however, emerging. Sri Lanka registered a growth rate of 6.1 percent in 1993 and a growth rate of over 5.5. percent is projected for 1994 and 1995. In 1992, industrial output grew by over 9 percent in India from a very low level of 3 to 4 percent in the previous.

A number of factors account for the trends outlined above. The first is the lagged response to many policies. This is the so-called J-curve effect. The second is the issue of design and sequencing policy reforms. Is the sluggish economic performance of the real sector of South Asia an inevitable outcome of the stabilization program? Or is the real sector sluggishness due to inappropriate sequencing and design of the various policies? Let us answer this question by examining the case of Bangladesh.

Bangladesh Reforms Since 1991

Fiscal Reforms

A major effort in the area of tax reform has been the successful introduction of the VAT in FY1992. As a result, the tax/GDP ratio has shown an increasing trend. Although efforts have been made to expand the tax base and compliance rates for the VAT, more needs to be done. Tax administration has also to be improved further as outstanding tax arrears are still high.

On the side of expenditures, a number of procedural changes have been introduced in relation to the implementation of the annual development program including the introduction of the three-year rolling plan. There is, however, a need for further delegation of authority. It is also necessary to establish a coordinating mechanism to take decisive and continuous steps in resolving problems identified in relation to project implementation.

Financial Sector Reforms

Perhaps the single most important reform in this sector relates to interest rates which are now essentially market-determined except for the floors on deposit rates. The role of directed credit has also declined; the NCBs have been partially recapitalized; a new loan provisioning system has been introduced; and several new private banks have been established.

Despite the progress made, Bangladesh is nowhere near establishing an efficient financial sector. Action is necessary to enhance the efficiency of both the banking system and capital markets. At the more micro level, there is a need to improve the technology (e.g., computerization) and the accounting and auditing system of the sector; there is also a need to strengthen the legal framework by enacting the Bankruptcy Bill and the Foreign Investment Protection and Promotion Act, and by amending the Financial Courts Act. At a more macro level, there is a need to make the sector more competitive by, among others, rationalizing yields on government savings schemes and allowing more private banks and restructuring and privatizing more NCBs. The provision of term credit to the private sector has also to be addressed.

External Trade

While progress in liberalizing imports through the reduction of tariffs and quantitative restrictions has been encouraging, success in reforming export policies has been limited. Although the system of export incentives has been deepened by introducing bonded warehouses, duty drawback schemes and back-to-back letters of credit, the implementation system is neither simple or transparent. Also, these incentives are available only to the direct exporters and not to the indirect exporters.

Exchange Rates

Although the government abolished the multiple exchange rate regime in 1992 and subsequently made the taka convertible for current account transactions, it still intervenes in foreign exchange markets to avoid the appreciation of the real exchange rate.

Agriculture

Most of the distortions in the sector had been eliminated by the removal of subsidies and privatization of the input distribution system. This, in turn, had partially contributed to placing the country close to self-sufficiency in rice production. More recently, however, some government intervention in the distribution of fertilizers has been witnessed at the district level. This may have an adverse impact on foodgrain production.

Industrial Policy and Public Enterprise Reforms

While the investment sanctioning regulations (for both domestic and foreign investors) have been relaxed significantly, progress in restructuring and privatizing enterprises has been slow. In 1991, the government had announced a list of 26 state-owned enterprises slated for the first stage of privatization. However, privatization has been finalized for only a total of 18 enterprises of which only 11 have actually been handed over to the private sector. Losses of public enterprises amount to nearly 1 percent of GDP and the pace of privatization has to be accelerated significantly.

Public Administration Reforms

Various studies and reports have been prepared but actions have been slow. The government has declared that by December 1994 it would have in place a time-bound action plan of practical reforms including personnel management and training, but it has failed to do so.

Labor Markets

Flexible labor markets are important for the country's economic growth. To this end there is an urgent need to institute a market-based collective bargaining system that is free from government intervention and a system of severance liabilities that is in line with market conditions.

The first column of Table 2.3 summarizes the status of policy reforms in Bangladesh in terms of the typology which we have developed. It is clear from the table that while the country has achieved a moderate amount of success in macroeconomic and sector reforms, reforms in the more microeconomic areas except agriculture have remained weak. The reform strategy of Bangladesh to date might, therefore, be labelled as a "macro-first" strategy.

The "macro-first" reform strategy has led to commendable success in macrostability as noted earlier and in reforming the incentive system

Table 2.3
Policy Reforms in Bangladesh: Status and Actions Required

	Status[a]	*Actions Required*
I. Macroeconomic and Sector Reforms		
A. Fiscal Reforms and Public Resource Management	Moderate Progress	Tax base and compliance rates for VAT to be expanded continuously.
		Need for improving tax administration.
		Need for delegating authority and establishing a coordinating mechanism to take decision and continuous actions in resolving problems identified in relation to project implementation.
B. Financial Sector	Moderate Progress	Urgent need to strengthen Bangladesh Bank by improving its supervisory powers, organization, management, and human resource development.
		Improve the technology (e.g. computerization) and the accounting and auditing system of the banking sector.
		Need for making banking sector competitive by allowing more private banks and restructuring and privatizing NCBs.
		Provision of term credit for private sector.
		Phase out directed credit programs.
		Further liberalize interest rates by removing floors on deposit rates.
		Expand credit guarantee schemes for small investors.
		Rationalize yields on GOB savings schemes.
		Legal framework to be strengthened: Bankruptcy Bill and the Foreign Investment Protection and Promotion Act have to be enacted by the Parliament; Financial Courts Act has to be amended.
C. Trade	Moderate Progress	Restructure institutions administering incentives (e.g. Export Promotion Bureau, Duty Exemption and Drawback Office, and Board of Investment).
		Introduce dialogue with private sector and promote a partnership approach.
		Discontinue the use of tariff values.
		Eliminate the remaining trade related quantitative restrictions.
		Simplify and administer the export incentive scheme more transparently (make it available to indirect exporters as well).
D. Exchange Rate	Moderate Progress	Reduce intervention by the Bangladesh Bank.

(Continued next page)

Table 2.3 *(continued)*

	Status[a]	Actions Required
II. Microeconomic Reforms		
E. *Agriculture Sector and Land Issues*	Moderate Progress	Need to develop a strategy for diversification. Eliminate exemption and raise agricultural land tax rates (after productivity has gone up!). Need to reassess land ceiling and provide support services to farmers to enhance land productivity further.
F. *Industrial Policy and Public Enterprise*	Limited Progress	Introduce a comprehensive restructuring program comprising: (i) liquidation of non-viable enterprises (need for safety nets); (ii) restructuring and good governance of enterprises to remain in the public sector; and (iii) privatization of the restructured enterprises. Reduce losses of public enterprises (Taka 20 billion or about one-quarter of 1992-1993 ADP or one per cent of GDP) by, among others, removing subsidies and/or price reforms.
G. *Public Administration*	Limited Progress	Develop and implement an action plan addressing various issues such as efficiency and accountability.
H. *Labor Market*	Limited Progress	Decentralize wage fixation. Stand against lawlessness should be taken by political leaders in the country. Enforcement of labor laws; code of conduct for management and laborers.

[a] Refer to Table 2.1 for the specific reform measures undertaken.

for the private sector. Supply responses have, however, been weak because of poor implementation of the announced measures and limited progress in the microeconomic areas. Many of the benefits of the macro reforms are not felt at the level of the entrepreneur because of inefficient institutions. A recent task force established by the government found that among the major reasons for the failure to attract foreign investments were the failure to implement policy incentives, lack of coordination among the different ministries, and lack of adequate infrastructure (including power). It is, therefore, felt that a more balanced design and sequencing of reforms, where certain aspects of micro reforms were implemented at an earlier stage of the process, together with macro and sector reforms could have enhanced the credibility of the package and placed the economy on a better footing by eliciting favorable supply responses to the reformed incentive structure. Such a supply-augmenting strategy would also perhaps have been less painful in terms of adjustment costs compared to demand restraint. It would also perhaps have been a more "bottom-up" grassroots-oriented approach to reforms. But micro reforms are also more difficult as they involve, among others, streamlining the bureaucracy and retrenching workers.

The present environment of macroeconomic stability in Bangladesh, however, presents an important window of opportunity and a base for more aggressive actions in policy reforms. Fiscal stability permits "pump-priming" activity while the comfortable balance of payments situation permits further opportunity for trade liberalization. The major components of a reform agenda recommended for higher levels of economic growth and investment, which are necessary for poverty alleviation in the country are:

- implementation of the announced reforms in a simplified, transparent and nondiscretionary manner;

- deepening economic reforms in various macroeconomic areas;

- broadening the reform process to cover the micro areas of institutional and enterprise reforms in various sectors such as agriculture and industries, public administration, including reforms of the legal system and labor issues; and

- developing a consensus on policy reforms with the private sector, labor unions, and the political parties so that the resistance to reform can be overcome.

While the details of the recommended reform agenda are presented in the third column of Table 2.3, in relation to the question of consensus of policies there is an urgent need for increased public awareness and debates on policy matters. This is critically important because while the costs of a particular reform package is often well-known by those who stand to lose from its implementation, the benefits are less well understood by the general public, specially those people who live in an environment of political difficulty.

Prospects for South Asia

The growth performance of South Asia has diverged significantly from that of East and Southeast Asia. However, over the next few years the wide-ranging reform programs adopted by these countries can be expected to bear fruit. The political deadlock is also expected to ease somewhat because of the close nexus between economics and politics. This will, in turn, pave the way for more reforms. The gap, therefore, is expected to narrow. The growth performance of the South Asian region as a whole is expected to improve further in the coming years.

It is sometimes argued that the pace of reforms in South Asia is too slow. There may be some truth in this proposition. However, policy-makers have to deal with the realities at the ground level and proceed in a manner and pace that is politically sustainable. It is instructive to remember that it is now nearly two decades since reforms were first initiated in People's Republic of China. The South Asian countries have initiated serious reforms only during the 1990s and it may still take a few years before these reforms gain full momentum.

Issues related to sequencing and design of a reform program are critically important. They eventually determine the credibility of the reform agenda. A more balanced sequencing where microeconomic reforms are implemented simultaneously or even precede macroeconomic reforms will encourage the development of institutions capable of adjusting to market opportunities, elicit quick supply response, and reduce the social costs of adjustment. This is the major lesson for South Asia from the experience of East Asia and the Asian transitional economies (including People's Republic of China). Since micro reforms are more painful, the South Asian countries are in a dilemma, which has further worsened recently because of political difficulties facing these countries.

One important factor accounting for East Asian dynamism is the increasing economic integration in the region, namely, the increasing cross-border flows of resources, goods and services as well as information and technology (Asian Development Bank 1995). It is important to emphasize that this integration has been largely market-driven, based on underlying complementarities among neighboring countries rather than preferential trading arrangements. The extent of such integration in South Asia has, however, remained limited. The complementarities within the South Asian region and the potential synergies of integrated development have to be exploited further. The prospect for further cooperation is bright since many South Asian countries are pursuing promarket and outward-oriented economic reforms. Also, as signatories to the new General Agreement on Tariffs and Trade, all of the South Asian countries are committed to reducing their levels of protection in accordance with a specified timetable. What appears to be urgently required is for the governments to initiate policies that foster regional cooperation and generate an enabling environment for the private sector. Unfortunately, the achievements of the SAARC in the economic area are few. In addition to regional cooperation, the SAARC countries need to foster greater economic links with East Asia to benefit from the latter's economic dynamism.

Because of "aid fatigue" in many donor countries, South Asia will have to rely increasingly on private financial flows. The annual inflow of foreign direct investment amounts to billions of dollars in People's Republic of China, Malaysia, and Thailand. But in individual South Asian countries, despite the improvements in recent years, they add up to no more than a few hundred million dollars. It is, of course, important to note in this context that the region has witnessed a rapid inflow of portfolio investment in recent years. A lot more effort, however, has to be made to attract long-term foreign capital. International experience suggests that external capital usually follows high economic performance and rarely leads it. Therefore, the prospects of large-scale foreign investment in South Asia are somewhat limited at present, and will depend largely on the prior economic success of the reforms and the maintenance of political stability in the countries of the region.

Acknowledgment

An earlier version of this paper was presented at the National Professor Atwar Husain Trust Fund Lecture 1994 in Dhaka on 20 January 1995. Helpful comments were received from the participants at the lecture and from B. Horayangura, N. Huda, R.K. Khan, M.G. Quibria, V.B. Tulsidhar and R.O. Wada.

Notes

1. A situation where output initially falls before increasing during the adjustment process.

2. In all of these countries, the reform process was initiated earlier than 1991, but the pace of implementation and coverage picked up after 1991. For example, in Bangladesh, the new industrial policy was announced in 1989 and deregulation of agriculture was initiated in 1990.

3. In contrast, reforms of the agriculture sector in People's Republic of China and the Socialist Republic of Viet Nam have significantly augmented rural savings and investment (Rana and Hamid 1994).

References

Asian Development Bank, various years. *Asian Development Outlook.* Hong Kong: Oxford University Press for the Asian Development Bank.

Barro, R. J., 1990. "Government Spending in a Simple Model of Endogenous Growth." *Journal of Political Economy* 98:103-125.

———, 1991. "Economic Growth in a Cross Section of Countries." *Quarterly Journal of Economics* 106:407-43.

Chakravarty, S., 1990. "Development Strategies for Growth with Equity: The South Asian Experience." *Asian Development Review* 8(1):134-59.

De Long, J. B., and L. H. Summers, 1993. "How Strongly do Developing Economies Benefit from Equipment Investment?" *Journal of Monetary Economics* 32(3):395-415.

Diaz-Alejandro, C., 1985. "Good-Bye Financial Repression, Hello Financial Crash." *Journal of Development Economics* 19:1-24.

Easterly, W., M. Kremer, L. Pritchett, and L.H. Summers, 1993. "Good Policy or Good Luck?" *Journal of Monetary Economics* 32:459-83.

Fischer, S., 1993. "Macroeconomic Factors in Growth." *Journal of Monetary Economics* 32(3):485-512.

King, R., and S. Rebelo, 1990. "Public Policy and Economic Growth: Developing Neoclassical Implications." *Journal of Political Economy* 98:126-50.

Levine, R., 1991. "Stock Markets, Growth and Policy." *Journal of Finance* 46:1445-65.

Lucas, R. E., 1988. "On the Mechanics of Economic Development." *Journal of Monetary Economics* 221:3-42.

McKinnon, R., 1991. *The Order of Economic Liberalization: Financial Control in Transition to Market Economy.* Baltimore: The Johns Hopkins University Press.

Rana, P.B., 1990. "Foreign Capital and Asian Economic Growth." *Asian Development Review* 8(1):77-102.

———, 1995. "Reform Strategies in Transitional Economies: Lessons from Asia." *World Development*. Forthcoming.

Rana, P. B., and N. Hamid, ed., 1994. *From Centrally Planned to Market Economies: The Asian Approach.* Hong Kong: Oxford University Press.

Romer, P., 1986. "Increasing Returns and Long-run Growth." *Journal of Political Economy* 94(5):1002-37.

Sachs, J., and W. Woo, 1993. "Big Bang Smear Job." *The International Economy* November/December:48-51.

Young, A., 1991. "Learning by Doing and the Dynamic Effects of International Trade." *Quarterly Journal of Economics* 6:369-406.

3 CRITICAL ISSUES IN AGRICULTURE: POLICY RESPONSE AND UNFINISHED AGENDA

ABU ABDULLAH AND QUAZI SHAHABUDDIN

The past decade (or perhaps more accurately, decade-and-a-half) has seen far-reaching changes in agricultural policies in Bangladesh, and also some fairly significant changes in performance. Whether the two are causally linked is still not a completely settled issue, but, as we shall argue subsequently, the burden of evidence is overwhelmingly in favor of such a causal link.

The changes in performance have, however, been rather narrowly focused, affecting primarily the rice economy. These changes have basically consisted of a continuation of the trend toward increased production of modern rice varieties, particularly in the *boro* (winter) season, but in more recent years also in the *aman* (post-monsoon) season. Growth rates for different rice varieties (excluding *aus*, the monsoon rice, which has been declining in importance) are presented in Table 3.1.

Table 3.1
Growth Rate of Rice Production by Variety, 1979-1991

	Local Varieties	*Modern Varieties*	*Total*
Aman	-1.55	7.09	1.29
Boro	-4.58	10.44	8.49
Total rice	-1.69	7.48	2.66

Source: Abdullah (1993, 28, table 6).

It may be noted that the overall growth rate of 2.66 is in fact lower than the growth rate for the period 1971-1980, estimated at 3.1 (Hossain et al. 1992). However, this comparison is misleading because the earlier period includes a subperiod, the early 1970s, when growth rates were exceptionally high as a result of a "recovery boom" from the dislocations of the 1971 Liberation War. A more appropriate comparison would be with the growth rate of 2.28 percent reported for the period 1976-1987 (Government of Bangladesh 1989, 140). The overlap between the periods being compared suggests that the acceleration in the growth rate was particularly pronounced after 1987. As a result of these developments, the technical and temporal structure of rice production has changed very significantly:

- Modern varieties of rice now predominate. In 1979 the share of modern variety (MV) rice in total rice production was a little over 35 percent. By 1991 this had risen to almost 65 percent. For *boro*, the change over the same period was from 77.5 percent to 95.6 percent; for *aman*, from 23.4 percent to 50.2 percent.

- Between 1979 and 1991, the share of *aman* in total production fell from 58.2 percent to 50.8 percent, while the share of *boro* rose from 19.4 percent to 37.3 percent. These developments, specially the latter, mean that production and hence market arrivals are smoother over the year.[1]

Agriculture: Beyond Self-Sufficiency?[2]

In the census year 1990/1991, the population of Bangladesh was reported to be 108 million. This would imply that over the decade 1981-1990, the population growth rate was 1.85 percent per annum, compared to an intercensal growth rate of 2.32 percent in the preceding decade. If true, this represents a major breakthrough for population policy (there is evidence that fertility decline has taken place and is largely attributable to policy).[3] Skeptics suspect an undercount, pointing to a probable large increase in the urban "floating population" as one possible cause. However, pending definitive postenumeration checks, we have no overriding reasons to reject this figure.

In the same year total rice production in Bangladesh was 17.85 million metric tons (MT). Availability of rice from domestic production was therefore 165 kg per person per year for the year, or 0.45 kg per person per day. This is about 10 percent less than the Food and Agriculture Organization (FAO) recommended "norm" of 0.5 kg of cereals per day, which would be almost made up by the 1 million tons of wheat produced that year. Thus, in this sense, Bangladesh was already nearly self-sufficient in cereals in 1990.

Traditionally, food policy issues in Bangladesh have been posed in terms of "self-sufficiency", meaning the production of all requirements (of cereals, especially rice) from domestic production, with requirements again being mechanically derived from more or less arbitrary nutritional norms. Clearly, this opened the door to policies that would protect highly inefficient domestic production. It is tempting to interpret input subsidies and restriction on cereal imports by the private sector as policies embodying precisely this tendency. However, aggregate protection to agriculture has always been modest, especially when compared to industry. Recent analyses confirm that "Bangladesh farmers are efficient producers of rice for import substitution" (World Bank 1992, 21). This World Bank report found that out of 22 rice varieties (distinguished by season, local/MV, and land type), domestic resource costs (DRC) were less than unity for all except two varieties (at farm level, with border price = US$150/MT). With a border price of US$200, all varieties have domestic resource costs less than unity (World Bank 1992, 38). Self-sufficiency, that is, complete import substitution, is therefore not just a slogan, it is also the economically rational solution, and, in the absence of serious market imperfection, would be attained by the workings of the market itself.

Thus Bangladesh appears to be self-sufficient in rice in both the economic sense (domestic demand equals domestic supply, with prices determined competitively and approximating the border price) and the "normative" sense that the equilibrium quantity is, on average, nutritionally adequate.

This does not mean, of course, that access to food is equitable. According to the 1988/1989 Household Expenditure Survey, while the average consumption of rice was 0.44 kg per day, it was 0.31 kg per day for the bottom 20 percent of the population, and for the top 10 percent, 0.51 kg per day.[4] Clearly, food security and foodgrain self-sufficiency are not identical.

The implications of rice self-sufficiency were brought home dramatically to farmers as well as to the government in October and November 1992. Government stocks were about 1.2 million tons, and occasional off-takes had to be undertaken just to avoid spoilage. Private stocks with traders and consumers were possibly three times as much (Chowdhury and Shahabuddin 1992), bloated from three straight years of bumper crops. For the first time in recorded history, rice prices stagnated instead of peaking in the immediate preharvest period. When harvesting started (about mid-November), prices went down further to US$67-80 per metric ton of paddy, well below all available estimates of the average costs of production. The government had initially contemplated the possibility of doing all procurement through the open tender system, but was forced by circumstances to initiate mill-gate as well as direct procurement—the latter at a support price of US$141 per metric ton of paddy. It seems certain that a heavy loss will be incurred in disposing of the paddy/rice thus procured. To minimize disruptions to private trade, it has been decided that rice will be substituted for aid-funded wheat in the Food for Works and the Vulnerable Group Development Programmes. The government is also encouraging private sector exports of fine and medium quality rice. In fact, more recent developments suggest that even coarse rice may find a market, for example, in some African countries.

In a certain sense, therefore, Bangladesh is at the moment not just self-sufficient in rice, it even has a small export surplus.[5] The question is whether this is sustainable, and if so, what reorientation of agricultural and food policies might be necessary.

The events described above have made one thing clear: whatever may be the technical potential for increasing rice production, growth cannot be sustainable unless the product finds a growing market at remunerative prices. The market may be domestic, growing as noncereal (including nonagricultural), incomes grow; or it can be the export market. It may be the case that for Bangladesh agriculture, demand management has become more important than supply management. If so, this would have profound implications for policy.

A number of attempts have been made to estimate supply-demand balances for foodgrains in Bangladesh. The results differ, depending on assumptions about population and income growth rates, income elasticities of demand, irrigation potential by different modes, behavior of yields, and other related factors.

The Master Plan Organization (MPO) found that the results of their exercise depended crucially on assumptions about the behavior of yields, and less on assumptions about population growth rates and irrigation development strategies. They found, for example, that under the assumption that yields (of individual varieties) remain constant at current levels, demand will exceed supply in 1989/1990, 1994/1995, and 1999/2005. This is so irrespective of assumptions about irrigation strategy and demand. However, if yields are assumed to increase over time (at the rather heroic rates of 2-3 percent per year for high-yielding varieties [HYVs] and 1-2 percent for local varieties), then the two most productive irrigation strategies would yield an excess of supply over demand in every fifth year after 1994, up to 2009 (MPO 1991, chapter 7). See Table 3.2.

The World Bank (1992, 43-57) makes somewhat more realistic assumptions about the behavior of yields: *aus* and *aman* HYV yields increase by 1 percent per year up to a maximum yield of 2.25 MT/ha, and *boro* HYV yields increase by 0.4 percent per year to a maximum of 2.75 MT/ha. Their "base" assumption about rate of expansion of irrigation, 250,000 hectares per year until 2010, is however, much higher than the MPO assumptions, which contemplate, for the preferred strategy, a total additional irrigated area of 2.3 million hectares by 2010. The World Bank's preferred estimates of cereal supply fall between the MPO estimates of "present" and "future" yields. The Bank's estimates of demand, even for the higher (5 percent) gross national product (GNP) growth scenario, is below MPO's estimates, since lower income elasticities of demand are used. As a result, for the preferred combination of demand and supply scenarios, the World Bank predicts that Bangladesh will have an excess domestic supply of foodgrains in every year after 1991, and an excess supply of rice every year, amounting to as much as 4.456 million MT in 2006. See Table 3.3.

The above exercises are both based on the assumption that excess supply (or demand) does not induce price movements that eliminate the surplus/deficit. The World Bank document does attempt to analyze the effects of a downward price movement, and concludes that a price reduction of 15 percent would approximately equate demand and supply, while a decline of 23 percent (which in the World Bank's opinion would bring domestic prices in line with import parity prices) would result in excess domestic demand and rice imports. These results are almost certainly due to the choice of an inappropriately low-quality world rice price for comparison.

Without a rigorous reexamination of the issue, there is no way to say whether the MPO or the World Bank projections are nearer the mark. However, if the evidence from the latest census on declining population growth rate turns out to be well-founded, this will clearly tilt the balance of evidence in favor of an emerging rice surplus.

Table 3.2
Comparison of Projected Foodgrain Demands with Production under Alternative Plans in Different Plan Periods (million MT)

	Demand		*Estimated Production Under Alternative Plans*[e]			
Year	*Constant*	*Increasing*[a]	*I*	*II*	*III*	*IV*
Present Yield Levels[b]						
1989/1990	20.34	20.34	19.01	19.01	19.01	19.01
	(20.17)	(20.17)				
1994/1995	22.50	23.14	19.71	20.19	20.76	20.79
	(22.51)	(23.16)				
1999/2000	24.46	26.24	21.47	22.36	23.63	23.69
	(24.89)	(26.53)				
2004/2005	26.24	29.36	22.77	23.75	25.64	25.60
	(27.23)	(30.11)				
2009/2010[c]	27.52	32.19	24.01	25.02	27.32	27.38
	(29.53)	(33.82)				
2009/2010[d]	27.52	32.19	25.01	26.02	28.32	28.38
Future Yield Levels						
1989/1990	22.50	23.14	22.24	22.74	23.41	23.45
	(20.51)	(23.16)				
1999/2000	24.46	26.24	26.02	27.19	28.83	28.93
	(24.89)	(26.53)				
2004/2005	26.24	29.36	27.62	28.91	31.41	31.37
	(27.23)	(29.36)				
2009/2010[c]	27.52	32.19	29.13	30.75	33.53	33.60
	(29.53)	(33.82)				
2009/2010[d]	27.52	32.19	30.33	31.95	34.73	34.80
	(29.53)	(33.82)				

[a]Estimated at 4 percent GNP growth and on Planning Commission (1990) population estimates. Figures in parentheses are based on BBS population estimates (BBS-2). The 1989-1990 demand is assumed to be the same by both methods of calculation, although per capita demand based on income elasticity was slightly less than the constant consumption level.

[b]Production figures include foodgrain production from active floodplains, an area of 0.53 million hectares. Floodplain production estimates for 1989/1990, 1994/1995, 1999/2000, 2004/2005, and 2009/2010 are 0.72, 0.78, 0.85, 0.92, and 1.00 million metric tons respectively, for all the plans under both present and future yield levels.

[c]Without full development of main rivers.

[d]With 20 percent of the full production increase due to the full development potential of main rivers. Full production increases are assumed to be 5.00 million metric tons under current yields and 5.80 million metric tons under future yields.

[e] Plan I: Groundwater development limited to only shallow tubewells (STW).
Plan II: Groundwater development limited to only STW/DSSTW.
Plan III: Mixed mode groundwater development including DTWs limited to pumping depth of 15m below the village mound.
Plan IV: Same as Plan III, except the limit to pumping depth is increased to 20 meters from the surface elevation of nonflooded land.

Source: MPO (1991).

Table 3.3

Alternative Scenarios for Foodgrain Supply and Demand

('000 MT)

Demand Scenarios			*1990*	*1991*	*1992*	*1993*	*1994*	*1995*	*2000*	*2005*	*2010*
	Population decline	*Income growth*									
Demand I	gradual	3%	19,272	19,717	20,166	20,619	21,076	21,537	23,900	26,353	28,887
Demand II	gradual	5%	19,668	20,225	20,775	21,321	21,863	22,401	25,069	27,792	30,731
Supply Scenarios											
	Irrigation expansion										
Supply I	low		19,289	19,267	19,831	20,384	20,951	21,484	24,221	26,587	27,758
Supply II	medium		19,289	19,628	20,430	21,223	22,033	22,811	27,162	29,598	30,509
Supply III	high		19,289	20,324	21,467	22,631	23,888	25,220	29,173	30,971	33,984
Supply IV	hi/low		19,289	20,324	21,467	22,631	23,888	25,220	27,173	30,971	33,984
Base scenario (DI & SII)											
Foodgrain balance (supply-demand)			17	(89)	264	604	958	1,274	3,260	3,235	1,622
Percent surplus			0.1	-0.5	1.3	2.8	4.3	5.6	12.0	10.9	5.3
Rice balance (supply-demand)			1,220	600	987	1,362	1,751	2,103	4,277	4,456	3,040
Percent surplus			6.6	3.3	5.2	6.9	8.5	9.8	16.6	15.8	10.5

Source: World Bank (1992).

Implications for Agricultural Policy

It is evident that agricultural development during the 1980s and early 1990s has been led by rice, and in particular by HYV *boro* rice. With the advent of the 1990s, it may be said that the import-substituting phase of growth for rice has come to an end, and Bangladesh will probably be at least self-sufficient and possibly at a surplus in rice production. This would imply that unless technical constraints are binding, growth in rice output will, in the future, be constrained by demand. It is generally acknowledged that, in fact, there are no major technical constraints to sustained growth of rice output for the coming two decades, and output can go up to about 32 million MT without major FCD/FCDI schemes, that is, based almost entirely on minor irrigation. It would seem therefore that for the output potential to be realized, there must be sustained growth in domestic and/or international demand. Growth in domestic demand can only come from growth in noncereal income. While part of this growth in demand can be within agriculture (crop diversification), a large part will have to be outside of agriculture. This is, in any case, what economic development is all about.

The implications for policymakers would seem to be that they should modify their priorities somewhat, and pay more attention than they have so far done to noncereals, nonfood crops, noncrop agriculture, and to industry, small and large. Since industrial expansion is in turn constrained by the small size of the domestic market due to low incomes, an export-led industrial strategy is called for, at least for pump-priming.

In the absence of major technological breakthroughs, Bangladesh will probably reach a plateau in rice production at around 32-34 million MT by the year 2010. Any increase beyond this level would depend on major flood control, drainage, and surface irrigation schemes, which would be high-cost, have high operation and maintenance costs, severely strain administrative capacities, entail large repayment costs, and above all, have far-reaching and unpredictable ecological consequences. At this cost, it is highly unlikely that Bangladesh will continue to have a comparative advantage in future expansion of foodgrain production. Since population growth is unlikely to stop completely, this may well mean that foodgrain will again have to be imported. Thus, Bangladesh has about 20 years in which to become an efficient exporter of nonfood items (agricultural, industrial, or service-sector) with which to pay for these imports. Hopefully, by that time the economy of Bangladesh will have undergone significant structural transformation, with industry contributing more than 25 percent of GNP and agriculture less than 25 percent. Then Bangladesh will no longer need such large flows of concessional external resources. Given moderately optimistic assumptions about world economic prospects, this can happen provided stable, efficient, and "developmentalist" governments push through with the needed policy reforms, and donors/lenders target their assistance with this vision in mind.

Policy Response

As noted earlier, important changes have taken place in the agricultural policy regime over the last decade or so. We need only highlight the main points here.

Privatization of Fertilizer Distribution and Elimination of Subsidies

Up to 1978, fertilizer procurement and distribution down to the *thana* level was monopolized by the BADC. Appointed private dealers bought fertilizer from BADC's thana sale centers at an administered price well below economic or budgetary cost, and were legally bound to sell to farmers at the same price—their own income being the commission that BADC paid them. Subsidies were very high in the beginning, but came down over time as prices were sharply raised, for example, the retail sale price for urea was Tk 536 per ton in 1972, but Tk 1608 from 1975 to 1977 (Government of Bangladesh and UNDP 1989, 4).

This system, known as the Old Marketing System, was replaced, between 1979 and 1983, by the New Marketing System under which the BADC withdrew from retail trade by closing down most *thana* sales centers. BADC still monopolized the wholesale trade. Over time, the role of BADC in fertilizer distribution was further restricted, and now has been completely eliminated, except that BADC can still compete for tenders to imports, generally under aid-funded program loans. But the bulk of imports and all domestic procurement and distribution is handled by private traders.

Prices of urea, the main fertilizer and one produced domestically (and exported), continues to be set administratively (the producing factories are all in the public sector). Subsidies were eliminated in 1985, but since "issue" prices were held constant, a subsidy had reappeared by the late 1980s. This was brought down significantly by a number of adjustments over 1990-1992. According to one estimate, (Abdullah 1992,

42-48) the subsidy (measured as a deviation from border price) on different fertilizers in October 1992 was as follows: urea, 5-7 percent; total soluble phospates, 27.6; and muriate of potash, 25.1 percent. Since then, however, world prices have declined somewhat, and recently the government has also reduced its exfactory price from Tk 4725 to Tk 4075 per MT. The BCIC export (FOB bulk) prices would be the appropriate border-price. For June 1993, two export prices were available for BCIC exports, US$107.15 per MT from CUFL, and US$91.25 per MT from JFCL (IFDC 1993); these work out to Tk 4286 per MT and Tk 3650, respectively. At the first price, therefore, the subsidy (without correcting for handling costs) is marginally positive, about 5 percent, and at the latter price it is negative at about -12 percent. Triple super phosphate and muriate of potash are now freely tradeable; hence the question of subsidies does not arise.

Evolution of Minor Irrigation Policy

This policy has broadly been directed at increased private sector participation in procurement and distribution (though with occasional hesitations and partial retreats), and reduction of subsidies (in the case of shallow tubewells, currently the most important mode of irrigation, complete elimination). BADC's monopoly of shallow tubewell import and sales was abolished in 1978: Engine imports were, however, subject to a "standardization" requirement, that is, if imported "for agricultural purposes" (which had to be duly certified by the Ministry of Agriculture, and entitled the importer to pay duty at 15 percent instead of 50 percent), they had to be a brand on an approved list. Attempts were also made in 1987 to introduce a "Groundwater Ordinance" that would rigorously control the location of shallow as well as deep tubewells, out of a misplaced concern about drawdown externalities. However, these restrictions, as well as standardization, were removed in late 1988. All customs duties and sales taxes on shallow tubewell imports were also abolished. The siting restrictions were reimposed in January 1992, but re-abolished in July of the same year. More recently a 7.5 percent import duty has been reimposed on shallow tubewell engines as well as a 15 percent VAT.

Other changes in the policy regime have taken place in the early 1990s—opening up the cereal trade to the private sector with low (7.5 percent) import duty, rescinding[6] of antihoarding regulations, abolition of restrictions on bank lending to rice traders, and introduction of government procurement of rice through open tender—but it is too early to assess the impact of these changes.

The question therefore arises as to whether the relatively buoyant performance of rice production in the 1980s can be attributed to the policy changes.

In an earlier article (Abdullah 1993), an attempt was made to answer this question essentially by a process of elimination, or one might say by applying Mill's Method of Difference. It was suggested that between the postreform period (here taken roughly as the early 1980s to date) and the prereform period, there was no other significant change that could account for the difference. Weather conditions were not demonstrably better (if anything they were a bit worse, since the 1980s saw two of the worst floods in history), nor was there any significant technical breakthrough.

Another possible explanation is pressure, for instance, an unfavorable land-person ratio makes the rapid adoption of modern varieties the only option to maintain consumption. This, it could be maintained, would have happened in any case, irrespective of the policy regime.

There is indeed some empirical evidence that subsistence pressure does play a role in determining adoption of new technology. In a cross-section regression analysis (Hossain et al. 1992, 130), it was found that average land owned per household in a village had a significant negative impact, and the dependency ratio a positive impact (interestingly, significant for the wet and dry seasons together but not significant for the two taken separately) on the percentage of cultivated area under MVs. The first finding, however, is probably only a reflection of the familiar fact that larger landholdings tend to be more fragmented, making it difficult to irrigate, and hence to bring a large percentage of the cultivated area under MV. Another finding of the exercise, not easy to reconcile with the above, is that for the household-level indicator, farm size, the coefficient is insignificant, and for the dry season positive.

Even if one admits that subsistence pressure plays an independent role in determining adoption of MV, the question remains as to whether the change in this variable (however measured) between these two periods was large enough to make a qualitative difference in performance. Recall that between 1979 and 1991, MV coverage increased from 35 percent to 65 percent, an increase of 30 percentage points. Since the coefficient of (village-level) land owned per household is -25.25, average land owned would have needed to decline by about 1.9 acres if subsistence pressure alone is to explain the entire increase. In fact, comparing the 1983/1984 Agricultural Census figures with a 1991/1992 BIDS survey, average land owned per household declined only by about 0.17 acres. This gives an average (arithmetic) rate of decline of 0.02 acres per year, so for the years 1979 to 1983 one may add another 0.08 acres to get a total decline of 0.25 acres. The change in the percentage of cultivated area under HYV would therefore be about 6.3 percent. Thus at most one fifth of the total change is explained by "subsistence pressure" measured by cultivated land per household. Note that most of the other significant variables in Hossain's equation can be expected to have been relatively constant over the period, except "irrigation", which itself needs to be explained.

There is, however, one variable, rural electrification, which appears to have a major impact on adoption of new technology and has changed significantly over the period under consideration. The number of villages electrified rose from 2,181 in 1979 to 13,955 in 1990 (BBS various years), a rise of 11,774 villages or about 15 percent of all villages. According to Hossain's equation, electrification raises HYV acreage by as much as 50.39 percentage points for both seasons taken together. Making some heroic assumptions, we can make a crude estimate of the possible impact electrification may have had in the aggregate.

Suppose that before electrification, the villages electrified since 1979 had the same percentage of area under HYV as the national average, that is, 35 percent. (Since the extent of electrification was small, the resulting upward bias will, hopefully, be negligible.) Also, suppose on the average that the villages had the same area under rice cultivation as the national average. In that case, they accounted for 15 percent of total area under rice, of which 35 percent is under HYV which in turn is 15 percent of total area under HYV in all villages.

Now, if as a result of electrification, the area under HYV of this 15 percent of rice area increases by 50 percentage points, the increase amounts to 7.5 percent of the total nationwide area under HYV. This may account, therefore, for nearly another one fourth of the increase. Thus electrification and subsistence pressure together may have accounted for about 45 percent of the total increase in HYV acreage, still leaving 55 percent that can realistically be attributed only to policy changes.

These extremely rough-and-ready numbers are certainly not to be taken too seriously—if anything they merely indicate an area where more rigorous analysis is urgently needed. But we suggest that, broadly, the orders of magnitude may not be far out of line with reality.

It would seem, therefore, that available evidence clearly supports the contention that the policy changes have elicited a favorable response from farmers in terms of growth performance. In other words, input markets are functioning competitively and delivering inputs to farmers at the right time and in the right quantities, though one may argue whether this has always been at the "right" price. Rising input prices have obviously reduced farmers' profitabilities and incomes, which may be considered distributionally unfair. We return to this question later. Before that we cite some direct evidence to show that markets are indeed functioning competitively.[7]

As Table 3.4 shows, the markup of farmers' prices over "issue" prices has been fairly modest from 1990 to 1993, fluctuating between 14.5 to 19.5 for urea, 11.7 to 19.6 for triple super phosphate, and 19.5 to 29.3 for muriate of potash. For the last two, there is also a discernible trend toward lower markups. It may also be noted that month-to-month fluctuations in the markups were also not very high. There are some fluctuations for triple super phosphate and muriate of potash for the years 1991 and 1992, mainly attributable to abrupt and sharp rises in issue price, for example, between July and August 1992 the issue price of triple super phosphate rose from Tk 300.00 to Tk 343 (per 50 kg), with the markup dropping from 13.59 to 2.35, but then gradually recovering nearly to the earlier levels.

Given that these margins must cover transportation charges from factories and ports to the farmers and yield a "normal" profit to wholesalers and retailers, they must be considered quite moderate. The absence of wide seasonal swings also suggests a reasonable degree of temporal arbitrage.

The coefficient of variation of June prices has declined over the last four years; in June 1993, these coefficients were 2 percent for urea, 3 percent for triple super phosphate and muriate of potash, indicating a fairly high degree of market integration.

From Table 3.5, it can be seen that among 14 Asian countries, only four countries had lower urea (retail) prices than Bangladesh—and only to the extent of 10-20 percent. In contrast, nine countries have prices that are higher by 20 percent or more, in some cases (such as Iran and Myanmar) by more than 200 percent.

It should be noted, however, that footnotes 3 and 4 to the table, taken from our source (International Fertilizer Development Center 1993b), are misleading in that the meaning of "subsidy" is unclear. If the Myanmar price, for example, is "unsubsidized" at 2.6 times the Bangladesh price,

Table 3.4

Mark-up in Fertilizer Trade

Month	1990			1991			1992			1993		
	Farm-level price	*Issue price*	*Difference (%)*	*Farm-level price*	*Issue price*	*Difference (%)*	*Farm-level price*	*Issue price*	*Difference (%)*	*Farm-level price*	*Issue price*	*Difference (%)*
Urea												
January	226.69	201.25	12.64	233.36	203.25	14.81	243.97	216.35	12.77	268.00	232.71	15.16
February	227.43	201.25	13.01	236.06	205.00	15.15	258.08	218.75	17.07	277.00	234.58	18.08
March	233.19	205.38	13.54	257.44	203.25	26.66	265.52	220.00	20.69	302.38	234.58	28.90
April	230.03	201.25	14.30	235.94	197.85	19.25	252.21	220.00	14.64	278.56	234.58	18.75
May	228.55	201.25	13.57	235.45	198.60	18.55	249.64	220.00	13.47	267.00	231.67	15.25
June	227.56	201.25	13.07	237.74	203.98	16.55	257.45	220.00	17.02	265.00	231.67	14.39
July	228.90	201.25	13.74	243.63	187.81	29.72	259.94	220.31	17.99	252.00	204.00	23.53
August	230.02	201.25	14.30	251.75	201.98	24.64	259.92	229.25	13.38	236.00	204.00	15.69
September	240.94	201.25	19.72	259.55	211.53	22.70	267.27	235.21	13.63	234.00	204.00	14.71
October	232.77	201.25	15.66	241.37	204.70	17.91	256.86	232.71	10.38	226.00	202.08	11.84
November	231.95	201.25	15.25	238.86	209.50	14.01	262.18	232.71	12.66	226.00	...	...
December	234.60	203.25	15.42	242.38	212.00	14.33	263.06	232.71	13.04	...	...	...
Average	231.05	201.76	14.52	242.79	203.29	19.43	257.84	224.83	14.68	257.45	221.39	16.29
Triple super phosphate												
January	249.10	216.25	15.19	262.03	216.25	21.17	320.33	275.00	16.48	402.00	343.00	17.20
February	251.96	216.25	16.51	265.52	216.25	22.78	316.64	275.00	15.14	395.00	343.00	15.16
March	250.42	216.25	15.80	267.64	216.25	23.76	324.80	300.00	8.27	398.72	343.00	16.24
April	246.24	216.25	13.87	256.38	216.25	18.56	330.22	300.00	10.07	392.71	343.00	14.49
May	244.52	216.25	13.07	257.82	216.25	19.22	334.36	300.00	11.45	400.00	343.00	16.62
June	248.55	216.25	14.94	269.33	216.25	24.55	339.49	300.00	13.16	399.00	343.00	16.33

(Continued on next page)

Table 3.4 *(Continued)*

Month	*1990* Farm-level price	*1990* Issue price	*1990* Difference (%)	*1991* Farm-level price	*1991* Issue price	*1991* Difference (%)	*1992* Farm-level price	*1992* Issue price	*1992* Difference (%)	*1993* Farm-level price	*1993* Issue price	*1993* Difference (%)
July	256.05	216.25	18.40	267.21	216.25	23.57	340.78	300.00	13.59	404.00	343.00	17.78
August	254.46	216.25	17.67	265.03	250.00	6.01	351.07	343.00	2.35	403.00	343.00	17.49
September	259.10	216.25	19.82	288.12	250.00	15.25	382.10	343.00	11.40	403.00	343.00	17.49
October	259.10	216.25	19.82	322.03	250.00	28.81	382.71	343.00	11.58	390.00	343.00	13.70
November	300.92	216.25	39.15	314.88	250.00	25.95	390.28	343.00	13.78	394.00	...	...
December	283.67	216.25	31.18	326.00	275.00	18.55	394.00	343.00	14.87	...	...	...
Average	258.67	216.25	19.62	280.17	232.40	20.56	350.57	313.75	11.73	398.31	343.00	16.13
Muriate of Potash												
January	209.87	166.25	26.24	207.99	166.25	25.11	266.63	212.50	25.47	353.00	...	...
February	215.20	166.25	29.44	217.10	166.25	30.59	270.70	212.50	27.39	345.00	...	...
March	220.99	166.25	32.93	214.80	166.25	29.20	276.03	237.50	16.22	353.14	...	...
April	211.67	166.25	27.32	209.46	166.25	25.99	278.14	237.50	17.11	351.90	...	...
May	214.76	166.25	29.18	209.78	166.25	26.18	280.14	237.50	17.95	357.00	...	...
June	212.30	166.25	27.70	212.60	166.25	27.88	282.69	237.50	19.03	357.00	278.00	28.42
July	214.27	166.25	28.88	214.80	166.25	29.20	284.61	237.50	19.84	355.00	278.00	27.70
August	211.49	166.25	27.21	223.93	182.50	22.70	289.71	281.25	3.01	353.00	278.00	26.98
September	212.14	266.25	27.60	239.62	182.50	31.30	328.56	281.25	16.82	358.00	278.00	28.78
October	217.48	166.25	30.82	243.29	182.50	33.31	343.53	281.25	22.14	339.00	268.00	26.49
November	218.17	166.25	31.23	240.89	182.50	31.99	353.34	281.25	25.63	369.00	...	...
December	221.01	166.25	32.94	262.54	212.50	23.55	353.17	281.25	25.57	...	...	...
Average	214.95	166.25	29.29	224.73	175.52	28.04	300.60	251.56	19.49	353.73	276.00	28.16

... means data not available.

Table 3.5

Ratio of Retail Fertilizer Prices in Other Asian Countries to Bangladesh Prices, June 1993

Product	*Bangladesh*	*People's Rep. of China*	*India*	*Indo-nesia*	*Iran*	*Malaysia*	*Myanmar*	*Nepal*	*Pakistan*	*Philip-pines*	*Rep. of Korea*	*Sri Lanka*	*Thai-land*	*Viet Nam, Socialist Rep. of*
Urea	1.0 (133)	0.8	0.8	0.9	2.1	1.5	2.6	0.9	1.2	1.6	1.6	1.7	1.5	1.4
Triple super phosphate	1.0 (200)	-	-	0.8	1.5	1.1	4.0	0.9	0.8	-	-	1.1	-	-
Muriate of potash	1.0 (179)	0.4	1.2	1.0	-	0.8	3.6	0.8	-	1.2	0.8	1.2	-	-
Exchange rate	40	5.7198	25.890	2069	66.934	2.5350	6.1997	42.7	25.634	25.492	785.1	49.63	25.51	10670

Notes:
1. Prices are rounded off and shown within parentheses in US$ per MT for Bangladesh.
2. Bangladesh prices for May 1993.
3. Prices are subsidized in People's Republic of China, India, Indonesia, Iran, Myanmar, Nepal, Pakistan, and the Republic of Korea (International Fertilizer Development Center 1993b).
4. Malaysia, Philippines, Sri Lanka, Thailand, Socialist Republic of Viet Nam, and Bangladesh have no fertilizer subsidies (International Fertilizer Development Center 1993b).
5. US$ per unit of currency.

Source: Fertilizer Trade Information: FADINAP, March 1993.

how can the Bangladesh price be unsubsidized? "Border prices" can hardly be that different between the two countries. Internal handling margins may be a factor, but hardly to that extent. However, the overall picture would seem to be that of a competitive and efficient market for fertilizer.

Similarly, evidence suggests that the policy changes with regard to minor irrigation equipment has had salutary effects on irrigation expansion and agricultural production. Between 1987 and 1988, the number of shallow tubewells (and private force mode tubewells) fielded jumped from 183,000 to 223,000, by far the largest increase since 1979 not only in absolute number but also as a percentage (40 percent). Between 1988 and 1990 (there was no census in 1989) this increased further to 276,000, an increase of 53 percent over two years, hence lower than the initial reaction, but still very healthy (Guisselquist 1991, 4). This spectacular growth spurt was undoubtedly caused by the increased availability of cheaper Chinese and Korean engines consequent on destandardization and the abolition of customs duty and sales tax (see Table 3.6). Not only did this make available to farmers cheaper, if less durable brands of engines, but the resulting competition (as well as the elimination of duty) caused a fall in the prices of the "standardized" brands as well.

Table 3.6

Price Difference Between Complete Shallow Tubewell Sets

	Current Market Price (Tk)	*Market Price Before Tariff Reduction (Tk)*
Engine (Yanmar, TS 70C 8.5 HP)	18,500	26,000
Pump	3,900	2,600
Pipe (100 feet)	3,500	3,000
Others (strainer, accessories etc.)	1,500	1,200
	27,400	32,800
Engine (Dong-Feng 12 HP)	12,200	
Pump	3,100	
Pipe (100 feet)	3,500	
Others (strainer, accessories etc.)	1,500	
	20,300	

Source: Rahman (1992).

It is unlikely that irrigation expansion will continue at these rates, which are partly a "once-and-for-all" response to the policy change. But even an *arithmetic* growth at about 30,000 shallow tubewell equivalents per year should suffice for the MPO target.

The new policy regime, therefore, has been vindicated by ensuing developments, at least as far as production and attainment of self-sufficiency goes. The question naturally arises: What next? The fact remains that Bangladesh is a poor country and that farmers in particular remain, on the average, undernourished, ill-clad, ill-housed, ill-educated, and perpetually vulnerable to the vagaries of the weather and domestic and international markets.

One thing would appear certain—further success in raising cereal output, especially rice, can no longer remain a priority. Arguably, the only viable long-term strategy would be to get people off the land altogether and into remunerative employment outside of agriculture. However, this will take time. In the meantime, farmers' incomes can be augmented primarily by diversifying into noncereal agriculture. In our opinion this is the most critical "agenda for the future". The next section therefore attempts a fairly detailed examination of the potential for, and the constraints to, crop diversification.

Crop Diversification: Potential and Constraints

Rationale for Crop Diversification

Currently, crop agriculture accounts for more than 25 percent of GDP at market prices and nearly 60 percent of the commodity production in the economy. The crop sector is dominated by rice, which alone accounts for nearly 70 percent of the gross farm revenue from crop production. Over the last two decades, the growth in crop agriculture has been predominantly led by foodgrains, mostly rice. As the country now seems to be approaching self-sufficiency in rice, serious questions have been raised about the sustainability of rice-led agricultural growth. The success in accelerating rice production may have thus brought new challenges and opportunities to make agriculture more efficient and flexible. It is in this context that the issue of crop diversification needs to be addressed as part of the broader agricultural development strategy.

One of the recent concerns of the government has been to explore ways and means to improve efficiency and equity in irrigation management. Irrigation systems in Bangladesh are rice-based but irrigation water is sold or transacted for growing nonrice crops as well as rice crops. The diversification of crop production is thus recognized as an alternative strategy for improving the productivity and efficiency of performance of the irrigation water market.

Crop diversification also features prominently on valid agronomic and nutritional grounds in the overall agricultural development strategy in the Fourth Five-Year Plan. Cultivation of more labor-intensive and higher value-added crops would have a salutary impact on agricultural income and employment. The essential task of crop diversification will be to select appropriate crops and encourage farmers to adopt them through adequate incentives in terms of cost effectiveness and relative cost advantages and financial returns to farmers through adequate price, marketing, and other policy supports. The emphasis will be to promote gradual diversification of agriculture through changes in the cropping system away from the present monoculture in rice, paying attention to soil management and income generation.

Generally speaking, crop diversification implies, among other things, raising the efficiency of irrigation equipment, increasing farmers' income, reducing farmer's risk, and improving nutrition. The constraints to crop diversification include, among other things, inadequate marketing facilities, scarcity of suitable land, the spectre of food scarcity causing reliance on the rice staple, and inappropriate rice-based water management practices. Although there is general agreement on the broad characteristics of the potential of and constraints to crop diversification, further research efforts are needed to improve our understanding of how this potential can be harnessed and the constraints relaxed to promote crop diversification in the country.

In fact, the prospects of agricultural growth through crop diversification raises a great number of issues concerning agronomic sustainability, farm-level incentives, changing technologies, marketing efficiency, comparative advantage, and macrolevel supply-demand balances. There are even broader issues involving the income-distributional and nutritional linkages of crop diversification, and the longer run role of crop agriculture in an economy undergoing a process of structural change. Recently, Mahmud, Rahman, and Zohir (1993) carried out a study on agricultural growth through crop diversification in Bangladesh. Although the study fails to cover all the issues raised above, it deals exhaustively with a number of important issues related to such areas as agronomic sustainability, marketing efficiency, farm-level incentives, and comparative advantage and hence remains the most comprehensive work on the subject. In our discussion of the problems and prospects of crop diversification in Bangladesh, therefore, we shall draw heavily on the findings of this particular study.

Pattern of Land Allocation in Cereal and Noncereal Crops

It is now well-established that reallocation of cropped area, especially from traditional to modern varieties of rice, has been the predominant factor behind growth in crop agriculture. This is evident from the overall trends in the cropping pattern along with changes in irrigation coverage and in the cropping intensity of land. Mahmud, Rahman, and Zahir (1993) present some relevant estimates regarding these trends based on five-year averages for five overlapping periods (1973-1977, 1976-1980, 1979-1983, 1982-1986, and 1985-1989).

It is observed that the overall cropping intensity increased up to the early 1980s, and thereafter stagnated and even declined in more recent years. The increase in the cropping intensity in the earlier period is entirely due to the increase in the area under foodgrains. On the other hand, the area under nonfoodgrain crops taken together has continuously fallen since the late 1970s, mainly due to the displacement of pulses, oilseeds, and minor cereals. For rice crops, the increase in area under HYV *boro* rice has been accompanied by an almost equal decline in the area under local *aus* and broadcast *aman* rice. This is mostly explained by the fact that the growing seasons of the latter two crops partly overlap with that of *boro* rice. In the case of HYV *aman* rice, on the other hand, the area expansion in the earlier periods appears to have taken place through an increase in total area under transplanted *aman* (local and HYV taken together); but in the later periods, there has been a shift of area away from local transplanted *aman*. The increase in total transplanted *aman* area might have been due to the considerable expansion of coverage of flood control and drainage facilities that have taken place since the early 1970s.

Most nonrice crops, with the notable exception of jute, compete for land in the *boro* (dry) season. It is, therefore, the changes in the cropping pattern and the cropping intensity in the *boro* season, especially in response to the provision of irrigation, that are crucial to the prospects of agricultural growth through crop diversification. For the entire period under review, irrigation expansion in the *boro* season appears to have been exactly matched by the increase in the cropping intensity in that season. However, this conceals the fact that, in more recent periods, there has been a decline in nonirrigated cropped land in the *boro* season (a reversal of the earlier trend), presumably because additional irrigation has been provided partly on land already under dry-season cultivation. Between the early and the late 1980s (that is, the third and the fifth five-year period under review), net addition to the dry-season cropped area was only about half of the additional coverage of irrigation. This seems to have been the major factor behind the decline in the area under pulses and other nonirrigated dry-season crops.

The major share of irrigated land is accounted for by *boro* rice, especially HYV *boro*, which is generally grown under irrigated conditions. The expansion of HYV *boro* rice has been, therefore, closely linked with that of irrigation. Among nonrice crops, only wheat, potato, and vegetables are grown equally on both irrigated and nonirrigated land; most other dry-season crops, including the year-round crops, are grown predominantly on nonirrigated land. It is worth noting that the area under *boro* rice (as well as under *boro* rice and wheat combined) has been expanding all along on nonirrigated land as well. Thus, not only does irrigation tend to displace some nonfoodgrain crops, these crops seem to have lost ground to foodgrains even on nonirrigated land. These trends are clearly contrary to assumptions underlying the official plans for agricultural development, which project an increase in area under nonfoodgrain crops (Mahmud et al. 1993).

Determinants of Area Allocation in Cereal and Noncereal Crops

Mahmud et al. (1993) also made an in-depth inquiry into the determinants of area allocation, both physical and economic, while assessing the supply response in crop agriculture. The major findings of this study are reproduced below, starting with physical and technical constraints to crop production, in general, and crop diversification, in particular.

Physical and Technical Constraints

The cropping patterns in the country can be broadly classified into rainfed and irrigated patterns; which again vary according to the degree of seasonal flooding. Table 3.7 presents evidence of such variations in cropping patterns, based on data from a fairly representative nationwide farm survey.[8] The land categories according to flood-depth levels are similar to those of the National Water Plan (MPO 1991); these are mainly based on the suitability of land for growing different rice crops during the wet season. Irrigation is divided into modern and traditional; the former mainly includes mechanized irrigation by pumps and tubewells, while the latter includes labor-intensive methods requiring very little fixed investment.

There are certain important features of these cropping patterns that are particularly relevant for crop diversification. Irrigation appears to have a favorable impact on the annual cropping intensity on high and medium-high land, but a negative impact in the case of lower lands. The higher the land, the larger is the share of land devoted to noncereal crops within any of the irrigation categories. On the other hand, among all flood-depth levels, the proportion of land allocated to noncereal crops is markedly lower under irrigated conditions than under rainfed conditions. However, there is also a sharp contrast in the cropping patterns between modern and traditional irrigation, the latter being clearly more conducive to diversified cropping patterns.

Traditional irrigation on high land appears to strengthen the cultivation of not only wheat but also of high-value, noncereal crops like potato, vegetables, and spices. The production conditions here may not be suitable for HYV *boro* cultivation which needs continuous irrigation and flooding, and is therefore much more demanding of water compared to most other crops. But this still leaves unexplained why the high-value, noncereal crops cannot compete with HYV *boro* under modern irrigation.[9] The answer may lie in a combination of technical and economic factors. There are very high risks associated with the marketing of these high-value crops. At the same time, the existing irrigation and on-farm water management systems do not allow rice and nonrice crops to be planted in the same service units. Growing nonrice crops under modern irrigation would, therefore, often require the farmer to allocate his entire land (or the major part of it) to these crops—hardly a preferable option for a risk-averse farmer. Traditional irrigation, being of a divisible nature, allows farmers to grow these high-value, but risk-prone, crops on small parcels of land. It is only when there are large economies of scale in marketing and/or assured markets (as in the case of vegetable belts near urban centers) that noncereal crops are found to be grown under modern irrigation on any significant scale.

The currently practiced cropping patterns evidently offer little scope for crop diversification through expansion of modern irrigation. It is not surprising therefore that, in projection exercises for the crop sector, the prospects for crop diversification are often sought in more intensive cultivation of nonirrigated land (see, for example, MPO 1991). But there may not be much scope for this left, as would appear from the recent trends in cropping intensities, particularly with respect to dry-season, nonirrigated crops. The prospects for intensified cultivation of noncereal crops through the expansion of the area under traditional irrigation also do not seem promising. The official data in fact show a declining trend in

Table 3.7
Cropping Pattern by Land Type, 1987
(Crop Area as Percent of Net Cultivated Land)

Crops	High Land			Medium-High Land			Medium-Low Land			Low-Land			
	No Irrigation	Traditional Irrigation	Modern Irrigation	No Irrigation	Traditional Irrigation	Modern Irrigation	No Irrigation	Traditional Irrigation	Modern Irrigation	No Irrigation	Traditional Irrigation	Modern Irrigation	All Land
Local *aus*	32	47	12	37	45	11	57	9	1	59	0	2	32
MV *aus*	6	12	27	6	3	14	0	25	9	1	0	1	7
B. *aman*	0	0	1	12	16	6	46	5	24	45	2	10	15
Local T *aman*	31	50	18	55	49	44	29	19	33	12	0	4	37
MV *aman*	16	14	49	15	13	38	6	6	7	1	0	0	16
Local *boro*	0	5	1	3	3	2	2	2	6	6	9	4	3
MV *boro*	0	0	29	0	3	57	0	16	62	0	89	93	16
Wheat	2	42	16	5	23	5	5	19	6	6	0	0	6
Jute	7	12	11	11	15	6	5	23	2	6	0	0	7
Sugarcane	5	0	3	2	1	0	2	3	0	0	0	0	2
Potato	2	8	2	4	2	1	2	4	0	1	0	0	2
Spices	2	3	2	4	1	1	2	3	0	7	0	2	2
Vegetables	6	9	1	1	4	0	1	0	0	1	0	0	2
Oil seeds	2	1	1	5	1	2	10	0	6	7	0	1	4
Pulses	10	3	6	18	8	6	23	2	4	13	0	2	13
Orchards	20	2	0	0	0	0	0	0	0	0	0	0	4
Other crops	14	11	0	1	12	1	1	0	0	3	0	1	4
All crops (cropping intensity)	156	218	180	179	200	194	191	138	165	165	100	120	173
of which:													
All rice	85	128	137	128	135	172	140	86	142	121	100	114	126
All cereals	87	170	153	133	158	177	145	105	148	127	100	114	132
Noncereal	69	48	27	46	41	17	46	33	17	38	0	6	41
Share of land type in total land (%)	21.86	2.66	3.32	28.06	1.86	11.75	15.07	0.54	5.41	3.79	2.35	3.33	100.00

Source: Mahmud, Rahman, and Zahir (1993).

the area covered by traditional modes of irrigation. An important policy implication in this context is the potential scope for promoting such "intermediate" irrigation technology as represented by hand-tubewells and treadle pumps. These labor-intensive irrigation techniques are found to be particularly advantageous for small farmers and for growing crops like potato, vegetables, and spices.

There is considerable scope for increasing the yields of noncereal crops through better farm practices and varietal improvements even under nonirrigated or semi-irrigated conditions. Such yield improvements, rather than more intensive cultivation of land, perhaps offer better growth prospects for these crops. The real prospects for crop diversification, however, would still depend on how competitive technological innovations could make noncereal crops under conditions of modern irrigation. Research and extension activities in the past were mainly concentrated on HYV rice to the neglect of most other crops. Among noncereal crops, the HYV technology is well-established only in potato cultivation. However, HYVs with very high yield potentials are now available for some vegetables and fruits like tomatoes, beans, watermelons, and bananas. Significantly improved technologies are also available for pulses, mustard, jute, sugarcane, maize, sweet potato, and some country vegetables. However, the technical and socioeconomic constraints to the diffusion of improved technologies in the case of noncereal crops are still little understood. Much will depend on how far adaptive research and extension activities can be strengthened to identify and overcome these constraints (Mahmud et al. 1993).

Area Response to Prices

The flexibility of the cropping patterns in adjusting to changes in prices and profitability is an issue of considerable interest in the context of crop diversification. Mahmud et al. (1993) estimated area response equations for a number of crops and crop groups using a Nerlovian-type supply response model, and national level time series data for the period from 1972 to 1989.[10] It appears that there is hardly any price response in the case of total rice area as well as *aus* area; but both *boro* and *aman* rice show some degree of price responsiveness. The short-run price elasticity for *boro* varies from 0.24 to 0.50 depending on whether the price effect is controlled for irrigation or not. These results suggest that the rice crops may respond to seasonal rice prices and that such a response may involve substitution among rice crops (thus canceling out the effect at the aggregate level). The estimated short-run price response for wheat, jute, tobacco, and melon is fairly modest and of high statistical significance. Sugarcane and oilseeds also show statistically significant price elasticities, although of relatively low magnitudes. For most other crops, the price responses are weak in terms of the magnitudes of short-run price elasticities and/or in terms of the statistical significance of the estimated price parameters.

The weak supply response in the case of such low-value crops as pulses, oilseeds, and minor cereals may be explained by the fact that the choice of these crops in the rice-based cropping patterns is mostly of a residual nature. However, this cannot be a plausible explanation in the case of such high-value crops as spices, potato, and vegetables. The problem may instead lie in the extremely high price fluctuations that often characterize the markets for these products, thus inhibiting any rational price expectations. It cannot be argued that the price fluctuations themselves are caused by Cobweb-type supply responses, since such a price response, even if present, seems to be rather weak in most cases. The reason for supply instability may in fact lie elsewhere.[11] Survey findings of the study carried out by Mahmud et al. (1993) suggest that the high-value, but risk-prone, crops are generally grown on small parcels of land and are usually rotated from year to year within the rice-based cropping patterns. By and large, it may not be, therefore, the same set of farmers who produce these crops in different years. There is thus an element of randomness in the choice of these crops, which may make supply both unstable and nonresponsive to price. If so, greater specialization through the adoption of improved production technologies with respect to these crops would probably lead to a more stable supply response behavior.

For a number of crops, the response of area to yield changes is found to be strong and statistically significant. In nearly all of these cases, the estimated yield elasticities are several times higher than the price elasticities. This suggests that farmers respond much more strongly to yield improvements (or declines) than to price changes. This gives an added importance to policy measures supporting technological improvements with respect to high-value crops such as vegetables and spices. Such technological improvements would contribute to the growth of the crop sector not only through increased yields, but also through the induced shift of land toward these high-value crops (Mahmud et al. 1993).

Marketing of Crops

As mentioned earlier, agricultural marketing, and the associated storage and processing functions are crucial to agricultural supply responses and prospects for crop diversification. There are likely to be considerable variations across agricultural commodities with respect to the degree of market integration, reliability of price formation, and extent of market participation by farmers. While the marketing of rice has been a subject of frequent investigation in Bangladesh, there is far less information available about the marketing of other crops.

The study carried out by Mahmud et al. (1993) provides some information about the crop-wise disposal of agricultural output of farm households by using unpublished primary data from the 1988/1989 round of the BBS Household Expenditure Survey (HES) conducted by the Bangladesh Bureau of Statistics. The estimates presented in Table 3.8 show that, compared to rice, the proportions of output marketed are generally much higher for other crops. The marketing proportions for cash crops (for example, jute and oilseeds) are high for obvious reasons; but the proportion may also be high if production is geographically concentrated (for example, wheat and potato) and/or if the urban consumer demand is relatively high compared to rural demand. Per capita consumption of most agricultural products is found to be significantly higher in urban areas compared to rural areas, while the reverse is true in the case of rice consumption (Asaduzzaman 1989).

Table 3.8

Proportions of Agricultural Output Marketed and Self-Consumed by Farm Households; Household Expenditure Survey, 1988/1989

	Percentage Disposal of Output		
Crops	*Self-consumed*	*Marketed*	*Yearend stocks*
Paddy	53.6	38.7	7.7
Wheat	43.4	51.3	5.3
Jute	13.6	84.1	2.3
Mustard	33.6	62.9	3.5
Sesame	20.1	76.3	3.6
Pulses	44.2	50.3	5.5
Potato	36.6	60.4	3.0
Minor cereals	18.3	76.8	4.9
Vegetables			
Brinjal	35.7	64.3	-
Arum	38.4	61.6	-
Pumpkin	64.8	35.2	-
Other vegetables	58.5	41.5	

Source: Mahmud, Rahman, and Zohir (1993).

The computations with the unpublished HES data also show that, compared to rice, poorer farm households account for a much larger share of the marketed surplus of nonrice crops. This may be, in part, because of higher allocation of land to nonrice crops on smaller farms such as in the case of vegetables, potato, and spices. But this also reflects, in part, the pattern of self-consumption of rice and other food crops by poorer and richer farm households as dictated by the relative income elasticities of demand for these products. The estimates show that for certain items like vegetables and spices, small farms may in fact have a larger quantity of marketed surplus, in absolute terms, compared to large farms. If so, the impact of improved marketing and price incentives on the supply response behavior of smaller farms and on their incomes deserves particular consideration in the context of policies for crop diversification.

Perhaps the most important aspect of agricultural marketing in relation to prospects for crop diversification is the extent of year-to-year price fluctuations and the associated risks to farm incomes. Using the official series of average annual harvest prices of crops, Mahmud et al. (1993) estimated the trend growth rates of these prices and the average variability around the respective trend. Average variability is defined as the annual average of percent deviation (positive and negative signs ignored) of the observed prices from the estimated trend level. Also, the corresponding estimates for the annual wholesale level prices, as far as data permit, were derived. The estimates show that, compared to foodgrains, the price variability is higher for all nonfoodgrain crops (with the lone exception of sugarcane), and is in fact strikingly high for many crops. The estimates mostly fall in the range of 5-6 percent for foodgrains, 10-12 percent for oilseeds and pulses, 15-25 percent for fruits and vegetables including potato, and 20-40 percent for spices. Evidently, for many of the items in the latter groups, the price variability is too high to allow any "rational" price expectations.

The estimates also suggest that the variability of harvest prices is generally higher than that of the annual wholesale prices. Thus the price shocks seem to be most severe at the level of primary markets during the harvest seasons. On the other hand, there is some evidence of harvest prices growing generally at a higher rate compared to the respective wholesale prices; this would indicate a decline in marketing spreads over time, perhaps due to improved marketing and storage infrastructure. The evidence in this respect is, however, too weak to permit any firm conclusions.

Trade Policies, Structure of Incentives, and Comparative Advantage in Crop Agriculture

Bangladesh has pursued a highly restrictive trade and exchange rate regime characterized by high import tariffs and pervasive quantitative restrictions. The heavy taxation of imports provided a convenient source of government revenues while providing protection to import-competing domestic industries. The trade regime has been even more severely restrictive in the case of agricultural commodities. Until 1992, the export of foodgrains was not permitted, and the government had a monopoly on importing.[12] Most other agricultural commodities can be imported only under licensing schemes while many are subject to an outright export ban. Even in the case of jute, the main export crop, severe restrictions have been imposed on its export in years of scarcity in order to maintain supplies to domestic jute mills. These restrictive trade policies have been variously justified on the grounds of protecting domestic producers from external competition, ensuring domestic availability of essential consumer items, and insulating domestic markets from the instability in world commodity prices.

As a result of the structural adjustment measures carried out since the early 1980s, Bangladesh has now moved considerably toward a liberalized trade regime with flexible exchange rate management. The policy reforms in this area have been generally aimed at lowering tariff rates and freeing imports from quantitative restrictions. However, trade in agricultural commodities has continued to be highly restrictive. The way trade policies affect producer incentives in agriculture would of course depend on the actual and potential trading status of the agricultural and agriculture-based commodities. Foodgrains, mostly wheat, have constituted the major agricultural import item and most have come as food aid. The import of rice has varied widely from year to year and the recent trends in import and domestic production would suggest that the country is nearing self-sufficiency in rice. Besides wheat, mustard seed, edible oils, sugar, and cotton are clearly importables in terms of the proportion of domestic supply met from imports. Some quantities of onion, chili, lentils, and other pulses are also imported, especially in deficit years and lean seasons. Tobacco is both imported and exported because of differentiated product quality. There is virtually no foreign trade in potato, while some exports of vegetables and fruits have been taking place in recent years, mainly to cater to the needs of Bangladeshi communities living in the United Kingdom and the Arab Middle East.

There is some potential for exporting spices in the future, provided domestic production can grow (Mahmud et al. 1993).

Trends in Domestic-to-Border Price Ratio

To assess the effect of trade and exchange rate policies on agricultural incentives, the Mahmud et al. (1993) study computed domestic-to-border price comparisons for a selected number of commodities both at the official and the estimated equilibrium exchange rate. The time-series estimates of these ratios can help explain how the trade policy environment may have changed over time with respect to these commodities. The estimates of import parity prices are based on the assumption that imports compete with domestic production at the wholesale level.[13] However, for wheat and rapeseed, the price comparisons are made at the farmgate level since reliable time-series of domestic wholesale prices are not available.

Given the predominance of rice in crop agriculture, the impact of trade policy on agricultural incentives would be largely determined by what happens in the case of rice. The border price comparison for rice is made with respect to coarse-quality rice, which accounts for most of the rice produced in the country.[14] At the official exchange rate, the domestic rice price has mostly remained within the band of import and export parity prices. This implies that in most years, there has not been any positive or negative protection for rice through import or export taxation or trade restrictions. The trade policy, nevertheless, can be held responsible for lowering the domestic rice price through public import of foodgrains, mostly under food aid. The effect of such imports on the domestic rice price is equivalent to an import subsidy as measured by the nominal rate of protection (NRP) at the import parity price. However, the meaning of an estimate of NRP in such a situation is not straightforward.

When we consider the equilibrium exchange rate, however, there appears to have been negative protection for rice in relation to the import parity price throughout the entire period under review. Even at the export parity price, there was substantial negative protection (about 25 to 30 percent) during the late 1970s. The domestic price of rice has therefore remained lower, at times by very substantial margins, compared to its opportunity cost in border price terms (which, in a rice-import regime, would be represented by the import parity price at the shadow or equilibrium exchange rate). However, all of this is now changing as the country approaches self-sufficiency in rice, while the implicit subsidy on wheat import has also been virtually eliminated. As a result, in the evolving scenario trade policies have increasingly become neutral to domestic rice price determination.

The trends in the domestic-to-border price ratio for wheat are very similar to those for rice. In most years, however, the extent of divergence between the domestic price and the import parity price has been less for wheat than for rice. In fact, in recent years, the domestic wheat market appears to have been somewhat protected at the official exchange rate, although not at the equilibrium rate.

The nominal rate of protection for sugar and mustard seed (represented by rapeseed) has been consistently positive and at times vary highly.[15] Even at the equilibrium exchange rate, these two items appear to have been heavily protected (with the exception of rapeseed in the early 1980s). Among crops and crop-based products, these are the two major items found to enjoy substantial protection after taking into account the direct and indirect effects of trade policies. Much of the protection to sugar is absorbed by the highly inefficient public refineries, which procure sugarcane at administered prices. But protection to sugarcane at the farm level is also provided through higher prices of *gur* (raw sugar) which is an inferior substitute for imported white sugar.[16] Lentil appears to be somewhat protected in recent years, but only at the official exchange rate. It is during this recent period that the country has turned into an importer from being self-sufficient in pulses. With regard to potato, there is virtually no foreign trade, with imports limited to seed potato only.[17] The domestic price of potato has mostly remained within the band of import and export parity prices both at the official and equilibrium exchange rates, implying that the effect of trade policy has been neutral (Mahmud et al. 1993).

Private Versus Economic Profitability of Rice and Nonrice Crops

Private profitability, on the basis of which farmers take decisions, is based on the calculation of prices farmers actually receive or pay. These prices may diverge from society's opportunity costs of inputs and outputs because of many distortions in the product and factor markets, such as those arising from trade restrictions, government taxes or subsidies, monopoly elements in marketing, surplus labor conditions, and segmentation in the capital market. Earlier, we discussed the effects of tariffs and trade policies on price formation in the domestic markets. We now present the results of a profitability exercise carried out by Mahmud et al. (1993) to assess the pattern of comparative advantage vis-a-vis private profitability in crop production. In this study, economic profitability of crops, as distinct from private profitability, is estimated in terms of "net economic returns" per unit of cropped land (vis-a-vis net private returns). The methodology followed is essentially an annualized version of the Little-Mirrlees method of social cost-benefit analysis in which all costs and outputs are valued at their opportunity costs at border prices. But, unlike in social cost-benefit analysis, no social weights are applied regarding consumption, savings and income distribution. The capital costs (especially the costs of irrigation investments) are included as the annual rental charge so as to cover capital recovery at the social discount rate (that is, the accounting rate of interest). Land rents are not, however, included as costs, so that the profitability estimates represent net returns to land (and managerial skills). For assessing profitability, the crop production activities are distinguished by the irrigation-seed technology and are so chosen as to cover important areas of choice regarding crop diversification.[18]

The estimates of economic and private returns per hectare for rice and nonrice crops are presented in Tables 9 and 10 respectively. While for some crops the economic profitability estimates correspond to alternative assumptions regarding their tradability status, private profitability is estimated using only a single set of "normalized" farmgate prices for 1990-1991. Economic profitability at the projected 1995 real prices, whenever estimated, are shown by the figures within parentheses (Table 3.10). The implications of the profitability analysis regarding incentives for crop diversification are briefly summarized below.

The estimates of "economic" profitability of crops, as distinct from private profitability, can help to derive meaningful policy conclusions regarding how to reorient farming systems toward socially profitable patterns. The profitability analysis yields a number of conclusions, which appear robust in spite of many conceptual and data limitations. An important aspect of the profitability estimates for rice crops is the implied incentives for shifting from local to modern varieties, which remain the main source of growth in rice production. The economic gains from such a shift are found to be quite substantial in the import and nontraded situations, and also in terms of private returns at the existing level of domestic rice price. However, if we move to the export parity price, the economic gains from the adoption of the HYVs are greatly reduced and may even be eliminated in some cases. Moving to a rice-export regime would generally imply a very substantial decline in the profitability of agricultural production (and in the returns from irrigation investments) as a whole,

Table 3.9
Private and Economic Profitability of Rice Crops (farm level),[a] 1990-1991

Rice Crop[b]	*Irrigation Technique*[c]	*Net Private Returns (Tk/hectare)*	*Economic Returns (Tk/hectare)*		
			Export parity	*Nontraded*	*Import parity*
Boro					
HYV	Modern	8,335	5,442	11,132	16,485
Local-T	All	4,643	3,763	6,554	9,170
Aman					
HYV	Modern	5,805	3,626	8,563	13,202
HYV	Rainfed	10,238	8,071	13,106	17,699
HYV	All	9,550	7,429	12,262	16,804
Pajam	All	6,401	4,924	8,997	12,824
Local T	Rainfed	3,786	3,019	5,856	8,515
Local B	Rainfed	2,772	2,274	4,470	6,525
Aus					
HYV	Rainfed	7,048	5,430	9,395	13,119
HYV	Modern	5,908	3,574	8,382	12,899
HYV	All	6,418	4,738	8,833	12,681
Local B	Rainfed Traditional	-165	-306	-1,605	3,383

[a]Profitability is estimated as net of all costs except land rent and is therefore a measure of return to land (and management). The estimates are based on "normalized" domestic and world prices of rice for 1990-1991.

[b]B: Broadcast; T: Transplant; Pajam: A locally improved variety.

[c]Modern irrigation includes mechanized irrigation by pumps and tubewells. The category "All" includes different irrigation techniques and represents the entire sample of the respective crop in the farm survey underlying this study.

Source: Mahmud et al. (1993).

given the dominance of rice in crop agriculture. Judging from the profitability estimates of many nonrice crops, it would appear that the country has more profitable options compared to rice export at the prevailing world price of rice. This in turn, raises the question of sustaining the profitability of other crops as well. It also remains doubtful whether the implied decline in private profitability would allow rice production to grow rapidly enough so as to actually generate an exportable surplus.[19] This does not, however, rule out the possibility that the export of certain special varieties of rice (such as high-quality aromatic rice) can be highly profitable, both in terms of private and economic returns.

Table 3.10
Private and Economic Profitability of Nonrice crops (farm level),[a] 1990-1991

Crop	*Irrigation Technique*	*Price Parity Basis*	*Net Economic Returns (Tk/hectare)*[b]		*Net Private Returns (Tk/hectare)*
Wheat	Modern	Import	747	(446)	184
	Nonirrigated	Import	2,701	(2,445)	2,046
	All	Import	1,757	(1,469)	1,149
Jute (white)	Rainfed	Export	5,809	(1,918)	-1,437
Jute (tossa)	All	Export	10,822	(5,693)	2,115
Cotton	Rainfed	Import	16,625	(13,135)	10,130
Tobacco (heat-cured)	Modern	Export	90,383		10,896
	All	Export	83,537		11,276
Sugarcane (for gur-making)	Modern	Import (Sugar)	3,106	(8,812)	44,534
	Nonirrigated	Import (Sugar)	-839	(3,525)	28,973
Oilseeds					
Mustard	Traditional/ Nonirrigated	Import (Oilseed)	-726		2,730
	Traditional/ Nonirrigated	Import (Oil)	-2,907		2,730
Sesame	Traditional/ Nonirrigated	Import (Oil)	-6,692		-2,197
Linseed	Traditional/ Nonirrigated	Import (Oil)	-719		2,256
Pulses					
Masur (lentil)	Traditional/ Nonirrigated	Import	10,131	(6,971)	5,816
	Traditional/ Nonirrigated	Export	6,320		
Gram	Traditional/ Nonirrigated	Import	7,698	(5,263)	4,376
Khesari	Traditional/ Nonirrigated	Import	7,979	(5,807)	5,286
Spices					
Chili (dry)	Modern	Import	8,522		19,694
	Traditional/ Nonirrigated	Import	868		7,398
Onion	All	Import	36,697		41,538
Potato					
MV potato (fresh)	Modern	Nontraded	29,247		16,043
	Traditional	Nontraded	32,342		19,289
	Traditional	Export	9,206		19,289
	All	Nontraded	26,402		16,698
MV potato (chilled)	All	Import	45,947		16,698
	All	Nontraded	34,960		16,698
Local potato (fresh)	All	Import	18,699		-2,412
		Nontraded	3,229		-2,412

(Continued next page)

Table 3.10 *(continued)*

Crop	*Irrigation Technique*	*Price Parity Basis*	*Net Economic Returns (Tk/hectare)*[b]	*Net Private Returns (Tk/hectare)*
Vegetables				
Brinjal	Traditional	Export	274,623	23,721
	Traditional	Nontraded	39,417	23,721
	Modern	Nontraded	48,246	47,398
Radishes	Modern/ Traditional	Export	241,102	11,620
	Modern/ Traditional	Nontraded	21,608	11,620
Cucumbers	Modern/ Traditional	Export	191,219	25,946
	Modern/ Traditional	Nontraded	37,858	25,946
Barbati (long-yard beans)	Traditional/ Nonirrigated	Export	167,244	29,731
		Nontraded	46,245	29,731
Arum	Traditional/ Nonirrigated	Nontraded	51,305	33,139
Tomatoes	Modern/ Traditional	Nontraded	88,775	63,462
Cabbages	Modern/ Traditional	Nontraded	50,657	33,770

[a]Private and economic profitability estimates are based on "normalized" domestic and world prices for 1990-1991.

[b]Figures in parentheses correspond to the projected world price for 1995 deflated to the 1990-1991 base. For pulses, however, this figure corresponds to the alternative lower world price of lentils.

Source: Mahmud et al. (1993).

A striking feature of the profitability estimates is that a number of crops such as potato, vegetables, onion, and cotton show economic and private returns that can be significantly higher than those of HYV rice. Though this suggests that while the potential exists for reorienting existing cropping patterns in a socially profitable way, the constraints to such a reorientation of the crop economy need to be addressed. Jute also has a competitive edge over local rice at the prevailing world price of jute. By contrast, wheat, sugarcane, and oilseeds show very low, even negative, economic returns, although in the case of sugarcane, private returns are quite high. Sugarcane production appears to generate negative economic returns even for making *gur*.

The profitability estimates discussed above are intended to reflect actual rather than potential farm practice. The relative profitability of crops can, however, change with technological improvements. As mentioned earlier, research and extension activities in the past were mainly concentrated on HYV rice to the neglect of most other crops. Nevertheless, new technologies of some noncereal crops have already been developed and recommended for commercial cultivation (Ministry of Agriculture 1989). In order to assess the likely impact of technological improvements on comparative advantage, Mahmud et al. (1993) derived profitability estimates for a number of "synthetic" crop activities incorporating the improved production techniques.

The synthetic crop activities are constructed on the basis of data on fertilizer recommendations and expected yields with respect to particular improved crop varieties as reported in the publications of the Bangladesh Agricultural Research Council (BARC 1989). These data on fertilizer input and yield rates are combined with other production input data of a corresponding crop activity used in the earlier profitability exercise.[20] The labor input requirements are however estimated by applying an elasticity of 0.3 with respect to the envisaged increase in yield rates. Also, since irrigation in varying intensities is recommended for all of the crop varieties (except rainfed jute), the irrigation costs have been estimated as appropriate proportions of those for HYV *boro* rice.

The estimates of expected private and economic profitability of crops under technological innovations are presented in Table 3.11. As in the earlier table, the economic profitability estimates for some crops at the projected 1995 world prices are shown within parentheses. As expected, there is only a small increase in the profitability of HYV *boro* compared to the earlier estimates. But for most other crops, there are very substantial improvements in both economic and private profitability, reflecting the higher productivity of the crop varieties as well as the effect of better farm practice (as implicit in the BARC recommendations).

Wheat and sugarcane do not, however, appear promising even in spite of its improved profitability. Under certain cropping patterns, wheat may still barely compete with HYV *boro* if we take into account the higher irrigation coverage made possible by growing wheat instead of rice. But mustard seed is the most remarkable in that economic profitability remains negative, even though a substantial increase in yield (by about 40 percent) is envisaged. This has something to do with the low world price of oilseeds and the nature of the improved production technology that is currently available.

Table 3.11
Expected Private and Economic Profitability of Crops with Technological Innovations, 1990-1991[a]

Crop	*Price Parity Basis*	*Net Economic Returns (Taka/hectare)*[b]		*Net Private Returns (Taka/hectare)*
Paddy				
Boro HYV	Export	6,094		9,176
	Import	18,068		9,176
	Nontraded	12,263	(12,609)	9,176
Wheat	Import	6,930	(6,470)	6,227
Jute (white)	Export	12,186	(7,459)	1,621
Cotton	Import	24,247	(19,538)	15,741
Sugarcane (for gur-making)	Import	8,925	(15,796)	59,240
Mustard	Import (oil)	-3,473		4,823
	Import (oilseed)	-401		4,823
Masur (lentil)	Import (high price)	16,418		10,205
	Import (low price)	11,589		10,205
Potato (fresh)	Export	19,541		33,728
	Nontraded	52,135		33,728
Brinjal	Nontraded	120,393		88,759
Radishes	Nontraded	105,060		74,013
Tomatoes	Nontraded	125,845		91,696

[a]Crop yield and production costs underlying the profitability estimates are based on the assumption that modern-variety seeds are used with "medium" doses of fertilizers; see Table A.5.3 in Statistical Annex and discussion in the text.

[b]Figures in parentheses correspond to the projected world price for 1995 deflated to the 1990-1991 base.

Source: Mahmud et al. (1993).

On the other hand, the expected private and economic returns from the improved variety of lentils are as high as those of HYV *boro*; this would clearly make it a preferable crop because of its much lower irrigation intensity. Both cotton and jute (even of the inferior white variety) show the potential to become even more competitive in the respective *aus* and *aman* seasons. Modern-variety potato, which has a competitive edge even with existing farm practice, can potentially attain much higher profitability and a comparative advantage for export. However, the most spectacular gains in profitability would come from the adoption of certain high-yielding varieties of vegetables as demonstrated by this exercise.

Policy Implications

Although the agroclimatic situations of Bangladesh are suitable for the cultivation of a large variety of crops, more than 80 percent of the arable land is presently confined to the production of rice and wheat, the staple foods. Since the mid-1960s, all government programs have been primarily aimed at achieving self-sufficiency in foodgrain production. The self-sufficiency goal, which for long remained elusive, seems to be very much attainable now. This has been possible largely due to the rapid dissementation of biochemical technology in the last decade.

But this high growth in foodgrain production, particularly *boro* rice and wheat, has been achieved often at the expense of other crops. For example, wheat is responsible for the decrease in oilseeds acreage while pulses continue to lose out to irrigated *boro* paddy. As a result, many of the noncereal crops, which could profitably be grown within the country, are being imported. Moreover, the continuous monoculture of rice is believed to be causing severe depletion of soil fertility.

The time has come, therefore, to pay more attention to noncereal crops that have great potential. Fortunately, the government of Bangladesh seems to have realized the importance of crop diversification along nutritional lines. This is reflected, as mentioned earlier, in the Fourth Five-Year Plan which particularly emphasizes the production of high-value, labor-intensive nonrice crops such as pulses, oilseeds, spices, vegetables, and fruits. Crop diversification, it should be emphasized, does not mean the elbowing out of rice crops; rather, it is a systematic arrangement for growing a variety of crops in rotation with rice.

In a program of crop diversification, quick-maturing, high-yielding, and profitable crops are likely to succeed. Although the availability of land in Bangladesh remains limited, there is considerable scope for diversification through intensive cultivation of HYV crops. The rabi season with low cropping intensity seems to hold the best promise for diversified crops; this could be realized through an intensive irrigation program. In fact, the success of crop diversification is contingent upon irrigation facilities. However, nonrice crops need much less water than rice crops, especially *boro* rice. At present, the lion's share of irrigation water goes to rice and wheat while other crops, with the exception of potato, receive an insignificant proportion of water (Wennergren, Anholt, and Whitaker 1984).

There has been significant expansion of irrigation in Bangladesh. The shallow tubewells, in particular, have become vastly popular among the farmers for their economic and technical advantages. With the development of minor irrigation, a water market has emerged in which buying and selling of water largely remain limited to rice production. Another important feature is the increased privatization of irrigation equipment, including its procurement and distribution. However, in recent years the performance of the water market has suffered from a credit squeeze, declining profitability of irrigated rice production, and inadequate support services. Other factors contributing to the slowdown of irrigation growth are high equipment, operation, and maintenance costs; fuel and electricity problems; reduced availability of surface and groundwater; and poor management. Moreover, given the present unequal access to institutions for credit, equipment, and other facilities, the market has been far from perfect. In this highly inequitable market, the big landowners seem to enjoy greater control over water and a larger share of the benefits. Amid this scenario of a rice-based irrigation water market plagued by many problems, the scope of crop diversification assumes a new dimension. As a matter of fact, the crop diversification and the irrigation program in Bangladesh can mutually reinforce each other (Biswas and Mondal 1993).

The profitability analysis presented earlier gives rise to a number of conclusions regarding incentives for crop diversification. A striking feature of the profitability estimates is that a number of crops such as potato, vegetables, onion, and cotton show economic and private returns that are as high or higher than those of HYV rice. While this suggests that there exists considerable potential for crop diversification, it needs to be investigated as to why these crops have performed so poorly, compared to HYV rice, in terms of land allocation and output growth. The answer may lie in a combination of economic and physical factors, some of which have been mentioned earlier.

There are very high price risks associated with the marketing of such crops as potato, vegetables, and spices. On the other hand, the existing on-farm water management systems do not allow rice and nonrice crops to be planted in the same service units. As discussed earlier, this discourages the use of modern irrigation for growing high-value, but risky, nonrice crops, since it may often require farmers to allocate their entire land (or most of it) to such crops. This perhaps largely explains why land under modern irrigation is almost exclusively devoted to rice cultivation while high-value, nonrice crops are widely grown under traditional irrigation (which, being divisible, allows such crops to be grown on small parcels of land). This poses a serious problem for crop diversification, since the prospects for increasing the area under traditional irrigation is believed to be limited. The problem needs to be solved in several ways, namely, by (a) reducing the price risks through improved marketing, (b) making the nonrice crops more profitable through technological improvements so as to compensate for high price risks, and (c) introducing water management systems that would allow rice and nonrice crops to be grown within the same service units.[21]

The prospects for agricultural growth through crop diversification depend largely on how far noncereal crops can compete with HYV *boro* rice under dry-season, irrigated conditions. The estimates of potential profitability with technological improvements suggest that there is more unexploited technological potential with respect to dry-season, nonrice crops compared to *boro* rice, even with the existing available technologies. However, the technical and socioeconomic constraints to technology adoption in the case of nonrice crops are still little understood. The cultivation of high-value crops like vegetables with improved technologies is very resource-intensive. The improvement of marketing facilities that could reduce price risks as well as the provision of credit to meet farmers' cash needs are likely to be important determining factors in the diffusion of these technologies.

The profitability estimates bring out the critical role of marketing, storage, and processing functions in determining both the economic and private returns of crop production. While there is evidence of a relatively efficient rice marketing system that evolved over time, most noncereal crops have a disadvantage in this respect compared to rice. Marketing costs are generally high because of inadequate infrastructure and also because of high price risks and private traders' lack of access to institutional credit. The high cost of marketing, in turn, has a depressing effect on both the size of the market (by raising the consumer price) and on producer incentives (by lowering the farmgate price). The relatively high marketing costs in financial terms compared to those in economic terms can also be an important source of the divergence between the private and economic profitability of crops.

Another way of looking at the profitability estimates for nonrice crops is that the country does not seem to have a comparative advantage in those items which currently compete with major imports, namely, wheat, sugar, oilseeds, and edible oils.[22] On the other hand, the crops that show high economic profitability, such as potato and vegetables, are currently produced either entirely for the domestic market, or have only limited access to the world market. While import substitution, by its very nature, does not encounter a market problem, the profitability of non-traded crops would depend on the growth of domestic demand in relation to output growth. The domestic market for noncereal crops, specially the high-value ones, is limited in size because of the low living standards. This underscores the need to explore the possibility of export of crops for which there is a potential comparative advantage.[23] It should be noted, however, that in the past the production of vegetables, potato, spices, and fruits did not grow rapidly enough even to satisfy the growth in domestic demand, much less create an exportable surplus. Efforts at export promotion, therefore, need to be part of an integrated strategy of technological improvements and development of marketing and process-ing facilities that could elicit better supply responses (Mahmud et al. 1993).

The Political Economy of Agricultural Policy

Governments make policies with a variety of objectives and under a variety of constraints. Policies adopted are not always necessarily the "rational" ones—assuming that "rationality" can be more or less clearly defined. In particular, it certainly cannot be taken for granted that governments always and everywhere act in accordance with "the general interest" or "the people's will"—again assuming that these notions have any definable sense. When selecting policies, governments are inevitably subject to pressures and counterpressures from various interest groups, and will respond more readily to pressure when this is perceived to increase the ruling group's probability of holding on to power. However, there are also situations where effective pressure groups do not exist, or can be successfully set off against one another, and the state can pursue its own agenda, which could be purely "predatory", purely altruistic, or a blend of the two (see Grindle 1991).

The salient fact about the Bangladesh polity is the relative weakness of the peasantry as a pressure group. They are numerous, but their geographical dispersion, internal differentiation, ideological orientation, and poor resource base all contribute to making them largely ineffective. In contrast, the urban "formal sector" working class and the bureaucracy (a "pressure group" within the state apparatus), and more recently private entrepreneurs, constitute organized and powerful pressure groups that few governments, democratic or autocratic, would wish to antagonize.

In policy formulation and implementation in Bangladesh, there are other major players, consisting of the principal aid agencies—the World Bank, Asian Development Bank (ADB), and the United States Agency for International Development (USAID). They have played an especially important role in the evolution of agricultural policy by tying program loans and import credits to the fulfillment of policy reform measures. Indeed, hard-core radical critics of the policy reforms are inclined to attribute the policy changes entirely to donor pressure. Credibility was lent to these charges by the tactlessness and arrogance of some aid personnel. The following incident illustrates this.

In 1984, the World Bank commissioned a study on the fertilizer subsidy, to be jointly carried out by the Bangladesh Institute of Development Studies and the International Food Policy Research Institute. Abu Abdullah headed the BIDS team, the other members being Mahabub Hossain and M.A. Quasem.

At a start-up meeting, the then representative of the Bank said, "Let one thing be clear. The policy regarding subsidy is not dependent on the outcome of the study." When Abdullah asked, "In that case why is the Bank funding the study?", the answer, heavily laden with sarcasm, was, "Because the government considers the study to be terribly important."

And in fact, the final increases in fertilizer prices, which for the time being eliminated all economic subsidies, were announced well before the report was submitted. Soon after this, the then Secretary of Agriculture, known to be against the policy of subsidy removal, was transferred to Defence, allegedly at donor insistence.[24]

To put things in perspective, however, it should be recalled that the First Five-Year Plan of Bangladesh had, in 1973, already committed itself to eventual removal of subsidies, indeed it had gone so far as to say that: "... in some cases these inputs must be sold at a profit" (Government of Bangladesh 1973, 42). We have already seen that urea prices were raised drastically starting right from that year.

Nevertheless, donor pressure undoubtedly played a role, if only that of neutralizing the opposition, not of a genuine farmers' lobby (there is none), but of sections of the bureaucracy who were opposed to subsidy elimination and privatization of the distribution of fertilizer as well as irrigation equipment. This opposition was undoubtedly partly derived from the bureaucracy's universal reluctance to see its control and allocative powers curtailed. But in many instances a genuine, if at times misplaced, concern for the equity aspects of these changes played a major role. The removal of the fertilizer subsidy became the symbol, or index, of the government's proclivity to inflict costs on the weak and disorganized while pampering the strong and organized, for example, the industrialists, or even urban industrial workers. There is this much truth in this, that removing the subsidy would have been much harder, perhaps impossible, in the face of determined opposition from a strong and well-organized peasant lobby. A further implication is that introducing technically (that is, economically) "rational" policies has been, and will continue to be, easier in agriculture than in industry and trade, even for a democratically elected government.

The fact that a certain set of policies was adopted at least partly under donor pressure, and could be adopted because those adversely affected could not protest effectively, does not by itself prove that the policies were wrong. However, technically right policies must also be socially and politically acceptable (at least tolerable), otherwise they cannot be sustained. Either the regime in power will be forced to retreat to less "rational" policies, or it may be replaced by a more "populist" regime that will abandon economic rationality in an attempt to maximize instant support by giving something to everyone—thus sowing the seeds of their own eventual ouster when the economy runs aground.[25]

The policymaking process is further complicated by the fact that policymakers (and implementers) may and frequently do differ among themselves as to what the appropriate policies are. This may simply be the result of difference in social class and professional training, or it may be due to more systemic factors: the bureaucracy is unwilling to relinquish the levers of control even if the political leadership is committed to deregulation, the Ministry of Commerce may obstruct liberalization measures proposed by Finance, and so on. Nor do policy advisors (mainly economists) speak with one voice. The colonial experience, interpreted as exploitation by world capitalism; the apparent success of the former Soviet Union and, later, the People's Republic of China in transforming their economies of petit bourgeois or peasant origins; as well as the expe-rience of certain blatant examples of market failure, such as the Bengal famine of 1943, combined to produce in our intellectuals, including economists, a bias against the market and for "planning". Recent developments in the world and in the discipline of development studies have dissipated some of the illusion, but enough lingers to produce an articulate antimarket lobby among the intellectuals, helped, unfortunately, by sweeping, simplistic claims for the market made by its overzealous votaries.

Whenever the party in power tries to implement tough policies, either the victims themselves (and there always are victims—that is why the policies are tough) or some opposition party will try to mobilize enough support to subvert the reforms or at least discredit the party in power. This is, of course, part of the democratic process, but it makes policy reform an exceedingly hazardous process, and frequently renders the government ineffective.

To take a recent example, the Awami League has recently put forward an 11-point charter of demands ostensibly intended to "save the peasants, save the nation". The demands include "immediate withdrawal of certificate cases (for recovery of defaulted loans) and warrants of arrest against farmers, reduction of agricultural input prices, lower rates of interest on agriloans, ensuring fair prices of agriproducts, distribution of *khas* lands among the landless, end of 'politicization' in leasing out *haats* and bazaars, and waiving of interest on loans up to Tk 5000 for cooperatives as per the PM's earlier commitment" (*Daily Star*, 9 September 1993). All of these demands will no doubt have the peasants' complete approval, so this is good short-run political tactics. But most of them are economically irrational, and will involve high financial costs and an increase in government intervention in the market, which will lead to gross inefficiencies and rent-seeking. If the Awami League succeeds in mobilizing enough support behind them on this and other similar populist policies, they may get to power, but will then find themselves unable to implement their own program (or ruin the economy in trying to implement it) and get thrown out of power again. For correct policy formulation and its effective implementation, therefore, it would be highly desirable, indeed indispensable, for the two major political parties to arrive at a minimum consensus regarding economic policy. They should agree in particular to abstain from making irrational promises to the electorate. (Note that before the 1991 election, both major parties promised waivers on agricultural loans, thus worsening an already fragile repayment situation.) The parties should then take on, as a major part of their responsibility, the task of educating the people about the hard facts of economic life.

At the same time, the government can try to sweeten the pill of agricultural policy reforms by offering nondistortionary and much needed compensation in terms of greater local autonomy and participation, infrastructure development (roads, electrification), and better health and education services. The provision of social safety nets is fraught with administrative difficulties, (witness the ill-fated Palli ration system), but attempts to evolve innovative delivery mechanisms that would be relatively free from these problems must continue.

Donor-government relations present a dilemma. On the one hand, tough conditionalities can help the reform process by providing the government with a convenient scapegoat for its own reform agenda. On the other hand, this lays the government open to charges of being "agents" or "tools" of "imperialist vested interests". On the whole it is our impression that donors are being a little too tough. For example, the ADB suspended release of the second tranche of the Foodcrops Development Programme Loan because some of the conditionalities had not been fulfilled. In our opinion, there was in fact enough progress in meeting other conditionalities, and enough genuine reasons for at least some of the underfulfillment, to have justified release. It must also be said that while donors are not always sufficiently sensitive to the political constraints confronting the government (the refusal to condone an industrial minimum wage is possibly a case in point), the government also sometimes takes a stand on rather tenuous grounds. An example would be, in our opinion, the refusal of the Ministry of Agriculture to sell off BADC's stock of irrigation equipment by auction within the date stipulated (in spite of that date being extended twice) under the loan agreement for the ADB's Foodcrops Development Programme Loan.[26] What is needed is much more groundwork before drawing up a loan agreement or similar documents, so that problems can be anticipated and realistic targets set. Under the present circumstances, it would seem that both donor and recipient are in too much of a hurry to do this necessary homework.

In sum, the policy reform process has been surprisingly smooth so far. This has been partly due to the fact that the peasants do not constitute an organized lobby; otherwise the progressive rise in fertilizer prices (at least since 1991) would have been resisted. However, it is probably due in good part to the fact that the policy reforms have, by and large, benefited all classes of farmers—destandardization in particular must have been a popular move. The opposition so far has come more from the public sector (such as BADC) employees. If the current decline in rice prices continues, matters might become more complicated, making it harder for the government not to intervene in input and/or output markets. But with some consensus between contending political forces, and more informed and tactful firmness on the part of donors, the reform process can be successfully sustained.

Conclusion

In this paper, we have attempted three things. First, we have given an overview of recent policy changes in agriculture relating to input marketing, and tried to assess the impact of these changes on the rice economy. In particular, we have tried to draw out the implications of the achievement (possibly provisional) of self-sufficiency in cereals.

Second, we have been led by the logic of the attainment of self-sufficiency to an examination of the potentials for crop diversification. This in fact constitutes the bulk of the paper.

And thirdly, we have attempted a foray into the political economy of agricultural policy formulation and implementation.

We are keenly aware of the shortcomings of this exercise. For brevity, we have left out the consideration of a host of critical issues—rural credit, research and extension, and employment and poverty, to mention a few. Our broad overall conclusions are:

- Policy reforms in agriculture have been successful, and have made a major contribution to the attainment of self-sufficiency in foodgrains.

- While rice exports are a real possibility, and are already taking place, this is unlikely to provide an "engine of growth" for agriculture, which ultimately has to be found in the growth of domestic nonagricultural income, such as from industry and services.

- In the interim, emphasis within agriculture should shift from rice to other crops. Here, however, not enough is yet known about constraints that inhibit spontaneous crop diversification, hence not much can yet be said about concrete policies to attain this goal. However, research to develop HYVs, infrastructure development to ensure rapid access to (domestic and world) markets, and the introduction of water management systems that would allow rice and nonrice crops to be grown within the same service units would seem to be indicated as immediate policy initiatives. At the margin, a relaxation of export restrictions on raw jute, while squeezing the jute industry, may benefit farmers, and on balance, the economy. Sugarcane, on the other hand, seems needlessly overprotected. A number of crops appear to compare favorably with HYV *boro* in terms of private and economic profitability. The technical and policy constraints that inhibit their growth need to be carefully identified.

- The reform measures have on the whole benefited all farmers, which is one reason why their adoption has been politically feasible. Other major factors have been donor pressure and the lack of an effective farmer lobby, which would no doubt have opposed at least some components of reforms, in particular, the removal of subsidies on fertilizer and irrigation equipment. However, the main opposition has come from public employees threatened with redundancy, bureaucrats reluctant to relinquish control, and intellectuals concerned with equity and distrustful of the market. The importance of a minimum consensus on economic policies between the two major political parties has been emphasized. It has also been suggested that donors should be a little more sensitive to the political constraints operating on a government, and also that governments and donors should do their homework more thoroughly before agreeing on the conditionalities attached to loan agreements.

Notes

1. All figures are calculated from Abdullah (1993, 9-12, tables 1-4).
2. This section and the one that follows are taken from work done earlier by Shahabuddin, as a staff consultant with the ADB.
3. Comment made by Jim Philips at a Bangladesh BIDS Seminar, November 1992.
4. Reported in World Bank (1992, 15). Monthly figures converted to daily ones by dividing by 30.
5. A successful export drive would support rice prices and hence hurt poor deficit households—the "food price dilemma". This could be offset by increased production or import of cheaper foodgrains.
6. There was some confusion as to whether these regulations have been simply "suspended" rather than "rescinded", that is (as we understand it), they can be reimposed at the discretion of the Food Ministry rather than requiring an act of Parliament or a Presidential Ordinance. We were assured by a Food Ministry official that the laws had indeed been "rescinded".
7. The following information is from IFDC (1993a, b).

8. The farm survey was conducted in 1987 by the Bangladesh Institute of Development Studies in connection with a study on the adoption of HYV rice technology in Bangladesh agriculture; see Hossain et al. (1992).

9. The profitability estimates presented in the next section will show that the net returns from these crops are generally higher compared to HYV Boro.

10. It may be mentioned here that the time series data on minor crops are of dubious quality in Bangladesh. Therefore, the estimates of price elasticity based on the data should be taken with a grain of salt. Moreover, for vegetables and spices, farmers may respond to expected postharvest prices rather than the "average price" for the year.

11. Natural factors affecting crop yields are also a likely source of supply instability.

12. As a result of very recent policy changes, the import of foodgrains by private traders is now allowed in principle while the ban of rice export has been lifted.

13. In the case of rapeseed, at the millgate level.

14. The average of the price of 5 percent broken and 25 percent broken Thai rice is used to represent the price of coarse-quality rice in Bangladesh. Discussion with traders suggested that the coarse rice produced in the country is markedly superior to the internationally traded 25 percent broken Thai variety. Also, a recent market survey has shown that domestic coarse rice mainly consists of about 15 percent broken; see Chowdhury (1992). However, there is no internationally quoted price available for 15 percent broken Thai rice.

15. Mustard is also protected at the farm level through the very high protection provided to the edible oil industry.

16. The major share of the sugarcane produced in the country is used for *gur*-making by traditional methods.

17. In the earlier years, some small quantities of potato were imported by the government. On the other hand, a very small quantity has been exported under the government's initiative in the recent past.

18. For a detailed discussion on the methodology and sources of data used in the study, see Mahmud et al. (1993). One major weakness of their profitability analysis is that the estimates of net economic returns for rice and nonrice yield are for "average" quality of land. For low lands, the rice yield will be higher while the yield of most nonrice crops will be lower because of excessive moisture. The reverse is true for highlands. Thus the average estimates of economic returns are misleading indicators of land use potential for different land types.

19. To allow rice exports to take place, the actual farmgate price of rice would have to decline by about 25 to 30 percent compared to the price that has been used in the present estimates of private profitability.

20. The corresponding crop activities are so chosen as to best represent an improved technology scenario, for example, modern variety potato under modern irrigation.

21. This may require special preparation of plots, as is practiced in some Southeast Asian countries.

22. Cotton and onion seem to be exceptions, but cotton is a very minor crop and onion is not an important import item.

23. The list of such crops may include many horticultural products and spices that have not been included in the present profitability exercises.

24. Personal recollection.

25. For an interesting analysis of the oscillation of postcolonial regimes between "technocratic" and "populist" policies, see Huntington and Nelson (1976, ch. 2).

26. Personal recollection of interview with the Agriculture Secretary in October 1992.

References

Abdullah, A., 1992. "Progress in Policy Reform in the Foodcrops Sector." Report prepared for the ADB. Asian Development Bank, Manila.

———, 1993. "Evaluating the Impact of Privatisation and Deregulation in Bangladesh Agriculture." Paper presented at the BEA Conference, Dhaka.

Asaduzzaman, M., 1989. "Feeding our Future Towns: An Overview of Urbanisation and Associated Food Policy Issues." In *Bangladesh Planning Commission, Food Strategies in Bangladesh: Medium and Long Term Perspectives.* Dhaka: University Press Limited.

Bangladesh Agricultural Research Council, 1989. *Fertilizer Recommendation Guide.* Dhaka.

Bangladesh Bureau of Statistics, various years. *Statistical Yearbook of Bangladesh.* Dhaka.

Biswas, M. R., and M. A. S. Mondal, 1993. *Irrigation Management for Crop Diversification in Bangladesh.* Dhaka: University Press Limited.

Chowdhury, N., 1992. *Rice Market in Bangladesh: A Study in Structure, Conduct, and Performance.* Dhaka: IFPRI.

Chowdhury, O. H., and Q. Shahabuddin, 1992. "A Study of Food Situation and Outlook of Asia: Country Report on Bangladesh." IFPRI/ADP. Mimeographed.

FAO/NAP, 1993. *Fertilizer Trade Information.* ESCAP/FAO/UNIDO Fertilizer Advisory, Development and Information Network for Asia and the Pacific, Bangkok, Thailand.

Government of Bangladesh, 1973. *The First Five-Year Plan.* Ministry of Planning, Dhaka.

Government of Bangladesh and United Nations Development Programme, 1989. *Agricultural Sector Review, Compendium,* Volume IV.

Grindle, M. S., 1991. "The New Political Economy: Positive Economics and Negative Politics." In G. M. Meier, ed., *Politics and Policy Making in Developing Countries.* San Francisco: ICS Press.

Guisselquist, D., 1991. "Development Potential of Minor Irrigation in Bangladesh." AST/CIDA, Ministry of Agriculture, Dhaka. Unpublished.

Hossain, M., et al., 1992. "Differential Impact of Modern Rice Technology: The Bangladesh Case." Bangladesh Institute of Development Studies, Dhaka. Unpublished.

Huntingon, S., and J. Nelson, 1976. *No Easy Choice.* Cambridge: Harvard University Press.

International Fertilizer Development Center, 1993a. "Monitoring Report on Fertilizer Distribution in Bangladesh." Dhaka.

———, 1993b. "Survey of Farm-Level Prices and Availability." Dhaka.

Mahmud, W., S. H. Rahman, and S. Zohir, 1993. "Agricultural Growth through Crop Diversification in Bangladesh." IFPRI/BIDS Study. Mimeographed.

Master Plan Organization, 1991. *National Water Plan (Phase-II),* Vol. 2. Ministry of Irrigation, Water Development and Flood Control, Government of Bangladesh. Dhaka.

Ministry of Agriculture, 1989. *Crop Diversification Programme for the Fourth Five-Year Plan.* Dhaka: Agricultural Division.

Planning Commission, 1990. *The Fourth Five Year Plan (Revised Draft).* Government of Bangladesh, Dhaka.

Rahman, S. H., 1992. "A New Tariff Structure for Agricultural Equipment Inputs." Report prepared for the Asian Development Bank. Manila, Philippines.

Wennergren, E. B., C. H. Anholt, and M. D. Whitaker, 1984. *Agricultural Development in Bangladesh.* Colorado: Westview Press.

World Bank, 1992. *Bangladesh Food Policy Review: Adjusting to the Green Revolution,* Vol. I. Washington, D. C.

4

Constraints to Industrial Development: Recent Reforms and Future Directions

Masihur Rahman and Zaid Bakht

Overview

Bangladesh, with a labor force estimated to grow at 4.5 percent per annum, and with an agricultural sector absorptive capacity limited to at most a third of the new entrants to the labor force, is faced with the pressing need to rapidly expand employment opportunities outside of agriculture, particularly in the industrial sector.

The importance of the industrial sector had been recognized even when the country was part of Pakistan, and industrial development had been attempted in the past under diverse policy regimes. At the time of the partition in 1947, East Pakistan was a primary product-producing region with little modern industry. The Pakistan government adopted a policy of private sector based industrialization with active public intervention. Initially, East Pakistanis were unable to generate private industrial initiatives, and the process of industrialization was started in this region by non-Bengali entrepreneurs with strong patronage from the government. By the early 1960s, however, a Bengali entrepreneurial class began to emerge and receive active state sponsorship and support.

From a negligible position in 1947, the industrial base of East Pakistan reached a substantial level by the end of the 1960s, raising its share in gross domestic product (GDP) from less than 4 percent to nearly 8 percent. However, given the low base from which it started, this doubling of the share of the industrial sector in GDP was hardly spectacular in absolute terms and failed to make any perceptible impact on per capita income, which grew at a dismal rate of 0.4 percent per annum between 1949/50 and 1969/70.

Moreover, the generous system of public subsidy and protection under which the industrialization process was nurtured and sustained had several distortionary effects. Many industries suffered from over-capitalization and the resulting underutilization of capacity. Private profits were high at the cost of productive efficiency, the benefits of which accrued mainly to non-Bengali entrepreneurs.

At the time of independence in 1971, the Bangladesh government adopted a development philosophy that assigned the lead role in industrialization to the state. It also adopted import substitution as a key element of the industrialization strategy. This, however, was basically a continuation of the previous policy. In pursuance of this philosophy and faced with the abandonment of a large number of industrial enterprises by Pakistani entrepreneurs, the new government nationalized all such abandoned properties, as well as all industrial enterprises with fixed assets exceeding a certain threshold level. Jute textiles, cotton textiles and the sugar industry along with banking, insurance, and the export trade in jute were totally nationalized. The scope of the private sector was limited to small and cottage industry, and foreign investment was allowed only in collaboration with the public sector in minority equity participation. However, existing foreign investments (excluding those belonging to Pakistan) were spared from this sweeping nationalization drive, explicable by political rather than economic impulses.

Quantitative restrictions on imports were extensively used in the early 1970s in pursuance of the import-substituting industrialization strategy. A policy of fixed exchange rate was adopted in support of domestic market oriented industrialization to complement the high tariff and nontariff barriers. In the early years, the exchange rate was also substantially misaligned.

The government interventionist role in industry did not bring about desired results. Apart from the inherent difficulties of implementing a strategy of public sector-led industrialization, the country was poorly equipped politically and socially, and lacked adequate administrative and managerial machinery to implement such a strategy. The initial circumstances were also unfavorable. The war of liberation had caused major dislocations in both internal and external sectors of the economy. Mismatches occurred between supply and demand for inputs and outputs, partly for reasons beyond the control of the government. It was soon realized that there was a need to encourage the private sector to play an augmented role. Accordingly, the ceiling on private investment was raised, a modest tax holiday was granted to private investors, foreign investment was allowed to collaborate with local private entrepreneurs, and a 15-year moratorium on nationalization was announced. All these measures were taken within the first two to three years of independence. Another notable development during the early years was that the government, in response to the foreign exchange crisis, allowed Bangladeshi nationals earning foreign exchange abroad to import goods through the so-called Wage Earner's Scheme (WES).

With the change in government in 1975, the strategy of public sector-led industrialization was abandoned. In a bid to give more room to the private sector, a number of major policy changes were made between 1975 and 1982. These included further raising of the private investment ceiling, and its eventual removal in 1978, amendment of the constitution to allow denationalization, with actual denationalization of a number of public enterprises, making investment funds available through development finance institutions; reopening of the stock market, and reducing the number of industries reserved for the public sector. At the same time, the investment sanctioning procedure was somewhat relaxed. On the trade policy front, a major shift was a move to a managed floating exchange rate system and the introduction of a number of export promotion measures.

However, the reforms that were carried out in the late 1970s were limited in scope and were implemented slowly. Although export promotion measures were gradually introduced in the late 1970s, trade policies continued to be inward looking, and the economy in general, and the manufacturing sector in particular, remained overregulated.

A New Industrial Policy (NIP) was declared in June 1982 by the new government that came to power in March 1982 following the political change of 1981. Reform measures that were initiated during the earlier regime got a further boost under the new policy. Sanctioning procedures were further relaxed and a large number of public enterprises were denationalized expeditiously, if not hastily. Import control systems and industrial import procedures were liberalized and export promotion measures, initiated during the late 1970s, were further strengthened.

A Revised Industrial Policy (RIP), declared in 1986, aimed at further strengthening and expanding the privatization and liberalization measures initiated earlier. Fiscal incentives, introduced earlier, were further expanded under RIP. Included among these were tax holidays, accelerated depreciation allowances with carry-over benefits, and exemption from tax on capital gains.

The pace of reform in the 1980s was significantly influenced by donor conditionalities as the country sought greater access to concessional external assistance, particularly from the World Bank and the International Monetary Fund (IMF). Thus, the mid-1980s saw some initiatives toward trade policy reform under the auspices of the World Bank's Industrial Sector Adjustment Credit Program (ISAC-1). A large depreciation of the domestic currency took place in 1985 prior to the initiation of a three-year IMF Structural Adjustment Facility (SAF) in 1986, which also involved defining an economywide policy framework for the country. There was a reduction in the number of tariff rates and in the maximum customs duty (except on a few luxury items). A gradual removal of quantitative restrictions has been attempted by stipulating yearly reductions beginning in 1987. Finally, a number of measures were undertaken to simplify custom procedures. These included adoption of a harmonized coding system.

During 1988 and 1989, more reform measures were undertaken. Public sector enterprises were placed at par with private sector units in matters of finance, infrastructure facilities, and duty rebates. Sanctioning rules for foreign private investment were further relaxed, and sanctioning requirements for investments financed through credit from private financial institutions were withdrawn. Other measures included extension of the tax holiday benefit to 1990 and creation of the Board of Investment (BOI) as a one-stop service to facilitate industrial development. A number of financial sector reforms were also undertaken in 1989. These included a shift to a more flexible interest policy from the previously pursued fixed interest policy, replacement of the subsidized refinancing facility with a more general rediscount facility, and introduction of a financial court designed to improve debt recovery. Enhancement of the efficiency of the public sector was sought through greater management autonomy in operations, more flexible pricing policies, technical and financial restructuring, and reduction of the debt burden of public enterprises by converting government loans into equity. Rescheduling and partial condonement of interest provided comparable relief to the private sector.

Yet another political change occurred in 1990, and a democratic government assumed power after the general election in 1991. A new industrial policy was declared in July 1991, further relaxing investment sanctioning procedures. There is now a commitment to strengthen the ongoing privatization process. However, denationalization has been slow in recent times because of resistance from trade unions in public enterprises, as well as problems associated with the pricing of assets and the availability of enough buyers who have not defaulted on bank loans or earlier purchases of denationalized assets. Nevertheless, as part of the public enterprise reform measures, the government has identified excess manpower in a number of public undertakings, worked out modalities for redundancy adjustment, and partially put into effect the downsizing of these enterprises. In line with earlier efforts, further incentives have been provided to attract foreign investment and promote exports. One significant point of departure of the 1991 Industrial Policy from the RIP has been the elimination of concessionary interest rates and special credit facilities directed toward particular sectors. This has been done to ensure consistency with the ongoing financial sector reforms that entail flexible interest rates and other credit reform measures. As in the earlier phase, policy-based lending of the donor agencies continues to influence both the scope and pace of reforms. Thus, for example, under the Extended Structural Adjustment Facility (ESAF) which Bangladesh availed of in 1990, predetermined targets of macroeconomic parameters are required to be met within economywide structural adjustment guidelines.

Thus, a substantial number of policy reforms aimed at opening up industrial investment and production to market forces have been put in place during the past 10 to 15 years. Unfortunately, the industrial sector of Bangladesh does not seem to have responded well to this maze of policy reforms. Industrial investment during this period has been stagnant and growth in output has not contributed significantly to economic growth. There has also been little in the way of structural change within the sector.

This chapter attempts to review recent developments of the industrial sector of Bangladesh and explore various reasons for the failure of the sector to respond to policy stimuli. A profile of the industrial sector of Bangladesh, highlighting its narrow base and lack of diversity, will be provided, followed by an assessment of growth and structural change in the sector during the past two decades. Finally, key issues influencing industrial development in Bangladesh will be discussed, recent reform measures reviewed, and policy adjustments recommended.

Profile of the Industrial Sector

This section highlights the strengths and weaknesses of the industrial sector of Bangladesh as manifested in its current size, structure, and composition. The overview is intended to help assess the readiness of the sector to capitalize on appropriate policy reforms. It presents evidence with respect to such issues as industrial diversification, market orientation, size distribution, factor intensity, and ownership patterns. The size of the industrial sector in Bangladesh will be assessed in terms of three broad parameters, namely, value-added, employment, and capital assets.

Overall Size of the Manufacturing Industry in Bangladesh

The main source of industrial statistics in Bangladesh is the Bangladesh Bureau of Statistics (BBS), which provides value-added data for the manufacturing sector as part of the national income accounts. According to BBS, manufacturing value-added in 1991/92 stood at Tk 82,571 million in current prices and constituted 9.14 percent of GDP (BBS 1993a). However, BBS figures are suspected to be an underestimate. Other independent studies estimate the share of manufacturing in GDP to be about 12 percent (see for example, Bakht 1991, Islam 1991). Even with the extended coverage, however, the share of manufacturing appears relatively small in comparison with countries such as India, Pakistan, and Thailand, where manufacturing value-added constitutes 24 percent, 20 percent, and 16 percent of GDP, respectively (Economic and Social Commission for Asia and the Pacific 1991).

In terms of employment share, the manufacturing sector also constitutes a small segment of the economy. In 1989/90, BBS carried out three separate surveys of manufacturing industries in Bangladesh covering (i) all handloom enterprises (BBS 1990), (ii) all enterprises having 1 to 9 workers excluding handloom (BBS 1992a), and (iii) all enterprises having ten or more workers (BBS 1993b). Employment estimates obtained from these surveys put total industrial employment at around 3 million, that is, about 10 percent of total employment as opposed to agriculture's share of 57 percent.

However, the size of the manufacturing sector is difficult to assess with regard to capital assets, as reliable data on the capital structure of the sector is lacking. Some data on the public component of manufacturing investment is available from the recently installed System of Autonomous Bodies Reporting and Evaluation (SABRE). The SABRE data shows that between 1985 and 1989, public manufacturing investment constituted, on average, 1.21 percent of GDP (Ministry of Finance 1990). If one adds the SABRE estimate of public manufacturing investment to available estimates of private manufacturing investment (Bakht and Bhattacharya 1991), total manufacturing investment is estimated to be about 2 percent of GDP.

The small relative size of the manufacturing sector implies that it will have to grow at a fairly rapid rate to make any perceptible dent on the employment and income situation. Thus, for example, if the overall economy grows at a modest rate of 6 percent per annum then manufacturing value-added will have to grow at an annual rate of 11.8 percent to reach the target of 20 percent of GDP in ten years' time. If the incremental capital-output ratio is assumed to be about 3.5 then such a growth in manufacturing would warrant an annual investment level of nearly 4.9 percent of GDP. As will be shown in the following sections, neither the value-added growth nor the manufacturing investment has been anywhere close to these figures during the recent past.

Size Distribution

For administrative and other reasons, manufacturing industries in Bangladesh are divided into three categories: large (which includes medium enterprises), small, and cottage. But a consistent set of definitions of these size categories is difficult to find. The main source of official data on large industry is BBS. The BBS defines large industry on the basis of employment size. On the other hand, the Bangladesh Small and Cottage Industries Corporation (BSCIC), which is the official source of information for small and cottage industries, uses investment limits to differentiate between the size categories.

The BSCIC completed a survey of small and cottage industries during the late 1980s. If one combines information from the BBS with those from the recently completed BSCIC survey, then the size distribution of the manufacturing industry is as shown in Table 4.1.

Table 4.1
Structure of Manufacturing Industry in Bangladesh, 1989/90

Item	*Large*	*Small*	*Cottage*	*Total*
Employment ('000)	434 (13.2)	847 (25.8)	1996 (61.0)	3,277 (100)
Value-added at market price (million taka)	37,565 (47.7)	27,391 (34.7)	13,865 (17.6)	78,821 (100)

Note: Figures within parentheses give raw percentages.

Sources: Bangladesh Bureau of Statistics (1990, 1992b, 1993a) and unpublished tables of the latest survey of the Bangladesh Small and Cottage Industries Corporation.

As is evident from the table, large industry accounts for nearly half of manufacturing value-added but its share in employment is relatively less. On the other hand, cottage industry accommodates the bulk of manufacturing employment but contributes much less to manufacturing value-added. One thus observes a somewhat dualistic pattern in the manufacturing sector of Bangladesh, with the more productive large industry being important in terms of output but not in terms of employment, and the reverse situation being true in the case of traditional cottage industry.

Industry Composition

Large industry, in turn, is dominated by a few industry categories (BBS 1991). At the two-digit level,[1] (32) textiles, apparels and leather is the major category, accounting for 65 percent of employment and 47 percent of value-added within the large industry sector. Within this subsector, (3213) jute textiles is the dominant industry at the four-digit level, accounting for 37 percent of employment and 26 percent of value-added among all large industries. Other important four-digit industries within the textile subsector are: (3211) cotton textiles and (3231) readymade garments. Next to textiles, (35) chemicals, rubber, and plastics is the second most important subsector in terms of contribution to value-added, accounting for 24 percent of value-added within large industry. Important four-digit industries within this group are: (3524) fertilizer, (3541) petroleum refining, and (3511) allopathic medicine. The top five four-digit large industries (in terms of value-added share) account for only 7 percent of the enterprises but 55 percent of employment, and 54 percent of value-added. Average size of employment in these five industries is 846 persons per establishment as opposed to 109 persons per establishment in the case of all enterprises covered by the Census of Manufacturing Industries. In other words, the large industry in Bangladesh has a rather narrow base and a highly skewed size distribution with a few large enterprises dominating the scene.

Information on the structure of small industry in Bangladesh (excluding handloom) is available from the recent survey of small industry by the BSCIC. As is evident from this data, the small industry sector also has a narrow base, with the food manufacturing subsector accounting for nearly half of employment. At the four-digit level, three out of the top five industries (in terms of number of enterprises) belong to food manufacturing. However, with respect to value addition, the sector seems more diversified. The food manufacturing subsector, in spite of its predominant employment share, accounts for only 12 percent of value-added. This suggests that labor productivity in this group of industries is less than that in the rest of the sector. Metal and textiles are important subsectors in terms of value-added contribution. Major four-digit industries within these groups are: automobile servicing and repairing, light engineering, and hosiery and readymade garments. The sector also has a more even size distribution. Average size of employment in the five largest industries is about the same as in the rest of the sector (14 persons).

Information from BSCIC's cottage industry survey (excluding handloom) shows that the structure of this sector is more diversified than either large or small scale industries. Food processing, textiles, wood, cane and bamboo, and metal are important subsectors in terms of both employment and value-added share. The top ten four-digit industries, in terms of number of enterprises, originate from these diverse subsectors. None of them have a dominant share either in employment, value-added, or number of enterprises. The cottage sector is also less skewed in terms of size distribution, with average size of employment of 3.5 persons in the largest 10 industries as opposed to 3.3 in the overall sector.

If one combines information from the official as well as unofficial sources then the top ten four-digit industries (in terms of value-added share) within the overall manufacturing sector are those identified in Table 4.2.

Table 4.2

Top Ten Four-Digit Industries (in terms of Value-Added) in the Manufacturing Sector of Bangladesh, 1989/90

			Percentage Share in	
S1	*Industry*	*Industry*	*Value-added at factor cost*	*Employment*
1.	3216	Handloom	15.65	27.61
2.	3213	Jute textiles	11.84	6.30
3.	3211	Cotton textiles	7.09	3.88
4.	3231	Readymade garments	6.48	6.48
5.	3524	Fertilizers	3.58	0.20
6.	3541	Petroleum refining	3.01	0.02
7.	3511	Allopathic medicine	2.79	0.72
8.	3223	Knitting & hosiery	2.56	0.37
9.	3119	Rice mill	1.97	4.50
10.	3311	Saw mills	1.46	0.88
		Total	56.48	50.96

Several points are worth noting from this combined list of top ten (in terms of value-added share) four-digit level manufacturing industries:

- Textile occupies a crucial position in the manufacturing sector of Bangladesh. Five out of the top ten industries, namely, handloom, jute textiles, cotton textiles, readymade garments, and knitting and hosiery, belong to the textile subsector. Together they account for about 44 percent of manufacturing value-added and 45 percent of manufacturing employment.

- A striking aspect of the dominance of the textile sector is the singular importance of the handloom industry. Handloom tops the list both in terms of value-added and employment. The employment contribution of handloom industry is overwhelming. It accounts for more than one quarter of all manufacturing employment. Because of the small average employment size (4.8 persons) in this industry, it is also the most important source of decentralized manufacturing employment. It may be mentioned here that this traditional labor-intensive industry of Bangladesh caters mainly to the domestic market and accounts for almost 70 percent of the total cloth supply in the country.

- Jute textiles also occupies a very crucial position. It is by far the most important large industry in Bangladesh accounting for almost a quarter of value-added and more than one third of employment within the large industry sector. The industry also has a very important backward linkage with the agricultural sector and currently is the second most important manufactured export industry of Bangladesh.

- The readymade garments industry had a near-zero base in the economy in the mid-1970s. But it emerged as a dominant industry, both in terms of employment and value-added share, over a span of only 10 to 12 years. It is currently also the top export industry of the country. However, the import content of this industry is quite high and consequently, both value addition and net foreign exchange earning is relatively low.

- Three of the top ten industries belong to the chemicals subsector (fertilizer, petroleum refining, and allopathic medicine). These are fairly capital-intensive industries and rank quite low in terms of contribution to employment.

- Rice milling, belonging to the food manufacturing subsector, is important in terms of employment share but less so in terms of value-added share, indicating the low level of labor productivity entailed in this activity.

- The metal sector, which occupies an important position in most of the industrialized countries, is conspicuously missing from the list of top ten industries in the case of Bangladesh.

- Except for fertilizer and petroleum refining, almost all of the other industries in Table 4.2 are fairly labor-intensive activities. The fertilizer industry is based on domestic gas resources. Thus, in relation to resource endowment, the structure of the manufacturing industry in Bangladesh does not seem to suffer from much allocative inefficiency.

- Four of the ten industries, namely, handloom, rice mills, knitting and hosiery, and saw mills, belong to the small and cottage sector while a sizeable part of the readymade garment industry belongs to the small industry sector. Thus, although large industry accounts for most of manufacturing value-added, a number of small and cottage industries feature prominently, not only in terms of employment share but also in terms of share in manufacturing value-added. These industries, therefore, assume crucial importance as pivots of growth and employment expansion in the manufacturing sector of Bangladesh.

Factor Intensity and Factor Productivity

As mentioned earlier, available information on fixed assets in the manufacturing sector of Bangladesh, including those relating to large industry, is highly unsatisfactory. The current practice of recording value of fixed assets at historical cost results in gross underestimation of fixed assets. To get a conservative approximate estimate of replacement cost, we have multiplied book value of fixed assets recorded in the Census of

Manufacturing Industries (CMI) by a factor of 2. For small and cottage industries, the estimates from the BSCIC surveys and the Handloom Census of BBS are used. The comparative picture with respect to factor intensity and factor productivity is shown in Table 4.3.

Table 4.3
Factor Intensity and Factor Productivity in the Manufacturing Sector

Industry Group	*Year*	*Fixed Assets per Worker ('000 Tk)*	*Value-Added[a] per Worker ('000 Tk)*	*Value-Added[a] Fixed Assets Ratio*
Large	1987/88	138.0	87	0.45
Small	1989/90	36.2	32	0.89
Cottage	1989/90	4.4	7	1.60

[a]At market price.

The picture portrayed in Table 4.3 seems consistent with the setting. Fixed assets per worker are much higher in the predominantly modern large industry than in the small and cottage industries. What is worth noting, however, is that even the large industry sector is not highly capital-intensive by modern standards. The average value of fixed assets per worker in the large industry is only Tk 138,000 (US$4,417).[2] The dominant two-digit large industry is (32) textiles, apparels and leather, with fixed assets per worker in this subsector only around Tk 55,000 (US$1,760). The most capital-intensive subsector is (35) chemicals, rubber, and plastics with fixed assets per worker estimated at Tk 659,000 (US$21,000). At the four-digit level, the most capital-intensive industry is fertilizer with fixed assets per worker estimated in excess of Tk 2 million (US $64,000). However, the share of fertilizer in manufacturing value-added is only 3.58 percent while that of the large-scale (35) chemicals subsector is about 11 percent. Thus, on the whole, the large industry sector in Bangladesh may be termed as only moderately capital-intensive.

Because of the observed pattern of capital intensity, labor productivity is highest in large industry followed by small and cottage industry, in that order. However, labor productivity seems to vary by a smaller magnitude than variations in capital intensity. Thus, fixed assets per worker in large industry is nearly 3.8 times higher than that in small industry. But the difference in labor productivity is only of the order of 2.7 times. Similarly, labor productivity in small industry is nearly 4.6

times higher compared to that in cottage industry, while capital intensity is nearly 8.2 times higher. This is reflected in the rising level of capital productivity as one moves from the large to small and from small to cottage category.

The other point to note from Table 4.3 is that labor productivity is abysmally low in cottage industry—less than one third of the sector average. It is true that there exists significant interindustry variations in productivity levels within the cottage sector. Available evidence points toward differences in capital intensity and variations in the degree of underemployment as the two proximate factors explaining differences in labor productivity within the sector (Ahmad 1984, Bakht 1984). However, the fact remains that the large majority of cottage industries use only rudimentary technologies and provide residual employment to unemployed workers with earnings, often at less than agricultural wage rates.

Ownership Pattern

According to the CMI 1988/89, there were some 210 manufacturing enterprises in the public sector in the reference year. But these are very large enterprises with average employment per establishment recorded at 1,386 as opposed to 49 in all the CMI-covered enterprises. Total employment in the public manufacturing sector accounted for 67 percent of employment recorded under the large industry category. The public manufacturing enterprises are also much more capital-intensive (with fixed assets of Tk 370,000 per worker), compared to the overall large sector, and accounted for 65 percent of the book value of fixed assets recorded under CMI in 1988/89. The share of the public sector in the value-added by large industry is estimated at about 59 percent. Thus, the public sector constitutes a significant part of large industry in terms of all three parameters, namely, fixed assets, value-added, and employment, even after the massive denationalization program carried out during the 1980s. Nearly half of the public enterprises fall in the textiles subsector and another one fifth in the food manufacturing subsector. Public enterprises belonging to the chemicals subsector are fewer in number, but are important in terms of share in value-added and fixed assets.

In contrast, private enterprises dominate in number but consist mainly of small and medium-sized enterprises. The small and cottage industries, which constitute a significant proportion of the sector in terms of number of enterprises and employment share, belong wholly to the private sector. Even within the large industry category, private enterprises are of relatively small size.

Foreign enterprises do not feature very prominently in the manufacturing sector of Bangladesh. The CMI 1988/89 recorded 79 joint venture units, which accounted for about 14 percent of value-added in the large industry sector.

Market Orientation and End Use

Manufactured exports of Bangladesh constitute less than a quarter of the gross value of manufactured output. Thus, with respect to market orientation, one would unmistakably characterize the manufacturing sector in Bangladesh as import-substituting.

Major manufactured exports include readymade garments, jute textiles, leather and leather products, processed fish and seafood, tea, fertilizer, chemicals, petroleum products, hosiery, machinery, and capital items. Of these, the first five may be considered as major export industries because these industries cater largely or wholly to the export market. Among these, jute textiles and tea belong to the large industry category. The other three export industries have a mix of large and small enterprises.

Manufactured exports from Bangladesh come mainly from the private sector. The share of the public sector in manufactured exports in 1989/90 amounted to about 10 percent of total manufactured exports (BBS 1993b).

The manufactured industry in Bangladesh is also undiversified in terms of end use. The bulk of the industries fall in the consumer goods category. Capital goods industries account for only about 6 percent of manufacturing employment and 9 percent of value-added.

Growth Performance of the Industrial Sector

Notwithstanding the limitations of the available industrial statistics, the balance of empirical evidence tends to suggest that the industrial sector in Bangladesh grew rather slowly during the last two decades. According to official BBS data, industrial value-added grew at an annual compound rate of approximately 3 percent between 1973 and 1993, while the GDP growth rate was around 4 percent during the same period. If these two decades are divided according to the Plan periods, we find that the rate of growth of industrial value-added was about 7 percent during the First

Five-Year Plan (1973-1977) period, 6.2 percent during the Two- Year Plan (1978-1979), around 1 percent during the Second Five-Year Plan (1980-1984), and 4.2 percent during the Third Five-Year Plan (1985-1989). Thus, the sector seems to have performed poorly during the decade of the 1980s when the most intensive implementation of the reform measures took place. Evidence from other independent surveys also corroborates the fact that the decade of the 1980s was a decade of industrial stagnation for Bangladesh.[3]

According to official statistics, the sector has shown signs of improvement during recent years. Average annual growth in industrial value-added during the first three years (1990-1992) of the Fourth Five-Year Plan period has been estimated to be around 7.4 percent.

The proximate reason behind low growth of manufacturing output is the stagnant level of manufacturing investment (public as well as private). Available evidence suggests that public manufacturing investment declined almost steadily during the Second Five-Year Plan period (1980-1984) except for a brief rise in 1981/82 (Bakht and Bhattacharya 1991). There were significant increases in public investment during the first two years of the Third Five-Year Plan, but this was largely due to lumpy investments in the fertilizer industry. Available evidence on private manufacturing investment also portrays a similar picture of stagnation and decline. During the entire decade of the 1980s, the sum of public and private manufacturing investment remained virtually stagnant at a level of 2 to 3 percent of GDP. This is supported by the evidence on import data that shows that import of machinery and capital equipment declined from a level of 2.4 percent of GDP in 1980/81 to about 2.2 percent in 1989/90. The flow of foreign private investment has been equally discouraging.

The recent growth in industrial value-added seems to have resulted more from improvements in the capacity utilization level rather than from new investments. Estimates of manufacturing investment during this period are lacking. However, if one uses import of capital machinery and equipment as a proxy indicator of manufacturing investment, the situation does not appear to have improved significantly over the past three years. One exception is the readymade garments industry, which has expanded quite rapidly during recent years. According to the Bangladesh Garments Manufacturers' and Exporters' Association (BGMEA), the number of readymade garments manufacturing units increased from 934 in 1991 to 1,580 in 1993 with 1,395 units currently in operation and more than 800 units awaiting operation.

At the macro level, aggregate investment as a proportion of GDP has shown a slight rising trend. This, coupled with various fiscal stimuli and recent successes with stabilization measures, has contributed toward boosting domestic demand and thereby facilitated expansion of industrial output.

Changes in Market Orientation

While the aggregate industrial sector grew rather slowly during the last two decades, there has been a differential performance at the disaggregate level. A number of export industries performed fairly well during this period. This included readymade garments, processed fish and seafood, and tannery and leather finishing. Among these, readymade garments has been the fastest growing nontraditional export industry. From an export level of only US$0.67 million in 1978/79, Bangladesh's readymade garment exports reached US$1,310 million in 1992-1993, implying a growth rate of nearly 60 percent. In fact, nontraditional manufactured exports, in constant 1981 US$ prices, grew at a rate of 22 percent from 1980/81 to 1989/90.

While the abovementioned nontraditional export industries experienced significant growth, most of the traditional export industries stagnated or even declined. Thus, for example, jute textiles, which occupies a dominant position both within the export sector and the manufacturing sector as a whole, experienced a declining trend of -1.2 percent in value-added during the period 1980/81 to 1989/90. Another major traditional export industry, tea, also stagnated during the reference period. As a result, growth in overall manufactured exports was much less spectacular than what was observed in the case of nontraditional exports, and the overall domestic market orientation of the industrial sector remained unchanged (Ministry of Finance 1993).

Changes in Size Distribution

In 1973/74, the top ten large industries in terms of value-added were jute textiles, cotton textiles, cigarettes, sugar, fertilizer, pharmaceuticals, tea, matches, petroleum refining, and hydrogenated vegetable oil. They accounted for nearly 80 percent of value-added in large industry. Except for fertilizer, all other dominant industries listed above stagnated or declined during the decade of 1980s. Fertilizer expanded only due to planned public investment. By 1989/90, the share of the top ten large industries in value-added came down to 65 percent (Bakht 1991).

In contrast, small industry seems to have shown some amount of dynamism during this period. The BSCIC carried out surveys of small and cottage industries in Bangladesh during the late 1970s and early 1980s. Around the same time, a census of all handloom units was also conducted. If one combines information from these and the BBS sources, one finds that small industry (excluding handloom) accounted for less than 20 percent of industrial value-added during the early part of 1980s (Khan and Hossain 1989). Recently, another round of surveys of small and cottage industries in Bangladesh was completed by the BSCIC, and a census of handloom units was conducted by the BBS. Results from these surveys show that small industry's (excluding handloom) share in industrial value-added in 1989 was nearly 30 percent, implying a yearly growth in value-added of 10.3 percent in the small industry during 1977-1989. Thus, during the last decade there seems to have been some change in the structure of the industrial sector of Bangladesh in favor of small industry. However, because of the rather low weight of small industries in aggregate industrial value-added, this growth failed to carry forward the overall industrial sector of Bangladesh. Within the small industry sector, industries that experienced significant growth during this period included the following: bakery, oil mill, readymade garments, hosiery, wooden furniture and fixtures, printing and publishing, industrial chemicals, lime products, soap, cosmetics and perfumery, light engineering, automobile servicing and repairing, steel furniture, and jewellery.

The handloom industry experienced moderate levels of growth. However, growth performance differed between different size categories of handloom enterprises. A recent study of the handloom industry by the Bangladesh Institute of Development Studies (Chowdhury and Latif 1990) has shown that household units having fewer than ten looms stagnated or even declined. On the other hand, establishments having ten or more looms and belonging to the small industry category expanded in size. Technological upgradation in terms of a shift to more productive semiautomatic loom from the low productive fly-shuttle loom has also been more pronounced in the latter category of handloom enterprises.

The cottage industry experienced some increase in the employment level. But this has not been accompanied by any growth in value-added. Thus, this sector has been a source of residual employment for the growing labor force, reflecting failure on the part of agriculture to provide productive employment rather than indicating dynamic growth of the cottage sector itself.

Growth in Industrial Employment

The population census of 1974 recorded manufacturing employment to be 1.03 million. Latest official employment data suggest that under comparable definition, manufacturing employment in Bangladesh was to the tune of 3.0 million in 1989, implying an annual compound growth rate of nearly 7.4 percent.

There are three possible explanations to the apparent inconsistency between stagnating value-added levels and the relatively vibrant employment scenario. The first explanation, of course, relates to the better coverage of employment data in successive surveys while the statistical base of industrial value-added data has continued to remain very weak. The second explanation lies in the fact that whatever growth took place in the industrial sector during the last two decades occurred more in the labor-intensive industries, particularly in the more dynamic components of the small-scale and cottage industries. Finally, there has also been growth of residual employment in many cottage and informal activities which again is a reflection of the default option of the unemployed rural labor force facing decreasing opportunities in the farm sector. As we shall see in the next subsection, similar expansion of unproductive employment also took place in the public sector enterprises during the decade of the 1970s.

Trends in Productivity and Wages

Official data show that between 1973 and 1989, industrial value-added grew at an average annual rate of 3 percent while industrial employment grew at an annual rate of more than 7 percent. This suggests that at the aggregate level, labor productivity declined during the reference period.[4] To get a better understanding of the trend in labor productivity, however, one needs to look at the disaggregated level.

The CMI data shows that employment in the public sector enterprises increased steadily from 1973/74 until the early 1980s, and the number of nonproduction employees increased at a faster rate. The proportion of production workers in the large industries covered by the CMI declined from 85 percent of all employees in 1973/74 to 77 percent in 1983/84. This contributed to a declining trend in labor productivity in large industry. However, the denationalization program and the public enterprise reform measures, initiated in the early 1980s, put a stop to the expansion of employment in the public manufacturing enterprises beyond the required number. Since then the trend has reversed; the proportion of nonproduction employees steadily decreased, and by 1989/90 reached more or less the same level as before. There was also a commensurate increase in labor productivity. While there has been year-to-year fluctuations, the trend in labor productivity in large industry over the period 1973/74 to 1989/90 seems to form a U-shaped curve with the lowest level of productivity reached in 1981/82 (Rahman 1993). If one compares the two end points, that is 1973/74 and 1989/90, yearly growth in labor productivity during the reference period works out to around 1 percent. Although the productivity index of the production workers remained higher than that for all employees, it experienced the same trend as was observed in the case of all employees (Rahman 1994b).

In contrast, real wages of all employees in the industries covered by the CMI increased almost monotonically during this period. The trend rate of growth in real wage for this group of employees for the period 1973/74 to 1989/90 is estimated at about 7 percent. Real wages of production workers and all employees increased at more or less the same rate during this time (Rahman 1994b).

Wage commissions, periodically constituted by the government, determine wages for public sector enterprises. Public sector wage policy, as well as minimum wage rates fixed by the government for the private sector, significantly influence wage determination in large-scale private enterprises. However, the collective bargaining process is an accepted modality of wage determination in the private sector. The trend in the wage rate in large industry, thus, has been largely an outcome of the government's wage policy and does not seem to have any direct relationship with the trend in labor productivity in the sector (Rahman 1994a). Two qualifications regarding the wage increase of workers of large industry, however, needs to be made. First, in spite of the rising trend, real wages of industrial workers in large industry are still significantly lower than the real wage that prevailed in 1969/70. Secondly, wages of unskilled workers in most of the dominant large industries were lower than wages of unskilled workers in agriculture for a large part of the last two decades (Rahman 1994a, 1994b).

Capital productivity measured by the ratio of gross value-added to fixed assets shows a similarly declining trend for industries covered by CMI during the reference period. Recent attempts at estimating total factor productivity suggests that overall productivity in the sector remained depressed for much of the reference period (Sahota et al. 1991).

However, given the deficiency of the capital data in CMI, this needs further investigation before any conclusive opinion is formed.[5]

Reliable information on productivity and wages of industrial workers in small industry is lacking. The BSCIC survey of small industries shows that from 1977/78 to 1989/90, labor productivity increased at an annual compound rate of 5.9 percent while real emoluments per employee increased at a rate of 4.1 percent. A recent report of the World Bank (1992a) presented indices of real wages in the small industry sector quoting BBS sources that show that the trend growth in real wages in the sector was nearly 5.8 percent. This seems plausible in view of the observed growth of the small-scale sector.

In the case of the handloom industry, the BIDS study mentioned earlier found that the real wage of male workers who are mostly skilled increased at an annual rate of 1.7 percent during the period 1979/80 to 1986/87. However, the real wages of unskilled, female, and child workers registered a net decline. The wage condition in handloom industry seems symptomatic of the wage situation in the overall cottage industry sector. Skill requirements in most of the cottage industries are rather low. As mentioned earlier, these industries also experienced little growth in the past. With the rising level of the unemployed labor force and the entry of female and child workers into the labor force in increasing numbers, the cottage sector may have suffered from stagnant or even declining real wages. However, those cottage industries that are more skill-intensive and that have experienced some growth in the past, for example, the medium and large size handloom units, seem to have experienced some growth in real wages.

Constraints to Industrial Development

As discussed above, the industrial sector of Bangladesh has been subjected in the past to widely divergent policy regimes. During the Pakistan period, the private sector dominated industrialization. With strong patronage from the government, it received major policy support. After independence, the public sector was assigned the lead role in industrialization. From 1975 to 1981, the growth of the private sector was encouraged, side-by-side with emphasis on the public sector. Since 1982, the private sector has been reassigned the lead role in industrialization.

Policies with regard to market orientation also changed over time. During the Pakistan period and following the independence of Bangladesh, greater emphasis was placed on the development of import-substituting industries. Export development began to get more attention in the late 1970s.

Since the mid-1970s, there has been a move toward greater reliance on market forces. As noted earlier, regulatory barriers have been gradually dismantled to facilitate ease of entry. Trade liberalization has been carried out involving simplification of import procedures, rationalization of the tariff structure, lowering of tariff rates, reduction in quantitative restrictions, and so on. In addition, a market-oriented exchange rate policy has been followed. In the financial sector, there has been a move away from the administered credit regime to a market-determined one. Public enterprise reforms were carried out aimed at subjecting these undertakings to greater competitive pressure. Also, denationalization has significantly reduced the public sector's share in modern manufacturing. A number of incentives for foreign private investments have been put in place. Major policy reforms were initiated in the mid-1970s and intensified during the decade of the 1980s.

As previously noted, the manufacturing sector of Bangladesh does not seem to have responded well to these policy changes. Review of available evidence has shown that there has been little in the way of dynamic growth or structural change in the sector during the past two decades. Within this general scenario of stagnation, the small industries and a few nontraditional export industries have shown a certain amount of dynamism. But given their low output and employment share, they failed to carry the overall sector forward.

This section attempts to explain this apparent nonresponsiveness of the industrial sector of Bangladesh to policy changes. The issues that are raised in this analysis relate both to the structural limitations of the sector and the economy as well as the weaknesses of policy measures and their implementation. It must be emphasized in this context that many of the structural limitations have policy failures as the cause of their perpetuation.

Structural and Exogenous Constraints to Industrial Development

Small Size and Poor Growth of Domestic Economy

One of the basic constraints to growth of manufacturing in Bangladesh is the small size of the domestic market resulting from the low level of national income. As discussed earlier, the manufacturing sector of Bangladesh caters mainly to the domestic market. As a result, there is a strong association between manufacturing output growth and growth of the rest of the economy reflected in the high coefficient of correlation (0.95) between manufacturing value-added and GDP excluding manufacturing. Since the bulk of the income originates in the rural sector, the growth of the domestic market-oriented industrial sector depends largely on the invigoration of the rural economy. In this respect, the performance of the Bangladesh economy during the past two decades has been quite discouraging. As mentioned earlier, GDP growth during 1973 to 1992 was 4 percent while that in the agricultural sector was only 2.7 percent. The poor performance of the economy, in turn, was partly due to inadequate public investment, which grew at a low rate during the reference period. Growth was also affected by natural calamities in the form of severe droughts and floods, which have affected the country several times during the past two decades.

There is scope and need to revamp the domestic economy with the purpose of boosting aggregate demand. An important step in this respect is the enhancement of public investment directed particularly toward the agricultural and rural sectors which will raise the purchasing power of the poor. Since the demand structure of this segment of the population is oriented more to local products, it would act as a stimulus to growth and expansion of domestic market-oriented industries.

Declining World Demand for Jute Products

Jute textiles is the largest modern manufacturing industry in Bangladesh, accounting for nearly 26 percent of value-added in the large industry and 12 percent of value-added in the overall manufacturing sector. It is the second major manufactured export item of Bangladesh. The performance of this industry thus has a major influence on the growth performance of the overall sector. The industry experienced decline in the level of value-added largely because of falling world demand. While the world recession of the early 1980s contributed to this trend of decline, changes in cargo handling methods that reduce the use of bags, and competition from synthetic substitutes caused the market for jute products to shrink. The process could perhaps be reversed if a major program of product diversification could be initiated. But in the past, there has been little research and development efforts to identify and market new jute products.

Low Entrepreneurial Base

Growth of entrepreneurship has been slow in Bangladesh. During the British colonial period, trade and industry in Bengal was dominated by the Hindus. The vacuum created by their migration in 1947 was soon filled in by the West Pakistani and non-Bengali Muslim migrant entrepreneurs with active state support. East Pakistan lacked a wealthy trading class that could provide the basis for the rapid growth of an entrepreneurial class. The prevailing culture was also unfavorable for development of the business class. This relegated businessmen to an inferior position with respect to civil and professional services. However, during the late 1950s, a Bangladeshi entrepreneurial class emerged and signs of an entrepreneurial culture could be discerned. The growth process experienced a serious setback when after independence the government nationalized all large enterprises in jute textiles, cotton textiles, and the sugar industry, including banks and insurance companies, and export trade in jute. Nationalization alienated the nascent Bangladeshi entrepreneurs, and had a longer term impact in the form of slow growth of entrepreneurship in the late 1970s and 1980s when the policy environment was made favorable for the growth of the private sector.

Need for Finance

Finance is critical to rapid industrialization of Bangladesh. However, for some industries, credit constraints may not be as binding as in most other industries. Thus, for example, the rapid growth of the readymade garments industry was largely based on self-financing which became possible partly because of the low capital requirement of the industry. The industry also benefited from use of back-to-back letters of credit (L/C) facilities, use of deferred payment from suppliers, and inflow of foreign investment. However, given the low rate of domestic saving, estimated at 4 percent of GDP in 1991/92, any major attempt at private sector led industrialization will presumably need the support of adequate credit facilities. It is no wonder, therefore, that in a number of recent perception surveys, entrepreneurs have mentioned lack of access to credit as their single most important problem (Kane 1991).

Industrial financing has been attempted in the past under concessional terms, conditions, and interest rates. It was hoped that low interest rates and a high debt-equity ratio would make investment profitable and produce a large group of investors who would implement the necessary industrial investment. Lowering the cost of credit was one of the prime concerns under the administered credit regime. There were also provisions for preferential access to credit. Small and cottage industries, export industries, and units located in less developed areas were to be provided with special credit facilities. Ensuring credit availability to target groups was the prime concern behind such arrangements.

Bangladesh's experience with administered credit regimes shows that given the paucity of fiscal and administrative resources, lower priced credit to a few favored operators enabled them to force out other competitors, while corruption among the staff of the institutions providing administered credit made efficient targeting of low-priced loans difficult (World Bank 1992b). In fact, attempts to stimulate private industrial investment with public financing and administered interest rates during the late 1970s and early 1980s resulted in many pitfalls including inappropriate investments, inefficient resource use, overcrowding in certain sectors, and widespread debt defaults. The extent of default was so pervasive that the donors moved to freeze the credit pipe line. Thus, from 1984 onward there has been virtually no channeling of investment funds underwritten by donor agencies to the private sector. The failure of the lending mechanism, the weaknesses and immaturity of the equity market to supply funds, and lack of flow of foreign private investment all resulted in bringing down the level of private manufacturing investment (Bakht and Bhattacharya 1991). On the other hand, one can cite the example of the Grameen Bank as a success story in spite of the significantly higher interest rates at which lendings were made. Recent studies (World Bank 1992b) have shown that informal financing involving high interest rates has played a critical role in the emergence, survival, and growth of many small-scale industries in Bangladesh. Availability, rather than cost of credit, is thus the most binding constraint to growth in industrial investment.

The financial sector reform currently under way is aimed at moving away from the administered credit regime toward a market-oriented credit regime. Under the provisions of these reforms, interest rates have been made somewhat flexible and all government guidelines regarding terms and conditions of industrial lending have been withdrawn.

In this context, it should be noted that the retail banking industry in Bangladesh is fairly noncompetitive. One implication of this is that sectoral allocation of credit based on total reliance on the market mechanism may not yield the desired results. For example, in the case of private banks, loanable funds may get channeled to their own business houses at favorable terms and this may lead to inefficient resource use. The bankers may prefer trade credit over industrial finance because of higher turnover rates. Industrial term lending may get least preference. Depending on the creditworthiness of the borrower, some credit may flow into fixed capital investment. Such lendings, however, are likely to entail higher interest rates and the collateral requirements in the form of ownership of fixed assets are also likely to be quite stringent. The large majority of the potential borrowers, particularly those in the small and cottage sector, are likely to remain outside of the scope of institutional finance due to the preoccupation of institutional lenders with asset ownership as the basis of creditworthiness.

For these reform measures to have substantial positive impact on private industrial investment in Bangladesh, the structure of retail banking will have to be made more competitive and the necessary institutional reforms of public sector financial institutions will have to be carried out so that they can be freed from bureaucratic controls and political interventions. The incentive structure should be such that public sector bankers are encouraged to solicit deposit relationships with small entrepreneurs in a bid to bring them within the fold of institutional financing with cash flows rather than asset ownership as the criteria for creditworthiness.

To ease the financing situation, the use of nonbank forms of resource flows such as debt-equity swaps, industrial leasing, and BOT (build-operate-transfer) arrangements should be increased. In addition, there should be attempts at further development of the equity market. Developing a securities market and other ways of mobilizing domestic saving and attracting overseas funds is a prime necessity. In making use of BOT, however, the future transfer problem should be carefully examined.

Infrastructure

Although the current status of the physical infrastructure in Bangladesh has not yet become a binding constraint to industrial development (more because the pace of industrialization has been slow), access to requisite site services is far from satisfactory. Almost all the basic facilities such as power supply, telecommunications, water, and gas are owned and operated by the state. Procedures for availing of these infrastructural facilities is needlessly complex. One has to fill up numerous forms, visit several offices, and incur "transaction costs" to get any service. In certain cases, such as with telephone service, demand at the prevailing price grossly exceeds supply and as a result getting a telephone connection involves inordinate delays. Apart from the difficulties of getting an initial connection, an industrial unit also suffers from frequent disruptions of power and other infrastructural support services, and poor reliability in their operations. Earlier attempts at providing access to site services through "one stop" institutional arrangements did not prove very effective. The current arrangement of the Board of Investment (BOI) providing such one stop services suffers from the limitation that although the BOI provides the service package at the time of sanctioning projects, under the current regulatory framework only a small proportion of investment cases reach the BOI for sanctioning. Hence the BOI needs to extend its purview of support service. Also, in a situation where demand for various site services exceed supply, administrative allocations become difficult without special arrangements, opening up the scope for corruption.

There have also been government attempts to provide site services through industrial estates. But these have not been commensurate with the level of demand. In particular, the BSCIC's industrial estate program to provide infrastructural facilities to small and cottage industries does not seem to have much correspondence with felt needs; rather, it reflects politicized and bureaucratic misjudgments in allocation of resources and locational choices. As a result, many of the recently constructed BSCIC estates in nonindustrial district towns have remained underutilized for long periods due to lack of demand, while in the areas where industrial concentration exists there is excess demand in relation to the number of available plots.

Human Resource

With continued improvements in technology, the labor component in most production processes is increasingly becoming more skill-intensive. If Bangladesh is to retain its competitive edge in labor-intensive production, cheap labor will not be enough. Instead, the quality of labor will become a decisive factor. With the adult literacy rate at about 29 percent, improving the general education system is an essential priority for the Bangladesh government. Moreover, the current education system is not sufficiently oriented toward technical, professional, and vocational training. As a result, there is a shortage of practically all categories of skilled workers.

In the perception surveys mentioned earlier, the respondent entrepreneurs did not identify shortage of skilled labor as a major impediment to investment decisions. At the current stage of Bangladesh's industrial development, absence of skilled workers is not a binding constraint to industrial expansion. Moreover, Bangladeshi workers have demonstrated their ability to acquire skills if requisite training facilities can be made available. In the long run, however, education and training perhaps constitute the most important leverage points available to any country to attain a competitive edge. To form a national competitive advantage, Bangladesh will have to meet increased requirements for a skilled work-force, including managers, engineers, and technicians. Unfortunately, no systematic attempts have yet been made in Bangladesh to design a human resource development program for the industrial sector.

Technology

Productivity growth through technology upgrading is one of the most critical determinants of industrial development. In Bangladesh, there is a lack of commitment to the importance of sustained technology improvement. At the enterprise level, there is very little in-house effort to improve product quality, innovate improved technology, raise workers' skill levels, or improve management practices. At the national level, the institutional arrangement for scientific and research work relating to such issues as industrial applications, and acquisition and adaptation of new technology are grossly deficient. If Bangladesh wants to retain its advantage in the production of labor-intensive products, it will have to avail of technological changes that increase the diversity of products and improve quality and efficiency.

There is little need or scope for Bangladesh to undertake fundamental research in technology development. Technologies that have already been developed need to be acquired, adapted, and disseminated. Current incentives and arrangements for such acquisitions and adaptations of new and improved technologies must be considerably upgraded and the private sector should play an active role in the process. There should be fiscal incentives for stimulating technology improvements. Technological institutions and industries should have strong links with each other and technology upgrading should be achieved through an interactive process based on the felt needs of the industries. Financial support from the government could facilitate forging such links between an industry and the research institution and also in initiating research within the firm.

Policy-Induced Constraints to Industrial Development

Regulatory Barriers

Overregulation of the economy has long been considered as a major policy-induced constraint to industrial development in Bangladesh. During the past decade and a half, a number of measures have been taken toward reducing these regulatory barriers, particularly with regard to investment sanctioning procedures. However, private entrepreneurs still express frustration about the regulatory environment and the associated bureaucratic sloth and corruption. Some of their concerns include the following:

- Delegation of sanctioning power to financial institutions for investments up to a given size has not been effective in freeing the sanctioning procedure from bureaucratic restraint, political patronage, and corruption. In spite of all the guidelines that have been provided, entrepreneurs complain of procedural complexities, unofficial payments, and delay in processing institutional loan applications. The main reason behind this is that necessary reforms in the organizational and management structure of the public sector financial institutions have not yet been carried out. It should also be seriously considered whether publicly owned financial institutions that are simultaneously subject to the control of the government and the central bank—the latter being also controlled by the government—can ever be autonomous in the real sense.

- The procedure for registration with the sponsoring agency has been an irritant to entrepreneurs and serves little useful purpose. With regard to registration with the Inspector of Factories, the rules governing the role of the inspector seem to provide ample discretionary power and put the small industries in a relatively disadvantaged situation vis-a-vis the large-scale industries.

- Although existing regulations provide for equal treatment of domestic and foreign investors, certain discriminatory rules still continue with regard to foreign investment. Sanctioning requirements for particular categories of foreign investment, restrictions against capacity expansion, special regulations for supplier's credit and pay-as-you-earn-schemes are some of the areas of differential treatment.

- The current investment limit beyond which an enterprise must go public is far below the ceiling set for small industries and hence acts as a deterrent to the expansion of small enterprises.

Prior to the initiation of the reforms, the government used a variety of instruments such as investment schedules, project profiles, priority lists, and discouraged lists, to guide and regulate private investment. But these were mostly drawn up on an ad hoc basis and were never preceded by the preparation of a full-fledged industrial strategy that would spell out a longer term vision of industrialization of the country. The system, as a result, failed to channel private investment in a desired track. Instead, it worked as a major disincentive and barrier to growth of private investment.

The relaxation of the sanctioning procedure has been accompanied by the decision to limit the public sector's entrepreneurial role and to have a neutral trade regime. All these measures have moved the country to the other extreme and the process of industrialization is now completely left to the imperatives of the market. The private sector's investment choices, which in turn will be guided mainly by the entrepreneur's reading of the market, will primarily determine the future composition of the industrial sector in Bangladesh.

But there is nothing to guarantee that private investment flows will be consistent with efficient resource allocation given the fact that a host of factors inhibit free flow of information and factor markets are usually distorted. Clearly, there is a need for working out a long term industrialization strategy for the country that will be based on a carefully studied analysis of the changing structural features and comparative advantage of the domestic economy in relation to the dynamics of the global economy.

Given the state of development of the Bangladesh economy and its private sector in particular, there is no denying the fact that the government will have to play an important facilitative role in this regard. There should be close collaboration between the government and the private sector in matters of information collection and dissemination. Government efforts at influencing private investment in accordance with the predrawn industrialization strategy, however, should be limited to adequate pre-investment counseling and provision of indicative guidelines to the project-appraising cell of the financial institutions. The existing pre-investment counseling facility of the regulatory and promotional bodies, and the capability of the financing institutions to appraise projects have been found to be grossly deficient. Study results have shown that most entrepreneurs are unaware of the pre-investment counseling provided by these bodies. Those who are aware do not consider these services to be of much practical use. Investment schedules and project profiles prepared by these agencies are of a very broad nature and are not based on proper market surveys and rigorous data collection, and hence do not provide any useful guidance to potential entrepreneurs. In addition, entrepreneur organizations, such as chambers of trade and industry, should also establish facilities for dissemination of information and investment counseling.

Public Ownership, Public Enterprise Reforms and Privatization

In spite of the substantial denationalization measures of the late 1970s and early 1980s, the public sector continues to dominate the manufacturing scene of Bangladesh. While there exists wide variations in the level of performance of the individual units, the balance of evidence shows that the overall performance of the public sector has been much less than satisfactory (Bakht 1992). There is little difference of opinion regarding the need for major reforms to raise the efficiency of public enterprises. However, the pace of implementation of such reforms has so far been slow; in the meantime, many of these units continue to be a serious drag on public resources.

Unfortunately, the process of denationalization and privatization has also been mismanaged, and has not brought about the desired results, but instead has had a number of adverse effects on the economy. Denationalization was implemented in great haste without sufficient prior analysis, either with regard to the desired role of the state or the modalities of denationalization. It seems to have been induced mainly by the desire to get rid of a large portion of public enterprises at any cost. Divestiture often involved significant undervaluation of assets and stocks to serve the interest of clients and sale of units through noncompetitive bidding to persons with no entrepreneurial background. The denationalization process also involved passing on to the divested units a few disadvantageous legacies of the public sector, such as a large and inefficient labor force, while denying some of the facilities previously enjoyed by the public sector. The result of all this has been low efficiency and poor performance of the disinvested units and default on installment payments by the buyers of the public enterprises. A recent survey of the disinvested units carried out by the Ministry of Industries has shown that 57 percent of the disinvested enterprises are either closed down or liquidated. Available evidence also shows that the performance of the disinvested units that are in production are no better than their public sector counterparts (Selim 1990).

Labor Laws and Labor Institutions

Labor laws and industrial relations have important bearings on industrial growth. Under existing labor laws in Bangladesh, registered trade unions can be formed at the factory or plant level with at least one third of the workers as members. When there are more than one registered union, the collective bargaining agent (CBA) is elected by secret ballot. A federation of trade unions can be formed provided at least two trade unions are affiliated with it. Only a permanent worker can be a member of trade union, but no such eligibility criterion has been established for membership in trade union federations. There are roughly 700 trade union federations. Of these, the three largest federations, accounting for 64 percent of the total members, are the labor front organizations of the three major political parties. The close ties of the dominant federations with political parties has led to politicization of the trade unions. One adverse effect following from this is that there has been a high incidence of work disruptions for political reasons which has contributed to strained labor-management relations (Rahman 1994a).

The Labor Directorate is responsible for resolving industrial disputes that cannot be settled through negotiations with CBA. The directorate lacks administrative and legal capacity to resolve labor disputes expeditiously and satisfactorily. The low level of resolution of disputes and the high incidence of failure, together with the difficulty of filing of cases indicate the weaknesses of the Directorate as an institution for dispute resolution (Rahman 1994a, b).

The Labor Court is the next higher level of dispute settlement. Because of the absence of representatives of workers and employers in the Court, there have been long delays in the disposal of the cases. From 1971 to 1992, 40 to 60 percent of the cases remained pending at yearend (Rahman 1994a).

The Minimum Wage Board (MWB) was established to lay down minimum wages for factories or industries in which wages cannot be determined effectively through collective bargaining procedures. The MWB has so far covered only a handful of sectors, many of which have become dated by now. The MWB is also institutionally ill-equipped to carry out its responsibilities. It is constrained by procedures as well as a lack of critical economic and sociological data for determination of fair minimum wages (Rahman 1994a).

The limited efficacy of the formal labor institutions in settling labor disputes and determining minimum wages has led to the emergence of the United Front of Workers and Employees (SKOP) as the key apex body of workers. Since the early 1980s, SKOP has played an active role in gaining wage hikes in both the public and private sectors, pressing demands for upward revision of the minimum wage, and resisting government attempts at privatization of public sector units and retrenchment of redundant workers (Rahman 1994b).

The employers have opposed the role of SKOP on the ground that it has no legal *locus standi* and have argued in favor of decentralized collective bargaining at the plant or industry level (Rahman 1994a).

Because of these disputes, there have been strained relationships between management, employees, and government, resulting in a large number of strikes, lock-outs, and other forms of unrest, which have discouraged many enterprises from expanding their workforce. Foreign investors have also been discouraged by the perception that the labor situation in Bangladesh is difficult.

If Bangladesh is to overcome this problem of image, the government will have to improve labor-management-government relations. An important step in that direction will involve modifying the existing labor laws to provide a framework for improving the performance of official labor institutions.

Trade Policy

Trade policy in Bangladesh has been subjected to significant reforms in recent years. Major elements of trade policy reform consisted of liberalization of import procedure, rationalizing tariff structure, and reducing tariff rates and quantitative restrictions.

The case for trade liberalization is usually argued on the grounds of allocative and productive efficiency, elimination of anti-export bias, and favorable employment and income distribution effects. While this view has fairly broad-based support from academicians and policymakers, concerns have been expressed with regard to potential limitations of such measures and the possible adverse effects that sweeping trade liberalization measures may entail.

Trade reform measures aim at raising the efficiency of import substituting industries by exposing them to foreign competition. To be able to respond to this competitive pressure, the indigenous industries will need to adopt the right kind of technology and also undertake other measures to improve their performance. The proponents of reforms urge rapid implementation of the liberalization measures on the plea that the market will weed out only the intrinsically inefficient producers while others will adjust themselves to the competitive environment. However, one needs to be sensitive to the fact that many domestic industries, particularly those in the small and cottage sectors, need government support to gain access to new technologies and undertake various efficiency enhancement measures.

Experience from both Bangladesh and abroad suggest that trade liberalization without the provision of support for undertaking the necessary technology upgradation and efficiency enhancement measures is a sure way of wiping out large segments of indigenous industry in the face of foreign competition.

Export Promotion

During the period 1980-1989, nontraditional exports grew at a rate of 22 percent in nominal dollar values. The main source of export growth was readymade garments, which grew at a rate of nearly 60 percent. The success of this industry was an outcome of diverse factors, the most important of which was relocation of trade by international marketing intermediaries after being faced with binding quota restrictions in their own country. The low capital and skill requirement also induced the entry of Bangladeshi entrepreneurs in the industry. At the same time, quick government support in the form of back-to-back L/C, bonded warehouses, export performance benefits, access to subsidized credit, and so on, provided the needed incentive for the entrepreneurs to enter the industry in large numbers. However, in spite of these incentives, it has not been possible to replicate the success stories of the readymade garments industry in other industries.

There are problems with effective implementation of some of the export incentives such as duty draw back and export credit guarantee schemes. Others such as export performance benefits, back-to-back L/C, and bonded warehouses are not sufficiently broad-based. These factors may have partly constrained the growth of the export sector. However, the critical missing factor in the development of a potential export market is a comprehensive export promotion strategy that aims at identifying market opportunities on a dynamic basis and providing the needed support services for the development of such industries, including technology diffusion, R&D, and human resource development. For the expansion of nontraditional exports, a search needs to be initiated to determine which industries will have a global comparative advantage, spot market trends and sources of competition in these sectors, and discover backward linkage potential of these industries. To ensure that such industries develop, adequate incentives and support services should then be provided. This type of active search for an export market, and the associated product diversification and quality improvements, have not been undertaken to date.

Conclusion

One of the most significant lessons that has emerged in recent decades with regard to economic management is that industrial and economic development has to be led by the private sector. This renewed faith in the role of the private sector is, by now, a fairly universal phenomenon. There now exists little confusion regarding the envisaged function of this sector. But what is the expected role of the government in this private sector led growth scenario? Can the government simply declare the market to be free, and then step back and watch the economy boom?

There is a general consensus that government should play a facilitative role in the private sector led development process. But what actions on the part of the government are likely to facilitate private sector development? Is the choice of such actions invariant with the level of development of a country? Also, in undertaking such actions, how does the government interact with the private sector?

In this respect, one extreme view is that it is not action but lack of action on the part of the government that facilitates private sector development, which, in fact, is the case for laissez faire. The problems with this position are all too well-known. The world is not frictionless, price signals are not always undistorted, and information is not without cost. In fact, a wide variety of factors inhibit the free functioning of market forces.

If we look at Bangladesh we see that government regulatory barriers were once considered the major impediments to industrialization. During the last decade, these barriers have been removed or relaxed to a significant degree. It is true that a lot more needs to be done in this direction. But even with whatever form of deregulation has been carried out, a commensurate improvement in the industrialization situation has not followed. This implies that in addition to removing the regulatory barriers, government actions are necessary to break other structural bottlenecks to the industrialization process.

It would be relatively straightforward to identify the areas where the government needs to play a facilitative role. The prime one, of course, is with regard to maintenance of a congenial macropolicy environment. This includes trade and exchange rate policy, monetary policy, fiscal policy, labor policy, and legal policy framework. In addition, government support is also needed in the area of information collection and dissemination, infrastructure creation, skill development, access to foreign technology, development of indigenous technology through R&D, and so on.

There will be broad agreement with the view that the nature and extent of the facilitative role that the government needs to play for private sector promotion varies with the level of development of the country. However, the point to be emphasized is that in the early stage of development, the government may need to play a complementary role beyond the recommended supportive and facilitative role. This means that the government may have to undertake entrepreneurial responsibilities to facilitate the development of particular private sector industries. Two points, however, need to be noted here. First, the purpose of the public enterprise should be to complement private sector development effort and not to substitute it. Second, public involvement will have to be of a transitory nature aimed solely at facilitating private sector development. This has been the dominant feature of government action for private sector growth not only in Japan but also in the Republic of Korea and Singapore.

For any form of facilitative function on the part of the government to be effective, however, there is a need for close interaction between the government and the private sector. The prime reason behind this is to determine the felt needs. Since the government intends to facilitate private sector development through its actions, it is only logical that it should find out what the felt needs are. Secondly, there may be differences of opinion between the government and the private sector regarding the direction of industrialization and the corresponding policies that need to be pursued. If facilitative functions of the government are to bear fruit, these differences will have to be bridged through a process of dialogue, and a common agenda of action will have to be agreed upon. Entrepreneurs often express concern about the slow pace of policy implementation, the problem of bureaucratic inefficiency, and poor administrative capabilities. Since the task of improving the performance of the sector must be done by the industry and the government in close cooperation, the working relationship between the government and the entrepreneurs must improve, and administration of policy must be made efficient.

In the developing countries, interactions between the government and the private sector often take place in an ad hoc manner. The model case of cooperation between the public and the private sector is, of course, illustrated by Japan. The Japanese model was replicated with their own variations by the Republic of Korea, Singapore, and Taipei,China. It is time for Bangladesh to come up with its own variation of "Bangladesh Inc." and develop an institutional capacity to that end.

Finally—and perhaps at the cost of repeating a banality—it may be suggested that the performance of the government, as well as that of the entrepreneurs, be informed by an "enterprise culture" centered on the values of individual enterprise and a clear perception of the meaning of "market economy". The government should concentrate on the formulation and efficient implementation of policies that remove market distortions and set up appropriate incentive systems that reward individual enterprise. The entrepreneurs should also get rid of the "psychology of dependence" that requires the government to adopt policies which distort the price system but promise reward to particular groups not commensurate with their individual efforts. Examples of such dependence psychology-induced demands are: preferential and distortionary tax treatment, concessional interest rates, and loan condonation even when no natural calamity or unexpected change in the world trade situation afflicts a particular sector. Above all, there ought to be an effective exit policy based on an easy-to-enforce bankruptcy law so that "industrial adventures" are discouraged and appropriate policy support can be provided to the genuine entrepreneurs. One of the problems in the formulation and administration of policy is that it tries to perform two apparently conflicting objectives: make policies and procedures helpful for entrepreneurship, but have adequate safeguards against abuses. The result is the preponderance of "control" and "screening" elements at the cost of promotional elements.

Notes

1. Figures within parentheses give industry code at two and four digit levels.

2. An earlier estimate showed fixed assets per production worker in large industry in 1981-1982 to be Tk 78,438 or US$3,909 in current prices (Khan and Hossain 1989).

3. This is not to suggest that there is an inverse relationship between reform measures and growth performance of the industrial sector. As shown in the following sections, there has been differential growth at the disaggregate level, and certain subsectors, such as small and export industries, actually expanded taking advantage of the reforms. In some cases, the reform measures did not go far enough and hence failed to deliver desired results. It is also argued by some quarters that the lack of response is simply a reflection of the normal time lag involved.

4. In the absence of flow data, employment stock data have been used for estimating labor productivity.

5. The capital stock data provided by CMI are book values of the assets written down in initial prices to which new investments in current prices are added from time to time and from which some notional depreciation is deducted on an annual basis. It is thus a hodgepodge aggregation of different years' assets in different years' prices and is therefore not a very meaningful entity.

References

Ahmad, Q. K., ed., 1984. "Special Issue on Rural Industrialization in Bangladesh." *Bangladesh Development Studies* 12 (1, 2):iii-xi.

Bakht, Z., 1984. "Rural Industrialization in Bangladesh: A Review of Issues." Bangladesh Institute of Development Studies, Dhaka. Mimeographed.

———, 1991. "Time Series Estimate of Manufacturing Value Added at 4-digit Industry Level: 1980/81-1989/90." Bangladesh Institute of Development Studies, Dhaka. Mimeographed.

———, 1992. *Promoting Competitiveness of Public Sector Industries in Asian and the Pacific Region.* Bangkok: Economic and Social Commission for Asia and the Pacific.

Bakht, Z., and D. Bhattacharya, 1991. "Investment, Employment and Value Added in Bangladesh Manufacturing Sector in 1980s: Evidence and Estimate." *Bangladesh Development Studies* 19(1,2):1-50.

Bangladesh Bureau of Statistics (BBS), 1990. *Report on Bangladesh Handloom Census 1990.* Dhaka.

———, 1991. *Report on Census of Manufacturing Industries 1987-88.* Dhaka.
———, 1992a. *Report On Integrated Annual Survey of Non-Farm Economic Activities (Some Selected Industries).* Dhaka.
———, 1992b. *Report on Labor Force Survey 1989.* Dhaka.
———, 1993a. *Statistical Yearbook of Bangladesh 1992.* Dhaka.
———, 1993b. *Report on Census of Manufacturing Industries 1988-89.* Dhaka.
Chowdhury, N., and M.A. Latif, 1990. "Towards Understanding the Structural Adaptations within the Bangladesh Handloom Industry: 1978-87." Research Monograph No. 12. Bangladesh Institute of Development Studies, Dhaka.
Economic and Social Commission for Asia and the Pacific (ESCAP), 1991. *Industrial Restructuring in Asia and the Pacific.* Bangkok: United Nations.
———, 1993. *Economic Survey 1992-93.* Ministry of Finance, Dhaka.
Islam, T., et al., 1991. "Bangladesh Manufacturing Industry Survey." Metropolitan Chamber of Commerce and Industry, Dhaka. Mimeographed.
Kane, 1991. "Bangladesh: Private Sector Perception of Impediment to Industry." World Bank, Dhaka. Mimeographed.
Khan, A. R., and M. Hossain, 1989. *The Strategy of Development in Bangladesh.* London: Macmillan.
Ministry of Finance, 1990. "Autonomous Bodies Budgets using SABRE Formats." Dhaka.
Rahman, M., 1994a. "Structural Adjustment, Employment and Social Protection for Workers in Bangladesh." In R. Islam, ed., *Social Dimensions of Economic Reforms in Asia.* New Delhi: ILO-South Asia Multidisciplinary Advisory Team (SAAT).
———, 1994b. "Bangladesh: Structural Adjustment, Employment and Social Protection for Workers." SAAT Working Paper. ILO-South Asia Multidisciplinary Advisory Team (SAAT), New Delhi.
Sahota, G.S., et al., 1991. "South Asian Development Model and Productivity in Bangladesh." *Bangladesh Development Studies* 19 (1, 2):51-87.
Selim, R., 1990. "Public and Private Enterprises in Bangladesh: A Case Study of the Jute Manufacturing and Textile Mills." Dhaka. Mimeographed.
World Bank, 1992a. "Bangladesh: Selected Issues in External Competitiveness and Economy Efficiency." Report No. 10265-BD. Dhaka.
———, 1992b. "Studies on Small Firms Informally Financed." Dhaka. Mimeographed.

5 Poverty and Human Resource Development

Mustafa K. Mujeri and Salehuddin Ahmed

Introduction

In Bangladesh, with a per capita gross national product (GNP) of about US$210 and a population of around 112 million in 1992, the magnitude and depth of deprivation are extremely high. The majority of the people live in abject poverty and are susceptible to hunger, disease, and natural calamities. This calls for accelerated development with rapid improvement in the socioeconomic conditions of the poor and the disadvantaged.

Since its independence in 1971, the country has experienced intermittent economic turbulence, shocks, and disequilibria resulting in the failure to generate stable and resilient development. In Bangladesh, a macroenvironment conducive to efficient allocation and proper distribution of resources is a necessary prerequisite for rapid long-term growth. In the absence of such an environment, the short-term growth momentum also falters. With pervasive poverty, the short-term distributional and welfare concerns remain and indeed become the major dilemma in macropolicy in the country. This calls for an appropriate balance between short-term and the long-term considerations consistent with societal objectives.

Alleviation of poverty remains one of the prime objectives of development efforts in the country for which accelerated growth and expansion of employment opportunities are emphasized. Within a macro context, even the higher growth of around 4 percent (in real terms) achieved during the past decades may not be adequate to address the specific concerns of the poor. This calls for devising appropriate strategies for sustained and accelerated growth along with poverty alleviation measures.

The poor in Bangladesh include self-employed subsistence farmers, landless laborers, sharecroppers, artisans, and others mostly involved in the informal sector. Therefore, successful attempts at alleviating poverty would involve strategies to enhance the incomes of the above groups through measures that will accelerate the overall growth rate of the economy.

It is now increasingly realized that in Bangladesh it is necessary to adopt policy reforms that promote economic efficiency and growth and, in the process, also alleviate poverty. Some of the positive impacts of policy reform on poverty reduction can be accelerated by concentrating, particularly during the initial phase of reforms, on correcting policy distortions that disadvantage the poor and by directing public spending toward basic physical infrastructure and social services. It is believed that growth policies can be made more amenable to the poor by reinforcing them with investments in basic infrastructure and social services that facilitate the accumulation of physical and human capital by the poor.

In this chapter, development is interpreted as people-oriented development, which involves "a process for evolving a capacity to influence one's own future" (Bryant and White 1982, 19). Such an interpretation focuses on human development, a process of enhancing capability and expanding choices (see Sen 1990, UNDP 1993). The key issue becomes people's deprivation and degree of access to various options for human development. A definition of development where the human factor is the instrument as well as the ultimate objective of development has certain implications. First, it involves enhancement of capacity: to develop sociopolitical institutions for production and allocation, as well as an ability to invest in human beings to enhance their capabilities in shaping their own future. Second, development includes equitable access to benefits by removing socioeconomic and other constraints of the disadvantaged groups. Third, development is empowerment providing for built-in mechanisms for equitable growth. Finally, development is concerned with sustainability to ensure the proper long-term management of resources. In a real sense, therefore, development is enhancement of human capability with equitable access to resources. This involves development of the people and their macroenvironments and microenvironments so that human resource development (HRD) becomes an integral component of the development process.

It must be realized, however, that the link between poverty and HRD is rather complex. The economic conditions of households are the outcome of their command over resources: physical, financial, human, and others. Households differ in their degree of command over such resources and poverty, in particular, entails limited command over resources. The command over resources by households is determined by a number of structural and other features of the economy, for example, ownership of assets, available skills and their marketability, prices for use/sale of assets, prices of goods and services, and net transfers, as well as macropolicies determining the meso setting that affects the households. Therefore, HRD as a means to alleviate poverty is to be seen within the entire spectrum through which the human capabilities of the poor are expanded and utilized to progressively enhance their command over resources for adequate access to income and other basic needs. With the above background and rationale for HRD vis-a-vis poverty, this paper focuses on three major issues: trends in poverty in Bangladesh along with its major determinants and correlates, specific areas of intervention for HRD, and finally, major policy implications.

Income Inequality and Poverty: Trends and Correlates

Trends in Income Inequality

Table 5.1 presents the findings from different studies on income inequality in rural and urban areas of Bangladesh. The findings are similar since the Gini coefficient has been used as the index of inequality based on the Household Expenditure Surveys (HES) carried out by the Bangladesh Bureau of Statistics (BBS). The data show that the level of inequality, as measured by the Gini coefficient, has remained virtually unchanged in the rural areas except for a peak in 1976-1977. Income inequality in the urban areas also reveals similar trends albeit with some fluctuations.

Table 5.1
Trends in Income Inequality in Bangladesh
(Gini coefficients at current prices)

	Rural			*Urban*		
Year	*Muqtada (1986)*	*Rahman and Haque (1988)*	*BBS (1991)*	*Muqtada (1986)*	*Rahman andHaque (1988)*	*BBS (1991)*
1973-1974	0.364		0.35	0.390	...	0.38
1976-1977	0.445	...	...	0.523	...	...
1977-1978	0.348	...	...	0.377	...	...
1978-1979	0.354	...	...	0.382	...	...
1981-1982	...	0.36	...	...	0.42	...
1983-1984	...	0.35	0.35	...	0.35	0.37
1985-1986	...	...	0.36	...	...	0.37
1988-1989	...	...	0.368	...	...	0.381

... means data not available.

Trends in Poverty

Poverty estimates are mostly based on the HES as conducted by the BBS. Using available estimates, Table 5.2 shows that rural poverty continuously increased until fiscal year (FY) 1981/1982 and then fell dramatically to 48 percent in FY1988/1989. Similarly, urban poverty also fell to 44 percent in FY1988/1989.[1]

Hossain and Sen (1992) used a standard methodology to calculate headcount ratios for rural areas on the basis of available HES data. Their findings are reported in Table 5.3. The table shows that absolute poverty in terms of per household expenditure increased sharply from 60 percent in FY1973/1974 to 79 percent in FY1976/1977, and declined thereafter to 37 percent in FY1985/1986. It then increased to 43 percent in FY1988/1989. The figures seem to indicate that the improvements in the rural poverty situation started during the late 1970s with some deterioration in recent years. More importantly, the findings regarding the change in the direction of poverty remain similar to studies based on different methodologies. While the changes in the incidence of poverty may not remove the controversies regarding the extent of poverty at different time periods, several studies (for example, Khan 1990, Osmani 1990a) have pointed out the observed incompatibility in poverty findings of HES data and changes in relevant macroeconomic indicators.

Table 5.2
Percentage of Population below Poverty Line

	Rural			*Urban*		
Year	*Muqtada (1986)*	*Rahman and Haque (1988)*	*BBS (1991)*	*Muqtada (1986)*	*Rahman and Haque (1988)*	*BBS (1991)*
1973-1974	55.9	65.27	82.9	37.8	32.3	81.4
1976-1977	68.2	...	...	40.3	...	...
1977-1978	...	...	...	...	...	...
1978-1979	68.7	...	...	40.8	...	...
1981-1982	...	79.12	73.8	...	50.66	66.0
1983-1984	...	49.81	57.0	...	39.52	66.0
1985-1986	...	47.08	51.0	...	29.11	56.0
1988-1989	...	...	48.0	...	...	44.0

... means data not available.

Besides the controversy, the above unidimensional measure of poverty overlooks many other important factors in the complex phenomenon of poverty. It is often emphasized that an essential prerequisite in the design of effective policies for poverty alleviation is a comprehensive analysis of the poverty syndrome incorporating all the major aspects of its "state" and "process" dimensions. The effective approach should be able to analyze poverty so as to identify the causal factors that bring about poverty and those that perpetuate it. It is important to realize that although vast in numbers, the poor are effectively unseen and rarely understood.[2] In particular, it is necessary that the formulation of policies be based on a sound understanding of the poor as "people, not statistics" who have many more dimensions than can be gleaned from calorie intake or per capita income.

Table 5.3
Trends in Rural Poverty in Bangladesh

	1973-1974	*1976-1977*	*1977-1978*	*1978-1979*	*1981-1982*	*1983-1984*	*1985-1986*	*1988-1989*
Poverty line income (Tk per annum)	1,150	1,633	1,894	2,064	2,227	3,150	3,701	4,340
Headcount Ratio(%)								
Per capita expenditure	71.3	...	...	...	65.3	50.0	41.3	43.8
Per capita income	...	...	...	...	60.0	42.8	38.9	38.7
Per household expenditure	60.3	78.9	77.4	65.8	55.3	46.3	37.3	43.4
Per household income	...	73.1	72.8	60.7	51.3	39.8	35.9	40.0

... means data not available.
Source: Hossain and Sen (1992).

In recent years, attempts have been made to study poverty incorporating a multidimensional index in its analysis (see for example, Rahman and Hossain 1992). However, no mechanism nor institutional framework as yet exists that encompasses the major dimensions of poverty for adequate and regular monitoring of poverty.

Development of a Poverty Monitoring System

In view of the above considerations, the Centre on Integrated Rural Development for Asia and the Pacific (CIRDAP) recently completed the first phase of a project, Monitoring Adjustment and Poverty (MAP) in Bangladesh, which aimed to pilot test, among others, a set of poverty indicators and recommend the methodology for the establishment of a regular system to monitor the multidimensional indicators of poverty. The system includes core indicators in 12 areas: income; nutrition; health; education; housing; access to community services (for example, potable water, sanitation, public health services); access to land; people's participation; crisis-coping capacity; economic diversification; employment; and public expenditure. To test and validate the multidimensional indicators of the Poverty Monitoring System, microlevel data were collected to provide an empirical basis to the indicators and make recommendations for a methodology for regular data collection by suitable national institutions. In developing the modules, multidimensional indicators in both rural and urban areas and those related to nutritional aspects were specifically considered (see Chowdhury 1993; Mujeri, Shahabuddin, and Ahmed 1993; Rahman 1993; Sen and Islam 1993).

The basic concern of the approach has been to recognize that, for policy purposes, poverty should be conceptualized in a continuum rather than in a discrete fashion so that a strict and static cut-off point to identify the poor is inadequate. In reality, the actual outcomes of poverty at the household level are the result of a complex and interacting set of factors rooted in broader structural processes. This suggests that a unidimensional approach to poverty with a focus on narrowly conceived performance indicators may not adequately capture the dynamics of poverty at the household and individual levels. For that purpose, a multidimensional approach to poverty is necessary, including both quantitative and qualitative indicators at individual, household, and community levels. A number of methodological and empirical issues that are important to poverty analysis in Bangladesh emerge from the studies.

Poverty Analysis: Rural Poor Households

An examination of various poverty correlates such as growth and growth-related linkages; landlessness, unemployment and trends in real wages; and food and nutrient intake, is warranted both for adducing additional evidence to corroborate the trends in poverty and for understanding how these correlates influence and determine poverty levels (for details, see Rahman et al., 1988; Hossain and Sen 1992; Mujeri, Shahabuddin, and Ahmed 1993).

In the context of poverty, the existence of rural households can be usefully analyzed in terms of three related aspects: productive activities, household instability, and state of vulnerability (Rahman 1993). Conceptually, the productive activities of poor households are of two distinct natures: income-earning and expenditure-saving. While income-earning activities are usually covered in income or expenditure accounting, cost-saving activities remain outside the purview of such accounting. However, a significant proportion of the productive time of rural households is devoted to such activities in Bangladesh and their significance extends much beyond their distress nature. In addition to income-earning activities, expenditure-saving scopes are important determinants of the well-being and survival strategy of the poor. From a dynamic point of view, the nature and durability of expenditure-saving scopes can shed important light on routine survival and crisis-coping capacities of rural households. In the latter case, expenditure-saving scopes may also be seen as a "safety net" in the survival process of the rural poor. According to the CIRDAP survey, expenditure-saving activities contribute as much as one fifth to the annual household income of the rural poor. The scope of such activities is, to a large extent, dependent on the size and availability of ecological reserves in an area. In a real sense, such expenditure-saving activities are not substitutes, rather they are complements to the income-earning activities of the poor, having long antecedents in the community culture of rural Bangladesh. The development of ecological reserves with adequate access to the poor not only has a poverty alleviation dimension as emphasized above, but an environment-sustaining dimension as well. Another distinguishing feature of income-earning activities relates to the existence of a widely variable range of earning sources with their markedly seasonal character. In this respect, four broad groups can be distinguished: self-provisioning agriculture, homestead production, petty entrepreneurial income, and wage income. Each has its own connotation requiring appropriate measures.

One of the key dimensions of the poverty process in rural Bangladesh is the marked instability of the household as a family unit. This has both social and economic ingredients. It also raises the issue of the adequacy of treating the household as a stable family unit since household instability itself becomes an aspect of the dynamics of poverty. This points to the need to accommodate, in addition to households, subnuclear units and vulnerable or transitory membership of kin household units in poverty analysis. In this respect, the gender dimension indicates substantial diversity with significant implications for women in poverty.

In rural Bangladesh, poverty, in addition to being a state of deprivation, is also a state of vulnerability. The persistence of crises that the rural households routinely face significantly affect the household's ability to sustain, let alone raise current welfare levels. In this respect, it becomes worthwhile to distinguish between anticipated and unanticipated threats to welfare losses. While anticipated threats, such as seasonal unemployment, are part of the normal cycle of household existence, unforeseen crises such as natural disasters and illness, have random elements with severe consequences for household welfare.

In the survey conducted under the CIRDAP study, three independent indicators were used to measure the extent of rural poverty:

- per capita annual income (with a poverty line income of Tk 4,608 per person per annum at FY1987/1988 prices) ;
- the household's self-evaluation about status, based on self-categorization in terms of four groups: chronically in deficit, occasionally in deficit, self-sufficient, and surplus;
- housing condition, based on roofing material and number of rooms.

Table 5.4 provides a picture of the incidence of rural poverty for each of the above indicators. It is seen that the rural poor are made up of two distinct bands, one of which may be categorized as "hardcore" poor living in extreme distress, and the other as "vulnerable" poor subsisting on or around the poverty line income. The "hardcore" poor constitute a distinct rural class averaging roughly a quarter of the rural population, while the "vulnerable" group accounts for a wider band ranging from 31 percent by the housing criterion to 50 percent by the self-evaluation criterion.

Table 5.4
Incidence of Rural Poverty, 1989-1990

Per Capita Annual Income		*Self-Evaluation*		*Housing Condition*	
Size group (in Tk)	*Percent of Population*	*Category*	*Percent of households*	*Category*	*Percent of households*
Up to 2,500	26.9	Chronic deficit	23	Leaf roof	9
2,500-3,500	18.3	Occasional deficit	50	Thatch/1 room	12
3,500-4,608[a]	16.6	Self-sufficient	17	Thatch/1+ room	31
4,608-6,000	13.3	Surplus	10	Tin roof	45
6,000 & above	24.8			Pucca roof	2
Total	100.0		100		100

[a] Poverty line income
Source : Rahman (1993).

Profile of the Rural Poor

The profile of the rural poor, as revealed from the CIRDAP study, points to the following important characteristics:

- The landless and functionally landless households constitute the bulk of the chronically deficit households. The differential access to land largely explains the growth of vulnerable households. Inequality in land ownership underlies the unequal distribution of personal incomes and the rapid increase in rural poverty.

- Rural labor households constitute the overwhelming majority of the hardcore poor group. Compared to farm households, a greater proportion of households engaged in nonagricultural self-employment are vulnerable to poverty, revealing low rates of return in these activities. With the dominance of labor households among the poor, their survival strategy critically depends on the availability of wage employment to support subsistence. The land-poor households engage in multiple occupations to compensate for low wages and underemployment in the crop sector.

The sharp distinctions brought out between the "hardcore" poor and the "vulnerable" poor have important implications for development policy in Bangladesh. The "hardcore" poor will need targeted policies of asset transfers and income creation to lift them out of poverty. On the other hand, the "vulnerable" poor are mainly the victims of distortions and imperfections, which preclude them from availing of opportunities. The successful implementation of poverty-sensitive structural adjustment (SA) policies, along with the creation of "safety nets" during the intervening period, can go a long way in ameliorating their poverty. Therefore, rural poverty alleviation in Bangladesh calls for an appropriate combination of SA measures to remove distortions, and direct intervention through asset transfers/creation and employment/income generation, thus making HRD critical.

Analysis of Urban Poverty

The state and the dynamics of urban poverty are best captured by a set of indicators with a focus on the entitlement of the urban poor including critical inputs relating to security, welfare, and living standard (Sen and Islam 1993). The following major dimensions of urban poverty have been emphasized in the CIRDAP study: economic status, human resource status, routine vulnerability, and crisis-coping capacity.

The economic status of the urban poor is captured in terms of indicators such as income, self-categorization, housing, and access to minimum clothing. The human resource status can be measured through two broad indicators: education, and health and sanitation.

It has also been pointed out that urban poverty is often reflected as a process of vulnerability, which is revealed through the degree of crisis proneness of poor households. A number of aspects of routine vulnerability can be recorded: crisis events related to natural disasters, illness, life-cycle factors (such as the death of income-earning members), personal insecurity (such as threat of eviction from slums, theft/robbery, serious physical assault, or harassment by police). The poverty implications of the above crisis-events relate to the critical problem of income erosion both through crisis-related expenditures as well as reduction in income-earning capabilities of the household. A marked inadequacy in crisis coping capacity is an important dimension of urban poverty; it is filled through a number of methods, for example, negative coping (such as sale of assets or injurious borrowing), positive coping (such as mobilization of soft loans, social network, or administrative support), and dissaving.

On the basis of various criteria, the survey found it useful to identify the "extremely poor" and "moderately poor" urban households. Such a differentiation brings out a number of aspects of urban poverty that are critical for policy: compared to the moderately poor, the extremely poor have a significantly lower male labor force participation rate, a greater proportion of children below 10 years of age, lower educational involvement rate, lower housing space, higher incidence of morbidity, and reduced networking capacity. The extremely poor display greater incidence of female-headed households and a higher female participation rate under compulsion, reflecting the importance of the gender dimension in urban poverty. The limited access, often at the cost of high "transaction costs" to basic social services also emerges as a critical aspect of their vulnerability.

Moreover, the pursuit of structural adjustments and associated stabilization policies in Bangladesh also have certain developments with adverse implications for the urban small-scale manufacturing sector and informal sector activities (Mujeri 1993, Sen and Islam 1993). Within the purview of privatization policy, for example, one unintended consequence has been the severe shortage of loanable funds for small entrepreneurs. The crisis in recovery of industrial loans to large enterprises has led to a crisis of recycling of funds to small borrowers from the financial institutions. The private banking sector also has a very small share for small enterprises in their credit portfolio. The general credit crunch, as a consequence of tight monetary policy, has squeezed the availability of financial resources to the small and informal sectors more than the organized sector (see for example, Sobhan and Sen 1989). These sectors are critical for expansion of employment opportunities for the urban poor. The economic situation of the urban poor has also been mitigated only marginally through target-oriented government programs. Even the efforts of nongovernment organizations (NGOs) to address the problems of the urban poor have been rather limited, although during recent years, in many rural areas, NGOs have emerged as an alternative delivery mechanism.

Some Issues in Urban Poverty

Migration from rural areas is a major factor in the continuously increasing aggregate burden of urban poverty. Therefore, issues in urban poverty are closely linked to, and are a reflection of, developments in the rural economy (see, for example, Afsar and Hossain 1992). Various studies suggest that the rural-urban migration process reflects both "pull" and "push" factors with some positive impact on the living standards of the migrants compared to their premigration situation (Afsar and Hossain 1992, Sen and Islam 1993). Thus, urban poverty is largely a spillover of the vast mass of rural poverty in Bangladesh requiring an economywide strategy for poverty alleviation. With increasing landlessness in rural areas, the incremental labor force has been increasingly absorbed in nonfarm activities and the informal sector in both rural and urban areas.

In general, the income-earning activities of the urban poor have strong links with capital and skill acquisition with implications for HRD. Skill formation in the informal sector takes place almost entirely through apprenticeship or on-the-job training. In this respect, two considerations are important for HRD as major elements of urban poverty alleviation (see Siddiqui et al. 1990). First, the more disadvantaged groups (such as female workers) in the informal sector have less opportunities for skill acquisition and thus a limited scope for upward mobility. Human development and skill training among these groups can, therefore, be an important element in creating income-earning opportunities for the poorest urban dweller. Second, upgrading of skills in many informal activities can lead to improvement in quality of products/services with consequent expansion of demand for such products.

Nutritional Aspects of Poverty

The nutritional aspects of poverty are likely to come first since the satisfaction of physiological needs is a precondition to satisfying other human needs. In the context of poverty, the sequence of development of nutritional deficiencies emerges from inadequate dietary intake and/or poor absorption leading to various physical symptoms of malnutrition. Poverty considerations, therefore, need to focus on both input-based and outcome-based indicators to combine various nutritional aspects to provide adequate guidance to policy (Chowdhury 1993).

The findings on socioeconomic determinants of nutritional status, particularly in the rural areas, indicate that both the food and nonfood environments are important factors in nutritional status (Chowdhury 1993). While poverty is the primary cause of inadequate food intake, it is also reported that ignorance about the nutritive value of various food items is a major factor in multiple deficiencies in nutrient intakes and the high incidence of various nutrition-related diseases. Such problems can possibly be addressed most effectively through HRD, linked to increasing awareness regarding the importance of particular nutrients and their common sources, rather than by raising income or intake of all food items.

In general, nutritional problems are complex, involving not only the broad issue of poverty but also specific health-related interventions. The differences in nutritional status between regions, seasons, and age-sex groups are determined not only by access to food and the nonfood physical environment but also by variations in socioeconomic and family characteristics.

Poverty and Human Resources

The above review of the poverty situation in Bangladesh suggests that the majority of the rural poor are marginal and landless farmers, agricultural laborers, and other assetless nonagricultural workers. Similarly, the urban poor are overwhelmingly dominated by the participants in the informal sector. Therefore, examination of the changing conditions of these groups is likely to provide an understanding of the relationship between poverty and human resources.

Over the years, one of the marked structural changes in the status of employment has been the shift of labor from rural to urban areas and from farm to nonfarm activities in rural areas. The share of the urban sector in the labor force increased from 10 percent to 22 percent over the 1974-1989 period. Between 1974 and 1986, the share of agricultural labor declined from 78 percent to 57 percent (BBS 1992). Given the rapid growth in the civilian labor force and the sluggish growth of the economy, unemployment and underemployment rates are quite high in Bangladesh. Despite very low open unemployment rates (less than 3 percent) in census and other labor force surveys due to definitional and methodological factors, the underemployment rate is reported to vary between 31 to 40 percent if full employment norms are used (Islam 1986). Underemployment is the highest among casual as well as female laborers, particularly among those involved in agricultural activities.

Generally, rural workers can be divided into three categories: self-employed, regular wage/salary earners, and casual laborers. A similar categorization of the urban poor is also applicable. Although there are no reliable data on the trends in these categories of laborers, the share of casual laborers seems to have increased in both agriculture and non-agriculture and they form the majority of the hard-core poor. While the linkage effect of agricultural productivity growth and the trickle-down effects of such growth on rural poverty point to the importance of maximizing these elements, the overall impact on poverty of the above strategies has been limited due to the overwhelming magnitude and intensity of poverty in Bangladesh. Many poor households remain outside the purview of these growth-oriented programs and have to be provided with "safety-nets" through various wage and self-employment programs (Task Force 1991).

In light of the review of the experiences during the 1980s, three avenues for poverty alleviation have been identified (see Hossain and Sen 1992). These can be broadly categorized as: fostering growth-oriented programs with a strong immediate impact on poverty; enforcing higher investment in social sectors leading to increased human capital formation and improved living standards; and promoting targeted income and employment-generating programs designed to support the vulnerable poor, particularly those left out of the mainstream of the market-based development process.

The first strategy refers to acceleration of growth in both the farm and nonfarm sectors. While appropriate technological and other innovations can play major roles in the farm sector, there exist significant potential for expansion of nonfarm activities in the rural areas. The urban industries have not provided significant growth linkages so far with the possible exception of the garment industry. A large number of semiskilled female workers (mostly migrants from the rural areas) are now employed in the garment industry.[3] Although the value added in the industry is rather low, its employment creation capacity is high, especially for poor women. To further enhance the benefits to the rural poor, garments and other similar industries could be relocated to the peri-urban areas as well as to the rural areas, along with required infrastructure facilities. In a broad sense, the general strategy should focus on identification and acceleration of poverty-focused growth elements in the economy.

The second strategy brings into focus the importance of HRD as a sustainable strategy for poverty alleviation. In particular, efficient investments in selected areas of social sectors, such as health and education, can contribute toward poverty alleviation and facilitate the realization of the full growth potential of the economy. Good health and educational attainment are obviously important for the poor to raise their productivity and improve their living conditions. The limited access of the poor to educational opportunities (both for primary education and general or technical education) restricts the scope for enhancing their skills and productivity. It has been indicated that the benefits to the poor are substantially below the mean expenditure on education in the country (Khundker et al. 1994). In view of the existence of a segmented labor market, the poor are forced to become participants in the low-wage sector.

The third strategy refers to the targeted approach for the "hardcore" poor, both in the rural and urban areas. The expansion of targeted income and employment programs under both government and nongovernment initiatives like the Vulnerable Group Development, Maternity and Child Health, Small Farmers' Development Programs, and Rural Poor Program programs can become effective in providing "safety nets" to the poor in the short and medium run as well as contribute toward HRD.

Dimensions of Human Resource Development

Policies designed to expand the availability of basic social services and improve the quality of life of the people are important cornerstones in the poverty reduction strategy. One can mention at least two immediate concerns for this. First, investments in the human resources of the poor have substantial payoffs. Second, with appropriate targeting, the poor can be made to benefit directly from investments in basic services such as primary schools and primary health care services.

The above observations may be rationalized by observing the differences in the employment pattern and other characteristics of the poor that are instrumental to understanding the poverty and HRD linkages. As discussed earlier, the general trend in Bangladesh has been a decline in agricultural employment relative to increasing absorption in nonfarm sectors (for example, formal/informal manufacturing, trade, transport, and construction). Within the activities, the occupational profile of the poor, though varying with location, is dominated by industrial workers, day laborers, transport workers, and those engaged in petty trade, services, and other activities in the informal sector. The specific occupational pattern that the poor can avail of is largely determined by their skill levels and education (see, for example, Khundker 1989, Siddiqui et al. 1990, Majumdar and Choudhuri 1991). Intrafirm mobility of the poor is often characterized by skill upgrading from helper to semiskilled laborer, and then to skilled laborer, sometimes leading to individual setting up of their own enterprises. As such, for the poor in both formal and informal sectors, education and skill development occupy a critical position in occupational and vertical mobility.

The characteristics of the poor also reveal substantial differences in living standards in terms of clothing, housing, health, education and other basic services (see, for example, Sen and Islam 1993). It is suggested that a sharp distinction can be made between the poor in the formal and informal sectors, with the poor in the formal sector having higher levels of education and greater access to resources (see Siddiqui et al. 1990, 6). The interindustry wage differentials have also been found to reflect differences in the interindustry composition of occupations resulting from variations in human capital endowments of different groups (Mondal 1992). Among others, the level of education appears as a significant variable in explaining wage differentials among the poor (for example, Majumdar and Choudhuri 1991). It has also been observed that male-female wage differentials tend to decrease with education and skill levels indicating a direct relationship between educational status and skill levels of the poor on the one hand, and increases in earnings on the other, particularly for vulnerable groups like women. The above suggests that HRD in Bangladesh needs to be characterized as an integrated process with a clear focus and direction in three major areas: employment and manpower development, science and technology, and quality of life.

- *Employment and HRD.* Employment situations in the agrarian sector and the market for unskilled workers are particularly serious in Bangladesh. There is also an additional problem in matching labor demand and supply in particular skills. These are specific problems in addition to the overall employment situation, which is grossly inadequate to absorb the existing and potential labor supply. While the pursuit of labor-absorbing policies and acceleration of growth is the long-run solution, these have to be supplemented by policies with an emphasis on flexibility and the creation of a broad-based productive capacity, rather than geared to promoting narrowly skilled workers. This is necessary for the growth of new entrepreneurial skills to take advantage of emerging economic opportunities in a global context.

- *Science and technology.* The implications of recent scientific and technological progress, particularly in such fields as information, biotechnology, electronics, material sciences, and energy technologies, indicate the need to adapt human resources to these realities to take advantage of the development potential of science and technology. In this respect, the two-way causality between science and technology capabilities and the human resource profile of Bangladesh is important, i.e., generation of human resources for the promotion of science and technology to serve the country's development needs, and utilization of science and technology to upgrade available human resources.

- *Quality of life.* The success in realizing equitable and accelerated growth in Bangladesh is critically dependent upon the use of the potentials of the underutilized human resources of the vast majority of the poor and disadvantaged groups. A necessary condition to raise their productive capacities is to improve their capabilities through their level of participation in society. This requires coordinated efforts in a number of key sectors such as education, health, nutrition, and the environment.

  For the effective coordination and integration of various elements of HRD efforts, policies must encompass both the supply and the demand sides. The supply side requires the generation of the means of HRD, while the demand side is concerned with the utilization of these means. In Bangladesh, existing policies largely concentrate on supply-side issues. This has contributed to the ineffectiveness of the policies, suggesting the need for more demand-oriented strategies. The effective policies must take into account the institutional and structural constraints in the participation of the poor in human development efforts. The institutional context itself must become an explicit focus of HRD policy.

Structural Adjustments and Human Resource Development

After independence in 1971, largely ineffective results of orthodox stabilization measures since the 1980s to restore macroeconomic stability with satisfactory growth led to an emphasis on structural reforms. (For details of structural adjustment measures and their implications, see Mujeri et al. 1993.) The nature of structural adjustment (SA) programs pursued so far can be termed as largely corrective. They have been aimed at improving fiscal and external balances, reducing distortions, encouraging competition, and enhancing the role of the market to guide resource allocation. The interventions largely focus on demand management and structural and institutional reforms to remove market distortions and change the public-private mix to promote market development.

While the correction of distortions is important, it is necessary to examine how SA policies impinged upon different household groups. It is important to recognize that the goal for Bangladesh is adjustment with poverty reduction, not adjustment or poverty reduction requiring formulation and implementation of poverty-sensitive SA policies.

Under the SA package, wide-ranging reforms have been attempted to stimulate the economy through relaxation of government interventions to enhance internal and external competitiveness in various fields. The reform measures have affected virtually every sector and all aspects of economic management, including external sector adjustment, demand management measures, enhanced mobilization of domestic resources, increased role for the private sector, and improved efficiency of public enterprises. A comparison of the performance of the Bangladesh economy in terms of some major macroeconomic and HRD indicators is presented in Table 5.5. The first five-year period (1981-1985) may be seen as the preadjustment period since the Structural Adjustment Facility (SAF) program was initiated at the national level during 1986-1987. Since then the country has been following the SA programs under the SAF, Enhanced Structural Adjustment Facility (ESAF), and SA guidelines under the Policy Framework Paper (PFP). The second period, 1986-1990, is the period of adjustment. The results reveal very limited positive achievements, particularly in terms of changes in the real sector of the economy. The policy combination of expenditure switching and expenditure reduction, emphasizing demand management, adversely affected growth prospects.

In the face of resource constraints, the government squeezed development expenditure rather than current expenditures, thereby curtailing investment and growth. Infrastructure investment was inadequate and resource flows were directed more toward policy reforms than to capital formation in the economy. Similarly, the impact of trade liberalization and exchange rate adjustment proved to be of limited use in achieving external competitiveness. The provision of social services, particularly to the poor, and HRD efforts were not given due importance in the SA program (for details, see Mujeri et al. 1993). In view of the widespread existence of poverty in the country, it is imperative to identify the impact of SA policies on different household groups, particularly the poor. The critical policy issue for Bangladesh is to protect and assist the poor without distorting the economy. The correction of distortions is important since, if they persist, not only economic recovery and growth will be undermined, but also the attainment of social goals.

Table 5.5
Changes in Selected Macroeconomic and HRD Indicators

Indicators	*Preadjustment period (Average of 1981-1982 to 1985-1986)*	*Adjustment period (Average of 1986-1987 to 1990-1991)*
1. Macroeconomic		
Real GDP growth rate (percent)	4.3	3.9
Increase in CPI (percent)	11.3	9.6
As percent of GDP		
budget deficit	8.8	7.5
current account deficit	8.7	6.5
public expenditure development	8.4	7.2
nondevelopment	9.2	9.6
investment	13.2	11.8
domestic savings	1.3	2.5
2. Human Resource Development		
Infant mortality rate (per 1000 live births)	122 (1982)	111 (1991)
Primary enrolment ratio (net)	59 (1982-1983)	65 (1988-1990)
Secondary enrolment ratio (gross)	17 (1986-1988)	17 (1988-1990)
Public expenditure on education (as percent of GNP)	2.2 (1986)	2.2 (1988-1990)
Public expenditure on education (as percent of total public expenditure)	10.3 (1987-1988)	10.5 (1988-1990)
Public expenditure on primary education (as percent of all levels)	39.1 (1985-1988)	48.7 (1990-1991)

Sources: Calculated from BBS data and UNDP (1993).

In the context of HRD, another aspect of SA policies that also needs to be emphasized may be termed as "directive" structural adjustments. The emphasis in this case is on the anticipation of future trends and on restructuring the economy to respond flexibly and rapidly to such changes. For example, within the external context, this involves anticipation of the pattern and pace of the dynamic external competitiveness of Bangladesh, identifying sectoral implications, and promoting activities likely to become important to retain export competitiveness. For HRD, this would imply the promotion of appropriate adjustment processes to generate technological innovations and build up endowments of human skills through human resource planning, education, and training. The policy of SA consistent with HRD should include proper assessment of the requirements of different types of human resources, including institutional arrangements for training. In effect, Bangladesh needs to supplement the currently pursued "corrective" SA with a deliberate strategy of "directive" SA to develop a flexible and adaptable human resource strategy that can respond to changing demands of dynamic production technology and market requirements.

Policy Implications of a Human Resource Development Strategy

To promote HRD, national plans and policies must be based on a clear recognition of the central importance of human resources in the development process of Bangladesh. For this, a longer-term perspective must be adopted within a framework to explore the full policy implications of placing human elements at the center of development.

The ultimate aim should be to develop the full human potential. The thrust of the efforts should be the recognition of the fact that investment in human resources of the poor is the most effective strategy for increasing their participation in development. This is also likely to be easier to implement compared to the efforts to increase their ownership and access to other assets through redistributive policies. Moreover, HRD and poverty alleviation are complementary goals; a focus on human development implies a major emphasis on poverty alleviation.

The framework of HRD must accommodate the impact of new technologies. In Bangladesh, this requires more technical and vocational training rather than a continuation of the traditional emphasis on general education. The attainment of universal primary education and literacy within the shortest possible time is a precondition that would require a major reordering of investment priorities. For education, three major issues need to be addressed: priorities among different levels and types of education, women as a target group, and reorientation of the education system to create the necessary human skills to take advantage of emerging technologies.

The informal sector plays a significant role in Bangladesh. Its existence and growth is closely linked to macroeconomic policies and trends as well as global situations. The specific policies in this respect should be geared toward creating employment, enhancing skills and raising incomes. The informal sector policy should be comprehensive in the areas of productivity, institutional and organizational viability, and human resources.

Human resource policies should facilitate structural adjustment while minimizing the costs to those affected by the necessary transformation of the economy. Further, such policies should be participatory. At the micro level, better management of human development requires a sensitive balance between efforts to enhance productivity and efforts to improve working conditions. The private sector can play a significant role and contribute to education and training with awareness of social responsibility.

Any HRD effort in Bangladesh must address the problems of the poor and strive to bring them into the mainstream of the development process. This is limited by inadequate understanding of the poor: who they are, how they behave, and how they manage to survive. Some evidence presented in this paper as well as other evidence (for example, Grameen Bank) reveal that:

- The poor are in a better position to realize the real opportunities to improve their quality of life than the existing institutional mechanisms to help them.

- The poor have economic rationality, the development of which is constrained by the availability of resources.

- To be effective, the poor should be approached with a flexible combination of formal and informal mechanisms.

- Organizing the poor is a key factor in developing a system.

- The urgent need for the poor is the enhancement of productivity within a package of human development efforts.

- The enhancement of productivity and institutional arrangements for the poor needs to be supplemented with the development of an appropriate macroeconomic setting.

- Within existing macroeconomic policies, the strategies for development need to focus on women and youth as explicit target groups.

The HRD strategy needs to consider the above in designing appropriate policies. The major economic issue is that the poor are constrained in making the required investment to harness the full productive potential of their human labor, thus adversely affecting their economic productivity. Constantly under pressure to eke out a living, the poor only have low-productivity activities as their options. The productivity of the poor as human capital is low and HRD can increase their productivity.

A major factor in the worsening quality of life of the poor in rural areas has been the widespread degradation and encroachment of common property resources. Local management of such resources is vital to ensure sustainable development with equity. Similarly, provision of safe drinking water, sanitation improvement, primary health care, and immunization schemes form priority areas to improve the health of the poor and promote human development.

Another key consideration is to address the issue of acceleration of the process of rural-to-urban migration. Several studies on migration reveal that the condition prior to migration, particularly in terms of skill and asset holding, has a strong impact on postmigration occupation within the informal sector (for example, Afsar and Hossain 1992). The large majority of the urban poor tend to be either unemployed or engaged in agriculture prior to migration. The urban poor usually improve their position over time largely through acquiring skills, which open up opportunities for them to move up the income ladder. Skills improvement also creates opportunities to move out of low remunerative marginal occupations (see Siddiqui et al. 1990). Analysis of the poor in both the formal and informal sectors also reveals a close link between skill levels and transition from informal to formal, and from casual to regular employment. This suggests that the major focus for dealing with urban poverty must be directed toward skill improvement through appropriately focused HRD.

Conclusion

In this paper, an attempt has been made to provide the broad links between poverty and HRD in Bangladesh. In this respect, the major thrust has been to delineate the channels through which HRD efforts can be accelerated and effectively pursued for sustained poverty alleviation.

The arguments basically follow two broad strands. First, due to inadequate access to and ownership of physical assets, the "hardcore" rural and urban poor must be lifted out of poverty through investments in such areas as health, education, skill training, and other human development efforts in order to transform their available labor into productive human capital. The currently pursued target group approach should be designed to progressively utilize human capital in productive income-generating activities. To the extent that the hardcore poor and the vulnerable groups are located in resource-poor households, such a strategy would create productive self-employment and wage-employment opportunities that are critical for their survival and ultimate graduation out of poverty. Second, growth-oriented activities in both the rural and urban areas should be accelerated. Acceleration of growth is necessary, otherwise, the cumulative impact on poverty for both the hardcore and the vulnerable poor cannot be sustained. In this respect, it is critical to integrate micro interventions with the overall growth strategy and macropolicies in the country.

In this context, it becomes important to redefine the goals of development consistent with the human potential and sociocultural characteristics of Bangladesh society. For this purpose, the development strategy must focus on integration of HRD with the growth elements of the economy. The formulation of such an integrated human development strategy requires the preparation of the existing "human development profile" and the setting up of appropriate "human development goals". The profile must address a broad range of social indicators of national concern (for example, health, nutrition, education, and skill level) in terms of different socioeconomic groups, particularly for the poor. The profile would indicate the current status in terms of human development and help to define the long-term goals for the high-priority indicators. This would also help to accommodate human development goals within the overall development strategy. For poverty alleviation, it is critical to ascertain the extent and causes of relative deprivation of the poor along with efforts to enhance their capability through HRD for innovative rather than imitative decision making.

The analysis in the paper indicates that poverty in Bangladesh should be seen within the context of low economic growth and consequent slow expansion of employment opportunities. With the limited scope of employment in the agricultural sector, the poor are mostly involved in off-farm activities in the rural areas and in the informal sector in the urban areas.

This calls for proper integration of strategies to organize the poor and their interests within the organizational hierarchy, and their implementation through servicing of the organizations in a productive manner. Such capacity-building programs can be made to improve the lot of the poor by generating and sustaining their willingness to organize, generate capital through savings, upgrade their human skills, and assume responsibility for managing their own affairs. Within the above conceptual package, HRD to upgrade skills is essential in making the best use of available resources. While the poor have skills and a traditional knowledge base, these need to be expanded to realize new and profitable opportunities.

To upgrade human and technical skills, the basic requirement is to provide inputs and services to the poor. In this respect, the conventional focus has been on specific skills through extension and training on a particular craft. However, with modernization and change, the traditional focus of HRD needs to be expanded to encompass the ability of the poor to perceive and exploit profitable opportunities emerging from the dynamics of market changes and external linkages. In effect, HRD efforts for the poor indicate the need for a well-integrated strategy to enhance their entrepreneurial abilities. Without such entrepreneurial abilities, the poor have little prospect for changing their subsistence environment. The poor need to be transformed into entrepreneurs who are well-trained in management, setting up microenterprises, marketing techniques, and making productive investment decisions. Poverty-focused HRD must include programs for acquiring managerial, productive, and other skills to exploit emerging opportunities. However, to be effective, the measures would require improved provision of infrastructure and access to credit.

The examination of the poverty correlates in this chapter also indicates that the poor are not homogenous; there exist differentiations with respect to socioeconomic conditions, agroecological situations, and cultural patterns. While adequate HRD efforts much recognize such differences, the general strategy can be based on observed commonalities: landlessness and small subsistence holding, the unorganized nature of economic activity with lack of capital and access to credit, lack of marketable skills, and alienation from the mainstream of organized economic activities. These elements, in effect, translate into a lack of capacity of the poor to change their own conditions. The human development focus, therefore, requires measures for the creation of incentives, opportunities, and organizational capacity for the poor to develop skills and the capability to plan and implement income-generating activities, in order to exploit economies of scale in the production and marketing processes, and compete effectively in the input, output, and capital markets. The success in such efforts would, however, largely depend on the creation of a macroenvironment designed to promote accelerated growth and support the initiatives of the poor.

Although expansion in the supply of necessary public services to promote HRD is crucial, increased supply must be complemented by effective policies and institutions to ensure availability to the poor. In this respect, major areas that need to be addressed include delivery systems and institutions, special measures for targeting services to the poor, development of innovative and cost-effective means to reach the poor, and replicability and sustainability of effective programs. Within the resource-constrained environment, reallocation of expenditures and improvement in the efficiency and equity of the service delivery system and expansion of the role of NGOs can be effective in expanding availability to the poor.

The severity and persistence of poverty point to the fact that growth alone is not sufficient for its alleviation. Growth-promoting policies need to be complemented by a wide array of programs and policies to ensure that benefits of growth reach the poor.

Notes

1. However, such a large decline in the incidence of poverty within a short time remains a controversial issue (e.g. Rahman and Haque 1988; Khan 1990; Ravallion 1990; Osmani 1990a, 1990b). In particular, it has been pointed out that HES data have limitations for intertemporal comparisons of poverty (see Hossain and Sen 1992, Mujeri, Shahabuddin, and Ahmed 1993).

2. According to the World Bank (1988, 1), "There is still much to learn about how to alleviate poverty. Data on the poor—where and who they are, the constraints they face, changes in their number or condition—remain extremely limited even in statistically sophisticated countries. Moreover, these limited data and the complex relation between poverty and development make it very difficult for policy makers to gain more than a partial understanding of the effect of their policies and programs on the poor."

3. For an analysis of female workers in the garments industry and their socioeconomic characteristics, see Majumdar and Choudhuri (1991).

References

Afsar, R., and M. Hossain, 1992. *Urbanization and Urban Poor in Bangladesh: Issues, Trends and Challenges*. Dhaka: Bangladesh Institute of Development Studies.

Bangladesh Bureau of Statistics (BBS), 1991. *Report on the Household Expenditure Survey 1988/89*. Dhaka.

———, 1992. *Labor Force Survey 1989/90*. Dhaka.

Bryant, C., and L. G. White, 1982. *Managing Development in the Third World*. Colorado: Westview Press.

Chowdhury, O. H., 1993. "Nutritional Status Indicators of Poverty." In *Monitoring Adjustment and Poverty in Bangladesh: Report on the Framework Project*. Dhaka: Centre on Integrated Rural Development for Asia and the Pacific.

Hossain, M., and B. Sen, 1992. "Rural Poverty in Bangladesh: Trends and Determinants." *Asian Development Review* 10(1):1-34.

Islam, R., 1986. "Rural Unemployment and Underemployment: A Review." In R. Islam and M. Muqtada, eds., *Bangladesh: Selected Issues in Employment and Development*. New Delhi: International Labor Organization/Asian Employment Program (ARTEP).

Khan, A. R., 1990. "Poverty in Bangladesh: A Consequence of and a Constraint on Growth." *Bangladesh Development Studies* 18(3):19-34.

Khundker, N., 1989. "Technology Adaptation and Innovations in the Informal Sector of Dhaka (Bangladesh)." World Employment Program Research Working Paper. International Labor Organization (ILO), Geneva.

Khundker, N., et al., 1994. "Urban Poverty in Bangladesh: Trends, Determinants, and Policy Issues." *Asian Development Review* 12(1):1-31.

Majumdar, P., and S. Choudhuri, 1991. *The Socioeconomic Condition of the Female Workers in the Garment Industry of Bangladesh*. Bangladesh Institute of Development Studies.

Mondal, A. H., 1992. "Trade Unionism, Wage and Labor Productivity in Manufacturing Sector of Bangladesh." Research Report No. 133. Bangladesh Institute of Development Studies, Dhaka.

Mujeri, M. K., 1993. "A Framework for Monitoring the Distributional Implications of Structural Adjustment Policies and Poverty in Bangladesh: Overview, Synthesis and Recommendations." In *Monitoring Adjustment and Poverty in Bangladesh: Report on the Framework Project*. Dhaka: Centre on Integrated Rural Development for Asia and the Pacific.

Mujeri, M. K., Q. Shahabuddin, and S. Ahmed, 1993. "Macro-economic Performance, Structural Adjustments and Equity: A Framework for Analysis of Macro-Micro Transmission Mechanisms in Bangladesh." In *Monitoring Adjustment and Poverty in Bangladesh: Report on the Framework Project*. Dhaka: Centre on Integrated Rural Development for Asia and the Pacific (CIRDAP).

Muqtada, M., 1986. "Poverty and Inequality: Trends and Causes." In R. Islam and M. Muqtada, eds., *Bangladesh-Selected Issues in Employment and Development*. New Delhi: International Labor Organization/Asian Employment Programme.

Osmani, S. R., 1990a. "Structural Change and Poverty in Bangladesh: The Case of a False Turning Point." *Bangladesh Development Studies* 18(3):55-74.

———, 1990b. "Notes on Some Recent Estimates of Rural Poverty in Bangladesh." *Bangladesh Development Studies* 18(3):75-87.

Rahman, A., and T. Haque, 1988. *Poverty and Inequality in Bangladesh in the Eighties: An Analysis of Some Recent Evidence*. Dhaka: Bangladesh Institute of Development Studies.

Rahman, H. Z., 1993. "Monitoring Adjustment and Poverty: Methodological and Empirical Issues in Rural Poverty Analysis." In *Monitoring Adjustment and Poverty in Bangladesh: Report on the Framework Project*. Dhaka: Centre on Integrated Rural Development for Asia and the Pacific.

Rahman, H. Z., and M. Hossain, eds., 1992. *Re-Thinking Rural Poverty: A Case for Bangladesh*. Dhaka: Bangladesh Institute of Development Studies.

Rahman, S. H., et al., 1988. *A Critical Review of the Poverty Situation in Bangladesh in the Eighties*. Vol. 1. Dhaka: Bangladesh Institute of Development Studies.

Ravallion, M., 1990. "The Challenging Arithmetic of Poverty in Bangladesh." *Bangladesh Development Studies* 18(3):35-53.

Sen, A. K., 1990. "Development as Capability Expansion." In K. Griffin and J. Knight, eds., *Human Development and the International Development Strategy for the 1980s*. London: Macmillan.

Sen, B., and Q. T. Islam, 1993. "Monitoring Adjustment and Urban Poverty in Bangladesh: Issues, Dimensions, Tendencies." In *Monitoring Adjustment and Poverty in Bangladesh: Report on the Framework Project*. Dhaka: Centre on Integrated Rural Development for Asia and the Pacific (CIRDAP).

Siddiqui, K., et al., 1990. *Social Formation in Dhaka City*. Dhaka: University Press Limited.

Sobhan, R., and B. Sen, 1989. "Trends in Repayment Performance of the DFIs: Implications for the Development of Entrepreneurship in Bangladesh." *Bangladesh Development Studies* 17(3):21-66.

Task Force, 1991. "Task Force Report on Poverty Alleviation." In *Report of the Task Forces on Bangladesh Development Strategies for the 1990's*, Vol. 1. Dhaka: University Press Limited.

United Nations Development Programme (UNDP), 1993. *Human Development Report 1993*. New York: Oxford University Press.

World Bank, 1988. *The World Bank's Support for the Alleviation of Poverty*. Washington D.C.

6 NONTRADITIONAL EXPORTS AND ECONOMIC PERFORMANCE: REVIEW AND EMPIRICAL EVIDENCE

ZAIDI SATTAR

Since the early 1980s, Bangladesh has experienced vibrant export growth. In the category of nontraditional exports, the economy averaged 20 percent growth per year during the 1980s, and this trend seems unabated in the first three years of this decade. While it is correct to state that the considerable export potential of Bangladesh remains largely unfulfilled due to the lack of a more vigorous proexport policy environment, it is equally true that economic reforms introduced between 1983 to 1995, especially the intensive reforms from 1990 to 1995, have attempted to address the fundamental shortcomings in export policy. With an improved policy framework and given that a favorable world trading environment exists, it is now hoped that Bangladesh's recent record of vibrant export performance will not only be sustained but improved upon.

This chapter reviews the past export performance, assesses the supporting policy environment and highlights the positive linkages between export growth and economic growth.

Structural Change in the Bangladesh Economy

Table 6.1 summarizes some trends in the social and human development indicators of Bangladesh. Table 6.2 provides a survey of the structure and performance of the Bangladesh economy during the 1970s and 1980s. Table 6.3 presents glimpses of structural transformation that has been taking place, and Table 6.4 summarizes the changing structure of Bangladesh trade. At least two changes are noteworthy because of their profound long-term ramifications for the economy. First, in terms of share of gross

Table 6.1

Bangladesh Social and Human Development Indicators

	1973	*1985-1987*
Employment (% of labor force)		
Agriculture	79.0	57.0
Industry	5.0	10.0
Service	16.0	33.0
Human Development		
Life expectancy	45	52
Infant mortality rate	150	121
Crude birth rate	48	40
Daily calorie supply (% requirement)	91	83
School enrollment ratio, primary	73	60
Food Security		
Food production per capita index	100	88
Food import dependency	103	17

Source: United Nations Development Programme (1991).

Table 6.2

Structure and Performance of the Bangladesh Economy

	1970s (1973-1979)	*1980s (1980-1990)*
GDP growth	2.14	4.36
GDP share		
Agriculture	55.0	41.0
Industry	14.0	16.0
Service	31.0	43.0
Share of		
Nontraditional exports	16.0	36.0[a]
in total exports	n.a.	46.0[b]
Investment in GDP	10.0	13.0
Private investment in total investment	46.0	50.0
Gross national savings in total investment	22.0	41.0
Export earnings in imports	38.0	39.0
Foreign savings in imports	57.0	44.0
Foreign remittances in imports	4.0	18.0
Government size		
Public expenditure (% of GDP)	11.0	14.0
Revenues (% of GDP)	8.0	9.0

[a] Using conventional definition.

[b] Using modified definition.

Source: Author's estimates from World Bank data, World Bank (1991, 1992b).

domestic product (GDP), agriculture is no longer the predominant sector in Bangladesh; the country's service sector now contributes substantially more to GDP (48 percent in 1992) than agriculture (35 percent), though the labor force employed in agriculture (65 percent) still significantly exceeds service sector employment (20 percent). It needs to be pointed out that industry and service sector employment doubled in the past 20 years indicating the significant job creation potential of these sectors (particularly the latter) over the agricultural sector. The second most notable transformation occurred in the export sector where a decline in the share of traditional exports has been matched by a remarkable rise in the share of nontraditional exports (from a meager 7 percent in 1973 to 72 percent of exports in 1992). Though assessing the potential implications of this change is the main point of this paper, it makes sense to first examine these structural changes in the backdrop of the "patterns of development" approach of Chenery and Syrquin (1975) and Chenery (1979).

Table 6.3

Structural Change Indicators for the Bangladesh Economy

	1973	*1980*	*1990*
Shares of GDP			
Agriculture	57.0	50.0	38.0
Industry	12.0	16.0	16.0
Service	31.0	34.0	46.0
Nontraditional exports	7.0	23.0	56.0[a]
as share of total exports	n.a.	27.0	68.0[b]
Share of			
Investment in GDP	7.5	16.0	11.5
Private investment in total investment	35.0	39.0	48.0
Gross national savings in total investment	35.0	24.0	50.0
Capital spending (ADP) in public expenditure	58.0	63.0	43.0
Export as proportion of imports	50.0	32.0	44.0
Foreign aid as proportion of imports	45.0	56.0	37.0
Foreign remittance as proportion of imports	5.0	9.0	22.0
Government size			
Public expenditure	11.0	17.5	15.0
Revenues	5.0	10.5	9.0

[a] Using conventional definition.
[b] Using modified definition.
Source: Author's estimates from World Bank data, World Bank (1991, 1992b).

As Figures 6.1 and 6.2 show, Bangladesh presents the case of the "double scissors", one in the structure of production and another in exports. While the first scissors follows closely the predictions of the Chenery-Syrquin (1975) study, some differences need to be highlighted. The most pervasive features identified by Chenery were the transformation in production represented by the shift from agriculture to industrial production as well as the rise of the service sector. As may be observed in Figure 6.3, the Chenery-Syrquin study predicts the first cross at a per capita income of US$375–400 (in 1976 US$). Bangladesh seems to have reached that stage much earlier. The second cross, which is reached at about US$600 per capita income (when industry outstrips agriculture) is yet to be reached. What is obvious is that the growth of the service sector has been far more rapid than predicted, while industrial growth has traced a familiar pattern. Is the rise of the service sector a favorable institutional development? The leading industrial nations typically have a service sector GDP share between 50 percent and 60 percent. The Asian newly industrializing countries (NICs) have reached a share of between 46 and 54 percent with Singapore at 62 percent. Casual empiricism suggests that this is a promising development.

Figure 6.1
Structural Transformation in Production

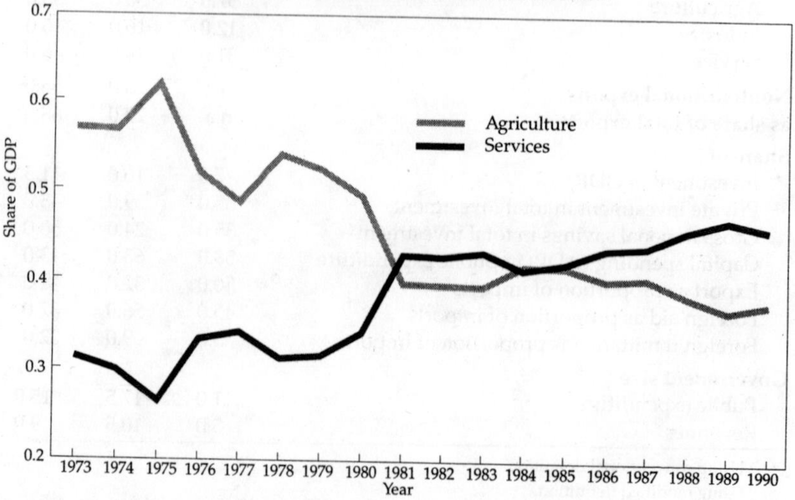

Source: World Bank (1979, 1992).

Figure 6.2
Structural Transformation in Composition of Exports

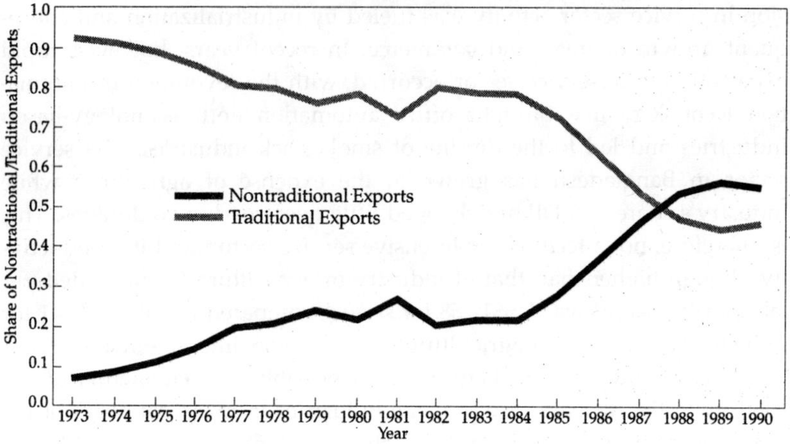

Source: World Bank (1991).

Figure 6.3
Patterns of Development

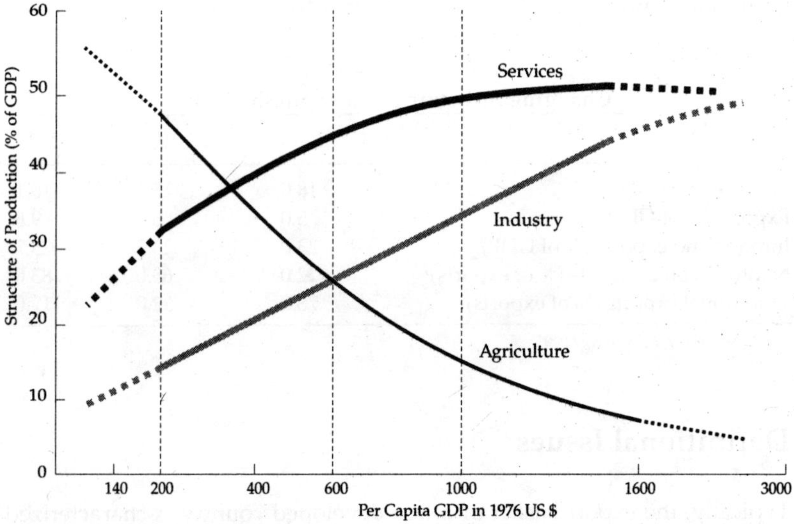

Source: Chenery and Syrquin (1975).

Service sector growth is linked to the expansion of industry and agriculture. For the developed economies and East Asian NICs, expansion in service sector activity was fueled by industrialization and consequent growth of trade and commerce. In recent years, however, rapid expansion of the service sector occurred, with the revolution in information technology that brought office automation and technology-based industries and led to the decline of smokestack industries. The service sector in Bangladesh has grown at the expense of agriculture while industry's share of GDP has changed little over nearly two decades. This is, therefore, not a technology-intensive service sector, and its productivity, though higher than that of industry or agriculture (value added per labor in 1992–1993 was US$1,258 for service compared to only US$541 for industry and US$252 for agriculture), is well below international levels.

The second scissors (Figure 6.2) is possibly a phenomenon of the 1980s with the meteoric rise of niche industries in many countries of the Pacific Rim, Indian Ocean, and Caribbean regions. A second "pattern of development" study for the post-1970 period is bound to capture this structural transformation in the export basket of many a previous primary exporter. It is too early to say whether Bangladesh is ahead in this game. This scissors portrays the progressively increasing share of nontraditional exports in the export basket with a corresponding decline in the share of traditional exports.

Table 6.4

Changing Structure of Bangladesh Trade

	1980	*1990*	*1993*
Imports (% of GDP)	18.0	16.6	16.1
Exports (% of GDP)	5.0	6.7	9.6
Imports and exports (% of GDP)	23.0	23.3	25.7
Nontraditional exports (% of exports)	22.0	68.0	83.0
Traditional exports (% of exports)	78.0	32.0	17.0

Source: World Bank (1993).

Definitional Issues

Typically, the export basket of a less developed country is characterized by the predominance of primary products based on mining extraction or agriculture. In recent decades, however, manufactured exports have grown in importance. Indeed, in textiles and some consumer durables, the cheap labor cost of less developed countries (LDCs) has resulted in the displacement of some developed country exports in the world market.[1]

Within the small manufacturing base of Bangladesh, jute manufactures, leather, and tea processing contribute significantly to exports. As a result, the correspondence between primary and traditional exports does not apply in the case of Bangladesh. Both primary products and manufactures (jute goods, processed tea, and leather products) make up the "traditional" exports of Bangladesh. In its "nontraditional" export category are processed primary products such as frozen fish and shrimps. Thus the "primary-traditional" and "manufactures-nontraditional" correspondence that one is likely to find in many developing country exports does not apply to Bangladesh (see Tables 6.5 and 6.5a).

Table 6.5
Exports List

Conventional	*Modified*
Traditional	
Raw jute	Raw jute
Jute manufactures	Jute manufactures
Tea	Tea
Jute specialty products	
Leather and leather products	
1992 share in exports (28%)	1992 share in exports (15%)
Nontraditional	
Readymade garments	Readymade garments
Frozen shrimps	Frozen shrimps
Fish and fish products	Fish and fish products
Frog's legs	Frog's legs
Newsprint, paper	Newsprint, paper
Urea	Urea
Naptha, furnace oil, bitumen	Naptha, furnace oil, bitumen
	Jute specialty products
	Leather and leather products
1992 share in exports (72%)	1992 share in exports (85%)

In its annual country economic memorandum, the World Bank has followed the practice of identifying as "traditional" exports those items that have historically dominated Bangladesh's export basket up until 1980. This classification of exports as "traditional" can be seen to depend on the "product" criteria, which suggests that historically predominant shares in the export basket determine "traditional" exports. Such "traditional" items include raw jute, jute manufactures, jute specialty products, tea, leather, and leather products. Among them, raw jute and tea are characterized by low income and price elasticities of foreign demand. While Bangladesh has a high market share in raw jute, its market share in jute specialty products and leather products is small but income and price elasticities are high. Such is the characteristic of most if not all "nontraditional" exports of Bangladesh.

Table 6.5a
Primary/Manufactures Versus Traditional/Nontraditional Exports
(value in million dollars)

Year	*Primary*	*Manufactures*	*Total*	*Traditional*	*Nontraditional*
1977	168.75	321.18	489.93	388.18	101.74
1978	232.16	377.58	409.74	462.97	146.78
1979	222.80	502.58	725.74	567.49	158.24
1980	209.33	504.08	713.41	527.14	186.26
1981	210.78	415.11	625.89	429.06	196.83
1982	243.17	443.43	686.60	473.69	212.91
1983	281.54	529.46	811.00	541.44	269.56
1984	316.62	617.81	934.43	599.90	334.53
1985	299.33	519.88	819.21	447.84	371.37
1986	298.37	778.24	1,076.61	435.65	641.07
1987	286.69	944.51	1,231.20	420.65	810.55
1988	300.72	990.84	1,291.56	416.78	874.78
1989	322.96	1,200.74	1,523.70	491.61	1,032.09
1990	306.13	1,411.42	1,717.55	431.99	1,285.56
1991	267.26	1,726.66	1,993.92	411.19	1,582.73
1992	313.91	2,068.98	2,382.89	399.36	1,982.53

Source: Exports Promotion Bureau of Bangladesh (1979, 1985, 1992).

The Exports Promotion Bureau of Bangladesh seems to take a somewhat modified approach by classifying items such as leather products and some jute specialty products as nontraditional exports in addition to what are historically classified as nontraditional exports of Bangladesh. We find this modified classification more amenable to economic analysis, as "traditional" and "nontraditional" exports could then be classified in accordance with uniform "elasticity" and "global market share" criteria as shown in Table 6.6.

Table 6.5b

Detailed List of Nontraditional Exports

Description	*Exports, 1992-1993 (million $)*
Manufactured Commodites	
Molasses	0.23
Petroleum by-products	36.81
Chemical products	57.64
Leather (crust/finished)	147.91
Jute manufactures	292.37
Handicrafts	5.43
Specialized textile and household linen	29.01
Knitwear and hosiery products	204.48
Readymade garments	1,240.48
Engineering products	17.51
Electronics	0.85
Other manufactured commodities	36.21
Subtotal	2,068.98
Primary Commodities	
Frozen foods	165.34
(frog's legs, shrimps, fish)	3.67
Subtotal	174.70
Total	2,243.68

Source: Exports Promotion Bureau of Bangladesh (1993c).

Thus, under this modified scheme, "traditional" exports appear to have a generally high market share and low elasticities, while "nontraditional" exports have a typically low market share and high elasticities.

The present paper pursues the modified route for classifying Bangladesh exports, opting for the "elasticity" and "global market share" criteria for classifying exports as traditional and nontraditional. The conceptual basis for this classification stems from the author's earlier work (Sattar 1984) as well as those of Schydlowsky and Rodrigues (1982). The elasticity test under this scheme requires traditional exports to have relatively low foreign price and income elasticities of demand. Primary products (raw jute and tea) fit this test squarely and are classified as traditional exports.

Table 6.6
An Exports Classification Scheme

Export Commodities	*Market Share*	*Income Elasticity*	*Price Elasticity*
Traditional			
Raw jute	High	Low	Low
Jute manufactures	High	Low	High*
Tea	Low**	Low	Low
Nontraditional			
Jute specialty products	Low	High	High
Readymade garments	Low	High	High
Frozen fish/shrimps	Low	High	High
Other (e.g., urea and newsprint)	Low	High	High

* High but not infinitely so.
** Low but not infinitesimal.

In contrast, jute goods have a higher price elasticity. While Bangladesh exports constitute nearly 30 percent of world exports of jute goods, domestic production is also a significant proportion of world production. Jute manufactures are therefore classified as traditional exports using the global market share test. But because leather and leather goods and jute specialty products both display high foreign income and price elasticities of demand and/or because Bangladesh only has a small market share, conceptually at least, the economy faces infinitely elastic demand curves for these products, thus also satisfying the small economy test. These are, therefore, classified as nontraditional exports although, historically, they have been lumped with the traditional exports of Bangladesh. The "small economy" test (infinite price elasticities, high income elasticities, and minuscule market share) is satisfied by much of the exports that gained prominence in the 1980s, e.g., garments, frozen shrimp, frog's legs, fish products, and newsprint. Table 6.5b provides a breakdown of traditional and nontraditional exports of Bangladesh under this modified approach. We shall refer to this as the "market" criteria (as opposed to the "product" criteria) for classifying exports.

To test the empirical validity of the export classification scheme above, in keeping with most time-series work of import and export equations, infinite price elasticity of exports is postulated, which then permits the estimation of export demand functions by single equation methods (see Goldstein and Khan 1985). Adding the small country assumption (so that the dollar price of exports and imports and hence the terms of trade could be viewed as exogenous) allows estimation of the following reduced form equations:

$$X = f_0\ (Y_w,\ TOT,\ RER)$$
$$NTX = f_1\ (Y_w,\ TOT,\ RER)$$
$$TX = f_2\ (Y_w,\ TOT,\ RER)$$

where

X	=	total exports
NTX	=	nontraditional exports
TX	=	traditional exports
Y_w	=	world income
TOT	=	terms of trade
RER	=	real exchange rate

The estimated results are summarized in Table 6.7.

Table 6.7
Estimates of Export Demand Functions

	United States GNP	*Total*	*RER*	*D-W*	*ADJ R2*
EQN (1)	3.37	0.23	0.63	2.04	0.94
	(11.97)*	(1.16)	(3.94)*		
EQN (2)	7.31	-0.30	0.69	1.94	0.95
	(13.45)*	(-0.19)	(3.64)*		
EQN (3)	1.50	0.27	0.89	1.85	0.82
	(3.65)*	(1.59)	(7.05)*		

* significant at 5 percent level.
Source: Author's estimates based on World Bank data, 1973-1992.

The results indicate that the United States gross national product (a proxy for foreign income) has the greatest influence on Bangladesh exports. The United States is, by far, the largest importer of Bangladesh products. As expected, the foreign income elasticity of demand is higher for nontraditional exports. The coefficients for the real exchange rate have the appropriate signs (positive) and are significant. Terms of trade have no appreciable influence on either exports category.

The results suggest that real exchange rates could be a powerful tool for export promotion. With some reservation, the results validate the propositions made with regard to classification of exports.

Nontraditional Exports in Growth Theory

A rich literature exists confirming the evidence of a favorable link between exports and economic growth (see, for example, Keesing 1967, Michaely 1977, Balassa 1978, Tyler 1981, Feder 1982, and Ram 1985). The emphasis of most studies seems to be limited to growth-modeling with inclusion of an appropriate export variable and determination of the statistical significance of the coefficients. The theoretical issue seems to be the contribution of the exports sector on aggregate factor productivity. Among the studies cited, only the Keesing and Balassa pieces deal with the advantages for less developed countries (LDCs) of switching from reliance on primary exports to manufactures.

The case for export-led growth is of course founded on Adam Smith's classical comparative advantage deftly put into proper perspective for underdeveloped countries by Hla Myint (1968) in his statement of the "vent-for-surplus" theory. Unfortunately, the record of export-led growth for LDCs relying on primary exports (which is what vent-for-surplus theory argued for) was dismal, particularly in the years following World War II.

The fundamental problem that emerges from such a strategy of export-led growth is that growth in primary production, albeit at minimal resource cost, while ensuring greater utilization of hitherto unemployed domestic resources, is often accompanied by sluggish growth of world demand for such products, thus giving rise to "terms of trade" pessimism and the much-heralded Prebisch-Singer thesis (Prebisch-Singer 1950). Furthermore, low income elasticities for primary exports means that growth of these exports over time could trail behind world income growth, thus giving rise to "growth" pessimism and even a possible "immiserizing" effect a la Bhagwati (1958). Moreover, the "dependency" school was quick to point out the emergence of "enclave" economies whose exports were mainly directed to the markets of former colonial masters with clearly uneven distribution of gains.

The case appears strong for Bangladesh to reduce its dependence on traditional exports and move vigorously toward expansion of nontraditional exports. The argument is based not merely on the benefits from export diversification but also on the potential advantages of shifting dependence on exports whose price variability is significantly lower than those of such primary exports as raw jute and tea, not to mention the fact that the relative international price index has moved against these two exports throughout the last decade. It follows then that the improvement in Bangladesh's terms of trade over the same period must be accounted for by the improvement in the export price index of other exports. This improvement in the terms of trade (in contrast with earlier declines) could be attributed to the growing predominance of nontraditional exports (NTX) in the exports basket. Casual empiricism further reveals that Bangladesh experienced stable and higher GDP growth rates during the 1980s compared to the 1970s (see Table 6.2) and the changing composition of exports could only have a positive contribution to this development.

Figure 6.3 portrays graphically the close association between the improvement in Bangladesh's terms of trade during most of the 1980s (68.6 in 1981-1982 to 116.75 in 1992-1993) and the increasing share of nontraditional exports in the export basket (31.45 in 1981-1982 to 83.24 in 1992-1993).

Macroeconomic Implications of Nontraditional Exports

In the previous section, we have presented the arguments for expansion of nontraditional exports as a means to promote growth and economic welfare. This section will examine some of the favorable macroeconomic implications of such a strategy over the alternative strategy of growth with traditional exports dominating the export basket.

The Bangladesh economy has reached the stage where a structural transformation has occurred in its composition of exports. As of 1992, nontraditional exports made up 85 percent of total exports (under the modified definition), with the switch from the predominance of traditional to nontraditional exports occurring around 1987. The macroeconomic implications of such a shift may be examined in the backdrop of the recent experience of the Bangladesh economy.

It has been argued earlier that nontraditional exports that satisfy the elasticities and market share criteria are characterized by infinitely elastic foreign demand curves (horizontal demand curves at fob prices, externally determined). The implication of this for domestic production is that it is wholly supply and not demand determined, as is shown in Figure 6.4. Production is no longer dependent upon the internal balance between domestic supply and domestic use.

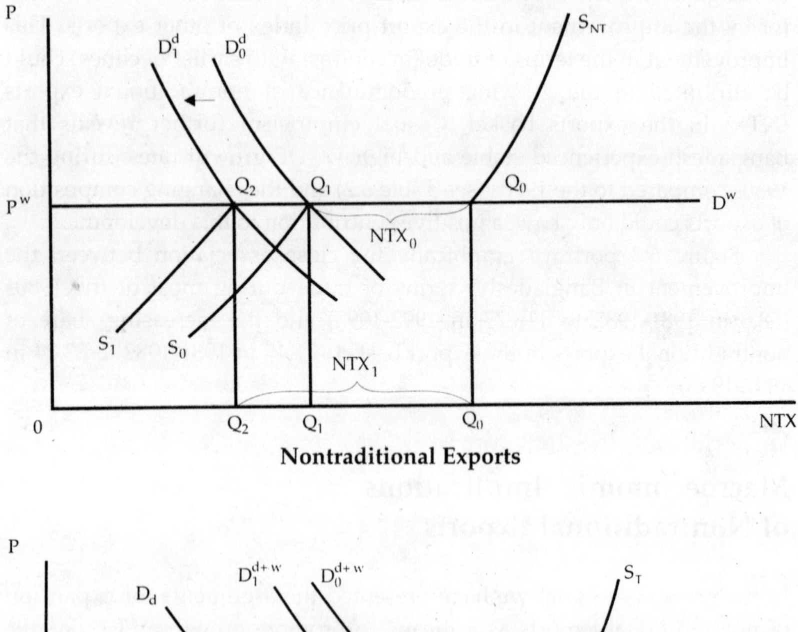

Nontraditional Exports

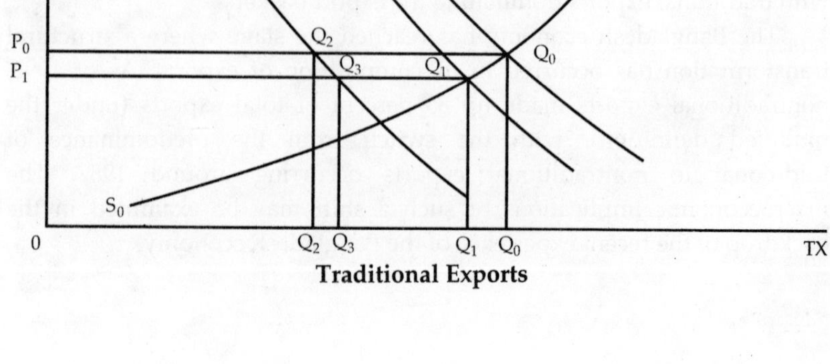

Traditional Exports

D^d is the domestic demand curve; the pinked curve, $S_\theta Q_1 S_{NT}$ is the domestic supply curve; and the horizontal line D^W represents world demand curve at price P^W. The quantity exported is Q_1 Q_0 which is the residual of domestic supply capacity and domestic demand. Clearly, the actual level of such exports depends not on changes in foreign demand but fluctuations in domestic demand. Given an infinitely elastic demand curve, domestic production is at maximum capacity (existence of excess capacity is unlikely). This ideal scenario is, in the real world, subject to two constraints that could significantly alter the final outcome: (a) to the extent that trade barriers (quotas or nontariff barriers) prevent the free entry of Bangladesh exports into world markets, the assumption of infinitely elastic demand curves will have to be replaced, perhaps with stepwise demand curves reflecting different levels of restrictions in segmented markets; (b) nontraditional exports production is geared entirely to the exports market under specific contracts that preclude the sale of these products in the domestic market. This gives rise to the nontraditional exports "enclave" scenario, which requires its own unique analysis not covered in the foregoing exposition (which was based on the assumption of an integrated production system catering to both domestic and foreign demand). It turns out that the leading nontraditional export of Bangladesh, namely, garments, falls in this category.

Figure 6.5 offers an exposition of a model with traditional exports. Note that the demand constraint for traditional exports production is the level of domestic demand plus foreign demand (*Dd+w*). This holds for primary production as well as processed materials (for example, jute manufactures) where the economy enjoys a significant market share. Consequently, the small country assumption does not apply and expansions of such exports can occur only at the expense of price reductions and some loss of export revenues. Dependence on traditional exports is no assurance for capacity production since the level of output is determined by domestic plus foreign demand which together could fall short of existing capacities. Total production is OQ_0 of which OQ_2 is the domestic demand and the balance, Q_2Q_0, is exported. Export supply in this case is constrained by world demand, *Dw*.

More importantly, it is possible to distinguish between the macro-economic impact of demand shocks for the two types of exportables. In Figure 6.4, for instance, a fall in domestic demand, from $D_0^{\,d}$ to $D_1^{\,d}$, leaves total activity $OP^wQ_0Q_0$ unchanged as the decline in domestic demand is compensated by an increase in exportable surplus (NTX_1 rather than NTX_0)

Figure 6.5
Trend in Real Exchange Rate Indices and Antiexport Bias

FY	AVG CPI	EPI	MPI	AVG ER	RPX	RPM	FY	RPX/RPM
1981	213	100.00	100.00	16.26	1.00	1.00	1980/81	1.00
1982	253	84.80	99.40	20.07	1.12	0.95	1981/82	1.18
1983	267	88.40	92.16	23.76	0.95	0.91	1982/83	1.04
1984	298	100.98	89.11	24.95	0.88	1.00	1983/84	0.88
1985	336	112.28	84.44	26.06	0.86	1.14	1984/85	0.75
1986	342	86.72	86.00	29.89	0.99	0.99	1985/86	1.00
1987	410	93.87	87.36	30.63	1.07	1.14	1986/87	0.94
1988	439	112.13	88.31	31.25	0.94	1.19	1987/88	0.79
1989	463	112.24	96.35	32.15	0.96	1.12	1988/89	0.86
1990	495	120.97	104.15	32.93	0.93	1.08	1989/90	0.86
1991	534	125.08	108.65	35.67	0.90	1.03	1990/91	0.87
1992	563	134.81	107.77	38.15	0.82	1.02	1991/92	0.80

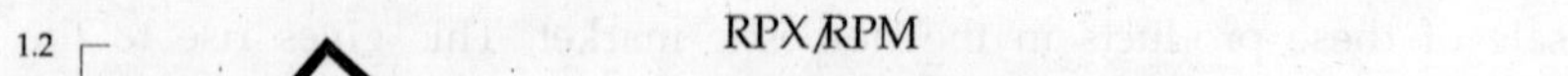

FY = Fiscal Year
AVG CPI = Average of rural and industrial CPI
EPI = Export price index
MPI = Import price index
AER = Average annual exchange rate
RPX = Real exchange rate for exports
RPM = Real exchange rate for imports
RPX/RPM = Measure of antiexport bias

Source: Bangladesh Bureau of Statistics (1994), World Bank (1992).

of nontraditional exports. This situation is contrasted by a decline in activity for traditional exports (Figure 6.5) as a consequence of a domestic demand shortfall that is not compensated by an increase of exportable surplus. The latter scenario implies a recessionary outcome (activity falling from $OP_0Q_0Q_0$ to $OP_1Q_1Q_1$) from adverse demand shocks with respect to traditional exports.

To study the macroeconomic implications of the existence or nonexistence of nontraditional exports in Bangladesh's export basket, we analyze the simulation results based on an open economy input-output model. Details of the model including a solution algorithm are presented in Appendix A and will be avoided here, for the sake of brevity.

The macroeconomic evaluation could be done in two phases: First, using the structure of the Bangladesh economy in the 1970s, when nontraditional exports were nonexistent, the economywide impact of introducing nontraditional exports may be simulated. The results might then be compared with actual data for the 1980s. Two sorts of results are worth examining: (a) output and income effects economywide, and (b) impact on growth and macroeconomic stability. Furthermore, a time series analysis of the linkage between nontraditional exports growth and economic performance (GDP growth) could point to the long-term relationship between the two variables.

Simulation results reveal the differential impact of export-led growth strategies based on traditional exports or nontraditional exports. In either case, the impact of activation is observed in economywide stimulation of activity levels (raising both income and spending). The expansionary impact is likely to be greater for the nontraditional exports regime in view of the fact that those manufacturing units that supply nontraditional exports are not subject to any demand constraint and, therefore, full capacity utilization is expected to be realized. No such possibility exists for the regime with only traditional exports where domestic production is limited by domestic use and income-inelastic foreign demand. It might be noted that activation effects for the nontraditional exports regime are a function, in the short term, of the degree of underutilization of capacities in the manufacturing sector. The World Bank-Boston University Study (1980) estimated such capacity utilization at 51 percent in 1976-1977, which was typical during the 1970s. The overall economywide impact will then depend on the size of the manufacturing sector in GDP, the linkage between this sector and the rest of the economy, input-output ratios, and so forth. Brief summaries of the simulation results are presented in Tables 6.8 and 6.9.

Table 6.8
Activation Effects of Trade Regimes Comparison of Traditional Exports and Nontraditional Export Trade Strategies
(in million Bangladesh taka)

	Benchmark	*TX* (Simulated)	*NTX* (Simulated)	*Share in* Benchmark	TX	NTX
GDP	109,822	119,322	129,837			
Agriculture	53,088	56,081	57,128	48%	47%	44%
Industry	13,272	19,092	24,669	12%	16%	19%
Service	43,462	44,149	48,040	40%	37%	37%

Note: TX = traditional exports.
NTX = nontraditional exports.

Source: Author's estimates from simulations.

For the sake of brevity, the impact on fiscal and trade balance of the two regimes is not stated here. Suffice it to say that the rise in activity levels stemming from greater utilization of industrial capacity generates higher tax revenues to reduce the current fiscal deficit while greater exports of both traditional and nontraditional categories produce an improved balance of trade picture. However, the rise in noncompetitive imports associated with higher output levels dampens the trade balance somewhat. In either case, the scenario is decidedly better for the nontraditional export regime.

A comparison of the simulation results with actual data for the 1980s reveals some remarkable similarities and some differences in trends. The model predicts the decline of the agricultural sector in GDP but fails to capture the growth of the service sector, both in terms of size and contribution to GDP growth.[2] As for the service sector, in reality, it grew dramatically in size, contributing as much as 44 percent of GDP growth during 1981-1990 with a GDP share of 46 percent in 1990. The service sector has demonstrated phenomenal growth instead of the declining growth predicted by the model. The model prediction is understandable in view of the fact that the nontraditional export regime relies entirely on the output increment of the manufacturing sector while service sector growth is merely expected to reflect the linkage effect. The model predicts the industrial sector growing at the expense of the agricultural sector while, in reality, during the 1980s, both service and industrial sectors expanded at the expense of agriculture.

Table 6.9
Increment in GDP, Sectoral Contributions

	TX	*NTX*
GDP	8.05	18.22
Agriculture	5.64%	18.22%
	(2.71)	(3.65)
Industry	43.85%	85.87%
	(5.18)	(10.30)
Service	1.32%	10.53%
	(0.16)	(4.27)

Note: TX = traditional exports.
NTX = nontraditional exports.

Source: Author's estimates from simulations.

Finally, the issue of macroeconomic stability in response to external shocks needs to be addressed. Bangladesh is an extremely open economy (exports and imports make up about 25 percent of GDP, not to mention all the foreign savings needed to cover the trade deficit each year); external developments have a significant impact on export levels, trade balance, and domestic economic activity. Two pertinent issues emerge with respect to the rise of nontraditional exports in its export basket:

- Since nontraditional exports have higher foreign income elasticities of demand, domestic economic activity will be more closely linked than before with developments in the industrialized nations, which are the main importers. Gains from world income growth are expected to be transmitted more easily; prosperity within will be closely linked to global prosperity but worldwide recession will likewise contribute to domestic decline. However, since the postwar period is characterized by roughly four years of expansion to each year of recession, the gains from this linkage are likely to more than offset losses.

- Export declines affecting traditional exports may lead to greater exports of nontraditional exports (resulting decline in domestic income and spending generates a higher exportable surplus of nontraditional exports in view of the absence of a demand constraint), thus ensuring greater macroeconomic stability.

Nontraditional Exports and Growth Performance

The record seems to suggest a relatively superior exports performance in the 1990s than in the 1970s mainly due to the rapid growth of nontraditional exports. Traditional exports did not grow at all in the 1970s and posted a sluggish growth of only 1.5 percent per annum in the 1980s. This compares with a 24 percent average growth for nontraditional exports in the 1970s and 14 percent for the 1980s. Thus most of the export growth for Bangladesh (14 percent in the 1970s, 9 percent in the 1980s, and 16 percent in the 1990s) is accounted for by expansion of nontraditional exports. How does this export performance affect the economy's growth performance? Since the economy's growth performance in the 1980s was relatively high (4.13 percent between 1980-1990) and stable, a plausible inference is that of a possible link between the two phenomena, though such a proposition needs to be tested empirically.

Research has established evidence of the positive impact of exports on growth performance of developing countries on the path of industrialization (see, for example, Balassa 1978 and Michaely 1977). Some have argued in terms of the beneficial effects of export production, namely, capacity utilization, scale economies from a larger market, and general competitive efficiency stemming from the incentives for technological and managerial innovations (Balassa 1978, Keesing 1967, Krueger 1980). Feder (1982) sums up these effects under the umbrella of the positive externality effect of the export sector, suggesting higher marginal factor productivities for the export sector. The present paper is based essentially on Feder's analysis with the addition that the externality effects and marginal factor productivities are relatively higher for nontraditional exports as compared to traditional exports, the implication being that transfer of resources from the latter to the former would raise aggregate factor productivity and economic growth.

The standard "sources of growth" approach (Solow 1956, Denison 1967) will be adopted here as the modeling framework with appropriate assumptions à la Feder about factor productivity differentials between export and nonexport sectors. A crucial assumption of this framework is that the nonexport sector enjoys positive "externalities" from exports production, stemming, for instance, from better-trained or more productive labor, innovative technology, or efficient management. Further modification to the Solow-Feder framework is provided by the bifurcation of investments attributable to public and private sources. (Model specifications including derivations are provided in Appendix B.)

For the present purpose, it is sufficient to report the estimated results from equation (7) of Appendix B, which are shown in Table 6.10.

Table 6.10
Exports and Growth Performance, 1979-92
(estimates from Modified Feder Model)

	POPN	*Ipr*	*Ipu*	*EXPORTS*	*ADJ R2*
Coefficient	0.9	0.07	-0.11	2.24	0.90
t-stat[a]	(0.12)	(3.49)[b]	(-4.91)[b]	(3.98)[b]	D-W=1.79 F=(15.9

[a] Though not reported, the equation is estimated with a constant term.
[b] Significant at the 5 percent level.

Note: Ipr = private investment
Ipu = public investment

Source: Author's estimates from World Bank data.

The results confirm the positive and significant impact of exports growth on GDP growth. As stated earlier, most of the growth in exports during the 1970s (14 percent), 1980s (9 percent), and 1990s (16 percent), is accounted for by nontraditional exports with traditional exports even declining in value over the entire period from US$463 million in 1978-1979 to a mere US$399 million in 1992-1993. Thus it is safe to conclude on the basis of empirical results reported that virtually all exports growth was accounted for by nontraditional exports and this contributed positively to the economy's growth performance. Another point worth noting is that the externality specified in the Feder model is a "static", not "dynamic", externality, in consequence of which the estimates might be understating the actual contribution of the nontraditional sector to economic performance. A more complete model would try to capture the knowledge and learning based productivity gains that accrue to the entire economy through input-output or backward linkages.

A curious though questionable result is the negative coefficient of the public investment variable (I_{pu}). This is in spite of several studies (for example, Taylor 1988, Sattar 1993) which cited evidence from many developing countries of the positive impact of public investments, particularly in infrastructure, on growth. However, the small sample size in the present instance precludes drawing firm conclusions on this issue.

Unlike public investments, private investments are shown to have a positive impact on growth. As expected, population growth is of no consequence to the growth of aggregate output. Until more time series data become available, these results need to be interpreted as being suggestive rather than conclusive.

Critical Issues in Nontraditional Exports Expansion

In the past decade, Bangladesh has been faced with a progressively shrinking market for its "traditional" exports, primarily due to the emergence of close substitutes for jute and jute goods and intense competition from rival suppliers (India and Thailand). Unless innovative changes are forthcoming in product quality or marketing strategy, the case for "traditional" exports expansion is all but lost.

An *exports expansion strategy* for the future must therefore focus on solidifying the gains already achieved in the nontraditional exports sector and must take effective steps to create new market opportunities globally and a supportive economic environment domestically.

The key ingredients of such a strategy must include:

- Identification of activities with proven or potential comparative advantage.
- Provision of a competitive cost structure to exporters by ensuring world-priced inputs (through an effective duty drawback scheme for dutiable imported inputs) and maintenance of real wages in line with productivity.
- Elimination of any antiexport bias in the tariff and quota rationing regime by scaling down nominal and effective protection while removing quota rations imposed for trade reasons.
- Assurance of the profitability of export production through effective exchange rate management to yield a favorable real exchange rate to the exporter.
- The streamlining of the regulatory and incentive framework while devising selective interventions for an export push.

A Review of Export Strategy

The government's commitment to exports with a particular emphasis on expansion of nontraditional exports is to be found in the Export Policy Order (EPO) 1993-1995. The EPO outlines the general thrust of the strategy with the incentive regime built around it. While most incentives address the profitability concerns of exporters in general, the strategy is clearly to promote the growth of nontraditional exports.

Identification of Potential Exports

On the basis of Bangladesh's resource endowment (cheap and abundant unskilled labor and plentiful proven reserves of natural gas), there is a presumption of potential comparative advantage in the following commodity groups: yarn and textile fabrics as inputs into the garments sector, various leather products (such as shoes, luggage, bags), fish processing, chemical products using natural gas as feed stock, and numerous specialty products based on jute fiber.

The task of identifying exports with proven or potential comparative advantage could be facilitated by undertaking exercises to determine effective rates of protection and domestic resource costs of existing or nonexistent activities. A study of this nature is soon to be undertaken by the Tariff Commission under the aegis of World Bank's ISAC-II[3] credit.

Mechanism for Providing a Competitive Cost Structure

Two facilities that have been operating successfully for garments exporters are the private bonded warehouse and the special bonded warehouse, both of which permit duty-free importation of inputs for readymade garments under back-to-back letters of credit (L/C). Recently, the special-bonded warehouse facility has been extended to cover nongarment export industries (such as leather products) and input imports under a more flexible arrangement without back-to-back L/Cs. More recently, NBR has taken a significant step forward in allowing duty-free imports of capital machinery to 100 percent export-oriented industries.[4] The Duty Exemption and Drawback Office (DEDO) of NBR was recently revamped under the Export Development Project (EDP) to streamline procedures and expedite disbursement of duty drawbacks on an actual or flat-rate basis. Estimation of input-output coefficients and calculation of flat rates is an ongoing task of DEDO, which has disbursed duty drawbacks of over Tk 145 crore in the past year. Setting up of export processing zones (EPZ) with tax and duty-free privileges and adequate provision of infrastructure facilities has encouraged some foreign and domestic investors to set up industries in the nongarments sector.

To maintain a competitive edge in the world market, it is imperative that real wages in Bangladesh do not fall out of line with labor productivity. There are disturbing trends, however. Firstly, during the decade of the 1980s, real wages in the textile sector have risen by 20-25 percent, but an evaluation of productivity trends (output per employed textile worker) shows no appreciable increase during the same period, implying an erosion of export competitiveness on this account. Unless this trend is halted, on an international scale, the exports sector might face the prospects of becoming a relatively high-wage, low-productivity sector. Secondly, the antagonistic relationship among management, labor unions, and the government is a hindrance to investments and growth in this sector. What is clearly needed for the nontraditional exports sector is a conducive environment for competitive wage setting.

Removing Antiexport Bias in the Trade Regime

Until recently, the trade regime in Bangladesh was geared toward a strategy of import-substituting industrialization with heavy protection to domestic activities without regard to considerations of efficiency or domestic resource costs. This scenario is changing, though not as rapidly as is warranted by the present highly competitive international trade scene.

The antiexport bias of the trade regime in Bangladesh is evident from the tariff structure consisting of high nominal and effective tariff rates, a quota rationing scheme that generates undue rents on imports, and an exchange rate that is typically overvalued. This situation is fast changing with trade policy switching from an inward-oriented strategy of import substitution to an outward-looking strategy of export promotion based on the economy's existing and potential comparative advantage.

The antiexport bias of the trade regime is being gradually eroded as average nominal protective tariffs keep crumbling under tariff reforms (the unweighted mean tariffs, which were 89 percent in funding year [FY] 1990/1991, came down to 39 percent for FY1993/1994, while the import-weighted mean was reduced from 42 percent in FY1990/1991 to 28 percent in FY1993/1994).

The government is committed to a policy of trade liberalization and the promotion of productive efficiency. Accordingly, tariff reforms have received high priority in its policy agenda and, until June 1993, the following significant measures have been adopted.

Reduction of High Tariffs

The average nominal tariff has been scaled down from 75 percent in 1991 to only 36 percent in June 1993. The new Bangladesh Customs Tariff 1993 sets a maximum statutory[5] duty at 100 percent for all commodities with the exception of two product groups: cigarette paper and alcoholic beverages. Over 100 percent rates are retained for these items for nontrade reasons.

Revenue neutrality of the tariff regime has been ensured by following a "concertino" approach whereby low rates (0 to 10 percent) have been raised to 15 percent with the exception of critical inputs into industry, agriculture, health, or education (for example, capital machinery, raw materials for pharmaceutical products, and agricultural insecticides still have tariffs between zero and 7.5 percent). Although inputs are subject to other taxes and fees (namely, VAT, supplementary duty, and license fees), the government has decided to use customs duties as the only protective instrument (nonquota rationing). Currently, protective rates of duty are 60, 75, or 100 percent for final consumer goods while 45 percent is the maximum operative tariff on such products for the purpose of revenue. Further, tariff realignment for inputs and outputs has led to the adoption of a "stage of processing" approach to rate setting whereby the lowest rates (7.5 or 15 percent) are set for basic raw material and capital machinery, higher rates (15 or 30 percent) for intermediate inputs, and the highest rate (45 percent) for final consumer goods.

Transparency in Tariff Administration

On the matter of tariffs, Bangladesh has taken only the first steps toward achieving the goal of uniform tariffs—a system that ensures nondiscriminatory protection, besides adding the qualities of clarity, simplicity, and transparency to tariff administration. To improve productive efficiency, several anomalies in the tariff structure have been addressed (e.g., eliminating multiplicity of rates for similar products, removing discriminatory rates between end-users, reducing dispersion in the tariff structure, and conforming to only seven tariff rates overall). Finally, the publication in July 1993 of the Bangladesh Operative Tariff Schedule 1993-1994 has presented in one document complete information on trade taxes and fees for the benefit of, among others, domestic producers and potential investors.

Reforming the Quota Rationing Regime

A key ingredient of trade liberalization is the replacement of quota rations with equivalent tariffs. The government of Bangladesh has, in most part, subscribed to the principle of having tariffs as the only protective instrument, and limiting quota rations to those imports that need to be restricted for nontrade reasons (e.g., health, religion, national security, or environment). Owing to the hitherto complex system of quota rations that often combined trade and nontrade arguments, no effort has been made to devise tariff equivalence of any sort. Instead, a principle of "dual CD maxima" has been accepted: 45 percent maximum CD on revenue grounds and 75 percent maximum CD on protection grounds.

The government's commitment to trade liberalization is evident in the diminished role of the Office of Chief Controller of Imports and Exports (CCI&E) that resulted from the drastic changes brought about in the Import Policy Order 1993-1995, which involved major cutbacks in the number of items whose importation is restricted (mainly on nontrade grounds).[6]

Exchange Rate Management for Export Competitiveness

Maintaining a favorable exchange rate for exports is critical for retaining incentives in export production. The key variable here is not the nominal but the real exchange rate (*RER*), suitably defined. Among the various measures of *RER*, one formulation that is becoming popular defines the *RER* in terms of the relative price of nontradables to tradables. An increase in the relative price of tradables would be construed as a depreciation of the exchange rate resulting in a rise in the profitability of exports.

The following formulation will illustrate this point:

Let $RER = RPNT = CPI/(e^{*}PT)$

where $RPRNT$ = relative price of nontraded to traded
CPI = consumer price index, conventionally used as proxy for price of nontraded
e = nominal exchange rate, Tk/$
PT = weighted average price of tradables, $mPM + xPX$

where *m* and *x* are shares of imports and exports in foreign trade, and *PM* and *PX* are US dollar price indices of imports and exports, respectively.

Based on the above formulation, export incentives could be ensured through a depreciation of the *RER*, which could result from: (a) depreciation of the nominal exchange rate, *e*; (b) improvement in the terms of trade[7]; and (c) a lowering of domestic inflation. While a structural transformation of the export basket has led to some improvement in Bangladesh's terms of trade, adverse shifts in the composition of fiscal expenditure contributed to an appreciation of the real exchange rate (Table 6.11):

Table 6.11
Trends in Real Exchange Rate

	RER
FY1981	1.00
FY1982	0.98
FY1983	0.96
FY1984	0.99
FY1985	1.06
FY1986	1.05
FY1987	1.10
FY1988	1.17
FY1989	1.16
FY1990	1.12

Note: An increase in the index is equivalent to an appreciation of the real exchange rate.
Source: World Bank (1992).

In the past decade, domestic inflation has been contained while the terms of trade have registered significant appreciation, thanks to the structural shift in exports toward nontraditional exports. Then it must be the case that nominal depreciation of the exchange rate, *e*, was not significant enough to offset the impact of other domestic policies that raise the relative price of nontradables. Matin (1991) has argued that a shift in composition of public expenditure in Bangladesh during the past decade has been responsible for the appreciation in the *RER*. He shows that current expenditures rose from 5.6 percent of GDP in FY1981 to 8.8 percent in FY1990 while the capital spending (ADP) component declined from 10.1 percent to 6.4 percent in FY1990 period. Current expenditures typically finance operations and maintenance costs and wage payments for nontradable services. It is the latter component that grew faster than the former. Again, the decline in the public investment share was most severe in the outlays on economic and physical infrastructure. The net result was an increase in the domestic demand for nontradables to tradables and, consequently, an increase in the relative price of nontradables.

This adverse trend in the composition of public expenditures has been somewhat halted in the 1990s except for the recent poor performance in ADP implementation, which continues to pose a problem. As a share of GDP, current expenditures (8.6 percent in FY1993) have remained static since 1989 while ADP expenditures (6.9 percent in FY1993) improved slightly.

Thus to maintain Bangladesh's export competitiveness in this decade, current trends in fiscal composition ought to change if the relative price of tradables is to be improved, and if significant depreciation of the nominal exchange rate is to be avoided to compensate for the adverse impact of our fiscal stance on export competitiveness.

Based on the alternative formulation of the real exchange rate, estimates of the relative returns to exports (*RPX*) and importables (*RPM*) could be computed using the formula:

$$RPX = CPI/(e^{*}EPI)$$
$$RPM = CPI/(e^{*}MPI)$$

The table and accompanying graph in Figure 5 describe the trend in relative real returns to exports and imports. A measure of antiexport bias can be obtained using the ratio *RPX/RPM*—a decline in this ratio being consistent with a lowering of antiexport bias inherent in the fiscal and trade regime. The estimates show that following a peak reached in 1985-1986, antiexport bias has been falling consistently, reaching a low of 0.80 in 1991-1992. With a further reduction in import duties, and a favorable shift in the composition of public expenditures via curbs on current expenditures in recent years, the momentum has been sustained. Most recently, the Bangladesh taka has been made convertible on the trade account, essentially unifying the exchange rate for exports and imports.

Streamlining Regulatory and Institutional Frameworks

Experience suggests that it is not enough to design a package of incentives for export expansion without simultaneously revamping the institutions responsible for implementing it. By all evidence, institutional weakness and stifling regulatory mechanisms are major stumbling blocks on the path to expansion of exports. Efforts are on, under the umbrella of ISAC-II, to remove many of the superfluous regulatory procedures relating to trade and investments, leaving only promotional tasks for such institutions as the Board of Investment and the Export Promotion Bureau, not to mention the considerably diminished role of the CCI&E. Needless to say, success of the financial packages for export promotion, such as the Export Credit Guarantee, Export Promotion Fund, Duty Drawback Facility, etc. depend squarely on the effectiveness of the institutions made responsible for operating these schemes. Much work remains to be done in this area before potential investors can perceive a real improvement in the profitability of exports.

Conclusion

The economy of Bangladesh has undergone structural transformation in two significant areas: composition of output and exports. The service sector now contributes more to GDP than agriculture and nontraditional exports dominate export trade. The emergence and rapid growth of nontraditional exports is a leap forward for the Bangladesh economy which, if sustained through appropriate incentives and liberalization strategies, has the potential to produce the breakthrough needed to reduce dependence on foreign aid and to embark on the path of sustained growth.

It is sobering to recognize that despite many favorable trends in the export sector, Bangladesh's growth performance at an average rate of 4 percent remains below its potential and well behind rates posted by high-performing Asian economies such as Malaysia, Thailand, and Indonesia, not to mention the People's Republic of China and other East Asian NICs. Quite apart from certain institutional weaknesses (such as poor infrastructure and inefficient bureaucracy) the most dynamic component of exports (readymade garments) is characterized by low domestic value added and negligible backward linkages to make a serious impact on the economy's growth performance. While potential exists both for diversification of exports and expansion of backward linkages, considerable improvement is warranted in the regulatory and policy environment before the export sector's performance in terms of output, employment, and investments can match those of competing nations in South and East Asia to significantly affect Bangladesh's growth performance.

The exports sector promises to be the focal point of policy attention in Bangladesh for much of this decade. The success or failure of its policies could well be judged by its export performance which, in turn, will have an impact on the economy's growth performance.

Appendix A

Macromodeling of the Economy with Traditional/Nontraditional Exports

The macroeconomic outcome of structural transformation in the composition of exports might be depicted within the framework of an open economy input-output model for Bangladesh. The sectoral demand-supply balances for the Bangladesh economy might be expressed, using an input-output system, in the following matrix form:

$$Q + CM + NCM = A^d Q + A^n Q + F + X \tag{1}$$

where

Q	=	vector of output
CM	=	vector of competitive imports
NCM	=	vector of noncompetitive imports
A^d	=	domestic input-output coefficient matrix
A^n	=	matrix of noncompetitive imports
F	=	vector of final demand (private and public consumption and investment)
X	=	vector of exports
$A^d Q$	=	domestic intermediate demand
$A^n Q$	=	NCM

To demonstrate the macroeconomic impacts of transformation in the exports sector, consider a break-up into traditional, nontraditional and service sectors such that output vector

$$Q = \begin{bmatrix} Q_t \\ Q_{nt} \\ Q_s \end{bmatrix} \tag{2}$$

where

Q_t comprises mostly agricultural output,

Q_{nt} covers industry and manufacturers, and

Q_s represents output of service or nontraded sectors.

To conform to this sectoral division of output, the exports vector may likewise be compartmentalized as follows:

$$X = \begin{bmatrix} X_t \\ X_{nt} \\ 0 \end{bmatrix} \tag{3}$$

X_t	=	traditional exports arising out of production in agricultural sectors
X_{nt}	=	nontraditional exports arising out of production mainly in the industrial or manufacturing sector
0	=	null vector indicating no exports for nontraded sectors

Two balance equations now emerge from the original equation (1) to reflect the existence or nonexistence of nontraditional exports. The solution algorithm for the two scenarios also differ as demonstrated below:

Case I: Only Traditional Exports Exist

The general balance equation for an economy that exports only traditional products (primary exports) may be expressed as

$$Q + CM = AQ + F + X_T \tag{4}$$

The exports vector, X_T, consists of nonzero elements for the traditional sector only, with zero elements for nontraditional and nontraded sector. Competing imports (*CM*) exist wherever domestic demand exceeds installed capacity such that

$$CM = D - Q^* \tag{5}$$

where Q^* represents capacity output and D reflects aggregate demand ($AQ+F+X$). The solution for output in this case will be given by the lesser of demand or installed capacity:

$$Q = \min[D, Q^*] \tag{6}$$

Hence, for any sector i,

$$D_i > Q_i^* \text{ implies } Q_i = Q_i^*, \text{ and } CM_i = D_i = Q_i$$
$$D_i < Q_i^* \text{ implies } Q_i = D_i^*, \; CM_i = 0$$

For Bangladesh, this means that production in such traditional sectors as jute manufactures will be constrained by the sum of domestic and foreign demand (inelastic) with the distinct possibility of excess capacities persisting in these sectors. Output determination in such sectors as jute and tea follow the same principle though capacities in these agricultural sectors would have to be treated as undefined.

Case II: Nontraditional Exports Emerge

To reflect the emergence of nontraditional exports (in an integrated production system rather than export enclaves) requires modification of the preceding balance equations as well as the output solution mechanism. The general system of balance equations might be restated as follows:

$$Q = AQ + F + XM \tag{7}$$

This is represented by essentially the same set of balance equations as in (4), except that one component of demand is characterized by the net export-import vector, [XM], such that

$$XM = \begin{bmatrix} X_T \\ XMnt \\ 0 \end{bmatrix} \tag{8}$$

Assuming that imports are nonexistent in the traditional sectors, competing imports are recorded for the nontraditional sectors such that the nontraditional part of the exports-import vector may consist of both positive (exports) and negative elements (imports). The solution system is also somewhat different from (6) and may be stated thus:

$$Q = \min\,[AQ + F + XM, Q^*] \tag{9}$$

The net exports-imports vector, [*XM*], might then be characterized as follows: for traditional sectors, traditional exports, X_T, are exogenously determined by foreign demand; for nontraditional sectors, there is endogeneity in both export and import determination.

For sector *i*,

$$\text{If } XM_i < 0, \text{ implies } CM_i > 0 \text{ and } X_i = 0$$
$$\text{If } XM_i > 0, \text{ implies } CM_i = 0 \text{ and } X_i > 0$$

Thus for any sector *i*,

$$D_i > Q_i^*, \text{ implies } Q_i = Q_i^*, \text{ and } CM_i = D_i - Q_i^*$$
$$D_i < Q_i^*, \text{ implies } Q_i = Q_i^*, \text{ and } X_i = Q_i^* - D_i$$

The solutions, $X_i = Q_i^* - D_i$ reflect the characteristics of nontraditional exports described earlier in the text.

Model Solution

Given the diverse nature of output determination for each category of sectors—output is demand-determined for sectors with traditional exports and supply-determined for sectors with nontraditional exports or competitive imports—the solution pattern is nonuniform. The model, therefore, needs to be solved through an iterative algorithm that can be readily devised on a microcomputer. This procedure was followed to stimulate the macroeconomic aggregates for the Bangladesh economy using a 47-sector input-output table and associated final demand vectors (Bangladesh Planning Commission 1980).

Appendix B

The economy is assumed to consist of two sectors: the nonexports sector (Y) and the exports sector (X), the latter being made up of traditional and nontraditional exports. The fact that production of Y benefits from the production of X is captured in the following production functions:

$$Y = f(K_y, L_y, X) \quad (1)$$

$$X = g(K_x, L_x) \quad (2)$$

$$\text{and } X = N(K_x, L_x) + T(K_x, L_x) \quad (3)$$

where Y = nonexports production
X = exports production
T = output of traditional exports
N = output of nontraditional exports
K_y, L_y = capital stock and labor force allocated to nonexports
K_x, L_x = capital stock and labor force allocated in exports production

By definition,

$$K = K_y + K_x,\ dK = dK_y + dK_x = I$$

$$I = I_{PR} + I_{PU} = dk_{PR} + dk_{PU}$$

where I_{PR} and I_{PU} are private and public investments respectively, and

Labor force, $L = L_y + L_x$,

and aggregate output, $Q = Y + X = Y + TX + NTX$ (4)

In addition, it is assumed that the marginal factor productivities diverge so that their ratios might be equal to $(1 + \phi)$:

$$\frac{g_k}{f_k} = \frac{g_L}{f_L} = 1 + \phi \quad (5)$$

where $f > 0$ implies marginal factor productivities in the exports sector. A final assumption of Feder is about the linear relationship between the marginal productivity of labor in each sector and average productivity for the economy:

$$f_L = \beta\ (Q/L) \text{ and } g_l = \alpha(Q/L) \quad (6)$$

Total differentiation of equations (1) and (2), manipulation of results by including equations (4) – (6), give us the following estimating equation:

$$dQ^* = \alpha d L^* + \beta_0 d K^*_{pr} + \beta_1 d K^*_{pu} + \delta dX^* \quad (7)$$

The following notations are observed:

$$dQ^* = (dQ\ /\ Q), + dL^* = (dL\ /\ L), dK^*_{pr} = (dK_{pr}\ /\ Q), dK^*_{pu} = (dk_{pu}\ /\ Q)$$

$$dX^* = (dX\ /\ X)(X\ /\ Q) = (dX\ /\ Q)$$

Notes

1. Growth of manufactured exports from low and middle income Asian countries in the 1980s was more rapid than that of the rest of the world. Consequently, the share of manufactured exports from developing countries rose from 10 percent in 1980 to an estimated 22 percent in 1993 (*The Economist*, 2 April 1994).

2. This is largely due to underestimates of service sector input-output coefficients in the 1976-1977 Input-Output table for Bangladesh (Bangladesh Planning Commission 1980).

3. Industrial Sector Adjustment Credit II of $100 million.

4. In general, export-oriented units are firms 70 percent of whose production are exported. Such firms can import capital machinery at a concessional duty rate of 5 percent and, if located in a less developed area of the country, at only 2.5 percent duty.

5. The applicable rate of duty (operative rate) may be equal to or less than the statutory rate. The National Board of Revenue is empowered under the Customs Act 1969 to grant exemptions from the statutory rates of duty to the extent that it deems necessary.

6. Negotiations between the government of Bangladesh and the World Bank are continuing for finalization of a fully codified Control List in Import Policy Order 1993-1995 that retains restrictions mostly on nontrade grounds.

7. Between 1981 and 1990, the terms of trade index rose 29 percent, with exports price index rising 36 percent and the import price index up only 12 percent.

References

Balassa, B., 1978. "Exports and Economic Growth: Further Evidence." *Journal of Development Economics* 5(2): 181-9.

Bangladesh Bureau of Statistics, 1994. *Statistical Yearbook of Bangladesh*. Dhaka.

Bangladesh Planning Commission (BPC), 1980. *The Structure of the Bangladesh Economy: An Input-Output Analysis*. Dhaka.

Bhagwati, J., 1958. "Immiserizing Growth: A Geometric Note." *Review of Economic Studies*.

Chenery, H., 1979. *Structural Change and Development Policy*. Baltimore: Johns Hopkins Press.

Chenery, H., and M. Syrquin, 1975. *Patterns of Development, 1950-1970*. London: Oxford University Press.

Denison, E., 1967. "Sources of Post-War Growth in Nine Western Countries." *American Journal of Developing Economies* 57.

The Economist, 1994. 2 April 1994.

Feder, G., 1982. "On Exports and Economic Growth." *Journal of Development Economics* 12:59-73.

Goldstein, M., and M. S. Khan, 1985. "Income and Price Effects in Foreign Trade." In *Handbook of International Trade.* Washington: International Monetary Fund.

Keesing , D., 1967. "Outward-Looking Policies and Economic Development." *Economic Journal* 77(306):303-20.

Krueger, A., 1980. "Trade Policy as an Input to Development." *American Economic Review* 70(2):288-92.

Matin, K., 1991. "How Composition of Public Expenditure Affects Competitiveness: The Case of Bangladesh." World Bank, Washington. Mimeographed.

Michaely, M., 1977. "Exports and Growth: An Empirical Investigation." *Journal of Development Economics* 4(1):49-53.

Myint, H., 1968. "The Classical Theory of International Trade and Underdeveloped Countries." *Economic Journal* 68.

Prebisch, R., 1950. *The Economic Development of Latin America and its Principal Problems.* New York: United Nations.

Ram, R., 1985. "Exports and Economic Growth: Some Additional Evidence." *Economic Development and Cultural Change* 33(2):415-25.

Sattar, Z., 1984. "Resource Allocation Impacts and Activation Effects of Trade Policies: A Case Study of Bangladesh." Ph.D. Dissertation. Boston University, Massachusetts.

———, 1993. "Public Expenditure and Economic Performance: A Comparison of Developed and Low-Income Developing Economies." *Journal of International Development* 5(1):27-49.

Schydlowsky, D., and M. Rodrigues, 1982. "Vulnerability of Small Semi-Industrialized Economies to External Shocks." In M. Syrquin and S. Teitel, eds. *Trade, Stability, Technology and Equity in Latin America.* New York: Academic Press.

Singer, H.W., 1950. "The Distribution of Gains Between Borrowing and Investing Countries." *American Economic Review* 40(2):473-98.

Solow, R.M., 1956. "A Contribution to the Theory of Economic Growth." *Quarterly Journal of Economics* 20(1):65-76.

Taylor, L., 1988. *Varieties of Stabilization Experience.* Oxford: Clarendon Press.

Tyler, W., 1981. "Growth and Export Expansion in Developing Countries: Some Empirical Evidence." *Journal of Development Economics* 9(3):121-30.

United Nations Development Programme, 1991. *Human Development Report 1991*. New York: Oxford University Press.

World Bank, 1979. Report No. 2870-BD, 1979. Washington, D.C.

———, 1991. "Bangladesh Managing Public Resources for Higher Growth." Report No. 9379-BD. Washington, D.C.

———, 1992a. "Bangladesh Selected Issues in External Competitiveness and Economic Efficiency." Report No. 10265-BD. Washington, D.C.

———, 1992b. *World Development Report*. Washington, D.C.

———, 1993. "Bangladesh Implementing Structural Reform." Report No. 11569-BD. Washington, D.C.

World Bank, and Boston University, 1980. "The Industrial Comparative Advantage of Bangladesh." Unpublished mimeo.

7 Foreign Direct Investment: Problems and Prospects

Sadrel Reza and M. Ali Rashid

In a broad sense, foreign direct investment (FDI) refers to the transfer of finance and intangible corporate assets, including global market links, by nonresidents who have an effective voice (in contrast to private portfolio investors) in the management of the enterprise in which they invest. Traditionally, such investments were in the form of whole or majority ownership. In recent times, however, there has been a proliferation of new forms of minority ownership including a variety of nonequity contractual arrangements such as licensing franchising; counter trade; coproduction agreements; managerial contracts; turnkey operations; joint projects in research, production and marketing; as well as some more complex arrangements under bilateral or multilateral government agreement.[1]

In recent years, particularly following the recession of 1981-1982, there has been a tremendous upsurge in the global FDI flow. During the period 1983-1989, for example, FDI is estimated to have grown by an unprecedented (nominal) rate of nearly 30 percent per annum, which was three times the corresponding growth rate of exports and four times that of world output (UNCTC 1989). More specifically, by the end of the eighties, the annual FDI flow was close to $200 billion, which was three to four times the average flow during 1975-1984. As a result, the global FDI stock tripled from about $500 billion in 1980 to over $1.5 trillion by 1990 (Oman 1993). This change was brought about by a combination of a sustained increase in world output, a spectacular growth in the services sector, a sharp rise in technological networking or *technoglobalism*, and the *globalization* of intercorporate competition and cooperation as evidenced by the proliferation of corporate mergers and takeovers. So dramatic has been the change that according to some observers (see Brewer 1991, 47) "a new FDI era has arrived—an era marked by a greater recognition of the benefits of FDI ...."

The new FDI era, in one sense, represents the final stage of the three interrelated, but analytically separable, phases of growing international linkages among countries since the end of the Second World War (Ostry 1992). The first phase, characterized as the golden age of the 1950s and 1960s, was driven by trade resulting from the dismantling of protectionist barriers in successive GATT rounds. The second phase was initiated by three massive commodity and oil shocks over the 1970s, and was characterized by financial integration via the recycling of the systems of the Organization of Pertroleum Exporting Countries (OPEC). The present third phase, beginning in the early 1980s, is called globalization and is led by waves of FDI.

Yet, most of the developing countries as a group, apart from the dynamic Asian economies, have largely been bypassed by the current FDI boom. For example, the share of the developing world in global FDI inflow fell from 20 percent in 1980-1984 to around 10 percent in 1988-1989. In fact, FDI is much more concentrated now than are trade flows: the Group of Five (France, Germany, Japan, United Kingdom, and United States) accounts for over 75 percent of FDI but just over 40 percent of world trade. Major changes have also occurred in sources and origin of FDI. By 1983, the United States became a net recipient of FDI, and, by 1985, Japan became the largest net direct investor followed by the United Kingdom and the former Federal Republic of Germany.[2]

As far as Bangladesh is concerned, its performance in attracting FDI until now has been extremely poor, although significant reform and liberalization measures have been instituted in recent years. This chapter makes an attempt to analyze the patterns of FDI inflows into Bangladesh, the policy frame surrounding the same, the problems that have hindered growth, and ways and means of improving future prospects.

Rationale of FDI Flows

While conventional trade theories do not permit any company-specific advantage because of the assumption of perfect competition, the theory of FDI draws specifically on the role of companies/firms as creators and exploiters of intangible assets (Hymer 1976). From this perspective, FDI is viewed to take place only in imperfect markets and it is the firm, not the country, that is the real actor causing FDI flows across national borders (Ozawa 1992).

The emergence of the multinational enterprise and associated internationalization of production has been viewed primarily as a response to the existence of transaction cost and factor cost incentives for global integration of related activities (Dunning 1981, Teece 1986, Kruggman 1990). The necessary conditions for international production have been specified as: (i) possession of owner-specific advantages by the firm (for example, a monopoly, brand name, a patent, or a superior knowledge of the market); (ii) local production under equity ownership or internationalization leading to enhanced exploitation of these advantages relative to arm's length transactions (such as licensing and exporting); and (iii) overseas locational factors (such as high-quality, low-wage labor; low transportation costs; or policy-determined advantages and direct incentives), which are more favorable than domestic ones.

In a dynamic setting, the comparative advantage itself changes as in Raymond Vernon's (1966) product life cycle theory of trade and investment, which explicitly brings in the factor of a hierarchy of economies as an additional element in the analysis. In this theory, new products are initially introduced in a high-income country, and then eventually introduced to the rest of the world as the products mature and become technologically standardized. Clearly, Vernon's description in terms of product cycle was a major explanation of the movement of production overseas, rather than just an explanation of international trade. Kojima (1975) has viewed foreign investment as being complementary to international trade; foreign investment creates an enlarged basis for trade through the transplantation of intangible assets from the source country's comparatively disadvantaged industries to the host country's comparatively advantaged ones.

Note that conceptually the following three types of foreign investments are possible: cost-oriented, market-oriented, and resource-oriented. Cost-oriented investment refers to foreign investment arising from an acute shortage of labor, increasing cost of production, and restructuring of the domestic industrial sector—all of which force investors in foreign countries to look for cheaper production bases outside of their own countries. Host market-oriented foreign investment arises out of the desire and need to avoid trade friction and market conflict (for example, Japanese investment in the United States, Canada, and European Community countries). Locational advantages may also be used for export-oriented investments, particularly when the host market is relatively small and there are some special considerations, such as the quota allocation under the Multi Fibre Arrangements (MFA).

It is well-known that the movement of production overseas is carried out primarily by multinationals or transnational corporations (TNCs). Two basic factors that attract TNCs to foreign locations are safety of investment and opportunity for profit. Their objectives in crossing borders include gaining access to foreign markets, access to inputs, freedom of decision making and operations, and reduction of risks. The objectives of host country governments, on the other hand, include the desire to gain economic efficiency, equity in TNC distribution of benefits, and participation in ownership, management, technology, and research and development (R&D). The objectives are not always conflicting; often there is similarity of interests between TNCs and host governments. Thus there is less need for regulation or coercion by governments on TNC activities.

In fact, opinions on the desirability of FDI from the host country's viewpoint have differed among scholars in this field. In the late 1960s through the mid-1970s, TNCs often came under severe criticism in developing countries. They were viewed as "suction pumps" in an overall imperialist design to perpetuate an exploitative economic system. Not surprisingly, therefore, this period witnessed a proliferation of restrictions on FDI inflows such as strict screening of such investments, limiting their entry into key sectors, and prohibiting takeovers of local firms by foreign firms. Analysts like Caves (1982) also pointed out many social and economic costs associated with FDI in the form of transfer pricing, fictitious and irrelevant transfer of technology, excessive product differentiation, need and taste creation, the crowding out of local capital and inhibiting the emergence and growth of domestic entrepreneurship, as well as political pressures leading to serious policy distortions. Moreover, Oman (1993) has argued that the procyclical tendency of FDI reduces its benefits to recipient developing countries.

By the early 1980s, the pendulum started to swing in the other direction when developing countries increasingly began courting FDI in the face of dramatic increases in real interest rates, the debt crisis, and the virtual disappearance of voluntary bank lending. At the theoretical level, it was pointed out by Grosse and Behrman (1992) that TNCs can offer major benefits to host countries in the form of: (i) assistance in improving their internal balance (for instance, income and employment) by providing access to investible funds, proprietary technology, and managerial and marketing skills; (ii) assistance in improving their external balance by providing low-cost inputs from abroad, access to export markets, and import substituting production; and (iii) assistance in achieving non-economic goals through such methods as placating pressure groups by providing jobs and other benefits, and by helping the host country in dealing with the firm's home government.

Another positive point is the nondebt-inducing nature of FDI. According to some observers, the larger inflow of FDI could itself help the indebted countries overcome their debt-servicing difficulties (Agosin 1985). In addition, there also simultaneously occurred the desire in the developing countries to set up export processing zones and eliminate anti-export policy biases. This liberalized the environment for foreign investment, particularly in the manufacturing sector. At the same time, it is worth noting that the preference of the developing countries, in general, shifted to the financial component of the traditional FDI "package", whereas a large number of investors came to prefer the "new" forms because of their risk-shedding advantages and their potential for greater financial leverage on certain nonfinancial assets (Oman 1993).

Be that as it may, nearly every developing country today is striving to attract investment from overseas, even at the risk of excessive policy competition among themselves; fears of diversion of foreign investment to the formerly socialist countries of Central and Eastern Europe have intensified such competition. So strong indeed is the current attitude in favor of foreign investment that "a restrictive attitude limiting the entry of FDI is regarded as foolish" (Williamson 1990, 7). In fact, policy on foreign investment has begun to vie with trade policy in importance in the arena of economic relations among countries.

Pattern of FDI Inflow

FDI inflow into Bangladesh has been scanty. Although the share of the Asian and Pacific region, to which Bangladesh belongs, has been rising over the last two decades,[3] Bangladesh has received a negligible amount of FDI. This is brought out in sharp relief in Table 7.1. During the period 1986-1991, Bangladesh received a meager FDI inflow of US$11 million.[4] Bangladesh's share in total FDI inflow into the Asian region during this period was only 0.01 percent. Average annual FDI inflow into Bangladesh during this period was about US$1.8 million, compared to US$3,105 million for the People's Republic of China. Bangladesh occupies the bottom position even within the South Asian region; compared to Bangladesh's average annual inflow of US$1.8 million, the corresponding figures for India, Pakistan, and Sri Lanka during 1986-1991 were US$223 million, US$189 million, and US$50 million, respectively.

Table 7.1
Foreign Direct Investment in Selected Asian Countries, 1986-1991
(US$ million)

	1986	*1987*	*1988*	*1989*	*1990*	*1991*	*1986-1991*
NIEs	2,471	4,152	5,485	5,132	5,906	5,971	29,117
Korea, Rep. of	435	601	871	758	715	1,116	4,496
Singapore	1,710	2,836	3,655	2,770	3,861	3,584	18,416
Taipei, China	326	715	959	1,604	1,330	1,271	6,205
PRC	1,875	2,314	3,194	3,393	3,489	4,366	18,631
Southeast Asia	1,137	1,467	3,336	4,688	6,581	7,494	24,703
Indonesia	258	385	576	682	1,093	1,482	4,476
Malaysia	489	423	719	1,668	2,514	3,454	9,267
Philippines	127	307	936	563	530	544	3,007
Thailand	263	352	1,105	1,775	2,444	2,014	7,953
South Asia	345	373	521	580	402	556	2,777
Bangladesh	2	3	2	-	3	1	11
India[a]	208	181	287	350	112	200	1,338
Pakistan	105	129	186	210	244	257	1,131
Sri Lanka	30	60	46	20	43	98	297
Pacific Islands	100	103	190	231	101	44	769
Fiji	8	(11)	23	13	75	7	115
Papua New Guinea	91	93	153	203	-	-	540
Solomon Islands	(1)	8	3	6	13	19	48
Vanuatu	2	13	11	9	13	18	66
TOTAL	5,928	8,409	12,726	14,024	16,479	18,431	75,997

[a] Data refer to net foreign direct investment.

Source: Asian Development Bank (1993).

Total sanctioned FDI in Bangladesh has been Tk 9,618.3 million (Table 7.2); of this, FDI sanctioned up to 1971 (year of independence) was Tk 283.2 million, the rest being sanctioned after independence. Actual inflows of FDI have been much less than the amounts sanctioned. No foreign investment proposals were approved between 1972 and 1976. This

Table 7.2
Flow of Foreign Direct Investment into Bangladesh
(Taka million)

Year	*Amount of Investment in Sanctioned Units*
Up to 1971	283.20
1972	nil
1973	nil
1974	nil
1975	nil
1976	nil
1977	10.47 (0.68)
1978	nil
1979	74.69 (4.91)
1980	53.97 (3.48)
1981	4.56 (0.28)
1982	403.90 (20.13)
1983	609.68 (25.62)
1984	75.10 (3.07)
1985	161.32 (6.21)
1986	96.80 (3.24)
1987	1,591.45 (51.96)
1988	1,571.41 (50.30)
1989	772.36 (24.03)
1990	1,945.00 (60.27)
1991	331.80 (9.30)
1992	1,245.31 (32.64)
1993 (till June)	387.28 (9.75)

Source: Board of Investment, Government of Bangladesh, unpublished documents.

Note: Figures in parentheses represent FDI inflows in millions of US dollars.

reflects the reluctance of foreign investors to move into a war-ravaged newly independent country that was constitutionally committed to socialism. FDI started flowing after the political change in 1975 when the new government adopted policy measures to attract foreign investment. The amounts of sanctioned FDI in the post-1975 period have fluctuated from year to year, but an upward trend is discernible. Sanctioned FDI increased from Tk 10.47 million in 1977 to a peak of Tk 1,945 million in 1990, but declined thereafter. The political change in 1981 was accompanied by a severe decline in sanctioned FDI to the level of Tk 4.56 million only. Similarly, the change of government in 1991 witnessed a sharp decline in sanctioned FDI to Tk 331.8 million. The volume of sanctioned FDI recovered to about Tk 1,245 million in 1992, but the proposed FDI flow of Tk 387.3 million during the first half of 1993 indicates that the level of sanctioned FDI is likely to decline in the current year.

As noted above, actual FDI inflows have been considerably less than the amounts sanctioned. As shown in Table 7.3, the number of FDI projects that have gone into production has been much less than the number of sanctioned units. The number of FDI projects sanctioned between 1972 and June 1993 is 170. Of these, only 82 units, that is, less than half the number of sanctioned units, went into actual production. In 1992-1993, only five units went into production out of a total of 24 units.

Table 7.3

Sanctioned Units and Units in Production

Year	*Number of Sanctioned Units*	*Number of Units in Production*
Up to 1971	23	23
1972-1973	nil	nil
1973-1974	nil	nil
1974-1975	nil	nil
1975-1976	nil	nil
1976-1977	2	2
1977-1978	2	1
1978-1979	3	3
1979-1980	2	2
1980-1981	12	11
1981-1982	nil	nil
1982-1983	9	8
1983-1984	18	14
1984-1985	6	4
1985-1986	5	1
1986-1987	16	4
1987-1988	17	3
1988-1989	19	...
1989-1990	...	...
1990-1991[a]	11	6
1991-1992	24	18
1992-1993	24	5

... means data not available.

[a] Period covered is March 1991 to June 1991.

Source: Board of Investment, unpublished documents.

The failure of many sanctioned units to go into production has meant that actual FDI inflow has been significantly lower than the amounts sanctioned. As seen from Table 7.4, total amount of FDI actually flowing in during the period 1979-1990 was Tk 2,293 million, compared to the sanctioned amount of Tk 7,360 million for the same period. Thus, actual inflow of FDI has been less than a third of the sanctioned amount. Table 7.4 also shows that the bulk (about three quarters) of foreign investment has been in the form of reinvested earnings. New infusions of cash have constituted about 22 percent of FDI inflow during 1979-1990, while only 3.6 percent of FDI has come in the form of capital equipment. Less than 0.5 percent of gross domestic investment has been financed by FDI in recent years.

Table 7.4

Flow of Net Foreign Direct Investment into Bangladesh

(Taka million)

Year	*Cash capital*		*Capital equipment*		*Reinvested earnings*		*Total investment*	
1979	30.39	(40.8)	11.09	(14.9)	32.93	(44.3)	74.41	(100)
1980	14.09	(20.7)	0.01	(neg.)	54.07	(79.3)	68.17	(100)
1981	27.17	(26.3)	5.03	(4.9)	71.05	(68.8)	103.25	(100)
1982	14.91	(14.6)	0.88	(0.9)	86.56	(84.5)	102.35	(100)
1983	21.29	(29.5)	25.67	(35.6)	25.21	(34.9)	72.17	(100)
1984	-10.83	(-13.4)	23.16	(28.7)	68.46	(84.7)	80.79	(100)
1985	88.28	(35.4)	3.70	(1.5)	157.28	(63.1)	249.26	(100)
1986	108.17	(57.7)	0.01	(neg.)	79.27	(42.3)	187.45	(100)
1987	107.47	(32.4)	0.73	(0.2)	223.78	(67.4)	331.98	(100)
1988	26.78	(9.5)	0.13	(neg.)	255.71	(90.5)	282.62	(100)
1989	41.26	(10.8)	7.78	(2.0)	331.94	(87.2)	380.98	(100)
1990	28.31	(7.9)	4.96	(1.4)	326.39	(90.7)	359.66	(100)
Total	497.29	(21.7)	83.15	(3.6)	1,712.65	(74.7)	2,293.09	(100)

Note: Figures in parentheses are percentage shares in total investment. Bangladesh Bank figures represent significant understatement of FDI flows because of its incomplete data collection method based on mailed surveys.

Source: Bangladesh Bank (1991).

Foreign direct investment in Bangladesh has mainly taken the form of joint ventures with local investors. Since independence, there have been only 11 sanctioned cases of 100 percent equity participation by foreign firms, mostly from the Republic of South Korea. The modal value of foreign equity share has been 49 percent; foreign equity share has however varied between 9 percent and 100 percent. Transnational corporations that have formed joint ventures with local investors include: Fisons, Rhone-Poulenc, General Electric Co., Reckitt and Colman, Lever Brothers, Glaxo, ICI, Berger Paints, Avery, and Burmah Eastern from the United Kingdom; Singer, Squibb, Pfizer, and producers of Coca-Cola and Pepsi from the United States; Bata and Milners from Canada; Siemens, BASF, and Hoechst from Germany; Philips and Organon from the Netherlands; and Swedish Motors from Sweden.

Even though equity participation continues to be the dominant form of foreign private involvement in independent Bangladesh, investments by foreigners have also taken various "nonequity" forms (Appendix Tables 7.1 and 7.2). Technical collaboration has been the dominant form of nonequity participation by TNCs in Bangladesh. Licensing and technical know-how, and royalty technical know-how and technical assistance have been two other major forms of nonequity participation by foreigners in Bangladesh. Industries in which technical collaboration has taken place include automobiles, diesel engines, electric bulbs, cycle and rickshaw tires and tubes, asbestos sheeting, accumulator batteries, tannery, road-making machines and equipment, oxygen gas, lift manufacturing, pharmaceuticals, rubber rolls and oil seals, deep sea fishing, dry cell batteries, electronics, nonalcoholic beverages, lubricating grease, and mosquito coils. Licensing agreements are in operation in pharmaceuticals, cosmetics, toilet soap, cigarettes, dyestuff, bicycle, motors, diesel engines, barley, accumulator batteries, motor lubricants, electric fuses, offset printing ink, paints and varnishes, leather footwear, tissue paper and napkins, mild steel products, electric motors, etc. The rate of royalty payment has generally been 1.5 percent. Once-and-for-all lumpsum payments have been agreed upon in most cases of technical collaboration. A technical know-how fee of 1.5 percent has generally been charged in cases of technical collaboration/assistance.

The sectoral composition of FDI has undergone significant change over the years. In the pre-independence period, the bulk of FDI inflow was attracted into the pharmaceutical and petroleum industries, while some foreign capital was tied up in the exploitation of natural resources like jute and tea.[5] The concentration of foreign investment in the pharmaceutical and petroleum industries can be attributed to the import-substituting industrialization strategy followed in Pakistan at that time. There was a ready domestic market for medicines and fuels since these were being imported. The government decided to save foreign exchange by stimulating domestic production of these commodities behind high protective walls. But since these industries were capital-intensive and used a high level of technology, and since it was unlikely that local initiative would be forthcoming in a capital-scarce, technologically backward country like Pakistan, the government allowed foreign firms to enter these two industries.

While manufacturing industry attracted most of the FDI inflow during the Pakistan period, the importance of this sector, in terms of the magnitude of FDI inflow, has declined in independent Bangladesh. This is seen from Table 7.5. Thus, while the manufacturing sector attracted nearly 42 percent of total FDI inflow in 1979, its share fell to a meager 1.6 percent in 1990; if the entire period 1979-1990 is considered, then it is seen that about 24 percent of total FDI inflow during this period was channeled into the manufacturing sector. The importance of commerce and financial services, which includes trading, banking, and insurance, has increased rapidly. By 1990, nearly 92 percent of annual FDI inflow came into commerce. During the period 1979-1990, 69 percent of total FDI inflow was attracted to trading, banking, and insurance, while the agricultural sector failed to attract even 1 percent of total foreign investment. Other nonfinancial service sectors received about 6 percent of FDI inflow during the same period.

A remarkable shift in FDI away from manufacturing to services is thus observed in Bangladesh. Within the service industry, financial services have received the single largest share of foreign investment. Movement of FDI from manufacturing to services is a feature not confined to Bangladesh alone but has been observed in developing countries as a whole during the 1980s. As in Bangladesh, financial services have been the dominant recipient of FDI in other developing countries, such as Argentina, Malaysia, and Pakistan. However, unlike in other developing countries, other service industries, including construction, transport, and communications, have failed to attract a significant flow of FDI to Bangladesh.[6]

A detailed breakdown of sanctioned FDI by major industrial sectors during the period 1973-1974 to 1992-1993 is presented in Table 7.6. The table shows that during the above-mentioned period, textiles (including readymade garments) has attracted the highest amount of FDI (Tk 3,117.9 million), followed by food processing (Tk 2,438 million), "other chemicals" (Tk 1,287.5 million), electrical goods (Tk 1,251.8 million), and metal industries (Tk 1,204.1 million). In relative terms, textiles, food processing, "other chemicals" and electrical goods have received 20 percent, 16 percent,

Table 7.5

Distribution of Foreign Direct Investment in Bangladesh by Broad Economic Sector

(percentage shares)

	1979	*1980*	*1981*	*1982*	*1983*	*1984*	*1985*	*1986*	*1987*	*1988*	*1989*	*1990*	*1979-90*
Agriculture	-0.03	nil	0.67	-0.29	1.34	nil	1.48	0.04	0.22	1.44	2.04	1.38	0.99
Manufacturing	41.65	20.25	27.02	24.86	81.61	49.68	45.21	51.72	38.14	1.37	0.47	1.62	23.76
Construction	-1.21	nil	nil	nil	nil	nil	nil	nil	nil	nil	nil	nil	-0.04
Commerce	41.05	68.74	66.09	69.07	15.07	48.44	51.72	42.08	54.55	88.75	91.70	91.60	69.11
Transport and communication	0.01	neg.	0.44	0.23	neg.	-0.36	-1.87	1.19	1.30	1.08	0.01	0.86	0.37
Miscellaneous services	18.53	11.01	5.78	6.13	2.10	2.24	3.46	4.97	5.79	7.36	5.78	4.54	5.81
All sectors	100	100	100	100	100	100	100	100	100	100	100	100	100

Source: Calculated using data from Bangladesh Bank (1991).

Notes: 1. Minus sign indicates creditor position.
2. Commerce sector includes trading, banking, and insurance.

Table 7.6

Annual FDI in Bangladesh by Major Industrial Sector

(taka million at current prices)

Year	*Food processing*	*Tobacco*	*Textiles*	*Pharma-ceuticals*	*Other chemicals*	*Metal industries*	*Electrical goods*	*Electronics*	*Machinery, spares and equipment*	*Leather and leather products*	*Plastic products*	*Paper and paper products*	*Miscella-neous*	*Total*
1973-1974	nil	nil	nil	nil	nil	nil	nil	nil	nil	nil	nil	nil	nil	nil
1974-1975	0.48	nil	nil	nil	nil	nil	nil	nil	nil	nil	nil	nil	nil	0.48
1975-1976	nil	nil	nil	nil	nil	nil	nil	nil	nil	nil	nil	nil	nil	nil
1976-1977	nil	nil	nil	2.80	nil	nil	nil	nil	nil	nil	nil	nil	0.90	3.70
1977-1978	nil	nil	nil	nil	nil	nil	nil	nil	30.87	nil	nil	nil	nil	30.87
1978-1979	251.70	nil	0.75	nil	nil	101.66	nil	nil	nil	nil	nil	nil	nil	354.11
1979-1980	nil	12.00	nil	nil	nil	nil	nil	nil	nil	nil	nil	nil	2.88	14.88
1980-1981	nil	nil	nil	23.87	nil	24.54	nil	4.5	35.00	8.55	20.38	nil	17.00	133.84
1981-1982	nil	nil	nil	nil	nil	nil	nil	nil	nil	nil	nil	nil	nil	nil
1982-1983	2.17	nil	39.75	nil	18.44	nil	nil	15.6	nil	442.00	nil	nil	nil	517.96
1983-1984	250.05	nil	18.65	nil	519.67	43.94	59.78	nil	nil	nil	198.4	nil	7.50	1,097.89
1984-1985	nil	12.91	nil	35.80	nil	232.91	nil	nil	nil	18.97	nil	nil	50.00	350.59
1985-1986	60.00	nil	nil	nil	nil	nil	nil	nil	5.26	nil	28.30	nil	nil	93.56
1986-1987	177.02	nil	240.39	300.00	52.28	nil	24.68	nil	7.57	nil	nil	nil	1,478.07	2,280.01
1987-1988	54.42	395.82	476.00	nil	242.54	592.20	23.50	1.75	111.7	nil	nil	615.64	33.40	2,546.97
1988-1989	397.10	nil	1,771.92	158.61	34.16	142.80	nil	nil	nil	nil	245.80	422.80	906.32	4,079.51
1990	43.75	nil	225.02	54.63	394.52	2.25	1,141.07	nil	nil	25.36	8.12	nil	50.29	1,945.00
1991	79.21	nil	99.09	nil	5.13	nil	1.96	17.58	7.01	57.34	nil	nil	64.48	331.80
1992	1,036.40	nil	119.60	nil	9.40	nil	0.77	nil	13.54	10.50	nil	326.00	51.84	1,245.31
1993 (up to June)	85.78	nil	126.74	nil	11.31	63.79	nil	23.09	7.04	21.15	nil	10.80	37.58	387.28
1973-1974-June 1993	2,438.08	420.73	3,117.91	575.71	1,287.45	1,204.09	1,251.76	62.52	217.99	583.86	501.00	1,052.50	2,700.16	15,413.76

Source: Board of Investment, Government of Bangaldesh, unpublished documents.

8 percent, and 8 percent, respectively, of total FDI inflow into Bangladesh between 1973-1974 and 1992-1993. In contrast to the pre-independence situation, the importance of the pharmaceutical industry has declined, its share in total FDI inflow being only 4 percent during the abovementioned period. It is noteworthy that prior to 1972 there was no foreign investment in food processing and only one foreign firm in the textile industry. In the postliberation period, 20 foreign firms had proposed to invest in food processing (particularly marine food processing) and 51 in textiles (of which 28 were in readymade garments).

This change in industry composition of foreign investment may be explained as follows. The industrialization strategy of Pakistan was import-substituting in nature. Hence, foreign investment in the petroleum and pharmaceutical industries was geared to meet domestic demand only and had no export potential. Since the domestic market was expanding very slowly with per capita income growing at a little more than 1 percent annually during the last decade, and since export potential was virtually absent in petroleum and pharmaceuticals, new foreign firms had little attraction to move into these sectors. The Drug Policy introduced about the mid-1980s, which prohibits production of several medicines/tonics mainly manufactured by TNCs, has doubtlessly discouraged foreign investment in the pharmaceutical industry. In contrast, marine food and readymade garments had excellent export prospects in addition to a local market, and hence foreign investment was attracted to these industries. An interesting characteristic of FDI in the readymade garments industry is the preponderance of foreign investors from Asian countries such as Hong Kong, India, Republic of Korea, and Singapore, that are exporters of readymade garments. Foreign investors from these countries presumably invested in Bangladesh to take advantage of its quota-free status in European and American markets.

A major contribution of FDI to the development of the recipient country is that it acts as a vehicle for technology transfer. It is difficult to determine the extent to which Bangladesh has benefited from FDI in this respect. It has been noted that less than 4 percent of FDI has come in the form of capital equipment. Even though technology does not necessarily have to be embodied in capital, the very small share of capital equipment in total FDI inflow nonetheless seems to indicate a limited contribution of foreign investment to technology transfer in Bangladesh. On the other hand, the fact that technical collaboration/assistance has been the major form of nonequity participation by TNCs would lead one to believe that some transfer of technology, however limited, must have occurred. Again, the relative concentration of FDI in the textile (mainly garments) and food industries, which can be considered as low-technology industries, would seem to point to limited technology transfer through foreign investment. A more precise answer to the question of what contribution FDI has made to technology transfer in Bangladesh can only be obtained by undertaking microlevel studies.

Remarkable change has also occurred in the distribution of investor countries, as revealed in Tables 7.7 and 7.8. In the pre-independence period, Western industrialized countries dominated foreign investment in Bangladesh; out of 37 foreign companies operating, 31 were from Western Europe and North America, while the remaining ones were from Asian countries (mainly Japan). This pattern has substantially changed after independence, with Asian countries emerging to be equally important as the developed market economies in terms of the volume of foreign investment. Geography, history, economic proximity, and strategies of TNCs have played major roles in determining sources of FDI in Bangladesh.

Table 7.7 shows that during the 1970s, developed market economies dominated foreign investment in Bangladesh. British and West German TNCs, which were operating in Bangladesh since the Pakistan days, continued to infuse new capital into their ventures. Japan joined this club in 1978-1979 with a large investment of nearly Tk 252 million. The 1970s also witnessed the entry of Asian firms into Bangladesh; firms from Hong Kong, India, Singapore, and Thailand began to invest in the country. Participation by Asian firms, particularly from the newly industrializing economies (NIEs), increased rapidly during the decade of the 1980s; during this period foreign investors from high-income countries also stepped up their operations in Bangladesh. Among the high-income countries, the United Kingdom continued to dominate, followed by the United States, Germany, and the Netherlands. Hong Kong dominated foreign investment from Asian countries, followed by the People's Republic of China and the Republic of Korea. A similar pattern is being observed during the 1990s.

In aggregate terms, however, the amount of foreign investment from the developed market economies has exceeded that from Asian countries in spite of increasing participation by the latter. Foreign investors from high-income countries contributed 56.7 percent of the total FDI inflow into Bangladesh between 1973-1974 and June 1993; 41.6 percent of FDI inflow came from middle-income Asian countries, particularly Hong

Table 7.7
FDI in Bangladesh by Country Source
(taka million)

Countries	*1973/74*	*1974/75*	*1975/76*	*1976/77*	*1977/78*	*1978/79*	*1979/80*	*1980/81*	*1981/82*	*1982/83*
High-Income Countries										
United Kingdom	nil	nil	nil	2.80 (75.68)	7.87 (25.49)	nil	2.88 (19.35)	15.50 (11.58)	nil	nil
United States	nil	nil	nil	nil	nil	0.75 (0.21)	nil	nil	nil	nil
Germany		nil	nil	nil	nil	nil	nil	36.45 (27.23)	nil	34.04 (6.57)
Netherlands		nil	nil	nil	nil	nil	nil	nil	nil	nil
France		nil	nil	nil	nil	nil	nil	nil	nil	nil
Switzerland		nil	nil	nil	nil	nil	nil	nil	nil	nil
Sweden		nil	nil	nil	23.00 (74.51)	nil	nil	nil	nil	nil
Canada		nil	nil	nil	nil	nil	nil	nil	nil	442.00 (85.33)
Belgium		nil	nil	nil	nil	nil	nil	nil	nil	nil
Italy		nil	nil	nil	nil	nil	nil	6.00 (4.48)	nil	nil

(Continued next page)

Table 7.7 *(Continued)*

Countries	*1973/74*	*1974/75*	*1975/76*	*1976/77*	*1977/78*	*1978/79*	*1979/80*	*1980/81*	*1981/82*	*1982/83*
Japan	nil	nil	nil	nil	nil	251.70	nil	nil	nil	nil
						(71.08)				
Australia	nil	nil	nil	nil	nil	nil	nil	nil	nil	nil
Sub-total	nil	nil	nil	2.80	30.87	252.45	2.88	57.95	476.04	nil
				(75.68)	(100.00)	(71.29)	(19.35)	(43.30)	(91.91)	
Middle-Income Countries										
Singapore	nil	nil	nil	nil	nil	nil	nil	16.00	nil	nil
								(11.95)		
Hong Kong	nil	0.48	nil	0.90	nil	nil	nil	nil	nil	16.16
		(100.00)		(24.32)						(3.12)
Korea, Rep. of	nil	nil	nil	nil	nil	nil	nil	nil	nil	25.76
										(4.97)
Thailand	nil	nil	nil	nil	nil	101.66	nil	24.88	nil	nil
						(28.71)		(18.59)		
China, People's Rep. of	nil	nil	nil	nil	nil	nil	nil	nil	nil	nil
Philippines	nil	nil	nil	nil	nil	nil	nil	nil	nil	nil
Sub-total	nil	0.48	nil	0.90	nil	101.66	nil	40.88	nil	41.92
		(100.0)		(24.32)		(28.71)		(30.54)		6.09

(Continued next page)

Table 7.7 *(Continued)*

Countries	*1973/74*	*1974/75*	*1975/76*	*1976/77*	*1977/78*	*1978/79*	*1979/80*	*1980/81*	*1981/82*	*1982/83*
Low-Income Countries										
Pakistan	nil	nil	nil	nil	nil	nil	nil	nil	nil	nil
India	nil	nil	nil	nil	nil	nil	12.00 (80.65)	35.00 (26.15)	nil	nil
Oman	nil	nil	nil	nil	nil	nil	nil	nil	nil	nil
Panama	nil	nil	nil	nil	nil	nil	nil	nil	nil	nil
Sub-total	nil	nil	nil	nil	nil	nil	12.00 (80.65)	35.00 (26.15)	nil	nil
GRAND TOTAL	nil	0.48 (100)	nil	3.70 (100)	30.87 (100)	354.11 (100)	14.88 (100)	133.84 (100)	nil	517.96 (100)

(Continued next page)

Table 7.7 *(Continued)*

Countries	*1983/84*	*1984/85*	*1985/86*	*1986/87*	*1987/88*	*1988/89*	*1990*	*1991*	*1992*	*1993 (up to June)*	*Total*
High-Income Countries											
United Kingdom	124.70	35.80	60.00	92.26	1,110.06[b]	1,820.59[c]	48.16	119.68	nil	38.89	3,479.19
	(11.36)	(10.21)	(64.13)	(4.05)	(44.63)	(44.63)	(2.80)	(36.07)		(16.19)	(23.14)
United States	11.60	nil	5.26	12.70	1.75	nil	5.20	nil	nil	22.49	59.75
	(1.06)		(5.62)	(0.56)	(0.07)		(0.30)			(9.36)	(0.40)
Germany	nil	50.00	nil	nil	nil	8.29	3.92	3.74	3.71	2.55	142.70
		(14.26)				(0.20)	(0.23)	(1.13)	(0.30)	(1.06)	(0.95)
Netherlands	198.40	18.97	nil	291.87	nil	nil	51.99	nil	nil	nil	561.23
	(18.07)	(5.41)		(12.80)			(3.03)				(3.73)
France	38.62	nil	10.00	nil	65.64	nil	nil	3.95	nil	nil	668.21
	(3.52)		(10.67)		(24.17)			(1.19)			(4.44)
Switzerland	4.95	nil	nil	300.00	nil	nil	18.00	nil	240.77	nil	563.72
	(0.45)			(13.16)			(1.05)		(19.37)		(3.75)
Sweden	453.45	nil	nil	nil	nil	nil	5.45	17.58	nil	nil	499.48
	(41.30)						(0.32)	(5.30)			(3.32)
Canada	5.32	nil	nil	nil	nil	558.61	nil	nil	nil	nil	1,005.93
	(0.48)					(13.69)					(6.69)
Belgium	nil	4.62	nil	nil	nil	nil	nil	nil	nil	nil	4.62
		(1.32)									(0.03)
Italy	nil	nil	nil	nil	592.20	500.89	nil	11.03	13.54	nil	1,123.66
					(23.25)	(12.28)		(3.32)	(1.09)		(7.47)

(Continued next page)

Table 7.7 *(Continued)*

Countries	*1983/84*	*1984/85*	*1985/86*	*1986/87*	*1987/88*	*1988/89*	*1990*	*1991*	*1992*	*1993 (up to June)*	*Total*
Japan	nil	nil	nil	40.57	nil	nil	12.32	45.28	14.19	36.02	400.08
				(1.78)			(0.72)	(13.65)	(1.14)	(14.99)	(2.66)
Australia	nil	nil	nil	nil	nil	21.60	nil	nil	nil	nil	21.60
						(0.53)					(0.14)
Sub-total	837.04	109.39	75.26	737.40	2,319.65	2,909.68	145.04	201.26	272.21	99.95	8,530.17
	(76.24)	(31.20)	(80.44)	(32.34)	(91.07)	(71.33)	(8.44)	(60.66)	(21.90)	(41.60)	(56.72)
Middle-Income Countries											
Singapore	230.45	nil	nil	nil	6.20	199.00	3.04	9.00	827.21	nil	1,290.90
							(0.18)	(2.71)	(66.56)		(8.58)
Hong Kong	4.80	8.29	4.90	1,398.50	11.00	176.50	1,521.33	41.94	58.91	18.96	3,262.67
	(0.44)	(2.36)	(5.24)	(61.34)	(0.34)	(4.33)	(88.52)	(12.64)	(4.74)	(7.89)	(21.70)
Korea, Rep. of	8.90	nil	nil	nil	63.76	205.27	15.97	59.84	73.09	93.53	546.12
	(0.81)				(2.50)	(5.03)	(0.93)	(18.04)	(5.88)	(38.93)	(3.63)
Thailand	nil	nil	nil	14.97	nil	nil	16.35	nil	nil	nil	157.86
							(0.95)				(1.05)
China, People's Rep. of	9.30	232.91	nil	5.55	135.76	565.60	7.81	nil	11.44	7.04	075.41
	(0.85)	(66.43)		(0.24)	(5.33)	(13.86)	(0.45)		(0.92)	(2.93)	(6.49)
Philippines	nil	nil	13.40	nil	nil	nil	nil	nil	nil	10.80	24.20
			(14.32)				nil			(4.49)	(0.16)
Sub-total	253.45	241.20	18.30	1,419.02	216.72	1,146.37	1,564.50	110.78	970.65	130.33	6,257.16
	(23.09)	(68.80)	(19.56)	(62.24)	(8.51)	(28.10)	(91.03)	(33.39)	(78.10)	(54.24)	(41.61)

(Continued next page)

Table 7.7 *(Continued)*

Countries	*1983/84*	*1984/85*	*1985/86*	*1986/87*	*1987/88*	*1988/89*	*1990*	*1991*	*1992*	*1993 (up to June)*	*Total*
Low-Income Countries											
Pakistan	nil	nil	nil	nil	1.00[b]	15.00	1.10	3.74	nil	nil	20.84
					(0.04)	(0.37)	(0.06)	(1.13)			(0.14)
India	nil	nil	nil	nil	9.60	8.16	7.98	16.00	nil	10.00	98.74
					(0.38)	(0.20)	(0.46)	(4.82)		(4.16)	(0.66)
Oman	nil	nil	nil	123.59	nil	nil	nil	nil	nil	nil	123.59
				(5.42)							(0.82)
Panama	7.40	nil	nil	nil	nil	nil	nil	nil	nil	nil	7.40
	(0.67)										(0.05)
Sub-total	7.40	nil	nil	123.59	10.60	23.16	9.08	19.74	nil	10.00	250.57
	(0.67)			(5.42)	(0.42)	(0.57)	(0.53)	(5.95)		(4.16)	(1.67)
GRAND TOTAL	1,097.89	350.59	93.56	2,280.01	2,546.97	4,079.51	1,718.62	331.78	1,242.86	240.28	15,037.90
	(100)	(100)	(100)	(100)	(100)	(100)	(100)	(100)	(100)	(100)	(100)

Note: There has been some collaboration among foreign sources, the extent of which are noted below:

[a] United States and Singapore: 0.75.

[b] United Kingdom and ADB: 448.20; Pakistan and Germany: 1.00.

[c] United Kingdom, India, and ADB: 245.80; United Kingdom and Netherlands: 580.00.

[d] United Kingdom, Netherlands, and Hong Kong: 40.04; Germany and United Kingdom: 8.92.

[e] Hong Kong and Sri Lanka: 28.99.

Source: Reza (1990).

Table 7.8
Equity Share of Foreign Firms in Bangladesh by Country of Origin, 1992-1993
(taka million)

Country	*Number of Firms*	*Total Capital Investment*[a]	*Foreign Equity Share*	*Foreign Equity Share as Percent of Total Capital Investment*
Developed Countries				
United Kingdom	26	2,239.810	1,292.397	57.70
United States	10	534.683	258.740	48.39
Germany	10	177.844	53.295	29.97
Netherlands	9	794.663	198.897	25.03
Switzerland	5	796.872	441.195	55.37
Sweden	4	514.935	436.655	84.80
Canada	6	1,248.923	736.248	58.95
France	3	54.510	19.601	35.96
Belgium	2	40.002	19.097	47.74
Italy	5	876.539	441.119	50.32
Japan	15	277.353	159.683	57.57
Others	4	191.419	97.238	50.80
Total developed countries	99	7,747.553	4,154.165	53.62
Asian Countries				
Singapore	12	1,173.560	962.847	82.04
Hong Kong	32	5,009.295	2,548.498	50.88
Korea, Rep. of	19	634.354	336.364	53.02
Thailand	6	165.507	81.647	49.33
India	7	134.711	51.713	38.39
Philippines	1	107.974	10.797	10.00
Pakistan	4	27.182	10.841	39.88
China, People's Rep. of	10	1,002.771	268.051	26.73
Other Asian countries	5	369.152	168.656	45.69
Total Asian countries	96	8,624.506	4,439.414	51.47
GRAND TOTAL	195	16,372.059	8,593.579	52.49

[a] at the time of permission/registration.
Source: Board of Investment, Government of Bangladesh, unpublished documents.

Kong and Singapore. During the postindependence period, the highest amount of FDI inflow has come from the United Kingdom (23.1 percent of total inflow), followed closely by Hong Kong (21.7 percent of total inflow).

A similar picture is observed from Table 7.8.[7] A total of 99 firms from developed market economies and 96 from Asian countries have invested (or proposed to invest) in Bangladesh. If the average foreign equity share is considered, it is seen that Swedish firms top the list with 84.8 percent equity participation, followed closely by Singapore (82 percent equity participation). Interestingly enough, equity participation by Asian firms

(Tk 4,439.4 million) has exceeded the equity share of firms from developed countries (Tk 4,154.2 million).

High-income Asian economies such as Hong Kong, Singapore, Republic of Korea, and People's Republic of China have thus been the major sources of FDI in Bangladesh.[8] In their quest for industrial restructuring these countries have been shifting their low-technology manufacturing activities to low-income countries like Bangladesh through FDI. Consequently, the bulk of Asian country-sourced FDI flowing into Bangladesh has been tied up in labor-intensive industries such as textiles, food processing, and leather.

FDI Policy Frame

Immediately after independence in 1971, private sector investment came under severe control and was limited to small and cottage industries. Initially being committed to socialism, the state policy also restricted FDI: it was allowed only in partnership with the public sector, which was to have at least 51 percent ownership of any such venture.

The gradual liberalization of industrial policy in Bangladesh started with the announcement of the Industrial Policy in 1982. This was followed by successive reforms and amendments within the broad framework of a liberalized and competitive market economy. The recent Industrial Policy, 1991, has clearly emphasized the importance of the role of the private sector in industrial development. In support of this policy, the scope of private domestic and foreign investment has been extended and registration and sanctioning procedures simplified. The government's role has been shifted from regulatory to promotional activities and attempts are being made to ensure transparency and accountability of administration to achieve an enabling environment for the successful operation of the private sector.

Investment policy now ensures equal treatment for local investment, joint venture, and even 100 percent foreign investment. No formal permission of the government is now necessary to set up industries and for BMR/BMRE (balancing, modernization, rehabilitation/expansion) of existing industries with the entrepreneur's own funds or with funds from private banks or private financing institutions. Industries set up under foreign loans and supplier's credit (subject to approval of the terms of financing by the concerned sponsoring agency), pay-as-you-earn (PAYE) scheme, and nonrepatriable foreign exchange are deemed to have been set up with their own funds.

However, to avail of institutional facilities, such as clearance of machinery under concessionary rates of import duty, import entitlement for raw materials and spare parts, and infrastructure facilities (like industrial plots, acquisition of land for setting up of an industry, electric/gas/telephone/water and sewerage connections, etc.) for industrial purposes, all industries are required to be registered in the simplified prescribed manner with the concerned sponsoring agency.

As far as private investment from overseas sources is concerned, it is welcome in all areas of the economy with the exception of only five industrial sectors (reserve list for public sector) that include arms, nuclear energy, security printing, forest extraction, and air transport. Such investments shall be made either independently or through joint ventures on mutually beneficial terms and conditions. In other words, 100 percent foreign investment, as well as joint ventures with local private partners or with the public sector, is allowed. Foreign investment, however, is especially desired in the following categories:

- export-oriented industries,
- industries in the export processing zones,
- high-technology products that will be either import substitutes or export-oriented,
- undertakings in which more diversified use of indigenous natural resources is possible,
- basic industries using mainly local raw materials, and
- investment toward improvement of quality and marketing of goods manufactured and/or increase of the production capacities of existing industries.

There are a host of incentives currently being provided by the government to foreign investors. These include fiscal and other incentives as well as relaxation or liberalization of exchange control regulations.

Fiscal Incentives

Tax Holiday

A tax holiday is available to industries subject to the relevant rules and procedures set by the National Board of Revenue (NBR). Presently, it extends for five, seven, nine, and 12 years for industries set up in the developed, less developed, least developed, and special economic zones respectively, and will remain effective until 1995. The period of the tax holiday will be calculated from the month of commencement of commercial production. Eligibility for the exemption of tax holiday is to be determined by the NBR. The time of commencement of production is certified by the respective sponsoring agencies.

Concessionary Duty on Imported Capital Machinery

Import duty is levied at the rate of 10 percent of payable on capital machinery and spares imported for initial installation or for BMR/BMRE of existing industries.

Accelerated Depreciation

Accelerated depreciation in lieu of a tax holiday is allowed at the rate of 80 percent of the actual cost of machinery or plant from the year the unit starts commercial production and 20 percent for the following year, if the industry is located in a developed area. If the unit is set up in a less developed area the rate of depreciation will be 100 percent.

Tariff Rationalization

Local industrial products are protected through tariff rationalization keeping in view the interest of entrepreneurs and consumers. Tariff protection is allowed to new industries for up to four years.

Incentives to Nonresident Bangladeshis

Special incentives are provided to encourage nonresident Bangladeshis to invest in industries. Nonresident Bangladeshi investors will enjoy facilities similar to those of foreign investors. Moreover, they can buy newly issued shares/debentures of Bangladeshi companies and can maintain foreign currency deposits in special accounts for up to five years.

Rationalization of Import Duty

Duties and taxes on the import of goods that are produced locally will be higher than those applicable to the import of raw materials for producing such goods.

Other Incentives

Other incentives and protection that are available for encouraging investments include:

- exemption of tax on interest of foreign loans;
- exemption of tax on royalties, technical know-how, and technical assistance fees, etc.;
- liberal investment allowance for tax assessment;
- tariff protection for up to four years to new industries;
- import of machinery under supplier's credit or pay-as-you-earn scheme is freely allowed on approved terms;
- availability of long-term credit facilities on liberal debt-equity ratio from industrial financing institutions;
- income tax exemption of foreign technicians employed in approved industries for a period of three years;
- remittance of 50 percent of the salary of foreign nationals employed in approved industries;
- remittance of savings from earnings, retirement benefits, and personal assets of individuals on retirement/termination of services; and
- remittance of approved royalties, technical know-how, and technical assistance fees.

Special facilities and incentives that are ensured to foreign investors include:

- tax exemption on royalties, technical know-how, and technical assistance fees and the facilities for their repatriation;
- tax exemption on the interest on foreign loans;
- tax exemption on capital gains from the transfer of shares by the investing company;
- avoidance of double taxation in the case of foreign investors on the basis of bilateral agreements;
- exemption of income tax for up to three years for foreign technicians employed under the approved industries;
- remittance of up to 50 percent of the salary of foreigners employed in Bangladesh and the facilities of repatriation of their savings and retirement benefits and personal assets at the time of their return;
- no restriction in issuing work permits to foreign nationals in Bangladesh;
- facilities for repatriation of invested capital, profits, and dividends;

- guarantee against expropriation and nationalization of foreign private investment as per the Foreign Private Investment (Promotion & Protection) Act 1980;
- provision for transfer of shares held by foreigners to local partners with the permission of the Board of Investment (BOI) and the Exchange Control Department of Bangladesh Bank;
- reinvestment of repatriable dividend is treated as new foreign investment;
- working capital loan from local commercial banks is allowed to the industries set up under foreign investment; and
- foreign investors are entitled to get concessionary financial benefits similar to local investors.

Relaxation/Liberalization of Exchange Control Regulations

To facilitate foreign investment:

- Foreign firms and companies operating in Bangladesh do not require prior approval of Bangladesh Bank for remittance of profits to their head office.
- Prior approval of Bangladesh Bank is no longer needed for issuance of shares to nonresidents in respect of investments for setting up industries in Bangladesh.
- Prior permission of Bangladesh Bank is not required for remittance of dividends on such shares to nonresident investors.
- Nonresidents, including foreign enterprises, can invest in shares and securities through the Dhaka Stock Exchange without prior approval from Bangladesh Bank.
- For details regarding investment in shares and securities, and remittance of profits and dividends, investors should contact any bank dealing in foreign exchange.
- Residents who bring their earnings from abroad through normal banking channels then invest in new industries, stocks, shares, or government bonds, or use such funds for purchasing industries sold in auction by state-owned financial institutions are exempted from payment of income tax on such investments.

To further improve the investment climate:

- Without prior clearance of Bangladesh Bank, banks may open letters of credit against the supplier's credit and other foreign borrowings contracted in the private sector in accordance with prescribed criteria of the BOI, subject to a maximum effective rate of interest of the London Inter-Bank Offered Rate (LIBOR) plus 4 percent and a repayment period of not less than seven years.

- Repayment of principal and payment of interest with respect to such loans will not require prior permission of Bangladesh Bank.
- Prior permission of Bangladesh Bank will also not be required by banks for remittance of technical fees and royalties, if the banks conform to Board of Investment guidelines.
- Banks may extend term loans on normal banking considerations to foreign firms operating in Bangladesh without prior approval of Bangladesh Bank.
- Banks may remit savings of expatriate personnel at the time of their leaving Bangladesh without prior approval of Bangladesh Bank as long as the salary benefits are clearly stated in the employment contract approved by the Board of Investment.
- Banks may remit, without prior approval of Bangladesh Bank, dividends and capital gains of foreign investors on shares and securities purchased through the Dhaka Stock Exchange after withholding any of the payable tax.

Bangladesh has also made some modest beginnings in setting up export processing zones (EPZs). These are industrial estates with the necessary infrastructure facilities for the promotion of export-oriented industries and the attraction of foreign investment. Such zones or areas, which enjoy customs-free privileges and other special incentives, have been established in many developing countries, particularly since the 1970s, with a view to accelerating the industrialization process.

In Bangladesh, the Bangladesh Export Processing Zones Authority was created in 1980 and the first EPZ in the country was formally opened in Chittagong (CEPZ) in January 1982. Moving slowly in the earlier years, CEPZ has achieved some notable successes in recent times, with 53 industries currently in operation and employment opportunities created for more than 8,000 people.

While CEPZ is making steady progress, another zone has recently been set up near Dhaka (DEPZ), where a few industries have already gone into production and about 30 more are in the implementation stage. Bangladesh has plans to further expand the EPZ system.

Note that the overall fiscal and other incentives in Bangladesh presently compare very favorably with the incentives provided by the highly successful member countries of the Association of Southeast Asian Nations (ASEAN) and other Asian NIEs. There are certain common features of policies, regulations, and institutional environments in those economies, as depicted in Appendix Table 7.1, which have made them attractive to foreign investors. These features include the prominent role of the private sector; liberal opening of fields of investments to foreign and domestic companies; lowering, simplification, and/or removal of tariffs and surcharges; relaxation/deregulation of investment and capacity licensing system; relaxation of foreign investment regulations; and liberal foreign exchange policies (Khan 1991). Bangladesh's move in the same direction should brighten its prospects with foreign investors.

Performance of FDI

Earlier we noted that although FDI flows have increased rapidly throughout the world, foreign investment in Bangladesh has more or less stagnated recently. There has even been some withdrawal of existing foreign investment. The pharmaceutical firm, ICI, has totally wound up its operations in Bangladesh, as has Philips.[9] Even neighboring South Asian countries with histories, cultures, values, and attitudes similar to Bangladesh have succeeded in attracting much larger amounts of FDI compared to Bangladesh. How can this poor performance of Bangladesh be explained?

At the very outset it should be noted that various policy changes have been implemented in Bangladesh since the mid-1980s to create an attractive atmosphere for FDI. The Industrial Policy of 1991 reflects the commitment to the principle of market economy wherein foreign investors have almost total freedom in choosing the field and size of investment. Foreign investment is welcome in all areas except for five sectors reserved for the public sector. The security of investment is guaranteed by the Foreign Private Investment (Promotion and Protection) Act of 1980. Bilateral investment protection agreements and bilateral agreements regarding avoidance of double taxation have been signed with several countries. Bangladesh is also a signatory member of Multilateral Investment Guarantee Agency (MIGA), Overseas Private Investment Corporation of America (OPIC), and International Centre for Settlement of Industrial Disputes (ICSID). Foreign investment with 100 percent equity is allowed. There is no discrimination between local and foreign-owned enterprises. Foreign investors can borrow necessary working capital from the commercial banks irrespective of their equity shares on the basis of the bank-customer relationship. Procedures for establishing an industrial unit have been simplified. Liberal repatriation facilities are available for capital (including capital gains), posttax dividend on foreign capital, royalty, and technical fees, and 50 percent of the salary of employed foreign nationals, etc. The BOI was created in 1989 to provide all types of services and assistance to private investment including foreign private investment. To make the BOI more effective, its status has been recently raised through an Act of Parliament by bringing it under the direct control of the Prime Minister. The import policy has been substantially liberalized to provide easier access to imported inputs. Exchange control regulations have also been liberalized.

In spite of these substantial changes in government policy, Bangladesh has failed to attract satisfactory levels of FDI. The reasons for this failure can be identified without much difficulty. Government policy is obviously an important factor influencing inflows of FDI. But there are other, perhaps equally important, factors that determine the volume of foreign investment flows. Even insofar as government policies are concerned, which are fine in spirit, their actual implementation continues to create obstacles for both local and foreign investors. An inefficient and not-too-honest bureaucratic system is primarily responsible for this problem. The future of FDI inflows will be significantly influenced by the confidence generated by the Bangladesh government through proper implementation of declared policy packages.

Conceptually, cost-oriented foreign investment can be expected in a labor-surplus economy like Bangladesh, which can offer a cheap labor supply. Such investments were made in the Republic of Korea; Malaysia; Taipei,China; Thailand; Singapore; and, more recently, the People's Republic of China. Although Bangladesh apparently offers the prospect of low wages to the foreign investor, the real picture is somewhat different. Labor unrest and political instability lead to frequent interruptions of working days. Furthermore, not only is the productivity of Bangladeshi labor lower compared to even neighboring South Asian countries, but wages too do not compare favorably. The effect of fewer working days and low productivity has been to raise labor costs in Bangladesh compared to countries that compete in attracting FDI. The law and order situation has also doubtlessly dampened interest among foreign investors to come into Bangladesh.

Another important factor that affects the level of foreign investment inflow into a country is its level of infrastructure development—this includes roads and highways, supply of electricity, air and seaport links, direct international telecommunication facilities, gas and water supplies, and the availability of dependable workshops for handling repair and servicing works. It can hardly be claimed that Bangladesh has reached a level of infrastructure development that will satisfy the foreign investor. Apart from physical infrastructure, the level of development of the social infrastructure is also not satisfactory. A foreign investor looks for easy availability of technicians, midlevel management cadre, and quality workers, all of which are in short supply in Bangladesh.

Political stability of the recipient country is a decisive factor in attracting FDI. It cannot be said with conviction that Bangladesh has achieved political stability. Unless the political environment stabilizes, foreign investors will shy away from coming into the country. Achievement of political stability aside, continuity of government policies has to be ensured if foreign investment is to be attracted. Unfortunately, Bangladesh has a tradition of changing government policies with changes in political regimes.

The size and growth of the domestic economy is another important determinant of foreign investment inflows (UNCTC 1992a). Sadly, the Bangladesh economy has not shown unusual dynamism during the last ten years. Unless domestic economic performance improves considerably, Bangladesh cannot hope to attract large amounts of FDI. After all, in a situation where local investors shy away from new investment, why should foreign investors move in?[10]

However, there is reason to be somewhat optimistic about the prospects of increasing flows of FDI into Bangladesh in the near future. But for this optimism to be realized, the problems mentioned above must be overcome. In this connection, it may be noted that Bangladesh offers several potential areas of investment to the foreign investor. These include the following: (i) textiles, particularly fabrics and accessories for meeting the demand of export-oriented, readymade garments and apparel industries; (ii) leather and leather goods; (iii) electronics, particularly assembly of electronic products and manufacturing of components requiring mainly semiskilled labor; (iv) marine food; (v) agrobased industries for processing of exotic and tropical fruits, spices, and vegetables for export; (vi) light industrial products like toys, and machine and hand tools, and (vii) chemical industries.

It is crucial to change the international image of Bangladesh from the existing picture of a distant country, ravaged frequently by cyclones and floods, where people live in utter poverty, and where political turmoil has assumed almost chronic proportions. Intensive investment promotional drives including image-building are absolutely essential. This can be done by holding investment seminars in prospective investing countries and disseminating information on Bangladesh to the business community in these countries.

Conclusion

Bangladesh has abundant low-cost labor and liberal policies to attract foreign investment. It provides quite an attractive incentive package and has reorganized its FDI-related administration with a view to simplifying procedures and regulations of foreign investment projects. Yet the FDI inflow has remained far below the desired level. While the country faces increasing competition in attracting foreign investment from other developing countries and the former socialist bloc countries, there still remains a host of internal problems of various dimensions (Reza 1990). For example, the domestic market is still limited in size because of lack of sufficient purchasing power. There are also shortcomings related to dissemination of information regarding the investment climate in the country, different incentive packages offered, and regulations guiding foreign investment. A number of other maladies discourage FDI: problematic organizational behavior, a policy framework that still favors trade and services over industry, lack of coordination of infrastructure support, poor management of financial resources, and a generally negative country image leading to uncertainty and decreased confidence in the minds of entrepreneurs (UNIDO 1989).

Recently, however, some marked improvements have been achieved in macroeconomic management and political stability. It is said that macroeconomic and sectoral development programs, "together with a smoothly working investment approval mechanism are often more important than financial incentives and regulatory policies" (Khan 1991, 6).

Of course, there are many other areas in which Bangladesh could improve the general operating environment to attract more direct investment. Adequate infrastructure facilities, including roads, railways, waterways, ports, and telecommunication facilities are considered as prerequisites for private investments to increase. Although basic infrastructure facilities are not unsatisfactory in Bangladesh, they are often difficult to obtain expeditiously. The government will have to pay serious attention to improving the situation.

A second area relates to training of officials and human resource development. Like many other developing countries, Bangladesh faces two seemingly diverse labor supply problems; it lacks persons with special skills in the industrial sector and, at the same time, there is surplus labor in both the modern and traditional sectors. Paradoxically, the existence of surplus labor is, to a certain extent, due to a shortage of skills. A meaningful human resource development policy would have to address both these problems simultaneously. Also, training of officials is needed to enhance job skills of personnel for the overall improvement of administrative efficiency, and development of professionalism in financial management, audit, and accounting. Note that the BOI has been assigned wide ranging powers for the promotion of industrial investment. The Board should now be developed into an efficient and effective organization by training officials who are responsible for policy execution and program management (Reza 1990). It must be remembered that foreign investors are often deterred by bureaucratic red tape and import-export bottlenecks.

Third, Bangladesh should encourage the growth of the necessary support industries to provide basic machinery and parts, material inputs, components, and testing services to foreign firms who would be willing to use more local inputs if they are made available at competitive terms with regard to quality and cost (Khan 1991).

Fourth, the information system plays a vital role in generating interest among foreign investors to locate in a particular country. A well integrated information system is a first step in any activity concerning FDI, and must work in two ways. First, Bangladesh itself requires information regarding interested foreign investors, potential markets for export products, and the export market conditions of its competitors. Second, the information system should be able to provide detailed information about the country's economy and the investment opportunities it provides. Both these issues are vital, as only through a good synchronization of both can a concrete form be given to any decision relating to FDI.

Fifth, it is necessary to appreciate the role of existing TNCs as marketing assets to attract direct investment. Any newcomer is likely to seek guidance and counseling from those foreign firms that are already operating in the country. Therefore, attempts should be made to retain the goodwill of existing TNCs. In Bangladesh, a crisis of confidence occurred among TNCs recently and a number have already left the country. Serious attempts need, therefore, to be taken to reverse the trend so that a sense of confidence can be generated among TNCs.

Sixth, it is the overall sociopolitical milieu that has a great bearing on the FDI inflow (Government of Bangladesh 1991). Although the country has achieved greater macroeconomic stability, Bangladesh still faces an image problem with prospective investors. The frequent natural calamities such as floods and cyclones severely affect the national economy. On the labor front, there are also problems relating to various unlawful acts, absenteeism, strikes, and a general lack of discipline. Politically, the democratic system is not yet rooted on a firm basis. All these call for concerted efforts by all relevant actors—the government and its administration, opposition political parties, the labor force, and various professional groups—for the country to improve its general investment climate and to be able to lure investment from overseas in the face of stiffening global competition.

Finally, it is important to note that favorable government policies do not constitute a sufficient condition for attracting FDI; it can at best create a conducive environment for foreign investment (UNCTC 1991b). Growth of the recipient economy is seen as a crucial factor affecting FDI inflow. The economic performance of Bangladesh has been mixed, and this has discouraged FDI inflows even though, over time, policies governing foreign investment have been made relatively attractive. This would seem to indicate that a target-oriented approach would be more effective in attracting FDI into Bangladesh compared to simply improving rules and regulations relating to foreign investment. Products and sectors in which Bangladesh enjoys comparative advantages need to be identified, and potential foreign investors contacted and persuaded to invest in these activities (UNCTC 1989). Since technology transfer and access to new export markets are two major benefits of FDI (UNCTC 1992b), particular attention should be paid to these aspects while adopting the target-oriented approach.

Appendix Table 7.1

Nonequity Forms of FDI Participation in Bangladesh, 1976-1993

Nature of Agreement	*Number of Agreements*
Licensing	8
Royalty	3
Technical assistance/collaboration	31
Licensing and technical know-how	15
Licensing, technical know-how, and technical collaboration	8
Royalty, technical know-how, and technical assistance	12
Technical know-how, project preparation, quality control, and production method	1
Technical assistance and know-how collaboration	4
Licensing and technology transfer	2
Licensing and formulation	1
Licensing, technical assistance, and project preparation services	6
Erection of machinery	2
Machinery designs, layout agreements, and technology transfer	1
Technical assistance, machinery installation, and marketing assistance	5
Management service	3
Consultancy service	3

Source: Board of Investment, Government of Bangladesh, unpublished documents.

Appendix Table 7.2

Nonequity Participation by Industrial Groups, 1976-July 1993

Industrial Group	*Number of Agreements*
Food processing	5
Tobacco	4
Textiles	2
Pharmaceuticals	9
Other chemicals	43
Electronics	5
Machinery spares and equipment	4
Engineering	17
Miscellaneous	12

Source: Board of Investment, Government of Bangladesh, unpublished documents.

Appendix Table 7.3
FDI Investment Incentives in ASEAN Countries

Country	*Government Attitude*	*Corporate Tax Incentives*	*Tariff Incentives*	*Export Incentives*	*Free Ports, Zones*	*Capital Incentives*	*R&D Incentives*	*State/Regional Incentive*
Indonesia	Jakarta introduced several incentives to woo foreign capital in 1985. Investors are required to form joint ventures with local partners.	None	Import duty and value-added tax (VAT) drawbacks available on goods made locally by investment board-approved ventures.	Export-oriented firms can buy materials at international prices and quality for VAT drawbacks or exemptions.	No imports/export duties or VAT in bonded (100 percent export processing) zones, where firms are not restricted by investment board regulations; 100 percent foreign equity available.	Local investor rights for some joint ventures (e.g., in distribution and investment in other projects): VAT on imported capital goods may be paid in installments over five years.	None	None
Malaysia	Kuala Lumpur offers a rich assortment of incentives to foreign investors.	Five-year exemption from income and development taxes, and tax-free dividends during this time; or up to a 100 percent investment-tax allowance on capital spending over a five-year span.	Waivers of import duties and various taxes on machinery and raw materials for approved projects are common.	Tax abatements for a firm's value-added exports are available. Exporters qualify for special depreciation schedules; expenses related to the export operation are also deductible. Specific sectors eligible for other exports.	Eight export processing zones, located mainly along the west coast of peninsular Malaysia. Offer tenants tariff assistance. Licensed manufacturing/warehousing facilities provide similar benefits.	The Malaysian Industrial Development Authority helps investors obtain loans from government-sponsored banks.	Firms can deduct 133 percent of R&D expenditures from their corporate tax.	Various states operate several popular industrial estates.

(Continued next page)

Appendix Table 7.3 *(continued)*

Country	*Government Attitude*	*Corporate Tax Incentives*	*Tariff Incentives*	*Export Incentives*	*Free Ports, Zones*	*Capital Incentives*	*R&D Incentives*	*State/Regional Incentive*
Philippines	Manila extends a wide range of incentives to foreign investors.	Five to eight-year tax holiday, accelerated depreciation, other deductions for labor-related expenses, tax credit for capital equipment purchased locally.	Post-operative tariff protection of up to 50 percent of import's dutiable value, no duty or tax on capital goods imports.	Exporters may import parts tax and duty-free. Tax exemptions, accelerated depreciation, deductions for training costs and waiver of local taxes and licensing for firms in EPZs.	Export processing zones in Bataan, Mactan, and Baguio City offer exemption from various taxes and other perks.	None	In the agricultural sector, 25 percent of R&D costs are tax-deductible up to 10 percent of taxable income.	Firms locating in less-developed areas receive tax deductions for infrastructure expenditures.
Singapore	Government fosters industrial, commercial, and technological development with a comprehensive investment incentive package.	Five to ten-year tax holiday (three-year extension possible), dividends tax-exempt during holiday. Profits arising from expansions qualify for holiday. Allowance deductions for some industries/services.	Nearly all goods enter Singapore duty-free.	Partial tax exemption on export earnings for up to 15 years, double tax deduction for export-related expenses, profit derived from exported services tax-exempt.	Singapore is a free port with six free trade zones.	Concessional loans in certain industries, grants and loans to fund employee development, financial aid for local partners of foreign firms, rent rebates available in well-developed industrial estates.	Tax holiday, up to 50 percent investment tax credit on capital outlays, double deduction on expenses for R&D, accelerated depreciation; lower withholding tax on royalties, tech fees, R&D stipends.	Not applicable

(Continued next page)

Appendix Table 7.3 *(continued)*

Country	*Government Attitude*	*Corporate Tax Incentives*	*Tariff Incentives*	*Export Incentives*	*Free Ports, Zones*	*Capital Incentives*	*R&D Incentives*	*State/Regional Incentive*
Thailand	While Bangkok offers various incentives to attract foreign companies, officials maintain a watchful eye over such enterprises.	Income from royalties, goodwill, etc. may be tax-exempt; three to five-year tax holiday, dividends paid by exempted firms not taxed.	Import duty waivers on machinery, construction materials etc., possible for select industries: tariff protection from import competition, lower duties on some materials.	No duty or business tax on imported inputs used in exports, which are also tax and duty-exempt: tax break for export increases: double deduction for export-related costs: tax credit on raw materials; lower tax for producers of intermediaries for export sector.	Two export processing zones provide exemption from export duties, import tariffs, and business taxes on new plant, equipment, and raw materials; also full repatriation of profits.	No loans, grants, or subsidies available, although government provides infrastructure support for large projects.	None	Tax credits for firms willing to locate outside Bangkok.

Source: Khan (1991).

Notes

1. For a detailed discussion see Oman (1984).

2. Note that technological networking is even more concentrated than investment: over 90 percent of technology agreements are made between companies with their home base in the Triad (Japan, United States, and the European Community) (Ostry 1992).

3. See Table II.2 in UNCTC (1993).

4. In contrast to this ADB data, the data provided by the Bangladesh Board of Investment show higher levels of FDI inflows (as reported in Table 7.7), when exchange rates of different years are used to convert taka into US dollars and actual investment is assumed to be one third of the sanctioned amount of FDI. One reason explaining part of this divergence may be that while the data provided by ADB are net figures, the Board does not specify the same—its data may well have been presented on a gross basis.

5. For details see Reza, Rashid, and Alam (1987).

6. For a detailed discussion of the sectoral composition of FDI flows to developing countries see World Bank (1993).

7. The differences in amounts of FDI as shown in Tables 7.7 and 7.8 are attributable to the different sources of data for these tables.

8. Japan has been a notable exception in this regard.

9. Global relocation policy of the concerned TNCs has been primarily responsible for these withdrawals. The restrictive nature of Bangladesh's drug policy has doubtlessly also contributed to the withdrawal of ICI from the country.

10. The average annual growth rate of gross domestic product (GDP) was only around 4 percent in the 1980s. Total investment-GDP ratio declined from 12.2 percent in 1988-1989 to 10.4 percent in 1991-1992; the proportion of domestic private investment in GDP fell from 6.5 percent to 5.7 percent during the same period.

References

Agosin, R., 1985. "Trends and Issues in FDI". *CTC Reporter.* New York. 19 March 1996.

Asian Development Bank, 1993. *Asian Development Outlook 1993.* Hong Kong: Oxford University Press.

Bangladesh Bank, 1991. *Foreign Liabilities and Assets and Foreign Investment in Private Sector in Bangladesh, 1989 and 1990.* Dhaka.

Board of Investment, 1992. *Guide to Investment in Bangladesh.* Dhaka: Government of Bangladesh.

Brewer, T. L., 1991. *Foreign Direct Investment in Developing Countries, Patterns, Policies and Prospects.* Washington: World Bank.

Caves, R. E., 1982. *Multinational Enterprise and Economic Analysis.* Cambridge: Cambridge University Press.

Dunning, J. H., 1981. *Explaining the International Direct Investment Position of Countries: Toward a Dynamic or Developmental Approach.* Weltwirtschaftliches Archiv 11.

Government of Bangladesh (GOB), 1991. *Report of the Task Force on the Bangladesh Economy.* Vol. 2. Dhaka: University Press Limited.

Grosse, R., and J. N. Behrman, 1992. "Theory in International Business." *Transnational Corporations* 1:93-126.

Hymer, S., 1976. *The International Operation of National Firms.* Cambridge: MIT Press.

Khan, Z. S., 1991. *Patterns of Direct Foreign Investment in China.* World Bank Discussion Papers 130, China and Mongolia Department Series. World Bank, Washington.

Kojima, K., 1975. "International Trade and Foreign Investment: Substitute or Complements". *Hitotsubashi Journal of Economics* 16:1-12.

Kruggman, P., 1990. *Rethinking International Trade.* Cambridge: MIT Press.

Oman, C., 1984. *New Forms of International Investment in Developing Countries.* Paris: Organisation for Economic Co-operation and Development.

———, 1993. "Trends in Global FDI and Latin America." In C. I. Bradford, ed., *Mobilizing International Investment in Latin America.* Paris: Organisation for Economic Co-operation and Development.

Ostry, S., 1992. "The Domestic Domain: The New International Policy Arena." *Transnational Corporations* 1:7-26.

Ozawa, T., 1992. "Foreign Direct Investment and Economic Development." Centre on Transnational Corporations, New York.

Reza, S., 1990. "The Role of Transnational Corporations in Bangladesh: An Assessment Study." United Nations Centre for Transnational Corporations, New York. Mimeographed.

Reza, S., M. A. Rashid, and M. Alam, 1987. *Private Foreign Investment in Bangladesh.* Dhaka: University Press Limited.

Teece, D.J., 1986. "Transaction Cost Economics and the Multinational Enterprise: An Assessment." *Journal of Economic Behavior and Organization* 7: 21-45.

United Nations Centre Transnational Corporations (UNCTC), 1989. "Transnational Corporations and International Economic Relations: Recent Developments and Selected Issues." UNCTC Current Studies Series A (11). United Nations, New York.

_____, 1991a. *World Investment Report 1991: The Triad in Foreign Direct Investment*. New York: United Nations.

_____, 1991b. *Government Policies and Foreign Direct Investment*. New York: United Nations.

_____, 1992a. *The Determinants of Foreign Direct Investment: A Survey of the Evidence*. New York: United Nations.

_____, 1992b. *World Investment Report, 1992: Transnational Corporations as Engines of Growth*. New York: United Nations.

_____, 1993. *World Investment Report, 1993. Transnational Corporations and Integrated International Production*. New York: United Nations.

United Nations Industrial Development Organization (UNIDO), 1989. "Preparation of Industrial Master Plan." Preparatory Assistance Report (BGD/87/034/A/06/37). Government of Bangladesh, Dhaka.

Vernon, R., 1966. "International Investment and International Trade in the Product Cycle." *Quarterly Journal of Economics* 80(2):190-207.

Williamson, J., 1990. "What Washington Means by Policy Reforms." In J. Williamson, ed., *Latin American Adjustment: How Much Has Happened*. Washington: Institute for International Economics.

World Bank, 1993. *World Debt Tables 1993-94; External Finance for Developing Countries*. Vol. 1. Washington: World Bank.

8 FINANCIAL SECTOR REFORM

AKHTAR HOSSAIN AND SALIM RASHID

An efficient and developed financial system is necessary for two reasons: first, to transfer capital from savers to investors, and secondly, to direct capital to productive and profitable investment projects. More productive saving and investment leads to faster growth (King and Levine 1993, Zahler 1993). An efficient financial system also enhances growth by pooling risks and facilitating transactions (World Bank 1989). Therefore, Joseph Stiglitz (1994, 23) considers it the brain of the economic system:

> Financial markets . . . can be thought of as the "brain" of the entire economic system, the central locus of decisionmaking: if they fail, not only will the sector's profits be lower than would otherwise have been, but the performance of the entire economic system may be impaired.

The importance that economists now attach to finance is quite different from what they had thought even a few decades ago. As Summers (1994, xiii) points out:

> At times economists—going back to John Stuart Mill—and policy-makers have viewed the financial sector as irrelevant, except in times of crises, and hence have tried to repress finance and use it for the convenience of government. More recently, the pendulum has swung back toward Schumpeter, who viewed finance as the key sector for its role in allocating credit efficiently.

The role of finance in economic growth is even greater in developing countries as their tolerable margin of errors in resource allocation is small. The importance of a developed financial system in a developing country originates from its contribution to growth through efficient resource allocation. This point is emphasized by the World Bank (1989, 26):

> The biggest difference between rich and poor [countries] is the efficiency with which they have used their resources. The financial system's contribution to growth lies precisely in its ability to increase efficiency.

The financial sector, broadly interpreted, has two major roles in the context of a market-based approach to economic growth. It not only has to link investors and savers efficiently, but also has to build up the "modern" habits of saving and investment. One of the main problems in Bangladesh has been that the second goal has dominated conscious policy, and needs to be replaced by the first. Bangladeshis are now market-oriented and their banking habits have developed. It is time to make this habit provide suitable dividends.

International financial institutions and the International Monetary Fund and leading economists in unison have been propagating the message since the early 1970s that the diverse and complex financial needs of savers and investors in growing economies can be best satisfied through a market-oriented financial system.

This message has reached the policymakers in Bangladesh whose underdeveloped and inefficient financial system has remained in distress since the late 1970s and is affecting the performance of the entire economy. Note that the Bangladesh economy is now in transition from a stagnant to a dynamic one. Its growth performance is respectable and can be attributed to the people's efforts and initiatives from below (Hossain et al. 1994). Therefore, it is imperative that the government should make an effort to create a dynamic financial system. The difficulty is that one cannot start creating a dynamic financial system from scratch. It has a range of financial institutions with various roles and responsi-bilities. As these institutions are problem-ridden, the aid donors are pushing for financial reforms to improve the performance of the financial sector. However, to make a real difference such reforms should be comprehensive, rather than microsurgical. Financial reforms are not merely a technical matter; there are deep-rooted economic, ideological, and political issues which need to be addressed by the government at the highest political level.

There are a number of basic requirements for the development of an efficient and a dynamic financial system. They include the following:

- Profit maximization should be the basic working principle of banks and other financial institutions.[1] In a competitive business environment, only the efficient, innovative and dynamic financial institutions will survive and thrive.

- Nonbanking financial institutions should be developed; while their functions may be specialized, the roles of banks and nonbanking financial institutions often overlap. Financial innovations can blur the traditional differences between banking and nonbanking financial institutions. Besides complementing the roles of banks, the nonbanking financial institutions in a deregulated financial environment can keep the banks honest and competitive.

- Money and capital markets should be developed. Medium and large firms should be encouraged to raise equity capital for investment in long-term projects. To develop money and capital markets, the government should introduce policies which make portfolio investment financially attractive and administratively less cumbersome. Besides attracting foreign portfolio investors, the development of money and capital markets may decrease capital flight and induce the return of capital.

- All financial institutions should operate under rules and regulations, which are well-defined and can be implemented by the central bank; they should also contain clauses that permit adaptation during periods of financial innovation. The goal of such rules and regulations should not be to undermine the autonomy of financial institutions in conducting their normal financial activities but to ensure that their lending operations do not cause systematic risk and thus pose a danger to the financial system.

- No rules and regulations can substitute for human factors in the development of the financial system. Keeping this in mind, financial institutions must develop an incentive system in which the personal interests of officials converge with institutional interests. For instance, the salaries, bonuses and promotions of officials may be linked with the profits of financial institutions. In addition, all officials can be regularly assessed to ascertain their individual and joint performance and then to duly reward them for their work, innovation, honesty and responsibility. A well-defined disciplinary system should be put in place so that corrupt and irresponsible officials can be promptly and appropriately disciplined.

Having identified the basic principles, the rest of this chapter will review key issues in financial liberalization reform in Bangladesh in the light of such reform experiences in other developing countries.[2] An historical account of the evolution of the financial system, a brief description of both the structure of financial system and the origins of financial repression and distress in Bangladesh is given below.

The Financial System

Structure

The financial system of Bangladesh comprises an organized or institutionalized banking system and an unorganized credit market. The banking system comprises a central bank, four nationalized commercial banks, 14 private commercial banks, six foreign commercial banks, and three nationalized specialized banks. The Investment Corporation of Bangladesh (ICB), Bangladesh Shilpa Rin Sangstha (Industrial Credit Corporation) (BSRS), Bangladesh Samabaya (Co-operative) Bank (BSB), Grameen Bank, and House Building Finance Corporation (HBFC) are important financial institutions. There are also 22 insurance companies; the two dominant ones are in the public sector (Bangladesh Bureau of Statistics 1993a).

The Bangladesh Bank is the central bank of Bangladesh. It is responsible for all traditional central bank functions, accepting deposits and collecting money for the government of Bangladesh, and for supervision and regulation of both nationalized and private commercial banks. It acts as the lender of last resort for both government and commercial banks. Besides these functions, according to the Bangladesh Bank Order 1972, the Bangladesh Bank is responsible for maintaining monetary and financial stability through appropriate policies and measures authorized by law.

In 1972 all the commercial banks (except the foreign-owned banks) in Bangladesh were nationalized, and, to foster development efforts, three specialized banks were established. At the moment there are four nationalized commercial banks—the Agrani Bank, Janata Bank, Rupali Bank, and Sonali Bank. These banks dominate the banking sector in terms of deposits and lending. Over the years the number of branches of nationalized banks has increased (Data Appendix) and they have particularly helped to develop banking habits among rural and small town people. Besides accepting deposits, they have also performed the role of dispensing subsidized credits to priority sectors operating under the guidelines of the Bangladesh Bank.

In 1983 the government allowed six private commercial banks to operate in the country in an attempt to encourage the expansion of credit facilities and to foster competition between nationalized and private commercial banks. The number of private commercial banks is now 14, but three of them started operations only recently (April 1995). Two previously nationalized banks (Pubali Bank and Uttara Bank) were denationalized in 1984.

The specialized banks are the Bangladesh Krishi (agricultural) Bank, the Bangladesh Shilpa (industrial) Bank, and the Rajshahi Krishi Unnayan (agricultural development) Bank. The Grameen Bank is another specialized financial institution. It was established by a government order in 1983 to provide credit to the rural poor. Except the Grameen Bank, all specialized financial institutions dispense subsidized (low interest) loans to priority sectors. The Bangladesh Shilpa Bank and the Bangladesh Shipa Rin Sangstha are traditional development banks. Their primary function has been to provide medium-term and long-term loans for private industrial projects. (The nationalized commercial banks also provide industrial loans.) The Bangladesh Krishi Bank provides loans for small agricultural projects. Except the Grameen Bank, the development financial institutions do not raise deposits from the public. They receive funds from both the government and foreign development banks and agencies. The Bangladesh Bank provides them with refinance facilities.

The Investment Corporation of Bangladesh (established in 1976) has the main objective of encouraging and broadening the base of industrial investment. It assists in raising equity capital for development bank projects through public offerings and has a substantial bridge financing program.

The Dhaka Stock Exchange is still in its infancy. After a period of suspension following the independence of Bangladesh in 1971, it was reactivated in 1976. Although with the disinvestment policy of the government and with the privatization of nationalized industries the stock exchange market grew slowly during the 1980s, it remained underdeveloped. Humphrey (1990, 88) called it a "relatively primitive institution." Since the early 1990s, with the considerable expansion of private business, including banks, insurance and industry and the emergence of private business as the main source of economic activity, trading activity in the stock exchange has significantly increased. Recently, a second stock exchange has been opened at Chittagong.

The government has taken a number of measures to encourage investment in the stock exchange. The Securities and Exchange Commission has been set up. It has a wide range of responsibilities and power to regulate the operations of the stock exchange. Commercial banks have been allowed to make loans against shares quoted in the stock exchange up to 40 percent of the market value of shares. Foreign exchange regulations have been relaxed to encourage foreign portfolio investment (Government of Bangladesh, 1995).

In Bangladesh, there is no national social security system. Insurance companies are the main contractual savings institutions. As mentioned above, there are 22 insurance companies. Two of them—the Jiban Bima (life-insurance) Corporation and the Sadaran Bima (general insurance) Corporation—are nationalized. They dominate the insurance industry as they have a virtual monopolistic control over the public sector. Private insurance companies are restricted to conduct business within the pri-vate sector. All insurance activities in Bangladesh are primarily concentrated in urban areas; the rural sector remains largely outside any insurance coverage. Unlike developed countries, the contribution of insurance companies to capital market development has been limited. The investment portfolios of insurance companies are dominated by government and government-guaranteed securities, real estate, and bank term deposits.

The Bangladesh House Building Finance Corporation was established in 1973 with the sole objective of providing credit facilities for the construction, repair, and remodeling of dwelling houses and apartments. It does not raise capital through public issues of securities. However, debentures issued by it are held by the Bangladesh Bank and the commercial banks. (Such debentures meet liquidity requirements of commercial banks.)

The rural sector has an unorganized credit market. As the coverage of the Grameen Bank is limited, the informal credit market meets the credit needs of most of the rural people. Some farmers borrow heavily subsidized loans from agricultural banks. The main lenders in the rural credit market are money lenders, friends and relatives, landlords, traders, shopkeepers, and commission agents. The nature and terms of their credit are not well-defined and publicized, although it is known that some of them combine lending with trading, employment, and other activities. The lender-borrower relationship is characterized by informality, secrecy, and promptness. Interest rates in the unorganized credit market are often higher than those in the formal banking sector.[3]

Origins of Financial Repression and Distress

The Pakistani government of the 1950s and 1960s used the commercial banks and other financial institutions as a cheap source of credits to the private sector for export processing and import substituting industrialization. To keep the loan rates of interest low, the government imposed controls over the deposit rates of interest. Controls over interest rates, selective credit allocation programs, suppression of money and capital markets by various rules and regulations, and maintenance of an overvalued domestic currency created a repressed financial system.

Upon independence from Pakistan in 1971, Bangladesh inherited this repressed financial system. Things got worse when in 1972 the government nationalized all commercial banks (excluding foreign banks) and other financial institutions. The nationalization of financial institutions was associated with the nationalization of heavy industries and foreign trade.

There is a broad consensus among political economists that the nationalization measures of the government were driven by politics, rather than ideology (Islam 1985, Jahan 1980). The economic viability of nationalized industries and financial institutions was not seriously studied. Humphrey (1990, 36) argues that the Mujib government went for nationalization under the influence of economic advisors with socialistic leanings:

> One cannot escape the thought that the principal advocates of the socialist solution were more motivated by ideology than economics. They constantly spoke and wrote about the danger to socialism posed by the bourgeoisie rather than centering on pragmatic considerations related to economic development. The academic economists did not understand reality; they misled the Mujib government, and few saw the private sector as the only real hope for growth. The obsession with ideological triumph is the only reason

> one can discover for taking over the Bengali-owned industrial enterprises, along with the abandoned properties.

It appears that the political leadership after independence fell in the trap of its agitation politics during the autonomy movement of the late 1960s when the feeling of deprivation and Pakistani exploitation provided an appeal for economic and political populism. The economic condition of the people in the 1960s was indeed conducive to political mobilization and recurrent rhetoric that inspired the people.

All nationalized industries (jute industries in particular) have incurred heavy losses since the early 1970s and, under the instruction of the government, the nationalized commercial banks have provided them credits to keep them alive (Hossain 1995a). Along with the increasing role of nationalized banks in the allocation of credits to priority sectors (including public enterprises), their primary role as mobilizer of financial resources diminished as the real deposit rates of interest were negative and fluctuated widely with inflation until recently (Data Appendix). As the loan rates of interest were negative and remained so until the early 1980s, bank credits became a scarce resource and the limited funds that were available for distribution in the private sector after meeting the needs of priority sectors were rationed among economically and politically powerful borrowers. It created inefficiency in investment and the nonrepayment of loans by borrowers. In the end the nationalized banking sector had to be recapitalized by the government during the late 1980s and early 1990s to keep them operationally solvent.

Financial Sector Reform Measures

The Bangladesh government has acknowledged the need for financial reforms since the early 1980s. In 1984 the government convened the National Commission on Money, Banking and Credit. It presented its report in June 1986. Based on its recommendations, the government has undertaken some reform measures. Although not comprehensive and carefully planned, the recommendations were important and are in the right direction. This section briefly reports some of the reform measures undertaken by the government since the late 1980s. The consequences of these reforms will be examined later.

Interest Rates

The major reform initiative was taken in November 1989 when the interest rates were partially deregulated. The aim was to introduce flexibility in the determination of both the deposit and lending rates of interest. The Bangladesh Bank set the ceilings and floors and individual banks were allowed to set their interest rates within the stipulated band. To ensure that the deposit rate of interest did not fall below the inflation rate, the Bangladesh Bank established a floor close to the inflation rate. A ceiling was also established to prevent banks from raising deposits at an unusually high interest rate because such deposits could only be loaned out for risky projects. The idea of a band around the deposit rate of interest was to maintain a positive real deposit rate of interest at a reasonable level. A band was also established for the lending rate of each category of loans. Banks were required to set their lending rates within the band. To establish the band the Bangladesh Bank calculated the shadow interest rate for each sector which was based on the long-run average cost of lending; such a cost included the costs of funds, the operational costs of banks, the earnings on capital, and the costs of bad loans. Once the shadow interest rate was determined, the band was set at, say, plus or minus two points around it.

The ceilings and floors of interest rates were reviewed and adjusted by the Bangladesh Bank a number of times and the commercial banks were allowed to adjust their interest rates once in a month within the revised bands. Some further flexibility in interest rates was introduced from June 1992. Commercial banks were permitted to differentiate interest rates to individual borrowers to include any risk premium of lending to priority sectors—agriculture, small and cottage industries, and exports. Most banks, however, did not differentiate interest rates to individual borrowers because they believed that they would not be able to make any systematic distinctions among borrowers and that any differences in interest rates originating from risk factors could not be effectively defended.

Besides these measures, the rate structure was simplified by redu-cing the number of lending categories from 29 to 12. As the government wanted to subsidize a number of priority sectors—agriculture, jute, exports, and small and cottage industries—provisions were made to provide interest subsidies through budgetary means. Further revision of the interest rate policy was made in April 1992. Except for three sectors—agriculture, small industries and exports—the interest rate bands for lending have been completely removed. For deposits, the ceilings have been removed, but the floors have been kept. Except for the Bangladesh Krishi Bank and the Rajshahi Krishi Unnayan Bank, the refinancing windows of the Bangladesh Bank have been closed and a rediscount window at the bank rate has been opened for commercial banks. The rediscount window operates to support monetary policy rather than to control banks. The Bank Rate was gradually lowered from 9.75 percent in January 1990 to 5.5 percent on March 3, 1994 (Government of Bangladesh 1995).

Monetary Management

Since 1990-1991 the Bangladesh Bank has gradually moved from direct to indirect instruments for monetary management. Credit ceilings and direct controls of interest rates have largely been removed. Although the presumptive targets for the expansion of money supply and credit are set as before, they are used to provide a framework for identifying the need to regulate the money supply through indirect manipulation of the reserve money. Since December 1990 the Bangladesh Bank has introduced a 91-day Bangladesh Bank bill for monetary intervention. This bill has been auctioned at market-related yields since then. To increase investable funds with commercial banks, there were also reductions in Statutory Reserve Requirements for a number of times during the period April 25, 1991 to May 28, 1992 (Government of Bangladesh 1995).

Provisions, Supervision, and Capital Adequacy

Over time all nationalized commercial banks have made large unrecoverable bad loans. However, provisions were not made for such loans until the Bangladesh Bank, as a part of the financial reforms, introduced regulations in 1989 which required the commercial banks to annually classify their loans into four categories—unclassified, substandard, doubtful, and bad/loss. Loans that were overdue by one year, three years and five years were classified as substandard, doubtful, and bad/loss loans. The rates of provision for unclassified, substandard, doubtful, and bad loans were set at 1, 10, 50, and 100 percent, respectively. Such a requirement replaced the general provision of 2.5 percent of total loans set in 1985.

In 1989 the Bangladesh Bank introduced the legal requirement of capital adequacy for banks. The aim of capital adequacy requirement has been to reduce the risk of depositors—particularly in the case of private banks. The private banks have so far maintained capital adequacy. The capital adequacy requirement of nationalized banks has been roughly met through the infusions of capital by the government. Over the 1990-1992 period, the government issued bonds of taka 34 billion, of different maturity and interest rates, to recapitalize nationalized banks. The government has also decided to recapitalize banks for the losses that originated from both the jute industry and agricultural bad loans (Asian Development Bank 1994).

Loan Recovery

Loan defaults have remained the major problem in the financial sector of Bangladesh. Some measures have been taken by the government for loan recovery, particularly from large defaulters.

In 1986 a loan recovery program was initiated that set loan recovery targets for both industrial and agricultural loans. An action program was adopted, which included prosecution of willful defaulters, prohibitions of defaulters from holding public offices or directorship of banks, limitations on access to new loans, and denial of import licenses to industrial loan defaulters. To induce agricultural loan repayments, an interest amnesty program was also introduced in 1986. These programs were followed by a debt collection strategy by each nationalized bank for its 100 largest loan defaulters. To close the legal loopholes and to expedite loan recovery, the Parliament enacted a Financial Loan Courts Act. On the basis of it, the government has established financial loan courts at the district level. An amendment has also been made in the Financial Loan Courts Act to allow for prosecution of defaulters (Asian Development Bank 1994, Hassan 1993). More recently, the government has attempted to shame defaulters by publishing lists of the most egregious offenders.

Privatization of Nationalized Banks

The government has recognized the need for privatizing the four remaining nationalized commercial banks to develop an efficient financial system. However, it has so far failed to do so for two main reasons. First, the nationalized commercial banks have remained in a financially unsound and distressed condition. As the performance of two previously nationalized banks (Uttara Bank and Pubali Bank) privatized in 1984 has been less than satisfactory, there was a lack of interest of investors for the Rupali Bank shares when they were offered for sale (Humphrey 1990). Second, the militant trade unions and other vested interest groups have been strongly opposing the privatization of these banks. Such an opposition has been effective because the government remains half-hearted about the privatization of both nationalized industries and banks. (The bureaucracy, as expected, is also not enthusiastic about privatization.) As Humphrey (1990, 155) comments on the government's indecisiveness in regard to privatization:

> The Bangladesh government has never really defined what role it should play in the development of the economy. It cannot restrain itself from interfering directly where it shouldn't, and would not resign itself to the role of planner, guru, coordinator, monitor, and pump primer, where it can be most productive. . . . Therefore, the government continues to give the ailing public enterprises one shot in the arm after another, while providing inconclusive encouragement to the private sector. Without coming to terms to reality or exerting the influence it should over powerful elites in the country, the government continues to drift and waver.

Exchange Rates

At the time of independence, the Bangladesh taka was pegged with the British pound sterling. Despite a large devaluation, it remained overvalued as the rate of inflation was high between 1972 to 1975. During this period there was no secondary foreign exchange market and the allocation of foreign exchange for imports was made through import licenses at the official exchange rate. In 1974 there was a major balance of payments crisis. In 1975 the exchange rate of the taka was devalued against the pound sterling. But it was not large enough to eliminate the overvaluation of the exchange rate of the taka.

Since the mid-1970s an active secondary foreign exchange market has been developed, where under the Wage Earners' Scheme, the foreign currency remittance of overseas Bangladeshi workers are transacted and used for financing of a list of imports. With the increasing inflows of such remittances, the secondary foreign exchange market has now become the important source of finance for nongovernment imports. The exchange rate of the Bangladesh taka determined in the secondary foreign exchange market is considered a proxy for the market-determined exchange rate. The difference between the official exchange rate and the secondary exchange rate as percentage of the official exchange rate is a measure of exchange rate premium. It was high throughout the 1970s, but narrowed down significantly during the 1980s. Ahammad and Fane (1994) found that the exchange rate premium declined from 31 percent in 1978 to just 1.8 percent in 1991.

In 1989 a reform program was introduced by the government to unify the two exchange rates. It was achieved in January 1992. The taka was made convertible for current account transactions in March 1994. In April 1994, the Bangladesh government accepted the status of Article VIII of the International Monetary Fund. It has made the government obligated to current account convertibility and the liberalization of exchange transactions on current account (Ahammad and Fane 1994, Government of Bangladesh 1995).

Issues in Financial Sector Reform

Financial Reforms: Economics, Ideology, and Politics

Financial Sector Problems and Financial Reforms

Proponents of financial reforms in Bangladesh have identified the problems of the financial sector and linked them with the performance of the economy. As the push for financial reforms have come from foreign aid donors, it is relevant to report Bangladesh's financial sector problems as they see them. The USAID Financial Sector Reform Project under way in Bangladesh in its Request for Proposal Document (1991, 9) stated the problems as follows:

> Major inadequacies in the financial market and institutions inhibit the formal financial sector from performing an effective and dynamic role in the economic development of the country. The existence of this deep-seated structural problem is manifest in various symptoms: non-existence of modern monetary policy instruments; inadequate bank supervision; inadequate mobilization of savings; misallocation of credit; widespread loan defaults and delinquencies; and inefficient credit delivery. The prevalence of these problems reduces the level of investment, the productivity of capital and the volume of savings. This results in a less than optimum utilization of resources and a lower economic growth rate, with consequent diminished employment opportunities. The weakness of the financial system adversely affects virtually all aspects of the economy and all regions of the country.

From the above list of problems, it is apparent that the objectives of financial sector reforms in Bangladesh are to develop a market-oriented, world-integrated financial system for mobilization of savings, efficient allocation of resources from domestic and foreign sources, and elimination of poverty through sustained economic growth.

Ideological Basis of Financial Reforms

Financial reforms in most developing countries during the past two decades have been carried out in the belief that financial liberalization reform promotes saving, investment, and economic growth (McKinnon 1973, Shaw 1973). Nevertheless, there is always a temptation among many to trace the idea of financial reforms in the extreme form of Monetarism. In fact, financial reforms in the Southern Cone of Latin American countries during the mid-1970s were treated as test cases for Monetarism—the "Chicago Boys" syndrome (Edwards and Edwards 1987).

Financial reforms are ultimately political decisions and they cannot succeed in achieving their goals unless there is an overwhelming political support for reforms. However, any linkage of financial reforms with politics could be counterproductive if not handled carefully. Perhaps ideological debate can be minimized by describing financial reforms as a strategy for resource mobilization and allocation with the objective of poverty reduction through economic growth.

For the success of financial reforms, political differences based on ideology should be kept aside to the extent feasible. While difficult, this is not impossible. It has been done in some developed countries, such as Australia and New Zealand. Abbott (1986, 343) reports their cases:

> Financial reform is very much the result of political decisions, although, perhaps, not of stereotypic political ideology. As the examples of Australia and New Zealand show, stereotypes can be misleading. Both countries have Labor Party governments which, according to stereotypes, favor control. Yet both governments have readily dismantled controls.

Government's Commitment to Financial Reforms

The major political debate in Bangladesh is not on the question of whether there is a need for financial reforms, it is about the pace and scope of reforms. Will the Bangladesh government move only to the extent that is required to satisfy aid conditionality? The government knows that there are political costs of financial reforms as they affect the interests of various organized groups. As such political costs are not compensated by the political support of unorganized, dispersed beneficiaries of financial reforms, the government remains prone to making excuses for the delay of reforms to aid donors. There is little doubt that political considerations have slowed the pace of reform in Bangladesh (Humphrey 1990). Many argue that for political reasons, reforms at a tortoise-pace are common in other developing countries. As Blair (1983, 187) makes the point in the context of rural subsidized credits:

> If the pain involved in imposing higher interest rates were to be borne by the economically poor and politically weak, we could rest assured that many governments would find the courage to set things right. But as is all too clear, it is the rural rich and powerful who would have to make the sacrifices, and few governments are willing to undermine their main support in the countryside.

Economic Growth and Poverty Alleviation

Most models of development consider poverty alleviation as the ultimate goal of economic growth. However, they differ in their approaches to poverty alleviation. Proponents of financial reforms are of the view that financial reforms would promote economic growth, and alleviate poverty, but not immediately.[4] As the development experiences of East Asian countries show, there is indeed a link between sustained economic growth and poverty alleviation (Chowdhury and Islam 1993). Based on the findings of a major study on poverty in developing Asia (including Bangladesh), Quibria and Srinivasan (1994, 63) have strongly endorsed this point:

> ... the countries which achieved the most success with poverty alleviation are those that achieved sustained growth. If ranked in terms of success in poverty alleviation, the three outstanding countries are [South] Korea, Thailand, and Indonesia which had remarkable success in terms of growth.

In the context of India, Hughes (1994, 593) comes to a similar conclusion:

> Poverty alleviation and equitable income distribution have been a major policy focus of countries such as India since the 1950s, but because national policies have not delivered growth, poverty persists.... Rapid growth is essential for poverty alleviation and improved income distribution.... With policies targeted toward rapid growth, "trickle down" from growth works very well. Even low-income countries can alleviate poverty markedly by removing policy-created distortions.

The Bangladesh Bank and Monetary Policy for Price Stability

Financial reforms must start from the Bangladesh Bank—the apex of the financial system. To begin with, the government must take a decision about the role of the Bangladesh Bank in the design and conduct of monetary policy. The main objective of monetary policy should be defined and the conduct of monetary policy should be simplified.

Presently the Bangladesh Bank does not exhibit independence within the government in the design and conduct of monetary policy. Experiences of many developed countries (e.g., Australia) show that even though under the British system of government the central bank remains under the control of the Ministry of Finance (or Treasury) because fiscal policy in these countries dominates or dictates the direction of monetary policy, the central bank can raise the standard of economic policy debate by articulating policies, conducting research on critical economic issues, and organizing and participating in policy discussion at national and international fora. The central bank is capable of raising its status and policymaking capability to such an extent that any government would find it difficult to ignore its views on economic matters. The Bangladesh Bank cannot and should not be an exception. It is not that the Bangladesh Bank does not have the legal basis to establish itself in a position of policy influence, it has not made any major efforts so far to create such a position for itself. By taking a low profile and restricting its role to the implementation of monetary and financial decisions taken by the Ministry of Finance, the Bank has failed to gain respect for its independent participation in financial policy. Therefore, both the government and the Bangladesh Bank must address the question of how the position of the Bank can be raised to a level where it can become an effective and independent source of policy advice to the government. In fact the success of financial reforms will depend largely on how well the Bangladesh Bank performs its increased role and responsibility in a deregulated financial environment.[5]

Objective of Monetary Policy

What should be the objective of monetary policy in a deregulated financial environment? Presently monetary policy in Bangladesh aims at achieving a multitude of objectives, such as economic growth, price and exchange rate stability, equilibria in the balance of payments, and development of money and capital markets (Bangladesh Bank Annual

Report various issues, Government of Bangladesh 1995, Rahim and Sohrabuddin 1988). Neither the order of priority of these objectives is explicit nor any conflict in the simultaneous achievement of multiple objectives is identified or acknowledged.

Monetary and financial stability are prerequisites for market-based economic growth. Fiscal and monetary discipline are cornerstones of macroeconomic stability. When feasible, monetary policy has a comparative advantage in achieving price stability. As Guitian (1994, 656) remarks,

> Although monetary developments cannot affect real variables sustainably, disorderly monetary conditions—leading to monetary instability—can and do hamper growth, employment, and economic activity.... Thus, there is at least full agreement that the target of monetary policy should be monetary stability. More frequently, this is interpreted as the achievement of domestic price stability--that is, stability in the internal value of money.

Conduct of Monetary Policy

In a developed financial system the debate on the conduct of monetary policy revolves around the choice between interest rate or a monetary aggregate as being the more appropriate intermediate target to achieve stability in the economy. In an underdeveloped financial system, it is difficult to use monetary policy to achieve short-term stability in the economy. If monetary policy is assigned the role of price stability, this should be conducted on a medium-term or long-term basis.

Presently Bangladesh Bank conducts monetary policy by targeting the growth rate of the broad money supply and using credit control and support measures to contain the growth rate of the money supply within a predetermined target level. Bangladesh Bank projects the growth rate of the broad money supply by taking into account the projected growth rate of real output, the rate of monetization of the subsistence sector, and a permissible rate of inflation. Once the projected growth rate of the money supply is determined, the Bank tries to keep the actual growth rate of the money supply within the projected rate by controlling the growth rate of bank credits (Rahim and Sohrabuddin 1988, Sohrabuddin 1986).

The implicit assumptions behind monetary targeting are that there exists a stable money demand function and the monetary authority has control over the money supply. The Bangladesh Bank is yet to specify and estimate a money demand function for Bangladesh and test for its stability. However, academic research suggests that the broad money demand function in Bangladesh is broadly stable and has remained so after whatever financial reforms have taken place since the late 1980s (Hossain 1993). However there is no guarantee that the money demand function will remain stable after a comprehensive financial reform[6] (Hossain 1994, Tseng and Corker 1991). The question of controllability of the money supply is yet to be rigorously investigated. Empirical results of a recent study (Hossain 1995b, 1995c) suggest that both the narrow and broad money multipliers in Bangladesh are unstable. Along with this problem, there remains an issue of whether a fixed or a flexible exchange rate system is appropriate for price stability in developing countries. A floating exchange rate system allows a country to control its money supply and conduct an independent monetary policy with the goal of achieving price stability. While it may be a strong argument for the flexible exchange rate system, in a developing country which lacks monetary-fiscal discipline, the fixed exchange rate system is often considered better as it can impose monetary-fiscal discipline and achieve price stability through promoting policy credibility and time consistency (Edwards 1993). In reality, as Aghevli et al. (1979) and later Pilbeam (1992, 269) found, for developing countries there is no clear-cut gain in choosing either the fixed or flexible exchange rate system in terms of its disciplinary role.

> The choice between the two regimes is seen to depend crucially upon the type of shock impinging upon the economy, the objectives of the authorities and the structural parameters of the economy....

Since the early 1980s the official exchange rate of the Bangladesh taka has been pegged to a basket of currencies and is frequently adjusted. This system has brought relative flexibility in the exchange rates of the taka against foreign currencies. It has an implication for the conduct of monetary policy. Under the fixed exchange rate system the money supply is endogenous and the monetary policy is often conducted by controlling bank credit with the objective of stabilizing balance of payments, rather than the price level. The gradual move of exchange rates in Bangladesh from fixed to managed floating might have brought the stock of money base under the control of the monetary authority. The money supply however cannot be considered completely under the control of the monetary authority because the money multiplier is unstable. It does not necessarily imply that the monetary authority should abandon the current practice of monetary targeting, especially since the authority is yet to develop an alternative approach to the conduct of monetary policy. Importantly, as most monetary relations (e.g., money demand and money multiplier) undergo changes with financial reforms and the spread of financial technology, the monetary authority in Bangladesh should remain cautious and adopt a money growth rule with feedback so that any changes in monetary relations during financial reforms can be incorporated.[7] While designing the money growth rule, it may also be necessary to take into account the shortcomings of the Quantity Theory in the Bangladesh economy.

The application of the quantity theory presupposes stable and widespread markets, stable velocity, and constant or predictable income. In the Bangladeshi context, the following caveats have to be made:

- Markets are not utilized in many areas and the subsistence sector is estimated to be as large as one third of the economy.

- Financial markets, in the textbook sense, do not exist. Banks assume that there is an infinite demand for credit and simply follow procedures in allocating the available credit. No intermediation via interest rates is done.

- In the banks' balance sheets, over 50 percent of assets are classified as "others". Hence no optimization models are appropriate.

- No reliable estimates exist for three types of money-using sets of transactions—smuggling, remittances outside the wage earners' scheme, and unreported transactions.

The National Income Accounts give no guide as to the appropriate orders of magnitude needed for making corrections for these caveats.

Fiscal policy discipline is a necessary requirement for monetary stability. Central bank autonomy can provide a necessary institutional limit on unsustainable monetization of budget deficits. However, it must be emphasized that central bank autonomy by itself cannot ensure monetary policy credibility, which depends ultimately on the credibility of government policy as a whole.

Given the constraints of the political system in Bangladesh on its inefficient government, constitutional safeguards may well be necessary on fiscal, debt, and money creation capacities. At an extreme it may involve the arrangement of some form of fiscal constitution. In fact fiscal constitutions exist in Indonesia; Thailand; and Taipei,China. Besides these institutional arrangements, the greater openness of the economy can serve as a further institutional constraint on macroeconomic misma-nagement and financial instability (Hossain and Chowdhury 1995).

The Commercial Banking System

The nationalized and private commercial banks are the backbone of the financial system in Bangladesh. Four nationalized banks dominate the banking sector. However, the private banks (domestic and foreign) are growing and increasing their market shares. Compared with the distressed nationalized banking sector, the growth of private banking is a healthy development. As the area of operation of private banks is still limited to a few city areas, they have not created any effective competition with nationalized banks.

Nationalized Commercial Banks

As pointed out above, all nationalized banks are technically insolvent and have remained in distress since the late 1970s. Inefficiency, mismanagement, corruption, and loan defaults are the main causes of banking distress. Loan defaults are linked with the government's industrial policy and directed credit programs to priority sectors. The problem started when the banks, industries, and foreign trade were nationalized in the early 1970s. Most subsidized credits have gone to loss-making nationalized industries, the jute industry in particular. Such loans were made at the direction of the government. As Humphrey (1990, 55) aptly described the lending procedure of nationalized commercial banks:

> Banks gave little scrutiny to loan requests from BJMC [Bangladesh Jute Mills Corporation] and BTMC [Bangladesh Textiles Mills Corporation]. Bad repayment experiences with these and other public institutions induced greater caution in bankers; but most of their reticence was directed, ironically, at private sector applicants. As Rahim [1978] points out, the lending strategy of commercial banks was not based on development, much less commercial, considerations. Politics had historically dominated in both the

official development financial institutions (DFIs) and the nationalized commercial banks (NCBs).

Privatization of nationalized industries has often been considered one way of improving their performance. Such a decision may improve the performance of nationalized banks as well. Thus financial reforms are linked with the government decision of privatization of nationalized industries. However, as expected, the government is dragging its feet for political reasons. The government has been facing opposition from vested interest groups, which include workers, trade unions, bureaucrats, and politicians (Humphrey 1990). Nevertheless, sooner or later the government will have to make hard decisions about the privatization of the bulk of nationalized industries. The government must realize that privatization of nationalized industries is good for these industries as well as for nationalized banks. Until such a decision is made, the nationalized banks should at least have the autonomy in lending to nationalized industries according to commercial principles. In fact it is widely argued that subsidized credits from nationalized banks have gone against the long-term viability of nationalized industries. Instead of improving their performance, they have operated under soft budget constraints. As personal and institutional interests diverged, the officials of both nationalized banks and industries have become involved in frauds and corruption and enriched themselves while their organizations have gone to bankruptcy in unison. Therefore, the future of nationalized banks are closely linked with that of nationalized industries.

Private Commercial Banks

The long-term solution of problems in the commercial banking sector is the development of the private banking system in terms of geographical coverage, deposit-taking, and commercial lending to all kinds of activities. As indicated above, 14 private banks now operate in the country. All of them are in the urban areas. They have not yet been able to generate any effective competition with nationalized commercial banks. There are newspaper reports (e.g., the *Bangladesh Observer*, several issues, April 1995) that some private banks are not following the rules and regulations of the Bangladesh Bank. Therefore, while the rapid growth of private banking should be considered a positive development, the Bangladesh Bank must keep an eye on private banks' lending activities. The development of a healthy private banking system will take some time and require the prudential supervision and guidance of the Bangladesh Bank. Like any other private business, private banks are likely to face various problems in the initial stages. The Bangladesh Bank must even be prepared to smooth out any potential private bank failures before they affect the financial system.

Although depositors have to be partly protected to develop confidence in the private banking system, the owners of private banks must bear the principal risk of banking. Risk taking and reckless gambling are two different things. As a precautionary measure, the Bangladesh Bank must ensure that the moral hazard problem induced by deposit insurance does not become endemic in the private banking sector. Provided that private banks are subject to well-defined lending constraints, they will take only necessary risks and adopt a cautious approach to lending. That is what the banking business is all about. It is the responsibility of the Bangladesh Bank to develop an ethic of banking in which both borrowers and lenders behave cautiously and conservatively.

To develop a sound private banking system, the government must make strenuous efforts to recover the enormous defaulted loans of nationalized banks. Loan recovery by stringent measures would be a signal to future borrowers that once loans are taken, they have to be repaid. Without banking discipline and responsibility of all concerned, the banking sector cannot survive and thrive. Laws may be legislated to blacklist loan defaulters and, unless they can prove their genuine creditworthiness, loans to them in the future should be restricted. Although the recent loan recovery measures taken by the government are in the right direction, they have not yet been successful in achieving any tangible result.

Development Financial Institutions

The government-owned development financial institutions in Bangladesh —the Bangladesh Krishi (agricultural) Bank, the Bangladesh Silpa (industrial) Bank, and the Bangladesh Silpa Rin Sangstha—are in real trouble. Many argue that their fate was decided when they were created on flawed economic principles. These government-owned institutions are not mobilizers of funds from the people. They are basically the dispensers of subsidized short-term and long-term funds from government and foreign sources to priority projects. They rarely evaluate the quality of such projects on the basis of economic criteria. In the industrial sector, persistent political pressure from above leave industrial banks no choice but to provide large loans to well-connected borrowers of dubious business and industrial backgrounds for unviable projects. Huge funds are also pumped into the agricultural sector with a feverish political zeal and a patronizing attitude with the belief that such loans would save the poor from unscrupulous money lenders and encourage borrowers to increase agricultural production. In the end a few rural rich get most of the loans with the connivance of corrupt bank officials. Adams and Vogel (1986, 479) explain the economic reasons behind the concentration of loans to the rural rich:

> Low interest rates induce both borrower and lender to concentrate loans in the hands of the well-to-do. Lenders have powerful incentives to minimize their cost of lending by concentrating cheap credit in loans to a select few: e.g., those who have borrowed previously, those with excellent loan collateral, and those who take large loans. At the same time, borrowers with clout have strong incentives to capture as much of the cheap credit as possible. These reinforcing incentives result in a small number of farmers getting most of the inexpensive credit.

Such loans are rarely repaid. Rural loan delinquency and default are not a unique Bangladeshi problem—it is common for agricultural development banks in all developing countries. Adams and Vogel (1986, 482) describe the situation:

> Loan delinquency and default have plagued agricultural credit programs in LICs [low income countries], especially agricultural development banks. It is not uncommon to find a quarter or more of loans outstanding with payments overdue, and this is often a substantial underestimation of the problem because of loan refinancing. Accounting practices used in many LICs also disguise the extent of loan recovery problems. . . . The main reasons given for the unwillingness to repay are that loans are viewed as grants or political patronage or simply that borrowers plan from the beginning not to repay.

What is true about agricultural loans is equally true for industrial loans. Industrial Banks' huge lending to projects of dubious quality and very low rate of loan recovery have left them in a moribund state. Industrial loan diversion is now an art form. There are cases where private sector borrowers have defaulted on legalistic but somewhat dubious grounds, such as loan defaults linked with the depreciation of the exchange rate of the taka. Sobhan and Ahsan (1987) examined the contribution of exchange rate fluctuations of the taka to the accumulation of debt overdues of private borrowers from the Bangladesh Silpa Bank and the Bangladesh Silpa Rin Sangstha. They found that (a) most borrowers did not face a significant exchange rate burden; (b) there was no causal connection between poor repayment performance of borrowers and their exchange rate burden; and (c) most borrowers who did face a significant exchange rate burden were able to compensate themselves through enhancement of their product prices.

Given the sorry state of development financial institutions, one needs to ask a hard question whether such institutions are really necessary for economic development. A country like Bangladesh may even be better off without them. Therefore, as in the case of nationalized banks, the government must take a hard political and economic decision about the justification for, and long-term viability of, these financial institutions.

True, the government will have to address some controversial issues, such as the role of industrial policy, and associated directed credit programs, in economic development. Unlike the popular view, recent development literature suggests that the role of industrial policy in economic development is somewhat exaggerated. Even East Asia is not a clear-cut case of industrial policy-induced economic miracle. As the World Bank (1993, 21) reports:

> Most East Asian governments have pursued sector-specific industrial policies to some degree. The best-known instances include Japan's heavy industry promotion policies of the 1950s and the subsequent imitation of these policies in Korea. These policies included import protection as well as subsidies for capital and other imported inputs. Malaysia, Singapore, Taiwan, China, and even Hong Kong have also established programs–typically with moderate incentives–to accelerate development of advanced industries. Despite these actions we find very little evidence that industrial policies have affected either the sectoral structure of industry or rates of productivity change. Indeed, industrial structures in Japan, Korea, and Taiwan, China, have evolved during the past thirty years as we would expect given factor-based comparative advantage and changing factor endowments.

Even if there are some benefits from directed credits to priority sectors, the question is whether the state of Bangladesh is strong enough to allocate credits efficiently and ensure their productive use. As indicated above, credit allocation decisions in Bangladesh are made on the basis of political and noneconomic considerations. Development projects are designed with conflicting objectives and they lack proper evaluation. Importantly, most credits go to loss-making public enterprises. Subsidized loans also have a built-in incentive for both bank officials and borrowers to engage in corrupt practices. The cruel hoax of the system is the willful loan delinquency and default by dubious borrowers who were supposed to be the entrepreneurs for economic development. Under such circumstances, the Japanese and Korean examples are misleading and should not be used to argue for directed credits in Bangladesh. Japan and Republic of Korea have strong institutional capacity for project design, appraisal, and monitoring. Because of it, directed credits have generally gone to projects that are creditworthy and viable. As the World Bank (1993) reports:

> Korea's directed-credit program for small and medium-size enterprises has been compatible from the outset with a disciplined, market-responsive financial system. Banks, which have had a large degree of autonomy in choosing borrowers, have preferred firms with an established track record: of 122 firms surveyed, only 20 drew on financial market resources during their start-up. The Korean program targeted firms without prior access to the banking sector. To keep enterprises going, the program provided for working as well as investment finance, with working capital for exports available on particularly liberal terms. Repayment rates in Korea have been in excess of 98 percent [p. 283].

> In Japan, public bank managers chose projects on basic economic criteria, employing rigorous credit evaluations to select among applicants that fell within government sectoral targets. In Korea, the government individually monitored the large conglomerates using market-oriented criteria such as exports and profitability. In some cases, major enterprises that failed to meet these tests were driven into bankruptcy [p. 20].

What was possible in Republic of Korea and Japan was not even possible in Malaysia and Indonesia—two recent success stories of rapid economic growth and development (World Bank 1993). Aid-based development strategy in Bangladesh has further corrupted the society and created an impression that bank loans do not have to be repaid. It will take considerable time and efforts for all concerned to reverse the situation. As Novak (1993, 6) describes the attitude of the Bangladeshi people:

> ... aid often ... corrupts the political processes. For what is the sense of democracy if the people are not required and refuse to pay taxes? ... As for the farmers, who pay no land tax and seldom pay income tax, they often come out net winners. Loans they have taken are forgiven by the aid-financed government, so they don't have to pay, for instance, for that tubewell they bought last year. Businesses often do not pay their government debts, knowing that sooner or later the aid-givers will refinance the banking system and past loans will be written off. Such debt forgiveness and lack of taxation fosters an unhealthy sense of irresponsibility toward scarce capital and an attitude that the aid-givers can afford to absorb the cost. Indeed, the notion that debts do not have to be repaid affects most classes of people, to the detriment of the country.

To put it bluntly, unless there is some radical change in the allocative efficiency and enforcing capability of the bureaucracy, development financial institutions should be phased out sooner or later. Over time private commercial banks would take care of the credit needs of genuine borrowers. For a rapid growth of the economy, there is no need for favor or discrimination of any sector of the economy. At an early stage of development, it is more important that resources are efficiently utilized. With economic growth, resources would flow to high productivity sectors because they would get high rates of return. The government's role should be to create competitive financial markets where there are no markets and to improve markets where they are distorted or imperfect. Market failures do exist but they should not be exaggerated. If feasible, they should be corrected at source.

Rapid investment is necessary for economic development but to promote investment, there is no need for subsidized credits. Subsidized credits do not necessarily make any nonviable project viable. If certain activities are profitable, it would be in the interests of commercial banks to lend and the genuine investors to borrow. In Bangladesh it may be more productive to focus on developing the long-run capabilities of the capital market. To many borrowers, the quality of financial services is important for the success of their businesses. For example, ready-to-wear garments are now a profitable export item. Private businesses have turned to foreign banks for their credit needs. It was not subsidized interest rates but the quality of banking services of foreign banks that encouraged such borrowers. The Grameen Bank is another example. Even the poorest of the poor are able to generate a high rate of return and repay high interest loans. The main reason is that they genuinely need loans and use them productively. Adams (1983, 75) has made strong arguments against cheap rural credits:

> Interest rates are critical in determining the performance of financial markets, and cheap-credit policies are a major reason for the poor performance of rural financial markets in low-income countries. They destroy the incentives for rural households to save in financial form and seriously distort the way lenders allocate loans. Arguments used to defend cheap agricultural credit are unsound, are based on value judgements, go counter to economic logic, and/or are not supported by empirical evidence.

Rural Private Lending and the Grameen Bank

As indicated above, most rural borrowers from development financial institutions are rich farmers. The rural poor do not have access to subsidized credits of development institutions. Even the rural branches of nationalized commercial banks do not cater to the needs of the rural poor. In a study on the Grameen Bank, Hossain (1988) reported that 7 percent of the rural poor took only 8 percent of rural institutional loans.

The poor borrow from informal sources—professional money lenders, well-to-do farmers, and friends and relatives. Those rich farmers who borrow from agricultural banks borrow not because they need working capital for agricultural activities, but because they take the advantage of subsidized credits which they are able to divert to other profitable activities because of the fungibility nature of loans (Adams and Vogel 1986). In two major volumes on rural finance in developing countries, Adams et al. (1984) and Von Pischke et al. (1983) have accumulated enough information to substantiate their view that subsidized rural credits are not in the interests of the rural poor and there are doubts that subsidized credits contribute to agricultural growth. With a prior impression that loans may not have to be repaid, there is an excess demand for subsidized loans. As interest rates are low and loans are rationed, rich farmers get such loans through their link with local politicians and corrupt bank officials. Once funds are borrowed, there are no incentives on the part of borrowers to utilize them for agricultural activities and they rarely are concerned about repaying the loans. In fact most borrowers consider agricultural loans as windfalls, provided that they can manipulate the system with the connivance of bank officials and support of lawyers and politicians.

To avoid such problems, rural credit needs are to be met through a system which can minimize loan defaults. Despite the common impression that private informal lending is exploitative, there is a need for investigation of the possibility of developing a competitive private lending system through a government licensing system. The question has to be investigated in an historical context with due emphasis on rural customs and traditions. For example, as money lending is not a respectable profession in the predominantly Muslim society of Bangladesh, until recently most rural money lenders were Hindu mahajans and shopkeepers. With the exodus of rich Hindus to India, a vacuum was created in the money lending business. Although by now some Muslims have taken up this business in a secretive way, their monopolistic position and the secretive nature of their business might have kept the interest rates high. Although exploitative, the rural informal credit system has been effective in meeting the short-term credit needs of the poor.

The idea behind a formal private lending system is to break the rural taboos of money lending and to encourage the money lenders to go public. Any government rural lending licensing system may make the money lending business competitive. The rural money lenders, who can minimize the problems of moral hazard and adverse selection, may not have to rely on commercial banks for their loanable funds. If they do not have adequate personal capital, they may be able to raise deposits from rich rural farmers. If lending is made an acceptable form of rural business and made competitive, there is no reason why interest rates should not remain low. The rural rich have excess funds and many of them will be willing to lend them through the organized money lenders. When the rural rich find that their own interests are at stake, they would be able to indirectly put economic and social pressure on borrowers to repay their loans.

One major criticism of such a system is that it may make the rural rich more powerful. But the question is whether there is any effective way of reducing the power of the rural rich in the midst of a high incidence of rural poverty. The higher the incidence of poverty, the more powerful the rich are. The rich cannot be made less powerful by making the poor poorer. The poor can gain economically, and even in terms of rural power, if they can improve their economic condition. Timely loans by private money lenders at competitive interest rates are at the interests of the rural poor. Cheap agricultural credit has been and will always be a political tool and the government should not be allowed to patronage the rural rich in the name of helping the poor. As Kane (1983, 187) writes:

> Subsidized credit programs, in sum, tend to succeed all too well in keeping governments in power through political patronage and in maintaining, and even enhancing, the position of rural elites. These programs do so because they are part of a dynamic political economy that serves the interest of both these groups in continuing a status quo that does not include much possibility for either equitable allocation of credit or optimal economic growth.

Although the area of operation of the Grameen Bank is small, it has certain noble features which can help to develop a viable rural credit system. One major lesson that can be learned from the Grameen Bank is that once the interests of borrowers are linked with loan repayments, even high interest loans can provide economic benefits to the poor and they do not create delinquency and defaults. After reviewing Grameen Bank performance, Hossain (1988, 80) has reached the following conclusion:

> The recent literature on rural financial markets emphasizes that the widespread failure of the rural credit program to achieve its objectives is attributable to following a low-interest rate policy. This policy led to rationing of credit, which benefited the upper-income groups and nonagricultural sectors because of their access to administrators, while it adversely affected mobilization of savings. The Grameen Bank experience shows that high-cost credit can keep the influential nontarget group away from a targeted credit program, but more importantly, it demonstrates the need to develop appropriate institutions for the delivery of loans.

Although the Grameen Bank is considered a success, the long-term viability of the Grameen Bank is not guaranteed unless it reduces its operation costs and widens its lending operations among medium farmers (Hossain 1988). Therefore, in the absence of alternatives, a large number of rural poor will remain dependent on money lenders. Even if Grameen Banks spread throughout the country, private licensed money lenders can provide a complementary source of credit to many poor and medium farm households.

Money and Capital Markets

Money and capital markets in Bangladesh are underdeveloped. In the absence of developed capital markets, large projects are debt-financed and, for the conduct of monetary policy, the government uses direct methods of credit control. Although equity financing is superior to debt financing for the development of the business sector,[8] large firms in Bangladesh prefer debt financing. Varley (1992, x) provides the reasons:

> ... firms prefer to finance capital projects with a minimum of equity. In the eyes of some firms, equity financing carries with it certain disadvantages that are not outweighed by the benefits. It was customary and is still possible in Bangladesh to undertake large projects with very little equity. Enforcement of debt repayment is lax; rescheduling is frequent and restructuring likely. Legal actions involve long delays, and enforcement of collection orders or foreclosure is rare. Insisting on additional equity from sponsors is not a technique used by banks to ration credit.... The low equity requirements by banks and the liberal terms under which debt is available and the lax enforcement of debt contracts all combine to make equity less necessary and debt more attractive as a financing alternative. In effect companies can arrange financing without approaching capital markets for long term risk capital.

As the rate of return on equity investment has been lower than that of the government-guaranteed savings certificate, private funds have flowed toward the savings certificate and funds for equity investment have dried up. Therefore the government should give priority to the development of private capital markets. Along with institutional reforms, the government should design and implement policies which make equity both as an attractive investment and as a means of investment financing. Varley (1992, xi) emphasizes this point:

> ... institutional reforms focused solely on improving the mechanics of trading or in strengthening institutions in the securities trading arena alone will probably not achieve the goal of developing a healthy securities market. Although such reforms are a necessary condition to development of capital markets, they will not be sufficient in themselves to correct more fundamental problems in

> the financial sector that have diminished the attractions of equity both as an investment and a means of financing. More work is necessary to create the foundations that will reward and motivate the private sector for initiating ventures aimed at mobilizing and properly allocating risk capital. For this to occur, the Government of Bangladesh must continue to pursue far reaching and fundamental reforms in the financial sector and the legal system underpinning the financial sector.

Despite capital shortages, there has been capital flight from Bangladesh since independence. In a recent study, Alam et al. (1995) have estimated the size of capital flight from Bangladesh by a number of estimation approaches. One approach finds that on average, around $176 million per year have fled Bangladesh during the period 1973 to 1992. The worst years were 1986, 1987, and 1990, when around $3 billion fled the country. Smuggling, political instability, and corruption at high places have been the important reasons for capital flight. A repressed financial system and an underdeveloped capital market provided additional inducement for capital flight. Such capital flight cannot be reduced unless there is political stability and an environment for private investment. Large-scale private investment is also necessary for the supply of corporate debt and equity securities. The development of capital markets would reduce the corporate sector dependence on banks for debt financing of investment. Provided that there is economic and political stability, portfolio investors may find domestic investment less risky but more profitable. It may reduce capital flight. There are reports all around that there is a section of people in Bangladesh who have large funds which they keep overseas and are hesitant to make long-term investment.[9] How they made such fortunes may never be known, but, if capital markets are developed and simplified, their personal fortunes may contribute to the development of the economy. To encourage remittances of overseas workers, domestic financial assets need to be made competitive in yield, risk, and liquidity.

Private Overseas Borrowing

In Bangladesh, the private sector's overseas borrowings have so far been limited and, whatever loans have flowed to the private sector, are implicitly or explicitly government-guaranteed.

Following financial reforms, if domestic commercial banks insist on large equity as a prerequisite for lending and debt contracts are strictly enforced, private borrowers may borrow heavily from international capital markets under less stringent conditions. Although in a deregulated, world-integrated financial system, private borrowers are entitled to borrow from the least-cost sources whether domestic or foreign, such private borrowings need to be carefully monitored to avoid any debt problem.[10]

It has been observed in Latin American countries that following financial reforms, the private sector borrowed heavily when foreign financial institutions were eager to lend without properly evaluating the credit risk and not charging the interest rates which include risk premium. McKinnon (1991) and Hanson and Melo (1985) considered it one main reason behind the debt crisis. McKinnon (1991) argues that when the government of a borrowing country explicitly or implicitly guarantees foreign loans by the private sector, an individual borrower in the foreign capital market faces a horizontal rather than an upward sloping curve for finance. It allows the private borrower to borrow more than what is optimal in the absence of a government guarantee. As private borrowers know that they would be bailed out by the govern-ment, they divert their borrowed funds and use them for more risky ventures than any projects they might have submitted to banks for approval (Edwards and Edwards 1987). Thus, to avoid an external debt problem following the opening of a capital account, there should be an indirect form of control over private foreign borrowings by phasing out implicit or explicit official guarantees of private loans. Any government policy or declaration in this regard must be time-consistent, or else it will not be credible and effective.

Prudential Regulation and Supervision

The success of financial reform largely depends on the establishment of a sound structure of prudential regulation and supervision. A weak regulatory and supervisory framework can be a barrier to financial deregulation because financial deregulation may place a different, and heavier, demand on the regulatory body than it does in a directed credit system. The skills required for smooth functioning of financial institutions in a regulated financial environment may also be different from those needed when interest rates and credits are controlled (Diaz-Alejandro 1985, Dooley and Mathieson 1987). The lack of adequate and effective supervision was one reason for financial crises in Chile, Philippines, and Turkey.

Therefore, financial deregulation in Bangladesh should not be understood as a laissez-faire approach to financial market. It should aim at regulatory reforms rather than simply one of deregulation. This entails overhauling of accounting, auditing, and information disclosure rules and bringing these items in line with current financial technology. The various laws governing companies, banks and financial institutions, and bankruptcies must also be updated and enforced to protect both debtors and creditors. Thus the focus of bank supervision should shift from the implementation of government directives, such as credit allocation, to the quality of loan portfolios, adequacy of capital, and the soundness of bank management. In other words, regulatory reforms should aim at enhancing the safety and efficiency of the financial system. As Long and Vittas (1991, 6) point out:

> [t]he line between economic and prudential regulation is thin. Any specific aspect of regulation may ... and most do ... have components of both. But the focus is different between using regulation to control credit allocation and pricing and using regulation to maintain a healthy and efficient financial system.

Interest Rate Reform and Credit Allocation

Although interest rate deregulation is often considered a major aspect of financial reforms, it should not be overemphasized. Interest rate determination by market forces is necessary but not sufficient for the development of the financial system. Market-determined interest rates can better allocate credits, provided that the financial system has a built-in structure that reduces moral hazard and adverse selection problems. As the financial system in Bangladesh is underdeveloped, the key question is whether the interest rates should be determined solely by market forces. The issue is complex because in an underdeveloped financial system the movement of free interest rates cannot be predicted. Because of market failures in the financial sector due to information asymmetry, moral hazard and the high transaction costs of monitoring and transferring information, a consensus is emerging that interest rates should not be left fully to markets until the money and capital markets are sufficiently developed (McKinnon 1989, 1991). A gradual approach to interest rate deregulation is suggested so that it can keep pace with the development of the financial system. Premature deregulation can lead to bankruptcy and instability (Sundararajan and Balino 1990).

One corollary of interest rate deregulation is that the government should allow the banking system to allocate credits on commercial principles. The pervasive system of administrative credit distribution should be phased out. In the absence of appropriate institutions and strict performance criteria, it is difficult to enforce the efficient utilization of subsidized credits. If necessary, the government should provide subsidies to small and poor borrowers through budgetary means and should avoid distorting credit markets.

The Political Economy of Financial Reform

Financial reform is both an economic as well as a political decision. Politicians and policymakers ask whether the reform package in question has sufficient political support; in a democratic country, this comes in various forms, chiefly electoral success. To be successful all reforms must deliver expected results, the sooner the better; and when the supply response is slow, enthusiasm for reform fades away, particularly as adjustment costs begin to hurt people (Asilis and Milesi-Ferretti 1994).

The first and foremost decision that the political leadership in Bangladesh must take is to define the role of the private sector in economic growth and development. If the private sector is given a major role in the development of the economy, then the financial system must be developed in accordance with market principles. To start with, Bangladesh has failed to follow a well-defined development philosophy. After independence the government adopted a socialist development strategy, not as an ideological commitment but in response to political necessity. As a result, without examining the economic costs and benefits of policy measures, the industries, banks and foreign trade were nationalized. Over time it has created an inefficient industrial and financial system, which is not only a burden to the national exchequer but is affecting the social foundation of the banking and economic system. In a country where every second person is a politician and where rent-seeking groups have proliferated since independence, the nationalized banking system and development financial institutions have created powerful vested interests who are now threatened by financial reforms. All political parties are aware of the political costs of reforms and therefore the reform process has been slow and ineffective.

The direction of financial reform should be based on the recognition that the character of the state in Bangladesh has changed since independence. The violent political process through which Bangladesh was liberated weakened the pillars of the strong, developmental state that Pakistan projected for itself. During the early years after independence, the elite bureaucracy was discredited, the authoritarian political system became unacceptable to the people, and the relationship between government and big business simply broke down.

The Awami League led the autonomy movement and later the Liberation War in Bangladesh. The Mujib government which came to power after independence initially distanced itself from the elites in the bureaucracy and even purged some of them because of their collaboration with the Pakistani occupation forces.

The support of radical students, workers, and left-wing political party members in the Awami League during both the autonomy movement and liberation war made it difficult for the Awami League government to develop any close relation with big business after independence. After the nationalization of heavy industries and financial institutions, imposition of state monopoly over foreign trade, and exodus of non-Bengali industrialists, the Awami League government also did not have to forge relations with any big business.

Therefore, given the weak nature of the state, what has been possible in the Republic of Korea, Japan, and Singapore cannot be replicated in Bangladesh. The present Bangladesh state is not capable of maintaining what Bardhan (1993, 46) calls "the discipline of the market ... against the inevitable lobbies of group predation" in distributive politics. Hence any deliberate distortion of relative prices in Bangladesh is unlikely to stimulate economic growth and development.

In Bangladesh, political stability is a must for making financial reforms a success. Politicians of all parties must reach consensus on key economic issues. Political instability has slowed the reform process, lowered the level of private investment, discouraged foreign investment, and encouraged capital flight. In a chaotic political environment, groups with vested interests have taken shelter under the political opponents of financial and other reforms.

Consequences of Financial Reforms

As discussed above, the Bangladesh government has undertaken some financial reform measures since the late 1980s. Their effects were not always as expected because of remaining distortions and problems in the financial sector.

Interest Rates

As a result of gradual reform measures, interest rates have now been largely freed. The upward adjustment of nominal interest rates and the reduction of the inflation rate have made the deposit and lending rates of interest positive in recent years (Data Appendix). But, for a number of reasons, such as an oligopolistic banking structure, bad loans, and bureaucratic management, the real lending rates have become stuck at a distressingly high level. Such high real interest rates might have lowered private investment and caused financial distress among firms with high debt-equity ratios. As the Bangladesh Bank does not have such monetary policy instruments which can lower the real interest rates, it has relied on moral suasion to reduce interest rates, but without any tangible effect.

As a consequence of positive real interest rates, the financial sector has been gradually growing (measured by an increase in the M2/GNP or M3/GNP ratio, see Data Appendix). Besides the interest rates, low and stable inflation might have contributed to the growth of financial assets. As Cho and Khatkhate (1989, 67) point out, "a relative price stability may be as crucial as (or even more crucial than) the achievement of rapid and sustained growth of the financial sector." It appears that high real interest rates on time deposits are attracting funds from the capital markets. The result has been that, in a depressed private investment environment, the nationalized banks have been holding more than the normal level of excess reserves.[11]

Shift in Demand from Demand Deposits to Currency and Time Deposits

The deposit-currency ratio is often considered a measure of economic development because with an increase in per-capita income, a country is expected to move from a cash-based economy toward a check-based economy. Despite some progress in the economic front, this did not happen in Bangladesh during the past two decades. In fact the deposit-currency ratio in Bangladesh has sharply declined since the early 1980s. Hossain (1995b) has examined the behavior of the deposit-currency ratio and found that with an increase in real income, the demand for currency has increased at a much higher rate than the demand for demand deposits. In fact the coefficient on real income in a regression equation of real demand deposits for the sample period 1972 to 1989 was found not significantly different from zero. This indicates that moneyholders have been holding cash relatively more than demand deposits as transaction balances. This finding is consistent with the result of a survey of 300 businesses in Dhaka conducted by Rashid (1990) where he did not find any significant use of checks by businesses for transactions. The relative decline in the demand for demand deposits does not indicate a lack of confidence of depositors' in the banking system. While the demand for demand deposits has not kept pace with an increase in demand for money, the demand for time deposits has increased rapidly since the mid-1980s, partly in response to a relatively high deposit rate of interest. Thus the conventional measure of financial deepening—the ratio of M2/GNP—suggests an increase in financial deepening following the rise in interest rates. However, it does not say why there has been no growth of demand deposits when both the number of bank branches increased and the people became richer. As the deposit-currency ratio has a positive effect on the money multiplier and hence the money supply, the decline in the deposit-currency ratio has an implication for the conduct of monetary policy. Here follows an explanation for the declining deposit-currency ratio; it highlights some socioeconomic problems which have broader implications for financial and fiscal reforms.

In Bangladesh, the level of per capita income at 1985 prices increased from taka 3494 in 1973 to taka 4688 in 1992. However such an increase in real income was associated with a decrease in real income of the urban people. Per-capita real output of the urban areas in 1973 was taka 10650, which declined to taka 8711 in 1992. By contrast, rural per-capita real GDP during the same period increased from taka 2904 to taka 3832 (Bangladesh Bureau of Statistics 1993b). This reveals that the increase in real income in Bangladesh during the past two decades was essentially due to an increase in rural real incomes. As rural people prefer currency to demand deposits with an increase in real income, the deposit-currency ratio has declined with an increase in real income.

There is another reason for the decline in the deposit-currency ratio in Bangladesh. Traditionally, urban people hold money in the form of bank deposits. It is common knowledge that illegal activity in Bangladesh has sharply increased since independence and has spread among all sections of the people, particularly in the urban areas (Taslim 1994). As many government officials, professionals, businessmen, and politicians now earn substantial sums through illegal means, they possibly hold currency relative to demand deposits to reduce the possibility of tracing their illegal earnings. The impetus for the change in the financial portfolio choice of the urban people might have originated from the common knowledge that the World Bank and the IMF have put pressure on the Bangladesh government to raise revenues from income taxes to reduce budget deficits. Expecting that the government would tighten the income tax rules, the professionals, businessmen, and other high income earners might have also increased cash transactions for income earning activity to conceal their incomes. Therefore, one can argue that the sharp increase in the demand for currency in Bangladesh has been associated with illegal activity, although such a claim cannot be substantiated for lack of data.

Provisions, Supervision, and Capital Adequacy

Provisions and the suspension of interests have helped to diagnose the health of the banking system better, but they did not make the problem of loan recovery simpler.[12] Nevertheless, it is a move toward the right direction. Before such measures were introduced, the profits of banks were overstated and banking sector problems were hidden. By bringing out to the light the extent of bad loans, the Bangladesh Bank has performed its supervisory function and exposed the inefficiencies and costs associated with directed credit programs in a largely nationalized banking system. It is expected that such an exposure will put pressure on banks and they will exert extra efforts to recover bad loans. The banks have been reluctant to write off their bad loans because such an action may reduce any chances of loan recovery.

As indicated above, in 1989 the Bangladesh Bank introduced the legal requirement of uniform capital adequacy for banks. Before that, different categories of banks were subject to different minimum capital requirements. Foreign banks were required to maintain capital and reserves equivalent to 5 percent of deposit liabilities. Each nationalized bank was required to maintain an absolute amount. The private banks under their licensing agreements were required to maintain capital and reserves at the equivalent of 6 percent of deposit liabilities. The aim of uniform capital adequacy requirement has been to reduce the risk of depositors—particularly in the case of private banks. The need to maintain an adequate capital-to-assets ratio is also expected to exert discipline on lending (World Bank 1989). The private banks have maintained their capital adequacy. While this has created depositor confidence in private banks, the dividends issued to share holders have somewhat been reduced. On balance, strict enforcement of the capital adequacy requirement has been beneficial for the long-run development of the private banking system. The enforcement of capital adequacy rule for nationalized banks has been necessary to allow both private and nationalized banks to operate under similar restrictions. The maintenance of capital adequacy would keep the nationalized banks operational for future privatization.

Competitiveness of the Financial System

The nationalized banking sector has remained uncompetitive. Private banks have a small number of branches in city areas and they are not a match for nationalized banks. Private banks have also concentrated their lending activities with clients engaged in profitable export and trading activities. As the capital market has remained underdeveloped, nationalized banks are the main source of term loans, especially since the Bangladesh Silpa Bank and the Bangladesh Silpa Rin Sangstha are in a moribund state.

Internationalization of Domestic Financial Markets

Despite some financial reforms, the financial sector of Bangladesh has not integrated with international money and capital markets. As indicated above, domestic interest rates have remained at high levels and shown no tendency to move along with international rates. After the removal of controls over interest rates, the interest rate differentials first narrowed down but have widened recently (Data Appendix). The main reasons for the insulation of domestic interest rates from foreign interest rates are limited capital mobility and the oligopolistic nature of the banking system.

Unless the domestic financial institutions face foreign competition, they would remain inefficient and would not broaden their range of services. Foreign competition is also essential for the transfer of international financial technology and the improvement of the quality of services. Integration with foreign markets will give domestic banks and borrowers access to foreign capital and to financial services, and increase the scope for risk diversification.

Conclusion

Financial reform measures that have been introduced in Bangladesh since the late 1980s have been inadequate and ineffective in solving financial sector problems. Nationalized banks and development financial institutions are operating with huge unrecoverable loans. They are in distress and technically insolvent. Loan recovery efforts so far have produced little success. Political interference in loan distribution and recovery is continuing. Money and capital markets have remain underdeveloped. Political decisions about the privatization of banks and industries and the future of development financial institutions are yet to be taken.

Despite the gloomy picture of the financial sector, there is a ray of hope in that the government is talking about reforms. Provided that an intense pressure is put on the government, it may come to its senses and undertake a comprehensive reform program to improve the financial system. The government may take the following steps and measures for the improvement of the financial system.

- The basic working principle of banks and other financial institutions should be profit maximization. Although it is possible in theory, in reality nationalized banks and development financial institutions cannot work according to this principle. They are subject to political interference and bureaucratic rules and controls and are required to meet multiplicity of conflicting objectives. Therefore the four nationalized commercial banks should be restructured, capitalized, and then privatized. Unless these banks are privatized, the banking sector is likely to remain uncompetitive, bureaucratic and inefficient.

- The private banking system should be expanded and developed. Nonbanking financial institutions, such as building societies, merchant banks, and finance companies should be allowed to operate under appropriate rules and guidelines. They will deepen the financial system and put pressure on commercial banks. Foreign banks and other financial institutions should be allowed to play a role in developing the financial system. If it is feasible, they should be allowed to form joint ventures with domestic private banks and other financial institutions. Foreign banks and other financial institutions provide maximum benefits only when the domestic financial sector is deregulated and competitive.

- Both the government and Bangladesh Bank should study the feasibility of rural private organized lending as a legitimate and respectable business. Like insurance companies, commercial banks may operate in rural areas through private commission agents, who would have the responsibility for allocating loans and collecting them on a commission basis. The aim of the government should be to create nonbureaucratic rural saving and credit institutions where the interests of borrowers and lenders converge in maintaining credit discipline. The operation of the Grameen Bank should be expanded to complement the operations of other rural credit institutions.

- Bangladesh Bank's supervisory and regulatory role should be strengthened to ensure that a financial crisis does not develop. The principles of bank supervision and regulation should be applied to other financial institutions, such as finance companies, insurance companies, pension funds, and mutual funds. To be effective, prudential regulation must be backed by a political commitment to supervision and enforcement. Importantly, the Bangladesh Bank as the supervisory body should be given well-defined policy goals and power to undertake measures which are required to achieve those goals (World Bank 1989).

- Bangladesh Bank has to change the impression that loans do not have to be repaid. The government directly, or through Bangladesh Bank, must stop using bank credits as a means of keeping sick industries alive. Bangladesh Bank must audit and make sure that private banks follow its directives with respect to lending and capital adequacy.

- Although the final responsibility for monetary policy is in the hands of government, Bangladesh Bank should be given adequate autonomy to design and conduct monetary policy with a well-defined objective (e.g., price stability). The present system of monetary targeting should be continued with an appropriate adjustment until the financial system is developed and an alternative approach to conduct monetary policy is found more suitable. The fact that Bangladesh Bank now auctions its bills for indirect monetary management is a positive development. However, until a secondary money market for government securities is developed, it may be difficult for the Bangladesh Bank to insulate the operations of monetary management from those of debt management as the intervention is concentrated in the primary market. Along with the development of secondary money markets, the exchange rate system should be made more flexible so that the monetary authority can establish effective control over the money base.

- The government must make serious efforts to develop the money and capital markets so that the monetary policy can be conducted through open market operations. Development of private capital markets is also necessary for any successful privatization of nationalized banks and industries.

- To reduce pressure on monetary policy, the government must maintain fiscal discipline. As financial repression is a source of government revenue, any potential decline in government revenue following financial reforms must be associated with an expenditure reduction and/or an increase in taxes.

- Private commercial banks must conduct risk assessment in a professional manner. Private credit rating and evaluating firms should be licensed under stringent rules and regulations. Banks would be encouraged to use their services on a routine basis. Such credit rating agencies could be the subsidiaries of reputed foreign credit rating firms to ensure professional standards and integrity. A strong accounting and auditing profession is essential for building efficient financial markets. Efforts should be made to improve the standards of domestic accounting and auditing firms.

- Provision of subsidized loans to priority sectors should be removed. If the government needs to subsidize any sector, it may do so through nonmonetary means. Specialized development banks have outlived their purpose. Sooner or later they have to be closed down. Until such a time comes, their sole task should be devoted to loan recovery by stringent means. At the time of closure Bangladesh Bank may open a unit to look after the loan recovery of specialized banks.

- Until the nationalized banks and industries are privatized, the nationalized industries have to arrange their loans from banks like other borrowers. They have to operate under hard budget constraints to raise their efficiency.

- While interest rates should be allowed to be determined by market forces, they should be closely monitored by Bangladesh Bank until the money and capital markets are adequately developed. Efforts should be made to integrate domestic financial markets with foreign money and capital markets so that domestic interest rates can align with foreign interest rates.

- Strong efforts are needed for loan recovery. Even at the risk of compromising the legal system, special loan recovery laws should be legislated to favor lenders so that loan defaulters cannot hide under legal loopholes. In fact the legal system must protect the integrity of the financial system. The massive default of loans by large industrial borrowers has created shortages of loanable funds for small borrowers who are better repayers of loans and have entrepreneurial capability (Hossain et al. 1994).

- Political interference should be considered an attempt to contempt the integrity of the financial system and should be treated as a crime. Banks and financial institutions should be encouraged to refer any political interference to Bangladesh Bank. A special financial ombudsman with clear responsibility may be created to charge anyone who contempts the integrity of the financial system.

- Dependence on foreign aid for financing of government deficits should be reduced. The government should raise funds from the private sector through issuing short-term and long-term securities with attractive yields. As the experiences of Indonesia, the Philippines, and Sri Lanka have shown, a market for government bills can be developed if the government is willing to pay the market interest rate. Development of a government bills market is often a first step toward building a market for corporate securities. The main aim of financial reform in Bangladesh should be to develop a secondary securities market so that Bangladesh Bank can conduct monetary policy through indirect means. Bangladesh Bank should be allowed to issue various short-term money market instruments with market related yields so that banks can invest their excess liquidity.

- The currency should gradually be made convertible for capital account transactions. However, until the money and capital markets are adequately developed, some restrictions may be necessary to avoid large-scale inflows and outflows of capital. Such capital flows may cause overshooting of both interest and exchange rates, which may lead to financial crisis. To avoid such problems, financial reforms should be accompanied by macroeconomic stability. The government must create credibility on the question of financial reform. Provided that macroeconomic stability is maintained, freer capital flows have an advantage that they promote the alignment of domestic interest rates with international rates, increase the availability of funds, and provide more opportunities for risk diversification (World Bank, 1989).

- Financial sector reforms involve risks and the authorities must remain prepared to minimize any damages to either the economy or the financial system, if mistakes are made.

- Financial deregulation does not guarantee competition in the financial sector because of the uncompetitive and oligopolistic nature of the financial system. Despite the presence of a number of small private banks, the banking system of Bangladesh has remained oligopolistic. Therefore, financial reform program should be supplemented with competition policy.

The steps suggested above are necessary requirements for the development of a dynamic financial system. Finance is a key to investment and a developed financial system is a conduit through which savings are accumulated and efficiently allocated for investment in productive projects. As an economy develops, the demand for diverse financial services arises. Without them, "an economy would be confined to self-sufficiency or barter, which would inhibit the specialization upon which modern economies depend" (World Bank 1989, 25). Diverse and complex financial services can only be provided by a financial system which is responsive and innovative to market demand. Competition is the key to innovation and the quality of services. Thus the contribution of a financial system to economic growth depends on the quantity and quality of financial services and the efficiency with which it provides them to households, businesses, and governments. The aim of financial reforms in Bangladesh should be to develop such a system. But, to be realistic, there are difficulties in, and obstacles to, the achievement of such a goal. The World Bank (1989, 132) aptly summed up the issues involved:

> Unlike the problems of industry, those of finance are not frozen in bricks and mortar, plant and machinery. Financial claims, together with the all important 'rules of the game', could be rewritten overnight by government decree. But this is not to imply that reforming a country's financial system can be accomplished quickly or easily. Time is needed for people to acquire the necessary skills in accounting, management, and bank supervision. Training staff, building institutions, and–perhaps hardest of all–getting people to revise their expectations have proved among the greatest challenges to development. Moreover, change is certain to encounter political opposition: people benefiting from the present arrangements will resist reform. Others–although they stand to benefit in the long run–will be hurt in the short run and may not choose to make the sacrifices demanded today for uncertain gains in the future. Change may be most resisted in the very countries where it is most necessary.

Appendix Table 8.1

Indicators of Bangladesh Financial System, 1973-1993

	1973	*1974*	*1975*	*1976*	*1977*	*1978*	*1979*	*1980*	*1981*	*1982*	*1983*
Number of Bank Branches											
Nationalized	1116	1291	1431	1523	1728	2366	2911	3290	3473	3697	3678
Specialized	108	142	153	158	177	206	261	426	573	667	873
Private	14	14	14	15	18	20	20	19	21	14	15
Domestic											
Foreign	14	14	14	15	18	20	20	19	21	21	20
Financial Deepening (monetary aggregate as percent of GNP)											
Narrow Money (M1)	13.1	10.1	6.6	8.4	8.8	8.8	9.1	9.2	8.9	8.0	9.1
Broad Money (M2)	18.5	16.9	10.4	13.3	15.7	15.4	15.5	17.2	18.5	18.1	20.3
Monetary Assets (M3)		17.4	10.7	13.7	16.0	15.7	16.8	17.4	18.7	18.3	20.5
Inflation Rate (%)	49.0	54.8	21.9	2.3	4.8	5.3	14.7	13.4	16.2	12.5	9.4
Rate of Interest (%)											
Deposits			3.5	4.2	4.3	4.2	4.3	4.3	6.8	7.3	7.4
Advance			11.3	11.6	11.0	10.7	11.1	11.0	13.1	13.5	13.6
Bank Rate		8.0	8.0	8.0	8.0	8.0	8.0	8.0	10.5	10.5	10.5
LIBOR									16.1	13.7	10.2
Exchange Rate											
Nominal											
Rate of Depreciation		7.9	13.7	15.0	15.5	15.1	15.6	14.8	17.8	22.2	24.5
Real Effective									16.4	23.0	11.3
Trade Account Balance (% of GNP)	-6	-7	-5	-14	-6	-10	-10	-13	-13	-15	-13
Current Account Balance (% of GNP)	-1	-4	-3	-10	-1	-5	-3	-6	-5	-7	-2
Capital Flight											
Estimation Method											
World Bank	270	369	-129	-35	85	73	-54	210	-488	-87	41
Morgan Guaranty	270	369	-132	-18	78	56	-49	118	-480	-74	46
Cline	268	367	-134	-21	73	50	-59	102	-492	-102	10
Cuddington	11	51	45	-13	14	-22	-44	25	-299	48	31

Appendix Table 8.1. continued.

	1984	*1985*	*1986*	*1987*	*1988*	*1989*	*1990*	*1991*	*1992*	*1993*
Number of Bank Branches										
Nationalized	3834	3343	3393	3435	3482	3536	3560	3581	3596	3603
Specialized	914	981	1028	1067	1104	1124	1146	1165	1167	1169
Private	18	648	673	715	737	793	846	887	920	962
Domestic		628	653	693	715	771	824	865	902	942
Foreign	20	20	20	22	22	22	22	22	18	20
Financial Deepening (monetary aggregate as percent of GNP)										
Narrow Money (M1)	10.2	10.7	10.9	10.0	8.6	8.5	8.9	8.8	9.4	9.7
Broad Money (M2)	24.1	26.8	27.3	27.4	28.1	29.6	31.1	30.8	32.3	33.7
Monetary Assets (M3)	24.3	27.0	27.5	27.6	28.3	29.9	31.4	31.2	32.6	34.1
Inflation Rate (%)	10.5	10.7	11.0	9.5	9.3	10.0	8.1	7.2	5.0	-2.4
Rate of Interest (%)										
Deposits	8.1	8.1	8.5	8.6	8.7	8.9	9.1	9.1	8.1	6.5
Advance	13.8	14.5	14.7	14.7	14.7	14.7	14.8	15.0	15.1	14.4
Bank Rate	11.0	11.3	10.8	10.8	9.8	9.8	9.8	9.8	8.5	6.5
LIBOR	11.8	9.1	7.0	7.6	8.4	9.3	8.5	6.3	4.2	3.6
Exchange Rate										
Nominal	25.2	28.0	30.3	31.0	31.5	32.2	30.9	35.7	39.0	39.8
Rate of Depreciation	3.0	10.4	8.6	1.8	2.5	1.7	7.1	5.9	6.4	1.6
Real Effective					83.9	91.7	86.8	84.8	84.4	81.9
Trade Account Balance (% of GNP)	-11	-11	-10	-10	-10	-10	-10	-8	-7	-8
Current Account Balance (% of GNP)	-2	-4	-3	-3	-2	-4	-4	-1	1	...
Capital Flight										
Estimation Method										
World Bank	-313	486	794	1504	118	-367	887	270	-116	
Morgan Guaranty	-313	435	810	1501	-87	-452	847	265	-36	
Cline	-343	412	796	149	-73	-470	828	244	-61	
Cuddington	28	21	...	144	-29	43	63	103	59	

... means negligible.

Notes:

1. M1 = Currency plus demand deposits; M2 = M1 + time deposits; and M3 = M2 + post office deposits.
2. Inflation rate is defined as the percentage change of the consumer price index for middle class people in Dhaka city.
3. Nominal interest rate on deposits represents the weighted average of interest rates on time deposits for different maturities, and the nominal interest rate on advances represents the weighted average of the interest rates on loans made for different activities. Interest rates are as at the last quarter of the fiscal year (July-June). LIBOR represents London Inter Bank Offer Rate of US one year deposits.
4. Rate of depreciation (%) is for the nominal exchange rate. Index for the real effective exchange rate is 1985 = 100.
5. Capital flight is in millions of US dollars.

Sources:

(a) Bank branches: *Economic Trends* (February 1994).
(b) GNP: BBS (1993b).
(c) Inflation Rate: Authors' computation based on *Bangladesh Bank Bulletin* (various years); *IFS Yearbook* (various years); and *Economic Trends* (various years).
(d) Interest Rates: *Economic Trends* (February 1994); *IFS Yearbook 1994.*
(e) Nominal Exchange Rate: *Economic Trends* (February 1994).
(f) Real Effective Exchange Rate: *Asian Development Outlook* (various years).
(g) Trade and current account balances: Authors' computations based on *IFS Yearbook* (various years); *Economic Trends* (various years); and BBS (1993b).
(h) Capital flight estimates by various methods are from Alam et al. (1995).

Notes

1. One reviewer of this paper argues that profit maximization should not be the working principle of banks because they function "more like a guardian of trust funds than a venture capitalist" under tight regulation and supervision. We do not see any difficulty in reconciling this view with our emphasis on profit maximization as a guiding principle of banks. We ourselves believe that banks should work under regulation and supervision and that they should maximize profits under such constraints. When the commercial banks are given an option of working to achieve social objectives, they are likely to operate inefficiently as they can always hide their failures under social goals and objectives which are often vaguely defined. In fact, depositors are safer in banks whose success or failure is measured in terms of profits than in banks which work to achieve vaguely defined social objectives.

2. Given the limited scope of the paper, it will briefly review key issues and not the technical details of the reform process.

3. These characteristics of the rural credit market have been identified in various survey-based studies. There are no official statistics on interest rates charged and loans transacted in the rural credit market. For details, see Ahmed (1980).

4. Although there are theoretical linkages between financial reforms and economic growth, empirical evidence on such a relation is weak. For a critical review of both theoretical and empirical literature on financial liberalization reform, see Chowdhury and Islam (1993).

5. As Partee (1986, 63) writes:

> Deregulation increases, rather than decreases, responsibility for close supervision and prompt supervisory action to prevent excessively risky behavior or abusive practices by individual managements. The opportunities for serious mistakes in the new environment are far greater than before, and they require commensurately closer monitoring and review.

6. Financial reform may affect the stability of the money demand function in a number of ways. First, in a financially repressed economy the roles of interest rates in the money demand function remain latent, which may become transparent once the interest rates are allowed to be determined by market forces. Second, reform measures that promote financial market development may create financial assets with attractive yields, which may lead to portfolio shifts away from monetary assets and thus to a shift of the intercept term of the money demand function. Third, any observed relationships among money, income, prices, and interest rates may alter following the relaxation of direct controls over banks' credits and interest and exchange rates, and the shift from direct to indirect monetary policy instruments (Jonson and Rankin 1986, Tseng and Corker 1991).

7. The money growth rule recommended here should not be interpreted in the Friedmanite sense. The aim of such a rule is necessary to bring monetary discipline, given the imperfect constraints of the political system in Bangladesh on its government. Since in an underdeveloped but deregulated financial system the conduct of monetary policy is complex, the Bangladesh Bank has to undertake an in-depth study on all technical aspects of monetary policy. Such a research program should be a major responsibility of the Bank.

8. Debt financing carries a high risk because it encourages risky projects and disrupts production when a debt problem develops.

9. As Alam et al. (1995, 20) write:

> In Bangladesh there is a group of nouveau rich who stay overseas for extended periods for medical treatment, child birth, and vacation. They also send their children to study in the United States, England, and even India. To finance these activities they need significant amount of foreign exchange. In the presence of exchange control and exchange rate risk, keeping money overseas is the most obvious means of financing these activities.

10. Although most of Bangladesh's foreign debt is government-guaranteed, its creditworthiness is very low. Since the Bangladesh government is courting foreign investment, any sign of debt problem may scare off foreign investors.

11. For instance, the excess reserves-deposits ratio increased from 1.3 percent in 1989 to 2.3 percent in 1992 and to 7.5 percent in 1993 (*Economic Trends* February 1994).

12. It remains as Humphrey (1990, 104) points out, a "national malaise that threatens economic progress".

References

Abbott, G. J., 1986. "The Political Economy of Financial Reform in Developing Economies." In H. S. Cheng, ed., *Financial Policy and Reform in Pacific Basin Countries.* Toronto: Lexington Books.

Adams, D. W., 1983. "Are the Arguments for Cheap Agricultural Credit Sound?" In D. W. Adams, D. H. Graham, and J. D. Von Pischke, eds., *Undermining Rural Development with Cheap Credit.* Boulder and London: Westview Press.

Adams, D. W., D. H. Graham, and J. D. Von Pischke, 1984. *Undermining Rural Development with Cheap Credit.* Boulder and London: Westview Press.

Adams, D.W., and R.C. Vogel, 1986. "Rural Financial Markets in Low Income Countries: Recent Controversies and Lessons." *World Development* 14(4):477-87.

Aghevli, B., M. Khan, P. Narvekar, and B. Short, 1979. "Monetary Policy in Selected Asian Countries." IMF Staff Papers 26. International Monetary Fund, Washington, D.C.

Ahammad, H., and G. Fane, 1994. "Exchange Rate Policy in Bangladesh." Paper presented at the Conference on Structural Adjustment in South Asia, November 29-30, Australia South Asia Research Centre, Australian National University, Canberra.

Ahmed, A., 1980. "An Assessment of a Special Credit Programme for Small Farmers in Bangladesh from the Viewpoint of Non-Participants." M.A. Dissertation. Australian National University, Canberra.

Alam, M. I., A. Dowla, and S. Rashid, 1995. "Capital Flight from Bangladesh." Processed. University of Illinois at Urbana-Champaign.

Asian Development Bank, various years. *Asian Development Outlook.* Hong Kong: Oxford University Press for Asian Development Bank.

———, 1994. *Bangladesh: Economic Review and Bank Operations.* Processed. Manila: Asian Development Bank.

Asilis, C. M., and G. M. Milesi-Ferretti, 1994. "On the Political Sustainability of Economic Reform." Paper on Policy Analysis and Assessment PPAA/94/3. International Monetary Fund, Washington, D.C.

Bangladesh Bank, various years. *Annual Report.* Dhaka.

———, various years. *Bangladesh Bank Bulletin.* Dhaka.

———, various years. *Economic Trends.* Dhaka.

Bangladesh Bureau of Statistics, 1993a. *Statistical Pocketbook of Bangladesh 1993.* Dhaka: Government of Bangladesh.

———, 1993b. *Twenty Years of National Accounting of Bangladesh.* Dhaka: Government of Bangladesh.

The Bangladesh Observer, various years. Dhaka, Bangladesh.

Bardhan, P., 1993. "Symposium on Democracy and Development." *Journal of Economic Perspectives* 7(3):45-9.

Blair, H. W., 1983. "Agricultural Credit, Political Economy, and Patronage." In D. Adams, et al., eds., *Undermining Rural Development with Cheap Credit.* Boulder and London: Westview Press.

Cho, Y. J., and D. Khatkhate, 1989. "Lessons of Financial Liberalization in Asia." Discussion Paper No. 50. World Bank, Washington, D.C.

Chowdhury, A., and I. Islam, 1993. *The Newly Industrialising Economies of East Asia.* London and New York: Routledge.

Diaz-Alejandro, C., 1985. "Good-Bye Financial Repression, Hello Financial Crash." *Journal of Development Economics* 19:1-24.

Dooley, M. P., and D. J. Mathieson, 1987. "Financial Liberalization and Stability in Developing Countries." Working Paper WP/87/19. International Monetary Fund, Washington, D.C.

Edwards, S., 1993. "Exchange Rates as Nominal Anchors." *Review of World Economics* 129(1):1-32.

Edwards, S., and A. C. Edwards, 1987. *Monetarism and Liberalization: The Chilean Experiment.* Cambridge, Massachusetts: Ballinger Publishing Company.

Government of Bangladesh, 1995. *Bangladesh: Economic Review June 1995.* Dhaka: Ministry of Finance.

Guitian, M., 1994. "Remarks." In T. J. T. Balino and C. Cottarelli, *Frameworks for Monetary Stability.* Washington, D.C.: International Monetary Fund.

Hanson, J., and J. de Melo, 1985. "External Shocks, Financial Reforms, and Stabilization Attempts in Uruguay During 1974-83." *World Development* 13(8):917-39.

Hassan, M. K., 1993. "The Financial Sector Reform of Bangladesh." *Thoughts on Economics* 3(1,2):40-64.

Hossain, A., 1993. "Financial Liberalisation, Stability of the Money Demand Function and Monetary Policy in Bangladesh." *Indian Economic Review* 28(1):85-100.

———, 1994. "Financial Innovation, Financial Deregulation and the Stability of the Australian Short Run Money Demand Function." *Economic Notes.* Forthcoming.

———, 1995a. *Inflation, Economic Growth and the Balance of Payments in Bangladesh: A Macroeconometric Study.* New Delhi: Oxford University Press.

———, 1995b. "The Money Supply Multiplier in Bangladesh." *Bangladesh Development Studies.* Forthcoming.

Hossain, A., and A. Chowdhury, 1995. *Monetary and Financial Policies in Developing Countries: Growth and Stabilisation.* London: Routledge.

Hossain, M., 1988. "Credit for Alleviation of Rural Poverty: The Grameen Bank in Bangladesh." Research Report 65. International Food Policy Research Institute, Washington, D.C.

Hossain, M., R. Mannan, H. Z. Rahman, and B. Sen, 1994. "Bangladesh." In M. G. Quibria, ed., *Rural Poverty in Developing Asia, Volume 1: Bangladesh, India and Sri Lanka.* Manila: Asian Development Bank.

Hughes, H., 1994. "Development Policies and Development Performance." In E. Grilli, and D. Salvatore, eds., *Economic Development.* London: Greenwood Press.

Humphrey, C. E., 1990. *Privatization in Bangladesh: Economic Transition in a Poor Country.* Boulder: Westview Press.

International Monetary Fund, various years. *IFS Yearbook.* Washington, D.C.

Islam, S. S., 1985. "The Role of the State in the Economic Development of Bangladesh During the Mujib Regime (1972-1975)." *Journal of Developing Areas* 19(2):185-208.

Jahan, R., 1980. *Bangladesh Politics: Problems and Issues.* Dhaka: University Press.

Jonson, P., and R. Rankin, 1986. "On Some Recent Developments in Monetary Economics." *Economic Record* 62:257-67.

Kane, E. J., 1983. "Good Intentions and Unintended Evil." In J.D. Von Pischke, D. W. Adams, and G. Donald, eds., *Rural Financial Markets in Developing Countries: Their Use and Abuse.* Baltimore and London: The Johns Hopkins University Press.

King, R. G., and R. Levine, 1993. "Financial Intermediation and Economic Development." In C. Mayer and X. Vives, eds., *Capital Markets and Financial Intermediation.* Cambridge: Cambridge University Press.

Long, M., and D. Vittas, 1991. "Financial Regulation: Changing the Rules of the Game." Policy Research Working Papers WPS803. World Bank, Washington, D.C.

McKinnon, R. I., 1973. *Money and Capital for Economic Development.* Washington, D.C.: The Brookings Institution.

———, 1989. "Financial Liberalization and Economic Development: A Reassessment of Interest Rate Policies in Asia and Latin America." *Oxford Review of Economic Policy* 5(4):29-54.

———, 1991. *The Order of Economic Liberalization: Financial Control in the Transition to a Market Economy.* Baltimore: Johns Hopkins University Press.

Novak, J. J., 1993. *Bangladesh: Reflections on the Water.* Bloomington: Indiana University Press.

Partee, J. C., 1986. "The Status of Banking Deregulation in the United States." In H. S. Cheng, ed., *Financial Policy and Reform in Pacific Basin Countries.* Lexington: D. C. Heath and Company.

Pilbeam, K., 1992. *International Finance.* London: Macmillan.

Quibria, M. G., and T. N. Srinivasan, 1994. "Introduction." In M. G. Quibria, ed., *Rural Poverty in Developing Asia, Volume I: Bangladesh, India and Sri Lanka.* Manila: Asian Development Bank.

Rahim, A. M. A., and M. Sohrabuddin, 1988. "Central Banking, Monetary Management and Related Issues with Reference to Bangladesh." *Bangladesh Journal of Political Economy* 8(1):182-201.

Rashid, S., 1990. "Tokten Report." Department of Economics, University of Illinois at Urbana-Champaign. Mimeographed.

Shaw, E. S., 1973. *Financial Deepening in Economic Development.* New York: Oxford University Press.

Sobhan, R., and A. Ahsan, 1987. "The Effect of Exchange Rate Depreciation on the Loan Repayment Performance of Private Enterprise in Bangladesh." *Bangladesh Development Studies* 15(4):1-52.

Sohrabuddin, M., 1986. "Monetary Policy in the Third Five Year Plan." *Bangladesh Journal of Political Economy* 7(1A):198-209.

Stiglitz, J. E., 1994. "The Role of the State in Financial Markets." Proceedings of the World Bank Annual Conference on Development Economics 1993. World Bank, Washington, D.C.

Summers, L. H., 1994. "Foreword." In Caprio, Jr., I. Atiyas, and J. A. Hanson, eds., *Financial Reform: Theory and Experience.* Cambridge: Cambridge University Press.

Sundararajan, V., and T. Balino, 1990. "Issues in Recent Banking Crises in Developing Countries." Working Paper WP/90/19. International Monetary Fund, Washington, D. C.

Taslim, M. A., 1994. "Public Corruption, External Interference, and Policy Making in a Dependent Regime." In H. Zafarullah, et al., eds., *Policy Issues in Bangladesh.* New Delhi: South Asian Publishers.

Tseng, W., and R. Corker, 1991. "Financial Liberalization, Money Demand, and Monetary Policy in Asian Countries." Occasional Paper 84. International Monetary Fund, Washington, D.C.

USAID, 1991. *Financial Sector Reform Project—Technical Assistance.* Ref. No. Bangladesh 91-02. United States Agency for International Development, Dhaka, Bangladesh.

Varley, J., 1992. "Returns, Risks and Capital Markets Development in Bangladesh." Paper presented at the Annual Conference of the Association for Economic and Development Studies on Bangladesh, November 21-22, 1992, Washington, D. C.

Von Pischke, J. D., D. W. Adams, and D. Gordon, eds., 1983. *Rural Financial Markets in Developing Countries.* Baltimore: Johns Hopkins University Press.

World Bank, 1989. *World Development Report.* New York: Oxford University Press.

———, 1993. *The East Asian Miracle: Economic Growth and Public Policy.* New York: Oxford University Press for the World Bank.

Zahler, R., 1993. "Financial Sector Reforms and Liberalization: Welcome Address." In S. Faruqi, ed., *Financial Sector Reforms in Asian and Latin American Countries: Lessons from Comparative Experience.* Washington, D.C.: The World Bank.

9 DOMESTIC RESOURCE MOBILIZATION IN THE PUBLIC SECTOR

M. ZAHID HOSSAIN

As in most other developing countries, there is an urgent need in Bangladesh to improve domestic resource mobilization. The existing level of resources mobilized domestically, both in the public and the private sector, is insufficient to attain a respectable level of economic growth and to reduce mass poverty in the country. The need to improve domestic resource mobilization has become all the more pressing in view of the fact that continued foreign resource inflow can no longer be taken for granted. On the one hand, the developed countries themselves are directing more of their resources to pull their economies out of recession and to reduce budget deficits, and on the other, the recent changes in Eastern Europe and the former Soviet Union have generated more competition for foreign assistance, the supply of which has diminished in recent years, owing mainly to the much reduced growth rates of the developed donor countries.

The existing rate of domestic saving is very low compared with the rate of investment, implying a sizable domestic resource gap. But even with the present 13 percent rate of investment, involving heavy reliance on foreign assistance, it has never been possible to attain a gross domestic product (GDP) growth rate of more than 3 to 4 percent. The experience of the last decade indicates that a much higher growth rate is necessary if poverty in the country is to be alleviated. It has been stated in the budget for fiscal year 1994 (FY1994) that in the medium term the government seeks to achieve a GDP growth rate of around 6 to 7 percent. To achieve this target, the rate of investment has to be raised from the existing 13 percent to around 18 percent within the next 5 to 6 years.

The rate of saving in Bangladesh has been low even by South Asian standards. The trends in domestic saving and investment of a number of South and Southeast Asian countries may be seen in Table 9.1. It is observed that for the periods stated, the rate of average gross domestic saving in Bangladesh is significantly lower than that of India, Nepal, or Pakistan, and much lower than Indonesia, Philippines, or Thailand.

Table 9.1
Domestic Saving in Selected Countries
(as percentage of GDP)

Country		*Saving Rate*
Bangladesh	I	3.2
	II	2.0
India	I	22.5
	II	22.6
Indonesia	I	23.0
	II	27.0
Nepal	I	12.1
	II	7.9
Pakistan	I	7.7
	II	4.8
Philippines	I	25.3
	II	21.8
Thailand	I	23.1
	II	19.1

Notes: I = Subperiod 1975/76 to 1979/80; II = Subperiod 1980/81 to 1984/85.
Source: Asian Development Bank (1988).

The only way to realize the level of investment required to attain a GDP growth rate of 6 to 7 percent in the medium term, given the grim reality of external resource inflow, is to raise the rate of saving in the public and private sectors. While public saving would imply mainly the surplus of public revenue, both tax and nontax over current expenditure, private saving would involve saving of the corporate and the household sectors.

This chapter seeks to examine the present position of resource mobilization in the public sector from tax and nontax sources and through current public expenditure management; identify problems in the areas of tax and nontax revenue collection and control of current expenditure; explore possibilities of enhancing mobilization of public resources; and suggest policy actions for increasing resource flows in the near future.

Present Position of Resource Mobilization in the Public Sector

Today a more active role is envisaged for the private sector to stimulate rapid economic growth. But there remains important roles for the public sector as well; on the one hand, there is the need to create an enabling environment, and on the other, to support technological and human resource development. Like other developing countries, the government in Bangladesh must generate a significant portion of the total investment and this requires a major mobilization of resources. These investment programs have to be financed mainly by revenue generation from tax and nontax sources.

The main source of public resource mobilization is tax revenue. The revenue-GDP ratio and the share of tax revenue in total revenue for different years are shown in Table 9.2. From this table it can be seen that the revenue-GDP ratio has increased from 5.2 in 1972/73–1974/75 to 11.0 in 1992/93. It can also be observed that tax receipts account for more than four fifths of the total revenue generated by the government.

Table 9.2
Revenue Structure of Bangladesh, 1972/73-1993/94

Year	*Total Revenue/GDP*	*Tax Revenue/Total Revenue*
1972/73-1974/75	5.2	83.00
1975/76-1979/80	8.8	85.30
1980/81-1984/85	9.2	84.00
1985/86-1987/88	9.0	83.90
1990/91	10.0	81.59
1992/93	11.0	81.60
1993/94 (Provisional)	11.5	81.35

Source: Chowdhury and Hossain (1988) and National Board of Revenue calculations.

Although the main burden of raising revenue is borne by taxes, the tax effort, as measured by the tax-GDP ratio, is low in Bangladesh compared with other Asian countries, as is evident in Table 9.3.

The structure of taxes in Bangladesh is quite inelastic, implying that it often becomes necessary to adopt discretionary budget measures to raise necessary revenue to meet the required public expenditure. The built-in elasticity and buoyancy in Bangladesh are shown in Table 9.4.

Table 9.3
Tax-GDP Ratio for Selected Countries
(Average of 1980-85, in percent)

Country	*Tax/GDP*
Bangladesh	7.3
India	16.2
Pakistan	10.7
Indonesia	20.1
Philippines	10.8
Thailand	13.1
Malaysia	22.8
Korea, Republic of	16.1
Less developed countries (82 countries)	17.5
South Asia (Average)	12.4
East Asia (Average)	16.8

Source: World Bank (1989).

It is necessary to mention here that since FY1992 sales tax and excise duty (mostly) have been replaced by the value-added tax (VAT) in Bangladesh. Since VAT has a larger tax base than the taxes it has replaced, the elasticity of VAT is expected to be a little higher than those of sales tax and excise duty.

Table 9.4
Elasticity and Buoyancy of Taxes in Bangladesh, 1972/73-1988/89

Tax	*Base*	*Elasticity*	*Buoyancy*
All taxes	GDP at current market prices	0.91	1.21
Import Duty	Dutiable value of imports	0.86	1.04
Sales Tax	Duty-paid value of imports	0.87	0.83
Excise Duty	GDP at current market prices	0.80	1.29
Income Tax	Nonagricultural GDP at current market prices	0.84	1.09

Source: Planning Commission (1990).

From Table 9.4 it can be observed that changes in tax revenue do not keep pace with increases in GDP as implied by the low elasticity, indicating that it is necessary to undertake discretionary measures to even maintain the existing tax-GDP ratio. To increase the responsiveness of the tax revenue to GDP changes, it is thus necessary to widen the tax base and strengthen compliance in the case of all taxes. The elasticities for different tax heads also declined over time, reflecting the inability of the country's tax system to bring the growing areas of the economy under the tax net.

The tax-GDP ratio in Bangladesh for the period FY1973 to FY1994 is shown in Table 9.5. It can be noted that the tax-GDP ratio remained more or less static from FY1976 to FY1985; thereafter it started increasing slowly. It thus appears that to attain a sharp increase in the tax-GDP ratio in the medium run, more than routine efforts would be necessary, and this would involve expansion of tax bases, procedural simplifications, and overall administrative improvements.

Table 9.5
Tax-GDP Ratio
(per cent)

Year	*Tax/GDP Ratio (%)*	*Year*	*Tax/GDP Ratio (%)*
FY1973	4.20	FY1984	6.80
FY1974	4.40	FY1985	7.10
FY1975	4.10	FY1986	7.20
FY1976	6.80	FY1987	7.40
FY1977	7.40	FY1988	7.90
FY1978	6.90	FY1989	7.90
FY1979	7.10	FY1990	8.00
FY1980	7.40	FY1991	8.20
FY1981	7.80	FY1992	8.42
FY1982	7.50	FY1993	8.90
FY1983	7.40	FY1994	9.40

FY = fiscal year.
Source: National Board of Revenue calculations.

Tax Structure

The following taxes are currently in existence in Bangladesh:

- Direct taxes: income taxes, land development tax, motor vehicles tax, stamp duty, registration, and other direct taxes.
- Indirect taxes: customs duty, value added tax, supplementary duty, and excise duty.

The indirect taxes may again be divided into foreign trade taxes and domestic goods and services taxes in the following way:

- Foreign trade taxes: customs duty, value added tax (VAT [I]), and supplementary duty (SD [I]).
- Domestic goods and services taxes: value added tax (VAT [D]), excise duty, and supplementary duty (SD [D]).

Table 9.6A gives a breakdown of the receipts of taxes under different heads from FY1992 to FY1994 (provisional). The proportionate contributions of direct and indirect taxes may be seen in Table 9.6b. From this table, it can be observed that indirect taxes account for about three fourths of total tax revenue. It is however found that the share of direct taxes is increasing, albeit slowly. For example, the share has increased from 24.76 percent in FY1992 to 25.11 percent in FY1993, and 27.10 percent in FY1994. Of the indirect taxes, foreign trade taxes are still dominant. For example in FY1992, the share of foreign trade taxes in total indirect taxes was 67.56 percent. This increased to 68.56 percent in FY1993 but declined slightly to 66.78 percent (provisional) in FY1994. It would be interesting to compare the relative shares of foreign trade taxes and domestic goods and services taxes before and after the introduction of VAT. It is however somewhat disappointing to note that the share of domestic goods and services is declining after the introduction of VAT. For example, the share of domestic goods and services taxes was 37.33 percent and 35.52 percent in FY1990 and FY1991 respectively. After the introduction of VAT during FY1992, the share declined to 32.44 percent in FY1992 and 31.44 percent in FY1993. The share is however expected to improve to 33.22 percent in FY1994.

It may also be deduced from Table 9.6a that the share of customs duties in total taxes is quite high, although the share is declining as a result of the massive tariff reductions that are taking place in the wake of ongoing tariff reform in the country. The relative share of customs duty is expected to decline further in the coming years.

The relative share of direct taxes in total tax revenue is still quite low although it is showing a trend to increase. Table 9.7 indicates that the ratio of direct taxes to total tax revenue in Bangladesh for the period 1980-1985 compares unfavorably with that of other developing countries for the same period. The ratio is much lower than the averages for the Sub-Saharan African and East Asian countries. The ratio is also lower than that of some 82 selected less developed countries (LDCs). The relatively low share of direct tax in total tax revenue in Bangladesh is accounted for by the low per capita income, light direct tax burden of the agricultural sector (which accounted for 35 percent of GDP in 1992), as well as the generous tax exemptions and incentive structure, still prevalent in the realm of direct taxes.

Table 9.6a
Tax Structure of Bangladesh
(crore taka)

Head of Revenue	*FY1992*	*FY1993*	*FY1994*
Customs duty	2,746.02	2,869.60	3,070.00
VAT (I)	1,269.74	1,731.77	1,785.00
SD (I)	25.71	31.12	130.00
VAT (D)	497.86	819.83	1,210.00
SD (D)	25.25	971.02	1,045.00
Excise duty	1,405.25	332.69	175.00
Income tax	1,294.03	1,603.88	1,900.00
Stamp (nonjudicial) duty	302.02	280.00	350.00
Land revenue	108.17	90.00	120.00
Registration	84.42	90.00	120.00
Motor vehicle tax	41.16	47.00	60.00
Other taxes	135.37	154.09	170.00
Total	7,935.00	9,021.00	10,035.00

VAT = value added tax.
SD = supplementary duty.
(I) = Import.
(D) = Domestic.

Source: National Board of Revenue calculations.

Table 9.6b
Contribution of Different Taxes to Total Tax Revenue

	Share in Total Taxes (%)		
Type of Tax	*FY1992*	*FY1993*	*FY1994*
I. Direct tax	24.76	25.11	27.10
II. Indirect tax	75.24	74.89	72.90
a. Trade taxes	(65.56)	(68.56)	(66.78)
b. Domestic goods and services taxes	(32.44)	(31.44)	(33.22)

Note: The figures in parentheses are proportionate shares of trade and domestic goods and services taxes in total indirect taxes.
Source: National Board of Revenue calculations.

Table 9.7
Percentage Share of Direct Tax in Total Tax Revenue for Selected Countries (1980-1985)

Country	*Direct Tax to Total Tax*
Malawi	38.1
India	30.1
Ghana	33.1
Pakistan	23.0
Indonesia (excluding oil revenue)	37.3
Thailand	22.1
Philippines	24.8
Malaysia	44.9
Korea, Republic of	26.2
Less developed countries (82 countries)	29.3
Sub-Saharan Africa	30.3
East Asia	43.3
Latin America	26.1

Source: World Bank (1989).

Existing Tax Systems

Income Tax

Income tax is the major source of direct taxes in Bangladesh. Of the two income taxes, corporate taxes predominate. Collection of corporate and personal income taxes is shown in Table 9.8. It can be observed that the share of corporate tax is much higher than that of noncorporate income tax although the former has been steadily declining over the years. This indicates that the base for noncorporate income tax is expanding at a faster pace than that for corporate income tax. In other words, more individuals are being brought under the tax net relative to corporate enterprises. That the growth rate in noncorporate income tax collection is higher than that of corporate income tax also signifies that the corporate industrial sector has been growing at a slower pace than the noncorporate sector assuming, of course, that the problems of tax compliance and avoidance in the corporate sector are not more pronounced than those in the noncorporate sector.

The coverage of income tax in Bangladesh is very narrow. As of June 1993, only 650,000 assessées are covered under income tax. The number of income taxpayers is found to grow at a modest rate of 5 percent every year.

Table 9.8
Composition of Income Taxes
(percent)

	FY1988	*FY1989*	*FY1990*	*FY1991*	*FY1992*
Corporate tax	77.20	76.39	67.55	65.05	62.42
Personal income tax	22.80	25.61	32.45	34.95	37.58

Source: National Board of Revenue calculations.

The structure of personal income tax as of FY1994 is as follows:

On the first Tk 50,000	Nil
On the next Tk 50,000	15 percent
On the next Tk 150,000	20 percent
On the balance of personal income	25 percent

On the face of it, the rate structure is progressive although it is less steep than before. But the structure is riddled with elaborate exemptions and concessions. In relation to the employment-related concessions, the allowances for housing and transportation are significant. The treatment of investment income is also generous in Bangladesh. Interest income up to Tk 20,000 and dividend income up to Tk 30,000 are exempt from income tax. Realized capital gains are subject to income tax under a separate schedule of graduated rates. However, these are entitled to tax deductions if reinvested in approved assets. Salaries of government workers are treated as if these are tax paid and thus incur no real tax liabilities.

It is doubtful if the above exemptions and concessions have encouraged more saving and investment in the country. Although the revenue losses implied by these tax expenditures have not been quantified, these are believed not to be negligible.

The corporate tax rates in Bangladesh are as follows:

- 40 percent for publicly traded companies other than banks, insurance companies, etc.;
- 45 percent for companies other than banks, insurance companies etc., that are not publicly traded; and
- 50 percent for banks, insurance, financial institutions, etc.

The statutory rates of corporate taxes are quite high in Bangladesh. However, the prevalence of liberal investment incentives like tax holidays and accelerated depreciation allowances serve to reduce the marginal effective tax rate (defined as the ratio of the difference between the pretax and after-tax rate of return to the pretax rate of return on investment).

Other Direct Taxes

Of the other direct taxes, stamp duty, registration, and land development taxes are important. Together, they will account for 5.70 percent of total tax revenue for FY1994. The land development tax and stamp duty collections have been increasing steadily in real terms albeit from narrow bases mainly as a result of periodic rate increases. The present land development tax introduced in 1982 is based solely on land area and is fixed in nominal terms. It has a progressive rate structure but the tax is inequitable as the rate is independent of land productivity. About half of the realizable tax on this account is reported to be collected every year. There is also the widespread problem of understating correct tax liability as well as the difficult problem of ascertaining the true ownership of land. The experience of other developing countries in Asia and Latin America leads one to believe that the land development tax in Bangladesh does not seem to hold the promise of becoming a major source of revenue.

The nonjudicial stamp duty yields more revenue than the land development tax. The rate structure for this tax has been revised upwards in the budget of FY1994 and is expected to bring about a 25 percent increase in revenue collection over FY1993.

Not only is less than half of the land development tax actually collected from agriculture, but the collection of income tax from agriculture is also negligible. It is difficult to identify agricultural income owners and quantify their incomes with any degree of precision. By all indications, agriculture in Bangladesh is quite lightly taxed compared with other countries at a similar stage of development. In the context of sectoral share in the overall GDP, which stands currently at around 35 percent, agriculture's contribution to total tax revenue is rather modest. Like many other developing countries, administrative difficulties would stand in the way of designing and implementing any comprehensive land tax system. Although the supply of land is inelastic and ownership patterns in rural Bangladesh are highly inequitable, land could ideally be considered a potential source of revenue for the government (see Ahsan 1991).

Customs Duties

Customs duties in Bangladesh are designed to meet the dual objectives of raising revenue and providing protection to domestic industries. Thus a well-balanced rate structure is needed to meet these objectives.

Bangladesh has historically maintained a highly protective tariff structure mainly to promote domestic industries. This has actually been counterproductive, helping only in the setting up of inefficient industries. This has also led to improper allocation of resources and discouraged export industries.

In view of the favorable experience with trade liberalization in different developing countries, a reform program to overhaul the country's tariff structure and remove quantitative restrictions has been initiated. Under this program, considerable rationalization of tariff rates has taken place in the form of lowering high rates, reducing the number of rates, and compressing tariff bands. The level of protection hitherto enjoyed by domestic industries has been moderated in the process. User-specific rates and the multiplicity of rates have also been drastically reduced to minimize distortions. The results of the reform exercise currently under way may be seen in Table 9.9.

Table 9.9
Impact of Ongoing Tariff Reform

	FY1992	*FY1993*	*FY1994*
Mean nominal (unweighted) duty rate	57%	47%	36%
Coefficient of variation of duty rate	72%	65%	62%
Mean weighted duty rate	24%	23%	22%
No. of duty rates	18	13	11
No. of harmonized system codes with duty rates above 100%	264	46	17
No. of harmonized system codes with zero rate of duty	395	323	296
Percentage of customs revenue realized from:			
Items with duty rate below 30%	29.78%	24.07%	20.49%
Items with duty rate within 30-60%	49.95%	58.29%	61.51%
Items with duty rate above 60% and not exceeding 100%	17.06%	16.24%	16.74%
Items with duty rate above 100%	3.21%	1.40%	1.26%

FY = fiscal year.
Source: National Board of Revenue calculations.

It may be observed from the table that the average nominal rate of duty has been steadily declining ever since major restructuring of duty rates was undertaken in FY1992. This has also meant a substantial reduction of dispersion, as measured by the coefficient of variation. The number of rates is also being progressively reduced from 18 in FY1992 to 13 in FY1993 to 11 in FY1994. The compression of duty rates is further evidenced by the reduction of the number of Harmonized System (HS) codes with duty rates of zero and above 100 percent over the period. By comparing the weighted mean duty rates for FY1992 and FY1993, it is found that the tariff reform was almost revenue-neutral. Although not necessarily designed to be so, an increase in the relative share of high duty goods in total imports left the trade-weighed duty rate more or less unchanged. However, with the static import level of FY1993, the duty structure for FY1994 is expected to be revenue reducing. In other words, in order to collect more revenue from customs duty in FY1994, the volume of imports has to increase significantly.

It thus appears that the dependence on import duties as a source of revenue is declining as a result of the downward adjustment of rates of customs duty. This is however fully in accord with the situation in other developing countries where the role of import duties is consciously being de-emphasized as a source of revenue although the tax base represented by the volume of imports is found to grow in tandem with the growth of per capita income. The revenue significance of import duties in Bangladesh is therefore expected to dwindle further over the medium run with further reform of the rate structure unless sustained increases in domestic economic activity cause import demand to respond more strongly to the changes in duty rates.

Value-Added Tax

The value-added tax introduced in FY1992 at a uniform rate of 15 percent has a wider tax base than that of the taxes it replaced, such as sales tax at the import stage and excise duty in the case of domestic goods and services. Unprocessed agricultural goods, forests, fisheries, and livestock are exempt from VAT. At the domestic production and import stages, supplementary duty at varying rates have been introduced for luxury goods or goods for which the government wants to discourage consumption. At the domestic production and service rendering stages, enterprises with turnover above Tk 7.5 lakhs are subject to VAT. The cottage industries (such as industries with installed machinery worth Tk 3 lakhs or below and annual turnover not above Tk 15 lakhs) are also exempt from VAT. For administrative and record keeping reasons, VAT in Bangladesh has been limited to the import-cum-manufacturing (and selected services) stages and has not yet been extended to the wholesale or retail stages.

The revenue performance of VAT in Bangladesh is more or less satisfactory although it has not yet been possible administratively to fully control the legal base of VAT, implying significant noncompliance, avoidance, and evasion, both at the domestic manufacturing and service rendering stages. Although VAT seeks to remedy much of the shortcomings of the previous tax systems, such as narrow tax base, cascading, inelasticity, and lack of transparency, it has not yet been possible to reap the full benefits of the new tax system owing to inadequate understanding or insufficient comprehension of the system on the part of both the taxpayers and tax collectors. To enhance the contribution of the taxes to domestic resource mobilization, the revenue performance of VAT (and supplementary duty) has to improve significantly.

Potential for Increasing Tax Revenue

Personal Income Tax

The record of the distribution of personal income earners in the Household Expenditure Survey indicates that there is considerable scope for increasing the number of personal income taxpayers. A study by Mansur and Khondker (1991) on the estimates for tax potential in Bangladesh indicates that tax returns could have been filed by approximately 3.1 million individual income taxpayers if employment-related allowances were abolished with an exemption limit of Tk 36,000 (in 1989). Since the exemption limit has been raised to Tk 50,000 in FY1994, this number would however be reduced to some extent, although it would be partly offset by the rise in the per capita income during the intervening period. But because of the overly generous employment-related allowances and treatment of investment income in Bangladesh, the number of potential income taxpayers would be around 0.9 million according to the above study. The same study suggests that even with this number of taxpayers, the potential collection of personal income tax in FY1989 could have been double the amount actually collected. This immediately implies that with the expansion and strengthening of administrative machinery, it should not be difficult to significantly increase the number of tax filers in Bangladesh.

The above study also indicates that tax revenue from personal income taxes could be further enhanced if the employment-related allowances were included in the tax base and the special exemptions of investment income were eliminated. Since the above study was undertaken, certain improvements in the position relating to the treatment of investment income have taken place in the form of replacement of investment allowance by investment tax credit, withdrawal of exemption of entertainment allowance, restriction of the exemption limit on dividend issued by public limited companies and withdrawal of partial exemption of dividends issued by private limited companies, and abolition of the provision for partially exempting interest on bank deposits. Other allowances have either been increased or retained, for example, house rent allowances for salaried taxpayers have been enhanced, capital gains arising out of disposal of approved securities and shares have been exempted from tax, and the exemption limit in case of interest on debentures has been raised. These, together with the high exemption limit of filing returns, place constraints on the possibilities of expanding the tax base. These exemptions and allowances create accounting and administrative problems as well. It is thus necessary to further scale down the exemptions and deductions in order to expand the tax base.

The experience of other developing countries (Table 9.10) also suggests that the base of personal income tax is usually sought to be broadened by eliminating incentives, reducing deductions and exemptions, including fringe benefits in the tax base, and taking recourse to presumptive taxation. Although the impact of these reforms may take time to become apparent, the directions of the reforms are in close conformity with the central message of modern tax theory, which suggests broadening of the tax base through lowering rates and reducing exemptions and deductions.

In Bangladesh, although personal income tax rates have been reduced substantially in the last couple of years, the simultaneous raising of the exemption limit has served to reduce the base. Since it is normally not easy to lower this exemption limit once it has been raised, care has to be taken to ensure that this limit is not further enhanced in the future without proper evaluation of income growth and the general price level as the current exemption limit (together with the generous allowances) works out at 12 to 13 times the per capita income, which is considerably higher than that in most other countries.

Table 9.10
Tax Reform Measures: Personal Income Tax Base Broadening

	Inclusion of Fringe Benefits[a]	*Presumptive Assessment*[b]	*Limited Deduction*[c]	*Increased Withholding*[d]
Bolivia		x	x	x
Colombia		x	x	
Indonesia	x		x	
Jamaica	x		x	x
Korea, Rep. of				
Malawi	x			
Mexico		x	x	
Morocco		x		
Turkey	x	x		x
Zimbabwe				

Note: x indicates that a particular measure was adopted.

[a]Indicates employer-provided benefits such as housing allowance (e.g., Jamaica), heating allowances (e.g., Turkey), and use of a company car (e.g., Malawi) have been incorporated in the definition of taxable income.

[b]Presumptive assessment of taxable income is based on gross turnover (e.g., Mexico), wealth holdings (e.g., Colombia), or consumption indicators (e.g., Turkey).

[c]Many countries have swept aside numerous personal deductions and replaced them with a single personal allowance.

[d]Withholding of tax at source may apply to labor income, all sources of income (e.g., Bolivia), interest income (e.g., Turkey), or product sales (e.g., Turkey).

Source: Bagchi (1991).

A study by Chowdhury and Hossain (1988) has shown (Table 9.11) that if the built-in tax elasticities in Bangladesh are decomposed (into the product of elasticity of the tax to its base and the elasticity of the base to income), it becomes immediately apparent that in the case of each of the taxes, the low overall elasticity stems from low tax to base elasticity. The base to income elasticity is found to be elastic in each case. This implies that tax yields under different heads did not keep pace with the increase in tax bases. This could be attributed to tax avoidance, owing to the generous exemptions and deductions on the one hand, and weak tax administration on the other. It is, therefore, obvious that one of the main reasons for the low level of income tax collection in Bangladesh is poor compliance. It may, however, be expected that once the ongoing administrative measures to strengthen the Income Tax Department are fully implemented and the computerization program takes shape, it would be possible to bring a larger number of personal income taxpayers under the income tax net as well as improve the quality of assessments in the case of the existing taxpayers.

Table 9.11
Decomposition of Tax Elasticities (1975/76-1984/85)

Tax Heads	*Built-in Tax to Base Elasticity*	*Base to Income Elasticity*
Direct tax	0.71	1.11
Income tax	0.85	1.11
Import duty	0.85	1.14
Excise duty	0.62	1.03

Source: Chowdhury and Hossain (1988).

In order to improve compliance, the coverage of self-assessment of income tax has been expanded and the procedure related thereto simplified in recent years. The income ceiling under self-assessment has been abolished and the scope has been extended to all assessees. The response to these changes has not however been encouraging so far. The requirement to pay a minimum tax of Tk 1500 seems to act as a deterrent to expansion of the self-assessment scheme as this amount exceeds the tax liability in case of many assessees.

Another important measure taken to expand the base of income tax recently has been to broaden the scope for presumptive assessment of income tax. The minimum presumptive tax has been fixed at Tk 2000 and Tk 1500 depending on the commercial importance of the area in which the assessee is located. In view of the low level of literacy, absence of tax culture, and weak tax administration, the problem of collecting taxes from small traders and the self-employed categories is quite serious in Bangladesh. The number of such potential taxpayers is believed to be large. Quite often, these taxpayers are incapable of calculating their true income and the government is unable to ascertain the same. In the absence of any dependable means of verifying a potential taxpayer's actual income, certain forms of external criteria or indications of wealth, such as number of employees, total sales, value of machinery used, or size of commercial operation, are used to make presumptive assessments. Such assessments or variants thereof have been in operation in France for a long time and are also to be found in many African countries with significant levels of effectiveness (Malik 1979). This system of assessment was introduced in Bangladesh in the FY1990 budget. With further streamlining of administrative procedures and preparation of groundwork relating to this system, it is expected to yield more revenues than what is presently being collected by way of presumptive assessment.

In order to widen the overall tax base, the scope of withholding income tax at source is being expanded in Bangladesh. This system of collecting tax in advance has been found to be extremely effective in countries where tax administration is particularly weak.

Corporate Income Tax

The level of collection of corporate income tax is obviously related to the stage of economic development of a country. Because of the low share of organized manufacturing and the low degree of urbanization, the collection of corporate income tax as a share of GDP is low (0.83 percent GDP) in Bangladesh. In addition, the rate structure is still high compared with the levels of noncorporate taxes, leaving scope for avoidance and noncompliance. Given the need to raise a certain amount of revenue from income taxes, these rates cannot conceivably be reduced further in the near future, unless there is a corresponding rise in the collection of noncorporate taxes.

Generous tax exemptions in the case of corporate taxes, mainly in the form of the tax holiday, exist in Bangladesh. The tax holiday, however, has not been found to be efficient in promoting industrial growth. Although the tax holiday helps entrepreneurs recover costs, there is a corresponding loss of revenue which increases with the length of the tax holiday period. No serious attempt has so far been made to quantify such tax expenditures arising out of the liberal tax holiday, owing mainly to the lack of adequate data, although the magnitude of revenue losses may be significant.

Tax incentives have been found to be ineffective instruments in promoting investment in other countries. For example, complicated and elaborate incentive structures were in place in Indonesia before 1983. In recognition of the deleterious consequences in terms of revenue and administrative and efficiency costs of different incentives such as the tax holiday, accelerated depreciation allowance, and investment allowance, these were abolished in Indonesia in 1983. In accordance with the current plans, the tax holiday in Bangladesh is to be abolished in 1995, to be replaced, if necessary, by alternative fiscal incentives such as accelerated depreciation allowance. It is, however, necessary to conduct detailed research in order to identify a suitable fiscal incentive structure for Bangladesh, keeping in view the experience of other countries with tax policies for industrial or export growth.

Agricultural Taxation

Historically, some form of land tax has been used as a preferred instrument to tax agriculture in view of the difficulties faced in designing a suitable agricultural income tax system. The relative importance of land revenue in Bangladesh has declined very significantly over the last couple of decades.

As the existing progressive tax structure of land development tax is complex in Bangladesh, a flat rate of tax, based on presumed income per acre of land (similar to the system that was in operation up to the 1960s), may replace the existing graduated tax structure (see Ahsan 1991). Such a tax system would make the taxes from land more equitable and revenue-productive, and would be simpler and less costly to administer as well. Ahsan (1991) also suggests that land revenue would be collected more effectively if the responsibility for collection is assigned to the local government, which would also be given the authority to retain the revenue so collected for its own expenditure. This could, to a large extent, solve the dual problem of collection and generation of funds for financing local development expenditure. As a new tax handle for agriculture, a tax on marketed surplus could be considered in a limited way. Hossain et al. (1987) estimate that a 5 percent ad valorem tax on the value of crops marketed could generate about Tk 161 crore, which is more than the amount of revenue collected from the land tax at present.

Customs Duties

The base of this tax cannot be broadened further by imposing customs duty afresh on any item. However, because of the ongoing procedural simplification and rationalization of the rate structure which should make the system more transparent, the compliance position is expected to improve in the near future.

Value-Added Tax

At present 60 percent of the VAT collected comes from imports. Dependence on import VAT will remain even as collection from domestic VAT increases. First of all, imported raw materials used in domestic industries will continue to generate VAT revenue at the import stage, although the same will be credited against VAT payable on domestic output. For accounting purposes, VAT would be shown to have been collected at the import stage while credit would be given at the domestic stage, thus reducing both cascading and domestic revenue correspondingly. Secondly, VAT on imported finished products would be maintained by design, following the principle of trade neutrality. Uniform trade-neutral VAT would not affect consumer allocation across goods, neither would it affect firms' allocation of inputs.

There does not appear to be any scope for further expanding the base of import VAT as most of the imported goods, except the primary or unprocessed agricultural goods such as livestock and forest products, have already been brought under the VAT. The compliance at the import stage is also more or less satisfactory and is expected to improve with the ongoing streamlining of customs procedures.

The same position prevails with regard to domestic goods because of the trade neutrality feature of VAT in Bangladesh. However, certain problems still exist with regard to domestic VAT. First, the dual threshold for small (Tk 0.75 million) and cottage industries (Tk 1.5 million) is anomalous. The exemption afforded by these thresholds is also quite high, keeping in view the average scale of industrial operations. This has reduced the tax base and created enforcement problems, in addition to the problem of market distortions resulting from dual cost structures relating to products coming from taxable and nontaxable firms. Efforts must therefore be made to unify the thresholds and not to raise the threshold(s) further unless dictated by a sustained rise in the general price level. Secondly, the compliance position is much less than satisfactory, both in the case of domestic goods and more so in the case of services. The current legal base remains far from being consolidated. To consolidate the base and thereby improve revenue collection significantly, it is necessary to educate both the taxpayers and tax collectors through continuous training and publicity campaigns. It is also necessary to develop improved supervisory or auditing capabilities of the tax officials through rapid computerization of the VAT system. Collection of VAT on a presumptive basis from hard-to-tax groups of taxpayers may also be tried along similar lines as existed in France and now exists in a number of African countries.

The share of organized manufacturing is only about 15 percent of value added in Bangladesh. To meaningfully expand the base of VAT in Bangladesh, it is necessary to bring more and more services under VAT. The share of the services sector in value added is about 50 percent. But the entire services sector cannot conceivably be brought under the VAT network. For example, services like education, public health, and administration will always remain outside VAT. This would leave around

20 percent of the value added in the services sector which could be covered under VAT. But it is really difficult to administer VAT when it relates to services. There are definitional and measurement problems, and problems relating to the location and time of supply. Since the value added in the main stage of production in case of services is very high, there is an irresistible tendency to evade. Nevertheless, for efficiency, distributional, and revenue considerations, all efforts should be made to expand VAT to cover more and more services.

Potential for Increasing Nontax Revenue

At present, nontax revenue accounts for 18 to 19 percent of total revenue in Bangladesh (Table 9.12) which works out to be 2 to 2.50 percent of GDP. The share of nontax revenue in total revenue has more or less remained steady over the last two decades.

Table 9.12
Share of Nontax Revenue in Total Revenue

Year	*Nontax Revenue/Total Revenue*
1972/73-1974/75	17.00
1975/76-1979/80	14.70
1980/81-1984/85	16.00
1985/86-1987/88	16.10
1990/91	19.41
1992/93	19.54
1993/94 (provisional)	18.64

Source: Chowdhury and Hossain (1988) and National Board of Revenue calculations.

The principal heads of nontax revenue are dividend and profit from public financial and nonfinancial institutions, interest income, and net contributions of the Bangladesh Telegraph and Telephone Board. The collection of nontax revenue from different sources during recent periods is shown in Table 9.13.

The dividend and profit from financial institutions include profits from Bangladesh Bank, nationalized commercial banks (NCBs), and financial institutions owned by the government, as well as from other banks and financial institutions in which the government has shares. Bangladesh Bank alone contributes more than 90 percent of total revenue against this head. The revenue from this head shows an upward trend because of increased profits earned by Bangladesh Bank resulting from its policy-driven interventions. The profit and dividend earned by public enterprises and corporations are the second largest source of nontax revenue. Against this head of revenue, the contribution of Bangladesh Petroleum Corporation is the largest. A very small contribution is received from public corporations while the manufacturing public enterprises maintain their positions as money-losing concerns. Thus, instead of contributing to the government exchequer, these enterprises live on government support in terms of equity infusion and capital restructuring. If the loss-making enterprises are closed down or disposed of by the public sector, it would in fact result in a one-time gain for the government in terms of capital income.

Table 9.13
Nontax Revenue by Source
(Tk in crore)

	FY1991	*FY1992*	*FY1993*	*FY1994*
1. Dividend and profit from public financial institutions	173	320	429	484
2. Dividend and profit from nonfinancial public enterprises	277	356	411	380
3. Interest income	298	242	252	350
4. Telegraph and telephone (net)	228	345	467	380
5. General administration and services	128	118	114	199
6. Economic services	138	148	189	148
7. Jamuna bridge surcharge	93	100	36	50
8. Post office department (net)	-29	-15	-43	-27
9. Railway (net)	-148	-106	-147	-84
10. Agriculture and allied services	40	67	43	68
11. Social and community services	51	59	62	90
12. Transport and communications	40	46	42	45
13. Other nontax revenue	143	149	176	152
14. Capital income	17	3	5	65
Total	1,448	1,832	2,034	2,300

Note: Figures for FY1994 are provisional.
Source: Calculated from Budget Summary Statements, Ministry of Finance (various years).

Interest on loans owed to the government comes under the head of Interest Income. This has remained more or less steady in recent years and is unlikely to register any sudden increase in the near future, unless attempts to recover interests on loans to the autonomous bodies are successful. Receipts from trade and commerce, like the fees collected under the Import and Export Control Act, registration fees paid by firms and companies, and audit fees account for the revenue collected under Economic Services.

The collection of revenue against the heads of General Administration and Services (such as defence receipts, health, education, and police); agriculture and allied services (sales proceeds from agricultural products, livestock, fishery, and forest products); social and community services (broadcasting, rent from government housing, and public health); transport, and communication (toll from roads, bridges, and ferry) show steady patterns and are unlikely to increase dramatically in the near future unless fees and user charges are raised.

Although the net revenue collected from Telegraph and Telephone is quite large and has been increasing over time, Railway and Post Office Departments have traditionally been money-losing sectors. Nontax revenue sources cannot be expected to play any major role in resource mobilization. However, there is potential for improving collection under several nontax revenue heads. As a result of measures taken under the ongoing financial sector reform program, the performance of public financial institutions is expected to improve over the medium run. The restructuring of public enterprises will also lead to improved financial performance on their part with consequent improvements of amounts of profits and dividend transferred to the government.

Current Expenditure

To mobilize resources for economic development it is not sufficient just to raise a certain amount of revenue, for no amount of revenue can contribute to development efforts unless considerable surplus is generated by keeping the government's current expenditure under tight control. Current expenditure in Bangladesh grew at a rapid rate of 18 percent annually between FY1984 and FY1990, which also exceeded the annual revenue growth of 14 percent during the same period, thus limiting the amount of resources available for development expenditure. Apart from the relatively large size of the government, subsidies (12 to 14 percent of revenue budget) for the loss-making departments and public sector enterprises accounted for much of the rise in current expenditure during the above period.

As a percentage of GDP, current expenditure rose from 5.6 percent in FY1981 to 9.7 percent in FY1991. After FY1991, the growth in current expenditure has been contained by maintaining it below the rate of growth of nominal GDP. Thus the share of current expenditure in GDP has been maintained at a level slightly lower than 9 percent since FY1991. Care has, however, been taken to ensure that relatively more resources are allocated to education, health and family planning, and social and community services with a view to contributing to human resource development and welfare. The relative shares of these heads of expenditure in total current expenditure during FY1991 to FY1994 (estimated) is shown in Table 9.14.

Table 9.14
Relative Shares of Selected Services in Current Expenditure

Head	*Share (%)*			
	FY1991	*FY1992*	*FY1993*	*FY1994*
1. Education	16.59	17.42	19.66	19.61
2. Health and population control	5.47	5.56	6.44	6.45
3. Social and community services	9.14	8.83	4.28	7.18
4. Agriculture, forest, fisheries, livestock	2.89	2.66	3.13	2.58

FY = fiscal year.
Note: Figures for FY1994 are provisional.
Source: Calculated from Budget Summary Statement, Ministry of Finance (various years).

It is observed from the table that the shares of education, health, and population control in current expenditure have been growing during recent years while those of social services and agriculture have remained more or less steady during the same period. Decomposition of current expenditure by economic classification (Table 9.15) indicates that consumption accounts for a large share of current expenditure. Within consumption, the expenditure on wages and salaries represents a higher proportion of expenditure than that relating to goods and services.

Table 9.15
Share of Current Expenditure (Economic) Categories in Total Current Expenditure
(percent)

	Consumption			*Transfers*	
	Wages/Salaries	*Maintenance*	*Goods*	*Interest*	*Subsidy and other transfers*
FY1992	35	5	20	14	26
FY1993	39	6	19	12	24
FY1994	37	7	18	13	25

FY = fiscal year.
Source: Calculated from Budget Summary Statements, Ministry of Finance (various issues).

Operation and maintenance is increasing steadily indicating that more attention has been paid in recent times to the maintenance of infrastructure projects from the current budget. Expenditure on interest payments has remained more or less steady at 12 to 14 percent of total current expenditure, underscoring the role of domestic and external debts in the financing of the national budget.

Careful designing of current expenditure policy is essential both for improving the productive capacity and welfare of the community as well as for generating sufficient revenue surplus for financing development outlays. It is necessary to eliminate expenditure that brings little benefit to the citizens of the country. At the same time, it is also necessary to ensure adequate expenditure in priority sectors like health, population, and social services while checking system losses in these sectors. This calls for a closer look at the current expenditure program of the government. Overstaffing in offices may be reduced by encouraging voluntary separation schemes and through redeployment of staff in productive activities. Careful scrutiny is also required to identify transfers that are not justified on economic grounds and thus deserve to be drastically cut down. Current expenditure monitoring and analyzing capabilities of the government also need to be strengthened. Losses of revenue-earning departmental enterprises like Railways and Post Office need to be reduced by improving the operational efficiency of such organizations. Finally, for reducing pressure on the government budget loss-making public enterprises should be privatized or closed down without further delay.

Conclusion

The existing level of domestic resource mobilization in Bangladesh is insufficient to achieve a reasonable rate of economic growth and reduce mass poverty. It is thus necessary to raise the level of domestic resources significantly within a short time. While the level of domestic resources mobilized in the private sector is equally unsatisfactory, the focus of this paper has been limited to an examination of the position relating to resource mobilization in the public sector only.

The public sector in Bangladesh is involved in the building of physical and financial infrastructure as well as in setting up basic industries requiring large investments. The close involvement of the public sector in building infrastructure is essential for generating positive externalities by way of enhancing the productivity of capital or returns for the private sector. For releasing resources for development expenditure, it is required, on the one hand, to raise more revenue from tax and nontax sources, and on the other, to restrain current expenditures as far as practicable.

The major sources of tax revenue in Bangladesh are customs duty, value-added tax (and supplementary duty), and income tax, while that of nontax revenue are the profit and dividend earned by the government from public financial and nonfinancial institutions and interest income. Around four fifths of the total revenue in Bangladesh is collected from tax sources and the remainder from nontax sources.

The contribution of direct taxes (income tax, land development tax, stamp duty, and registration) to total revenue and as a percentage of GDP is low compared with other less developed countries. The coverage of income tax is narrow and there are a large number of concessions and exclusions, both in the case of personal and corporate income taxes. The collection of income tax from agricultural income is negligible. The land development tax, in its existing form, also yields limited revenue. However, it appears feasible to improve collection of income tax through administrative strengthening, procedural improvements, and reduction or elimination of concessions, exclusions, and incentives. It is possible to bring more assessees under the income tax net and also ensure collection of due amounts of tax from the existing taxpayers by adopting the above measures effectively. The collection of land development tax could also be enhanced by simplifying the rate structure and linking taxes to land productivity.

Even after the general reduction of rates, custom duty still plays an important role in mobilizing domestic resources. Although dependence on customs duty as a source of revenue is being reduced by design, this will remain a major source of revenue as long as domestic-based direct and indirect taxes are not in a position to generate required revenue for the government. Since customs duty is not an efficient source of revenue in view of its distortionary effects on domestic production and its dependence on balance of payments situation, it is necessary for domestic taxes to take over the revenue role of customs duty as early as possible.

The value-added tax is an efficient, buoyant, and revenue-productive system of taxation. However, the transitional problems relating to its implementation are not yet over, as administrative and systemic weaknesses are still prevalent. It is, therefore, necessary to administratively consolidate the present legal base of VAT to improve revenue collection significantly. For small and hard-to-tax groups of taxpayers, the possibility of applying some form of presumptive taxation could be considered. Administrative improvement, through continuous training of tax collectors and computerization of the VAT department can have a major impact on revenue collection.

Nontax sources are not expected to play any major role in domestic resource mobilization although there is scope for improving the operational performance of departmental enterprises and sector corporations which could then raise the contribution of these agencies to the government exchequer.

Side by side with the measures taken to improve revenue collection, it is also essential to restrain current expenditure to the required minimum. While expenditure on human resource development and welfare activities should continue to get priority, wasteful expenditure should be reduced drastically. It is necessary to study the pattern, composition, and growth trend of current expenditure in order to identify the portion of expenditure which could be dispensed without affecting efficiency.

From the analysis here presented, it appears feasible to improve the tax effort in Bangladesh in the medium run by bringing about administrative and systemic improvements in relation to different taxes. At the same time, if current expenditure is kept under tight control, it would be possible to generate a larger amount of revenue surplus to support development activities in the country.

References

Ahsan, S. M., 1991. "Taxation in Bangladesh: Issues of Reform and Design. Concordia University." Mimeographed.

Asian Development Bank (ADB), 1988. *Financing Public Sector Development Expenditure in Selected Countries: An Overview*. Manila.

Bagchi, A., 1991. "Tax Reform in Developing Countries: Agenda for the 1990s." *Asian Development Review* 9(2):40-72.

Chowdhury, O. H., and M. Hossain, 1988. "Tax Structure of Bangladesh: An Overview." *Bangladesh Development Studies* 16(4):65-91.

Hossain, M., A. Rahman, and M. M. Akash, 1987. "A Study on Agricultural Taxation in Bangladesh: Potential and Politics." Bangladesh Institute of Development Studies. Mimeographed.

Malik, I. A., 1979. "Use of Presumptive Tax, Assessment Techniques in Taxation of Small Traders and Professionals in Africa." *Bulletin for International Fiscal Documentation* 33(4):162-78.

Mansur, A. H., and B. H. Khondker, 1991. "Bangladesh: Some Estimates for Tax Potential." Mimeographed.

Ministry of Finance, various years. *National Budget*. Government of Bangladesh.

Planning Commission, 1990. "The Fourth Five Year Plan." Government of Bangladesh.

World Bank, 1989. *Bangladesh: An Agenda for Tax Reform*. Washington, D. C.

10 DIMENSIONS OF GOVERNANCE

MOHAMMAD MOHABBAT KHAN AND
A.K. MONAW-WAR UDDIN AHMAD

The term governance, though not new, has attracted the attention of international donors, policy makers, development practitioners and scholars. However, there has not been a universal agreement about the meaning of the term. It has come to mean a number of things, including the following:

> ... a judgment on the quality of government (Jahan 1992, 3); how people are ruled, how the affairs of the state are administered and regulated ... a nation's system of politics ... in relation to public administration and law (Landell-Mills and Serageldin 1991, 304); exercise of political power to manage a nation's affairs (World Bank 1989, 5); and the manner in which power is exercised in the management of a country's economic and social resources for development (World Bank 1992, 1).

The definitions above point to the following. First, there is acceptance of the fact that governance includes exercise of authority or power. Second, the process through which authority or power is exercised and with what intent is important. Third, interrelations and interactions among politics, economics, administration, and law in a given society is of utmost importance for understanding governance. Fourth, such terms as "good" and "quality" tend to be equated with governance.

The aims of this chapter are to: (a) probe into the meaning and characteristics of good governance; (b) analyze principal components of governance in Bangladesh; and (c) show problems and progress of governance in development administration in Bangladesh.

Good governance denotes a desirable state of affairs. A precise definition of good governance is, however, still awaited. Because of the difficulties involved in defining the term, the overwhelming tendency has been to delineate aspects of good governance (OECD/DAC 1992, Landell-Mills and Serageldin 1992, 306).

To define and clarify the meaning of good governance, Sir Kenneth Stowe (1992, 388), a retired British permanent secretary, presents six desiderata. These are:

- political freedom, including free speech and a freely elected parliament;
- constitutional and judicial protection for the rights of the individual;
- maintenance of the rule of law by an independent judiciary;
- maintenance of a stable currency;
- development of society as a whole by education and health care; and
- executive accountability to a freely-elected legislature.

Good governance has two parallel meanings which often overlap (Leftwich 1993, 606). The first and more restricted meaning is associated with the World Bank which consistently interprets it in primarily administrative and managerial terms. Good governance, for the World Bank (1989, 15, 60-61, 192) includes some or all of the following features: "an efficient public service; an independent judicial system and legal framework to enforce contracts; the accountable administration of public funds; an independent public auditor, responsible to a representative legislature; respect for the law and human rights at all levels of government; a pluralistic institutional structure; and a free press." On the other hand, the second meaning, associated with Western governments, is more political as it includes an insistence on competitive democratic politics as well as concern for administrative improvement (Leftwich 1993, 606).

Ultimately, good governance depends on the extent to which "a government is perceived and accepted as legitimate, committed to improving the public welfare and responsive to the needs of its citizens, competent to assure law and order and deliver public services, able to create an enabling policy environment for productive activities and equitable in its conduct" (Landell-Mills and Serageldin 1991, 310).

Governance in Bangladesh

The citizens of Bangladesh at this juncture of the country's history deserve good governance for more than one reason. An authoritarian regime has been forced to quit power as a result of a mass upsurge and organized protests. During nine years of dictatorial rule which was sometimes given the garb of democracy, the economy was seriously ruined; productivity, efficiency and morale of public servants deteriorated sharply; indiscipline and mismanagement in the public sector was widespread, and there was serious misuse of public office and state power. So the people were not only interested in dislodging the dictator but also in demolishing what he stood for and the system he developed to "privatize" state resources and personnel. The people naturally aspired for a new system of governance, a system that would allow meaningful popular participation at all levels, protect their fundamental rights, and rid the nation from mismanagement and indiscipline.

The caretaker government was to play the role of catalyst in the transition from autocracy to democracy, and its main responsibility was to hold free and fair elections within 90 days. The polling was free, fair, impartial, and held under peaceful conditions. Undoubtedly, the holding of elections in such a manner was the singular and credible achievement of the caretaker government. The "all-powerful" dictator who called the shots for so many years was asked to explain his conduct while in office. This exercise means that in the future, chief executives would be held accountable for their actions even after their departure from power.

In the following subsections various aspects of two principal components of governance in Bangladesh are discussed and critically analyzed.

Political Accountability

Political accountability is an essential precondition for the functioning of a democratic system. It entails that those holding elective political offices must be accountable to the citizens for all their actions. It also necessitates that there should be appropriate checks and balances within the political system so that no one branch of the government dominates and controls others. The nature of political parties, the extent of independence enjoyed by the judiciary, and the credibility of the electoral process and opportunities allowed for expression of opinion and free flow of information, all influence political accountability in a particular country.

Political accountability in Bangladesh has been shaped by the influence of a number of factors. These are: dominant executive, weak legislature, distorted growth and low level of development of political parties, lack of independence of the judiciary, lack of credibility of the electoral system, and lack of respect for human rights.

(1)

Dominant Executive

Political institution building in Bangladesh over the years unmistakably indicates a growing trend to strengthen and consolidate all powers in the office of the chief executive, i.e. the presidency. This has been possible because of the support provided to such a move by the military, the bureaucracy, and the unprincipled politicians (Khan and Zafarullah 1988, 179). The imbalance, resultant of the growing power of the presidency, took a number of forms. But all these considerably eroded political accountability as all powers were concentrated in the hands of one man.

The constitutional policies of three past effective rulers of Bangladesh, Sheikh Mujibur Rahman (Mujib), General Ziaur Rahman (Zia), and General Hossain Mohammad Ershad (Ershad) clearly demonstrate that these were primarily confined to bringing undemocratic amendments to the constitution, suspending the constitution, and flagrantly violating the constitution to consolidate the power and position of the chief executive, i.e. the president (Khan 1992a, 179-181).

The constitutional amendments were mostly utilized to legitimize one-party rule, validate all actions under martial law, and legalize highly controversial issues. Through the fourth amendment of the constitution, Mujib replaced a multi-party parliamentary system with a one-party presidential system. This amendment closed all avenues to organize and sustain democratic opposition to the government, thereby creating tension, dissension, and frustration within the polity. The fifth amendment provided legal protection to General Zia's almost four years of military rule. This, among other things, opened up the prospect for future military intervention in Bangladesh politics. The seventh amendment, likewise, validated the four-and-a-half years of military rule of General Ershad. General Zia was also instrumental in amending the constitution to give it an Islamic character.

During a span of 20 years, i.e., 1971-1990, the country's constitution remained suspended for over eight years due to military takeover of state power. This allowed the two principal beneficiaries of the military coups, General Zia and General Ershad, to concentrate all power in their hands and rule the country by proclamations and directives.

The chief executives also resorted to ostensibly invoking the emergency provision of the constitution to tackle national emergencies. But in reality such a provision has been used to counter and suppress democratic opposition to the government in power. This meant further enhancement of the power of the presidency.

The present parliamentary form of government of Prime Minister Khaleda Zia is an elected one. The ruling Bangladesh Nationalist Party (BNP) was originally committed to the presidential system of government. When pressed by the main opposition party, i.e., Awami League, the BNP switched to the parliamentary system. This is an outcome of the ongoing democratic process in Bangladesh. While the present government has on occasion ignored the parliament on some issues of public importance, in most cases such major issues are discussed and debated in the parliament. The president, on the other hand, being advised by the prime minister, promulgated ordinances to abolish the elected *upazila* (subdistrict) council, to ban floor crossing by the members of the parliament and to contain terrorist activities by segments of the population (Khan 1993a, 18-19). But at the same time, there are a number of parliamentary committees consisting of members from all the political parties to examine various issues of national importance. It is worth noting that a committee was even formed to investigate into the corruption charges brought against an influential cabinet minister. As such it appears that things are slowly getting better.

Weak Legislature

One of the consequences of attempts to concentrate enormous power in the hands of the chief executive over the years has been the gradual and systematic weakening of the position of the parliament vis-a-vis the executive. The president was not accountable to the parliament. In fact, the president became and remained omnipotent. In other words, successive parliaments were made ineffective by all-powerful presidents.

None of the four previous parliaments were allowed to complete their five-year term. The first parliament lasted for only 2 years, 7 months, and 5 days. The second fared little better as it survived for 3 years, 8 months, and 12 days. The third parliament had the shortest life, i.e., a little over one-and-a-half years. The duration of the fourth parliament was 2 years and 8 months.

During the tenures of Mujib, Zia, and Ershad the parliament rubber-stamped the decisions of the executive; parliamentary approval of each and every executive act was taken for granted. Even amendments to the constitution which intended to radically transform the nature of the state and the governance system, i.e. the fourth amendment, was passed in the parliament with an overwhelming majority within a few minutes of its introduction. Of the 300 members, 294 voted for the amendment and none opposed it. Interestingly, no discussion was allowed on the amendment. Also, parliamentary control over ministries was restricted to raising harmless questions and holding meetings.

The present parliament, the fifth, was expected to play its designated role for two reasons. First, as mentioned earlier, the members were elected under the auspices of an interim government and the polls were the freest and fairest held in this country. Second, as also noted above, the members of parliament took a historic decision on August 6, 1991 when they voted unanimously for the passage of the twelfth amendment of the constitution to change the system of government from a presidential to a parliamentary one.

However, a number of factors have considerably weakened parliament's control over the executive. These are: (a) the inexperience of the majority of the legislators, i.e., 68 percent had been elected for the first time (Maniruzzaman 1992, 221); (b) the reluctance of the government to subject itself or its plans to debate; (c) the tendency of the opposition (political parties) to oppose only for the sake of opposition; (d) uncertainties concerning appropriate procedures resulting in part from the absence of institutional conventions or traditions; and (e) some fairly sharp differences between the two largest parties on major symbolic issues although there are seemingly few differences on substantive program issues (Blair et al. 1992, 36-37).

In a parliamentary system political accountability is ensured by making the executive accountable to legislature. The legislature keeps watch over the activities of the executive through a number of mechanisms such as various committees, questions raised by legislators, and debates on important issues.

But committees in the present parliament have faced difficulties in performing their designated role due to the following reasons (Khan 1994). First, many committees have been overwhelmed with workload due to past neglect. Second, committee members do not always get necessary information pertaining to a case under consideration. Third, recommendations of the committees are not acted upon on many occasions due to political influence-peddling and bureaucratic intransigence. Fourth, committees lack adequate staff and other logistic support. Fifth, the practice of having standing committees headed by concerned ministers has not helped the smooth functioning of such committees because it is almost impossible for the chairmen of these committees to be dispassionate when their actions and those of their senior civil servants are scrutinized. In addition, it has been found that on many occasions when discussions took place on issues of national importance, the prime minister, her cabinet colleagues, and senior opposition MPs including the leader of the opposition, have been conspicuous by their absence. In spite of these shortcomings, parliamentary committees formed for various ministries are working steadily and in many cases some progress has been made. One has to bear in mind here that a parliamentary culture takes time to develop.

In a parliamentary system the majority party governs with the consent of other parties. So the role of the ruling party, the Bangladesh Nationalist Party (BNP), is to present and defend its policies in the parliament. The opposition parties in the parliament, the Awami League (AL), Jatiya Party (JP), Jammat-e-Islami (JI), and others are supposed to point out and criticize genuine policy failures of the government and offer viable policy options to enable the BNP to better serve the people. Though some constraints have been faced in this process due to reasons mentioned earlier, there are indications that the parliament will have greater control over the executive. However, adequate mutual trust between the BNP and other opposition political parties, specially the AL, will be required to ensure good governance within the present democratic framework. The BNP leaders act on the premise that their main adversary is the AL. The logic subscribed to by the policy makers of the BNP is that AL is out to destabilize the government. The AL leaders, on the other hand, believe that BNP's policies and actions are primarily designed to discredit the past achievements and present programs of the AL. The recent demand for a caretaker government by the opposition parties is a challenge for the present parliament. At the time of writing, negotiations and proposals for reconciliation are in the process.

Nature and Character of Political Parties

One of the major problems of political accountability in Bangladesh can be attributed to the nature and character of its political parties. They have played a crucial role in the political development of the country. However, on many occasions they have not been able to lead and guide effectively at different crucial junctures. Fortunately, on such occasions, like the movement which finally toppled the Ershad regime, supplementary leadership was provided by students, labor, and professionals. The reasons for such a situation can be diagnosed if one looks at a number of factors. These are the weak nature of the leadership, fragmentation of political parties into smaller factions/groups, and the promotion and perpetuation of personality cults (Khan and Zafarullah 1990, 315-316); the failure to develop clear and cohesive socioeconomic programs, unstable membership, and lack of organizational discipline and democratic practice (Rahman 1993, 467).

Leaders of some political parties, irrespective of ideological moorings, supported military dictators and enabled them to legitimize their regimes. They did so by abandoning their parties and joining the parties floated by the military rulers, and by rushing into the election fray organized under the auspices of the military. This is how both the BNP and the JP were launched by General Zia and General Ershad, respectively. Fragmentation of political parties into smaller factions/groups has been a recurring phenomenon with party leaders using such split to obtain benefits for themselves and their key followers from the regime in power. Political parties have been dominated exclusively by personalities. The situation resulted in political parties building and cashing in on the images of a big leader rather than concentrating on formulating and implementing socioeconomic programs. The four major political parties continue to depend almost exclusively on the "charisma" of their leaders, i.e., AL on Mujib, BNP on Zia, JP on Ershad, and JI on Ghulam Azam. This situation has contributed to selection of leaders on the basis of heredity and perpetuation of undemocratic practices within political parties more than before. On the plus side, however, all parties now agree on the broad economic philosophy of a market-based economy. In spite of their many differences, the political leaders of different parties have sat together to discuss and debate a large number of economic and other policy issues. In particular, in the last three years there has been a positive trend among the politicians to respond to calls made by newspaper editors for open discussions on socioeconomic problems besetting the country.

Lack of Independence of the Judiciary

A sound judicial system, which is a must for good governance, is possible when the judiciary can exercise its authority independently. The judiciary was made subservient to the executive branch of the government by the fourth amendment in 1975. To reverse the process, a private member's bill was placed before the parliament in July 1991 by an AL member of parliament (*The Daily Star*, August 9, 1993). The bill was in accordance with the agreed outline of the three alliances, which was formed toward the end of the Ershad rule by political parties, for protection of the fundamental rights of the people and the independence of the judiciary, and for ensuring rule of law (*The Daily Star*, February 25, 1994). After a lapse of almost three years, the select committee report on the constitutional amendment bill seeking independence of the judiciary and rule of law was placed before parliament in late February 1994. All the opposition MPs, including the sponsor of the bill, vehemently opposed the introduction of the report and the amended bill. They maintained that such amendments would strike at the very root of the whole question of the independence of the judiciary and hamper the magistrates from exercising judicial functions. They felt that the amendments would allow greater executive inroads in the affairs of the supreme court through the modalities of making appointments of the judges. The parliament is yet to discuss the amended bill in a threadbare manner.

A number of actions taken by the present government has left some doubts about the sincerity of its stand on the issue of independence of the judiciary. In 1992 the government turned down a High Court Division decision relating to the promotion of subjudges (*The Daily Star*, November 10, 1992). This action violated the spirit and intent of articles 109 and 116 of the constitution. Article 109 states that "The High Court Division shall have superintendence and control over all courts" (*The Constitution of the People's Republic of Bangladesh* 1991, 93). On February 4, 1994, nine judges were appointed to the Supreme Court without prior consultations with the Chief Justice, even though it has always been the practice to consult the Chief Justice before making any appointment to the Supreme Court. Both Zia and Ershad observed this practice though they were not legally bound to do so as the relevant article requiring such consultation was amended by the fourth amendment in 1975. The leaders of the Supreme Court expressed their dissatisfaction regarding this matter and the government agreed to cancel its original order of appointment and issued a new order in consultation with the Chief Justice. Although there is some influence of the executive on the lower judiciary, the higher courts, particularly the High Court division and the appellate division of the Supreme Court, are independent in discharging their judicial responsibilities. This is evident from many important cases lost by the government.

Lack of Credibility of the Electoral System

The uncertain state of political accountability can be attributed, among other things, to the big question mark which hangs over the electoral system. This is not surprising because all the elections (local, subnational, and national) held between 1973 and 1990 were manipulated and rigged with the knowledge and blessings of the government in power. Only the nature and extent of electoral malpractices varied from government to government. To Ershad, who ruled Bangladesh for nine years, goes the credit of doing maximum damage to the credibility of the electoral system. The incidence of irregularities and manipulation in the electoral process increased at a frightening rate during his term of office. The Election Commission, till 1991, failed to play an independent role in the electoral process. It has been alleged that the Election Commission provided active assistance in the past to civil servants to manipulate election results in favor of candidates either belonging to or supported by the ruling party (Khan 1989, 105). In fact, elections became farces as these had been deliberately rigged and undermined during the Ershad era (Huq 1988, 74).

The interim government of Justice Shahbuddin Ahmed took a number of decisive steps to restore the credibility of the Election Commission and the electoral process. The action included reconstitution of the Election Commission with three judges of the Supreme Court who were known for their integrity and honesty; bestowal of broad powers to the commission to supervise and punish corrupt public officials acting as returning and presiding officers, preparation of a code of conduct in consultation with all political parties; and conferment of wide powers to local government bodies in the area of law and order during elections (Khan 1993a, 11).

But a recent parliamentary by-election result in the rural constituency of Magura has once again underlined the importance of holding free and fair elections. Unfortunately, the alleged massive rigging and fraud which took place during voting to fill up a seat which fell vacant due to the death of an MP has exposed the weaknesses of the electoral system and the inadequacies and ineffectiveness of the Election Commission. The incident in Magura has considerably strengthened the demand of all major opposition political parties, i.e., AL, JP, and JI, that in the future all national elections, to be free and fair, must be held under the auspices of a caretaker government. The government party, now under pressure from the opposition, has also agreed to make the Election Commission more effective and powerful to ensure justice and fairness in the elections.

Lack of Respect for Human Rights

Promotion and respect for human rights is one of the obligations of a modern government. Political freedom, including free speech, freedom of expression, assembly and movement, and availability of information are not only inalienable rights of a citizen but essential preconditions for ensuring political accountability.

The first significant attempt to curb the fundamental rights of citizens was initiated by the Mujib government. The process began with the second amendment to the constitution effected in 1973 which curtailed fundamental rights by making them subject to any constitutional amendment passed by the parliament (Hussain 1994). One of the outcomes of the amendment was the coming into force of the Special Powers Act 1974.

In Bangladesh, though a democratic government is in power, there are a number of repressive laws which in "in the name of security of the country violate the right to life, to liberty and security of the person; they are discriminatory in their application and they violate all safeguards against arrest, detention and provision on torture or cruel, degrading and inhuman punishment" (Farooq and Khan 1993, 5). Such special laws include the Special Power Act 1974, Special Security Forces Act 1986, and Suppression of Terrorist Offenses Act 1992.

Some of the human rights abuses which still continue unabated include maltreatment of people of low status by police and lack of trials for such abuses, confrontation, with the insurgent Shanti Bahini movement in Chittagong Hill Tracts which has led to violations by both sides; and denial of equality to women (Blair et al. 1992, 47).

Freedom of information and expression has been compromised to a large extent due to the government's control over television and radio. In this regard, the government could not break the tradition of the Zia and Ershad governments. It was not unreasonable to expect that the government would implement its pre-election pledge to transform the electronic media into self-governing institutions. Unfortunately, both television and radio regularly highlight the "achievements" and "successes" of the government in various fields while ignoring its policy and program failures. But the policies and programs of the major opposition political parties are not given adequate coverage by the media. On the contrary, television and radio have been consciously and systematically used to promote policies and programs of the ruling party and project attractive images of its leaders.

While it is true that newspapers and magazines under private ownership now enjoy more freedom of expression compared to the past, the government-owned and progovernment newspapers benefit from more liberal advertisements. On the other hand, the independent and antigovernment newspapers do not get enough advertisements. This practice of deliberate and selective discrimination in advertisement distribution is a government attempt to influence a newspaper's policies in its favor. Nevertheless, the general environment regarding freedom of the press has improved.

Bureaucratic Accountability

Bureaucratic accountability is possible only when political accountability is in place. Bureaucratic accountability requires effective performance of public agencies and officials in their relations with the public in a transparent manner (Halfani et al. 1994, 6). There is also the need to monitor the performance of civil servants and to institutionalize measures to correct their abuses, excesses, and deficiencies. To ensure bureaucratic accountability, civil servants must be aware of their responsibilities in a multiparty democratic system. These are (Stowe 1992, 390):

- To supply ministers and parliament with complete and accurate data presented objectively and on time.
- To advise ministers by analysis of data and appraisal of options in which they can have confidence.
- To implement ministerial decisions and administer the resultant legislation.
- To account to ministers and parliament for their actions (or inaction) with particular reference to the safeguarding of public funds and ensuring effective value-for-money.

But for civil servants to shoulder the four-fold responsibilities indicated above, they must be professional. Five attributes characterize a professional civil service. These are (Stowe 1992, 391):

- It is based on the merit principle.
- It guarantees financial probity.
- It respects political neutrality and impartiality under law.
- It is committed to serve any government well.
- It is accountable at all levels.

But whether it is possible for civil servants to act in a professional manner in view of the multifarious and adverse circumstances under which they have to function in developing or emerging democracies is another matter. Still, systems need to be designed to make civil servants accountable for their actions; at the same time it must be ensured that such systems do not leave open possibilities for political interference and bureaucratic manipulation. In Bangladesh, as in many other countries, civil servants are made accountable for their actions through two mechanisms—internal and external (Khan 1983, 684-688).

Internal Mechanisms

Internal mechanisms in Bangladesh are based on hierarchy and include such requirements as disposal of files within a specified time limit varying from 24 to 72 hours, depending on the level and status of the concerned civil servant; inspection; supervision; and annual confidential report (ACR). These internal mechanisms, however, have not ensured effective bureaucratic accountability. Time limits for disposal of files are not always complied with; supervision has not been strong enough in many cases and has been nonexistent in others; inspections are not conducted in an organized way and not done regularly; and the ACR is too subjective to be of much use. However, the ACR is an important means of evaluating an individual civil servant's eligibility for promotion. The problem has been exacerbated by nonexistence of position descriptions for most public sector jobs. As a UNDP study pointed out, "the performance of individuals (civil servants) is not evaluated by using objective criteria, and, therefore, individuals are not held accountable for performance through the ACR process" (UNDP 1993, 22). An earlier USAID-sponsored study found "lack of accountability within the organization of the government ... (and) supervision of personnel very weak in the entire system" (USAID 1989, 12, 16).

External Mechanisms

The external mechanisms for ensuring bureaucratic accountability in Bangladesh include specific actions of the executive and the legislature, the role of the judiciary, the press, and citizens' groups. All past governments failed to take decisive steps to define the role-relationship between political masters and public servants. The documents which incorporated such relationships were formulated during British rule and were slightly modified in the 1960s and hence had little utility in the vastly changed context of an independent country. Further, successive governments found it convenient not to change such documents as the Rules of Business and Warrant of Precedence (1985).

The Rules of Business as it exists stipulate the following: (a) the secretary is designated as the official head of the ministry/division; (b) he acts as the principal accounting officer of the ministry/division; and (c) he keeps the minister-in-charge generally informed of the working of the ministry/division (Rules of Business 1987, 2-3).

The Warrant of Precedence is an index of importance given to designated individuals for the purpose of state ceremonies and other important occasions. The senior civil and military servants have higher ranks in the Warrant of Precedence compared to the MPs.

The present government initially showed keen interest in making civil servants accountable to both the executive and the legislature (Khan 1992b). In November 1991 a new Rule of Business was prepared in draft form which envisaged changes in the role-relationship between the minister and the secretary. The minister was vested with more power and authority vis-a-vis the secretary in the running of the ministry. The minister was made responsible to the parliament for performance of his ministry. The minister was designated head of the ministry/division, and made responsible to parliament for the performance of his ministry. The secretary was to become the ministry's chief of administration and principal accounting officer. But this draft document has not as yet been formalized and will perhaps take some time for approval. It thus appears that the Warrant of Precedence has not been changed in the light of existing reality.

The civil servants can also be held accountable by the ministers through promotion and transfer. But this would require an objective criterion for promotion and transfer. There is a clear perception among a majority of the civil servants—generalists and technical-functional—that "merit is no longer the only basis for promotion and the government has not adhered to transfer policy, principles, and general conditions concerning civil servants" (Khan 1993b, 16-17, 23). This perception of civil servants partly reflects what is happening in practice. The validity of ACRs and interviews to judge a candidate's potential and suitability for promotion has yet to be established. So career mobility of civil servants is to some extent restricted because merit and performance are not clearly differentiated from seniority. A civil servant's aptitude, training, and relevant experience are not always given careful consideration while deciding on his transfer and posting.

It would appear that parliamentary control over ministries has been strengthened, as statutory standing committees like the Public Accounts,

Public Undertakings and Privileges are serving their purposes well. But as explained earlier, due to the prevalence of a number of factors, supervision and control of standing committees have not been satisfactory. One reason for such a state of affairs was elaborated by a member of parliament who said, "The Rules of Procedure of the (standing) committees were framed during the presidential form of government when the purpose of the committees was to discuss affairs of various ministries and not necessarily to make ministries accountable to the parliament. They (committees) were talking clubs and have essentially remained so under the present parliamentary form of government, as the rules governing them have not been altered to reflect the change in the system of government" (UNDP 1993, 19). But these are currently under scrutiny and one would expect them to change in the right direction.

The weaknesses of the court system often raises doubts about the credibility of the judicial system. The weaknesses include: (a) a large backlog of cases resulting from both slow procedures and a high degree of litigiousness in the society; (b) poor reporting of the decisions; and (c) either a reluctance or an inability to deal with cases of governmental maladministration (Blair et al. 1992, 46). In spite of these deficiencies, the judiciary, on occasions, have restricted the discretion and arbitrariness of public agencies and officials and redressed grievances of citizens. The major problem of the judiciary is its limited amount of resources in relation to the large number of pending cases.

The press has played a valuable role in investigating and reporting executive excesses, administrative irregularities, mismanagement, inefficiency, and corruption of civil servants. But such investigation and reporting have mostly been restricted to lower and midlevel civil servants.

Citizens' groups have not been able to play any significant role in influencing public policies and shaping behavior and actions of civil servants. Even the advocacy role of citizens' groups has mostly been limited to holding meetings and organizing seminars with no follow-up actions to determine the impact on civil servants of recommendations emanating from such gatherings.

Government and Development Administration

It is well known that Bangladesh has very limited natural resources, a high population density, and that the country is vulnerable to natural disasters. However, it is widely believed that Bangladesh has achieved considerable success not only in stabilizing the economy but also in improving economic growth since 1991. The emerging economic dynamism and the changing policy environment in the country necessitate greater efficiency from the government. It is interesting to note that the role of the government and the approaches to the role of public policy are now changing rapidly. It is important to determine what are the appropriate activities of the government in a competitive and rapidly changing world economy, and to find ways and means to achieve higher efficiency in the provision of government services (ADB 1994).

The proper role of different economic agents in efficient utilization of limited and scarce resources depends on the quality of governance as reflected in the dynamic administration of economic and development projects. Development administration thus refers mainly to the formulation and implementation of policies, programs, and projects relating to the development goals and activities of the government.

While the government of Bangladesh has played a major role in the country's economic development, its role is now changing because of growing incomes, a more open economy, and developing markets. Thus the question of the optimal size and function of the government is now being reassessed. It is now generally felt that there is less need for rigid controls and direct participation in the market by the government. As a result the ability of the government to influence economic affairs is being reduced.

The government policies regarding public expenditure and regulation need to be analyzed within the changing context. It is, therefore, necessary to redefine the boundaries of the public sector and redesign appropriate regulatory mechanisms. The issues related to government and development administration should be examined in the light of changing priorities and concerns of the Bangladesh economy and the global context. The performance and achievements of various economic projects rest on how they are formulated and implemented. In addition, good governance must take into consideration the welfare impact of projects, an issue which is also related to the nature of administration.

Privatization

Although privatization in Bangladesh began in 1975, denationalization of jute and textile mills was done in the first half of the 1980s. The government could intervene in the administration of the units if the owners failed to operate them or meet contractual obligations. In the second half of the 1980s, further efforts were made for the wider participation of investors in the privatization process. However, although the denationalization program made some progress in privatization from the mid-1970s to the end of the 1980s it could not make a major contribution to the government's capital receipts.

The major privatization attempt was made in 1991. Only air travel, railways, production, and distribution of power, and defence industries were retained for the public sector. Further privatization of state-owned enterprises in all other sectors and full foreign ownership of enterprises were carried out. The public sector reserve list was further narrowed down to make way for private investment in the power, telecommunication, and domestic air transport sector (World Bank 1994a).

Although there has been substantial progress on privatization since 1975, there are some formidable difficulties to be overcome in making it completely successful. First, the institutional problems and bureaucratic delays in changing the institutional arrangements for privatization have made it time-consuming. Second, a broad understanding of privatization among the public, the private sector, labor unions, and the state-owned enterprises has been lacking. Finally, the poor financial condition of majority of the state-owned enterprises identified for privatization has been a major disincentive for the private sector's interest in the program.

An Inter-Ministerial Committee on Privatization (ICOP) entrusted with the responsibility of developing privatization policy as well as considering, approving, and monitoring specific privatization proposals of the various line ministries was created in 1991. But it had no mandate and autonomy to implement privatization. In 1993 the ICOP was replaced by an autonomous Privatization Board with the responsibility of all privatization-related activities. However, the effectiveness and the success of the Privatization Board depends on a number of diverse, complex political economic factors currently prevailing in the country. Successful privatization can be achieved by creating a new and balanced regulatory environment in which competition can flourish. In addition, it is also important that the government undertake a deliberate policy of bringing the private sector to assume a greater role in the investment, operation, and maintenance of the utilities and in the basic economic infrastructure.

The Power Sector

It is widely known that in recent years, system losses in the power sector have often exceeded 40 percent of gross generation, and cash collections have been less than 80 percent of current billings. The cash income of the Bangladesh Power Development Board (BPDB) and Dhaka Electric Supply Authority (DESA) has been less than half of the sales value of the power generated. While the situation improved somewhat in FY1993, and the collection-to-generation ratio increased to 58 percent, due to the failure to bill or collect, foregone revenues amounted to over Taka 5 billion. On the other hand, the rural electricity cooperatives sustained only 16 percent system losses, and recorded a 101 percent collection and 85 percent collection-to-import ratio (World Bank 1994a).

Involvement of the government in the power sector has created an overlapping and confusing situation regarding responsibilities. The establishment of DESA in 1990 attempted to decentralize BPDB's distribution function. Measures were undertaken in 1992 to establish staff discipline and accountability, particularly in the distribution function. This was primarily directed to an improvement in the performance of the individual units regarding systems losses. Further attempts were made in 1993 through the establishment of an interministerial working group on the power sector to determine means to improve existing public utilities and create an incentive structure for private participation.

The Telecommunications Sector

The telecommunications sector provides an opportunity for the government to encourage majority private-owned operators to compete with the Bangladesh Telegraph and Telephone Board (BTTB) in the provision of basic services. To separate regulatory functions from operations, the government has approved the amendment to the 1979 BTTB Ordinance. Interministerial consultations on a telecommunications policy statement have been completed and preparations are now on to commercialize telecommunication services.

The Gas Sector

The gas sector is a major source of government revenue. The sector is wholly dominated by Petrobangla, a group of eight state-owned companies. The exploration, production, and delivery of natural gas is the sole responsibility of Petrobangla. However, the in-house capability of the group is not sufficient enough to plan, design, and supervise the sector's expansion programs. It has been estimated that during 1968-1993, annual system losses on average were around 4.5 percent of production. However, in fiscal year 1993, total system loss was about 7.8 percent, of which more than 80 percent was incurred by nonbulk industrial, commercial, and domestic customers (World Bank 1994a).

The government announced a new petroleum policy in 1993 to open up the gas sector for private participation. This is necessary to mobilize more capital to achieve accelerated development for the sector and improve its performance.

The privatization of Petrobangla group would be an effective alternative to transform the individual oil companies into efficient businesses. The government is also planning to float a portion of its shareholding in two oil companies—Bangladesh Gas Fields Company Limited and Titas Gas Transmission and Distribution Company—in the local capital market.

Financial Market Reform

The Bangladesh Bank has substantial powers to formulate and implement monetary and supervisory policies and to advise the government on economic policy. Recently its power has been extended to issuing directions to banks and financial institutions. It is generally felt that Bangladesh Bank operates the country's payments system reasonably well. It is, however, widely believed that Bangladesh Bank suffers from its past image of a weak and ineffective organization, without much autonomy or authority.

At present the four nationalized commercial banks exert oligopolistic market power over the banking system. The nationalized commercial banks have contributed to the government's socioeconomic objectives by expanding their rural branch network and lending to agriculture, small-scale and cottage industries, and by funding state-owned enterprises. But the combination of government ownership and attempts to achieve these objectives meant a high cost in bad loans.

At present there is a general stagnation of credit in both the agricultural and industrial sectors. This is a matter of serious concern because of its impact on the future economic growth of the country. Commercial banks are very reluctant to lend to industries for a number of reasons.

There has been a high default rate among nationalized commercialized bank borrowers. The management of these banks was poor and they had little incentive to make good loans. Government direction and interventions were quite serious in magnitude. Thus the nationalized commercial banks had to make high-risk loans to priority sectors, new entrepreneurs, public corporations, "sick" industries, and borrowers with political influence. In addition there was the financial burden of "loan forgiveness" programs by the government. The recent legal reforms within the financial sector have enabled the banks to obtain decrees in their favor in the cases against defaulters. But the ineffective legal enforcement system does not allow for liquidation of collateral. Thus, there is a need not only for further legal reforms but also for effective enforcement.

The two publicly owned industrial development banks, i.e., Bangladesh Shilpa Rin Sangstha (BSRS) and Bangladesh Shilpa Bank (BSB), are institutions with serious difficulties. They relied largely on international credit lines and Bangladesh Bank for funding. Their own fixed deposits amounted to only 25 percent of total resources. Unfortunately, foreign funding has ceased as BSB and BSRS could not improve their performance. Domestic funding was also curtailed at the same time, but, paradoxically, has been recommended again and again since 1989.

The credit needs of the agricultural sector are served by Bangladesh Krishi Bank, Rajshahi Krishi Unnayan Bank, and the nationalized commercialized banks. During the 1980s, the government directed these banks to expand their rural branch network and increase lending to agriculture. It was a period when credit discipline seriously deteriorated. The expansion took place at the cost of the institutions' ability to maintain the quality of its lending and recovery programs. The factors responsible for worsening the situation are the involvement of local government officials in borrower selection, loan amnesty, interest remission programs, and the use of credit for relief or patronage purposes. As such, these were serious violations of credit discipline and evidence of political pressures was quite apparent (World Bank 1994b).

The general guidelines for regulating the banking system in Bangladesh are outlined in the Banking Companies Act (BCA) 1991, and its amendments in 1993. Various circulars of BCA and Bangladesh Bank specify rules regarding the overall banking system. These have considerably improved the financial sector's regulatory environment. However, there remains further scope for improvement. Asset classification and provisioning rules have made the enormity of the bad debt problem transparent. Many substandard loans are actually bad, but it takes time for them to be classified as bad. Current borrowers pay high interest rates charged by banks to permit provisioning for bad loans made years ago. It is widely believed that a one-shot recapitalization would make current nationalized banks' performance transparent by removing the impact of past poor lending. The BCA 1991 and the Financial Institutions Act 1993 provide Bangladesh Bank with a sound legal basis for supervising banks and financial companies. They also allow it to take all necessary measures to ensure the safety and soundness of the financial system.

Legal Framework

Recently, legislation was passed in Bangladesh to improve its legal framework for the financial system. Among the legislations adopted were the Banking Companies Act, Financial Loan Courts Act, Securities and Companies Commission Act, and the Financial Institutions Act. Bankruptcy legislation is under preparation. At the moment, implementation of law court decrees is done under the Civil Procedure Code. As a result, it takes a long time for the nationalized commercial banks to collect on their collateral. The special foreclosure powers given to development banks have not been used. Thus, there remains a great scope to improve contract enforcement, especially to encourage private sector financial institution lending for industrial projects.

Labor Market Interventions

Unnecessary and disproportionate interventions in the labor markets have adversely affected the economic development of the country. Public wage policies and minimum wage regulation in effect have created wage increases faster than productivity. This has made both the public and private firms less competitive by international standards.

The direct intervention by the government in the past has created an excessive politicization of labor relations, resulting in a deep distrust between labor and management. In Bangladesh, the trade unions rely on general strikes and countrywide agitations to pressure the government. This is because of the absence of direct industrial negotiations with employers. Four national wages and productivity commissions (NWPC) were instituted in 1973, 1977, 1985, and 1991. The tripartite nature of the NWPCs did not provide any opportunity for collective bargaining. The government retains the right to accept, reject, or modify NWPC recommendations. Thus, in July 1993, the government announced a minimum basic wage for public workers of Taka 950 instead of Taka 1000 as recommended by the NWPC. It is essentially a process of consultation in a system where pay and allowances are determined unilaterally by the employer—the government. As a result, NWPCs have made their recommendations purely on social and political consideration without any reference to productivity.

The labor movement in Bangladesh is characterized by a large number of unions, a small percentage of unionized workers, and a division at the national level into many labor federations associated with different political parties. Because of the centralization of managerial authority in the public sector, labor unions cannot pursue their objectives (e.g., wage improvement) through the usual method of industrial relations. This makes them depend on political parties to achieve their objectives. The plurality of the political parties is automatically reflected in the trade union structure of the country. The political parties (the ruling and the opposition), trade unions, and the government have all contributed to the complex problems of governance in industrial relations in Bangladesh.

As a result of the ineffectiveness of the normal method for tripartite consultation, the alliance of the main national trade union federation, SKOP, has, in the past decade, made attempts to negotiate with government directly outside the existing legal framework. In compelling the government to accept negotiations or agree to concessions, SKOP has often resorted to well-publicized general strikes accompanied by countrywide agitations. This has resulted in major economic losses and inflicted critical damage on the image of industrial relations in Bangladesh. It is important that the government leave employers and trade unions to settle their differences with minimal political intervention.

Conclusion

It is now widely believed that good governance is the most desirable thing in Bangladesh. However, this is not easy to achieve mainly because of a host of social, cultural, economic, administrative, and legal variables which affect the nature, and consequently, determine the shape of governance in a particular country.

Political and bureaucratic accountability, two principal components of governance, are in an inadequate and ineffective state in Bangladesh. Political accountability could not be made effective due to the presence of a number of factors including dominant executive, weak legislature, slow growth and low level of development of political parties, lack of independence of the judiciary, weak electoral system, and lack of respect for human rights. Principal mechanisms used to secure accountability of bureaucrats are not also strong.

Some of the major problems of governance can be observed in the development administration of the government. The privatization program of the government has gone through several stages. The drive toward promarket policies has been accompanied by a major reform effort in the financial sector. Although there still remains problems in credit market management (both agricultural and industrial), substantial progress has already been made in creating a more liberalized environment needed for higher growth. The overall economic environment and the legal framework for the functioning of the financial market are healthier than in the past. The labor market and industrial relations are also slowly improving.

The most significant achievement of the government is its considerable success in stabilizing the economy. It is expected that reforms will be extended to include public enterprises and the structure, size, and functions of the civil service. As these reforms extend to other areas, there will be more success in the implementation of various government programs. However, ultimate results will depend on how the programs are implemented. The crucial importance of good governance lies in making the program a success. Factors determining good governance and development administration are large in number and they interact in a complex manner. Indications are already there that in most areas, things are moving in a healthier direction. However, what is most important is to continue open discussions about the current state of affairs and make things transparent for a better future in Bangladesh.

Acknowledgement

The authors are indebted to Professors Nurul Islam, Wahidul Huq, and Salim Rashid, Mr. A.M.M. Muhit, and Dr. M.G. Quibria for their comments on the earlier drafts of this chapter.

References

Asian Development Bank (ADB), 1994. *Asian Development Outlook.* Hong Kong: Oxford University Press for the Asian Development Bank.

Blair, H., et al., 1992. "The Bangladesh Democracy Program (BOP) Assessment: Final Report." Bureau for Asia, Democratic Affairs and Special Issues Branch, USAID, Dhaka.

Constitution of the People's Republic of Bangladesh, 1991. Dhaka.

The Daily Star, 1992. November 10. Dhaka.

———, 1993. August 9. Dhaka.

———, 1994. February 25. Dhaka.

Farooq, M., and A. R. Khan, 1993. "National Security Laws and the Violation of Human Rights in Bangladesh." *Holiday* July 30:3-4.

Halfani, M., et al., 1994. "Towards an Understanding of Governance: The Emergence of an Idea and Its Implications for Urban Research in Developing Countries." Center for Urban and Community Studies, University of Toronto. Unpublished.

Huq, A. F., 1988. "The Problem of Legitimacy and Elections in Bangladesh." *The Journal of Social Studies* 41(July):50-74.

Hussain, S. A., 1994. "Challenges of Democratic Governance in Bangladesh." Paper presented in the Conference on Bangladesh: Society, Polity and Economy. March 7-8, 1994, New Delhi, India.

Jahan, R., 1992. *Governance and Public Policy: A Programming Strategy*. Dhaka: The Ford Foundation.

Khan, M. M., 1983. "Administrative Accountability in Bangladesh." *Indian Journal of Public Administration* 29(3):682-89.

———, 1989. "The Electoral Process in Bangladesh." *Regional Studies* 7(3):95-111.

———, 1992a. "Politics and Democratization in Bangladesh, 1971-1990." In R.K. Arora, ed., *Politics and Administration in Changing Societies: Essays in Honour of Professor Fred W. Riggs*. New Delhi: Associated Publishing House.

———, 1992b. "Report on Public Administration Reform in Bangladesh." Dhaka, UNDP.

———, 1993a. "Process of Decentralization in Bangladesh." Paper presented at the SOG Mini-International Round Table on Governance in South Asia: Impact of Decentralization. January 18, 1993, New Delhi, India.

———, 1993b. "Civil Service Management in Bangladesh: Final Report." United Nations Development Program, Dhaka.

———, 1994. "Legislature in Bangladesh: Past Experience and Present Concerns." Keynote paper presented in a National Seminar/Workshop. May 7, 1994, Dhaka.

Khan, M. M., and H. M. Zafarullah, 1988. "Entrenched Strong Man Rule: The Governmental System in Bangladesh." In J. W. Langford and K. L. Brownsey, eds., *The Changing Shape of the Government in the Asia-Pacific Region*. Halifax, Nova Scotia: The Institute for Research on Public Policy.

———, 1990. "Trends in Bangladesh Politics, 1972-1988." *The Round Table* 315 (July):315-21.

Landell-Mills, P., and I. Serageldin, 1991. "Governance and the External Factor." Proceedings of the World Bank Annual Conference on Development Economics 1991. The World Bank, Washington, D.C.

Leftwich, A., 1993. "Governance, Democracy and Development in the Third World." *Third World Quarterly* 14(3):615-24.

Maniruzzaman, T., 1992. "The Fall of the Military Dictator 1991: Elections and the Prospects of Civilian Rule in Bangladesh." *Pacific Affairs* 65(2):203-24.

Ministry of Finance, 1993. Budget Speech of the Finance Minister. Dhaka.

OECD/DAC, 1992. *DAC Work on Participatory Development and Good Governance.* Paris: OECD.

Rahman, A., 1993. "Challenges of Governance in Bangladesh." *BIISS Journal* 14(4):461-77.

Rules of Business, 1987. Dhaka: Cabinet Division.

Stowe, K., 1992. "Good Piano Won't Play Bad Music: Administrative Reform and Good Governance." *Public Administration* 70(Autumn):387-94.

UNDP, 1993. *Report on Public Administration Sector Study in Bangladesh.* Dhaka: United Nations Development Programme.

USAID, 1989. *Report of the Public Administration Efficiency Study, Main Report.* Vol. 1. Dhaka: United States Agency for International Development.

Warrant of Precedence, 1985. Dhaka: Cabinet Division.

World Bank, 1989. *Sub-Saharan Africa: From Crisis to Sustainable Growth.* Washington, D. C.

———, 1992. *Governance and Development*. Washington, D. C.

———, 1994a. "Bangladesh: From Stabilization to Growth." Report No. 12724-BD. Washington, D. C.

———, 1994b. "Bangladesh: Privatization and Adjustment." Report No. 12318-BD. Washington, D. C.

AUTHOR INDEX

SUBJECT INDEX